WEATHER
and
CLIMATE
FORECASTING

The Scientific Method in Action

Kendall Hunt
publishing company

THOMAS A. KOVACS
Eastern Michigan University

Cover image: Shutterstock.com

Kendall Hunt
publishing company

www.kendallhunt.com
Send all inquiries to:
4050 Westmark Drive
Dubuque, IA 52004-1840

Brief Contents

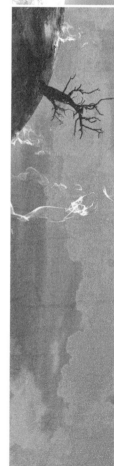

Contents

Preface

Weather and climate courses are a popular option to satisfy general education courses in the sciences because of the natural interest students have in the weather and climate, and given its impact on our everyday lives. This book attempts to put a greater emphasis then most on the students' topical interests, which are mostly weather forecasting, severe weather, and climate change. Furthermore, the main learning objective of university general education programs' natural science requirements is to apply the scientific method. Weather and climate forecasting provides the ideal focus for learning and applying the scientific method. Weather forecasting requires obtaining weather observations, developing empirically based weather relationships from testable hypotheses, and using these relationships and theories to develop forecasts. Climate forecasts are similar, but with some important differences. This book aims to provide students a real-world experience of applying the scientific method using weather and climate observations in real-time.

The primary goal of the textbook is to help non-science majors, beginning meteorology students, and science education students apply the scientific method to make weather and climate forecasts. The weather forecasts include the well-known daily and seven-day forecasts, and the special hazardous weather forecasts that often invoke weather watches and warnings. The climate forecasts include the future climate change and global warming forecasts and the shorter-term seasonal, monthly, and weekly outlooks.

Often, science concepts are provided in introductory scientific textbooks without instructing the reader how scientists mentally digest these concepts. Scientific practice and literacy is more than just the overarching scientific method. It is a group of unifying concepts within all sciences and a range of cognitive, social, and physical practices in which all scientists engage. This textbook intentionally focuses on literacy by including unifying concepts and scientific practices boxes throughout the chapters and in the context of the concepts being discussed. These unifying concepts and scientific practices help the reader to understand science literacy as well as model how scientists think and approach scientific concepts. Many of the textbook concepts are examples of these unifying concepts and they help them become more digestible to the novice scientist. The scientific practices help students understand how a scientist conceptualizes these concepts so they learn as a scientist.

These unifying concepts and scientific practices come from, "A Framework for K-12 Scientific Education" developed by the National Research Council of the National Academy of Sciences and serves as the foundation for the Next Generation Science Standards published by Achieve (https://www.nextgenscience.org/framework-k-12-science-education). Because of the explicit inclusion of themes from federal and state science standards, this textbook could be used in a weather and climate or physical science course for K-12 student teachers in science education courses. Many of the disciplinary core K-12 physical science national standards are included in this book. However, the book is primarily written for earth science, environmental science, geography, non-science general education, and meteorology majors.

The textbook units are organized similar to the linear progression in which the scientific method is often presented. Each unit in the book is a major subset of the scientific method. The first unit presents the gathering and presentation of observations to forecast weather and climate. The second unit presents the important laws, theories, and principles that ultimately allow us to use these observations to make weather and climate forecasts. The final unit presents how these observations and theories are used to make weather and climate forecasts. The

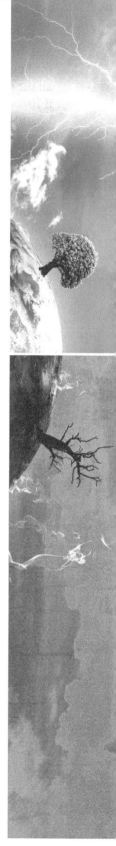

learning objectives of the final unit are to apply many of the tools and methods used on typical radio, television, and internet forecasts. In addition, the special techniques used to forecast hazardous weather including blizzards, ice storms, lake-effect snowstorms, floods, severe thunderstorms, tornadoes, hail, and tropical cyclones are included.

The book emphasizes freely accessible weather data within the chapters and the end-of-chapter questions and problems. It is risky to put web links in textbooks because they often change, but I am hopeful that the included links will remain stable, as they have for the many years I have used them. Nevertheless, I include all the links for data analysis at a website that I control to ensure that students and instructors can obtain data if links become broken. Please visit https://www.emich.edu/geography-geology/weather for links to useful weather data to go along with this textbook and contact information for conversation.

To the Instructor

This textbook is organized in a way that is slightly different from most science textbooks and in general weather and climate textbooks in particular. Although it covers many of the same concepts in other weather and climate textbooks, it does so with a focus on application of the scientific method. I have always been frustrated as a student and now as a professor that introductory science courses and textbooks often focused on scientific facts. However, they did not focus on doing science or how to think like a scientist. After several years of teaching weather and climate to K-12 science education students, but trained as a research scientist, I saw an opportunity to teach science courses differently. I have focused on the scientific method in non-science major courses and needed a textbook that fit that vision. Not only does this textbook focus on the scientific method using weather and climate forecasting, but it also includes the three-dimensional learning of unifying concepts and scientific practices that is the focus of the national science education standards.

The book is written at the level of an introductory weather course and a second year climate course. However, advanced topics have been placed in "Digging Deeper" boxes and I selectively omit some of the more advanced material from this text in my non-science and science education major courses. Nevertheless, the material is there for interested non-science and science education majors. In addition, I feel the focus on the scientific method, science practices, and unifying concepts are an important change in the way we teach science to non-science majors. The website that I include in this preface has my contact information and I am interested to hear from you on how we can improve upon science education. Standardized testing reveals that we need to find better ways to teach science. Issues such as our vulnerabilities to pandemics and climate change motivated me to teach science education courses and write this textbook. I appreciate any discussions with those that teach science.

If your course is for first or second year earth science, environmental science, geography, or meteorology majors, then I would include the "Digging Deeper" boxes and omit the unifying concepts and scientific practices boxes. Chapter 2 is about the extent of climate material normally taught in an introductory weather and climate course. Much of the climate material in Chapter 8 Circulation Models and Conservation Laws (e.g. deep ocean circulation and internal climate oscillations), Chapter 11 Climate Models, Chapter 12 Weather and Climate Forecast Products (e.g. climate outlooks), and Chapter 15 Climate Forecasting, are targeted for the second year science students.

To the Student

The material in this textbook is meant for learning the data collection, observations, laws, theories, and principles that go into weather and climate forecasting. Students often lament the detailed and trivial nature of science textbooks to me. I hope I have avoided this and got to the point of learning how science is done and how weather and climate forecasts are created. I invite you to https://www.emich.edu/geography-geology/weather to participate in discussions around these topics. Much goes into weather and climate forecasting and the actual forecasting does not start until Chapter 9. Nonetheless, some of the early chapters foreshadow the use of this early material in forecasting. All the material in the text uses freely available data that you can use outside of the course if you are or becoming a weather and climate enthusiast. Non-science major science courses often present science concepts and expect you to think like a scientist to understand them. Please read the unifying concepts and science practices to help you understand how scientists think to help in understanding the course concepts. You may want to look through these before the course begins to help you be better prepared.

Each chapter ends with a summary and list of key words. The key words are bolded within the chapters when they are first mentioned. They are also included in the glossary. It is less important to know the exact meaning of these words and more important to be familiar with them. If you asked me how to define any word, I would probably start with "Um …" and then feel the stress of saying something that probably would not be too educated-sounding. Yet, I implicitly know what the words mean and they would not stop me from being able to understand them in conversation. That is the familiarity you should have with these words so that you can focus on learning the concepts. Sometimes jargon in any field can be a barrier to learning.

If any links in the book are broken, please go to the above link to find updated links. If the links are not updated here, email me to tell me that you cannot access them. Now, please enjoy the weather.

Acknowledgements

Writing this book was enjoyable and exhausting and I have many to thank for making it more enjoyable than exhausting. First and foremost, my wife Ann. It always seemed cliché to me to acknowledge your family, but family really does participate in completing a book even if they do not actually write the book. No doubt, I have a year's worth of household chores to make up. Thanks for the emotional support, Ann. I also want to thank my publisher for helping me through the process and making it fairly painless. I also appreciate that my employer, Eastern Michigan University, gave me the time to devote to writing the book. Without that time, I certainly would not have been able to complete it.

Finally, I would like to thank the many reviewers that gave me confidence with their kind words. I also appreciate the time they took to provide mindful suggestions that certainly made the book better. So, I say thanks to the following:

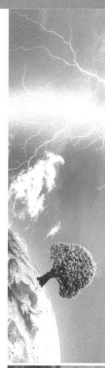

Scott Curtis
East Carolina University

Nyasha Dunkley
Georgia State University

Michael Feeley
Joliet Junior College

John Frye
University of Wisconsin - Whitewater

Kevin Goebbert
Valparaio University

Stephen K. Lentz
Penn State University – York

John McCuin
Dallas Baptist University

Ricardo Nogueira
Georgia State University

Thomas Patterson
The University of Southern Mississippi

Jeremy Spencer
The University of Akron

Aneesh Subramanian
University of Colorado Boulder

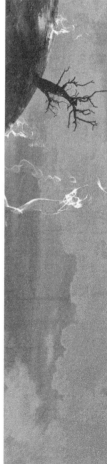

Unit 1

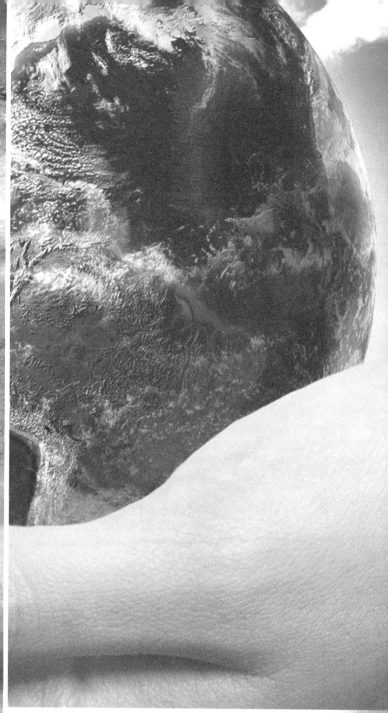

Weather and Climate Data

Chapter 1

Weather Data

Introduction

Observations are the foundation of science, so detailing the observations necessary for weather and climate forecasts is a logical starting point. Comparing weather parameters is possible because the instruments used to measure them have a scale developed for them. The unit of measurement on any scale is important to include with any measurement or calculation. The vast array of units of measurement often adds to the difficulty in understanding science concepts. It also makes it difficult to appreciate the magnitude of scientific phenomenon and weather parameters. The International System of Units (SI) helps standardize these units. However, scientists and non-scientists still use other units. In fact, mistakes with units of measurement happen to expert scientists. In 1998, units of measurement supplied by Lockheed Martin to adjust the approach of the Mars Climate Orbiter was not the SI units required by contract with NASA Jet Propulsion Laboratory. The mistake caused the orbiter to approach Mars at too low an altitude causing the $327.6 million dollar spacecraft to be lost. Therefore, this textbook will use the SI units with the more familiar units in parentheses throughout. Each section below introduces the basic weather parameters and their units of measurement.

Matter, Mass, and the Composition of the Atmosphere

Matter is the physical substance that composes all objects and organisms. The amount of matter determines an object's mass. The SI unit for mass is the kilogram, kg, which is also the most familiar unit. Mass and weight are different, but weight is covered later.

The matter that makes up the atmosphere can exist in three distinct states or phases of matter: solid, liquid, and gas. States and phases have slightly different meanings. States of matter are defined by how the component particles (i.e., atoms, molecules, ions, etc.) interact. Solids have a fixed volume and shape; liquids have a fixed volume, but not a fixed shape; and gases have neither a fixed volume nor shape. Lightning strikes and space weather lead to a fourth state known as plasma, which is an ionized gas, but is not a focus of this textbook. Phases of matter are defined by the arrangements of the component particles. For example, graphite and diamond are both solids composed of carbon atoms, but they are in different phases due to their atomic arrangement. Ice also has different phases, but all are in the solid state. Only one phase of ice is found at typical Earth temperatures and pressures, which is ice crystals that are six-sided. The transition between states or phases is always called a phase change. Figure 1.1 shows the different states and the phase changes that can occur between the states.

State of Water

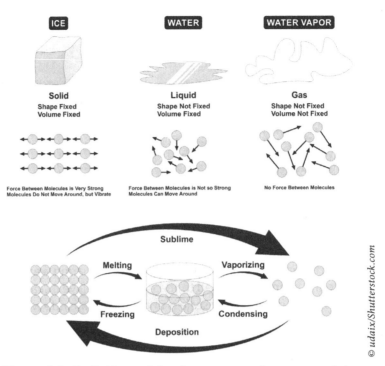

Figure 1.1 Definitions of the three states of matter and the phase changes that occur between them.

Proceeding from right-to-left in Figure 1.1, there are three possible phase changes: condensation (gas-to-liquid), freezing (liquid-to-solid), and deposition (gas-to-solid). Deposition is probably the least familiar, but it is how snow, frost, and ice clouds form. Frost does not form from liquid water freezing to the grass; it is, in fact, deposited. Likewise, snow does not form from liquid water freezing in the air, which is how ice pellets and hail form. Snow forms by crystal growth from the gas state to the solid state. Proceeding from left-to-right in Figure 1.1, there are three possible phase changes: melting (solid-to-liquid), evaporation (liquid-to-gas), and sublimation (solid-to-gas). Sublimation is probably the least familiar, but it is how dry ice (frozen carbon dioxide) turns to gas and how ice cubes in a freezer shrink.

Nitrogen (78%) and Oxygen (21%) make up 99% of the dry atmosphere (not including water). Argon and other trace gases make up the rest (Figure 1.2). These trace gases are small in concentration, but extremely important to life and climate. Ozone, for example, is necessary to support life on land; and carbon dioxide, methane, nitrous oxide and a few other gases have a significant effect on our climate. Water makes up a variable amount of the Earth's atmosphere and is present in all three states of matter. The variability and importance of water is discussed later in this chapter.

Temperature

Temperature comes about from the motion of the internal molecular components of all matter and is a measure of the energy of this molecular motion. These motions can be a movement from one location to another, a rotation, or a vibration of the molecular bonds themselves. This motion of the bonds themselves is why solid matter, like ice, still has a temperature even if the components that make up the solid matter does not appear to be in motion.

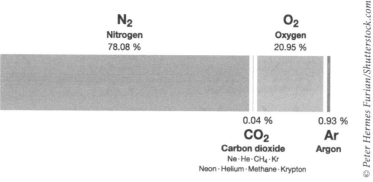

Air Composition of Earth's atmosphere by volume, excluding water vapor

N₂
Nitrogen
78.08 %

O₂
Oxygen
20.95 %

0.04 %
CO₂
Carbon dioxide
Ne · He · CH₄ · Kr
Neon · Helium · Methane · Krypton

0.93 %
Ar
Argon

© Peter Hermes Furian/Shutterstock.com

Figure 1.2 The composition of the Earth's atmosphere by volume excluding water vapor is shown.

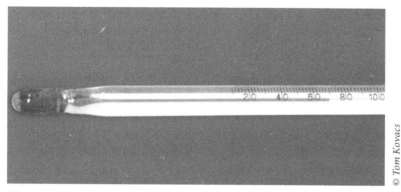

© Tom Kovacs

Figure 1.3 Liquid-in-glass thermometer showing a temperature of 70 °F

Thermometers measure temperature. The first modern or precision thermometer with a temperature scale was a mercury liquid-in-glass thermometer invented by Daniel Fahrenheit in 1709. The unit of measurement bears his name, degrees of Fahrenheit (°F). The liquid-in-glass thermometer has two concentric tubes of glass with a liquid in the inner tube and the scale on the outer tube. Both tubes end at the bottom as a bulb, which contains the reservoir of the liquid (Figure 1.3). The instrument works because most liquids expand as they are heated and, as they expand, liquid rises up the inner tube. The liquid is often mercury (silver color) or alcohol (non-silver color). If you drop these thermometers, they will break and the liquid will spill. For mercury, exposure to the air creates a toxic gas that can impair brain function, so clean-up should minimize air movements. As a child, I would play with the mercury ball, so a mercury spill is nothing to be deathly afraid of if you take the proper precautions.

Most countries, other than the U.S., use Celsius (°C), which is equal to a hundredth the distance between the temperatures that pure water freezes (0 °C) and boils (100 °C) at sea level. The SI base unit is the Kelvin (K). The Kelvin (K) scale, with its unit of measurement equal to the Celsius, has its zero point at the zero point of internal energy. Because temperature is an expression of the internal energy of a substance, the Kelvin scale is the only scale where doubling the internal energy doubles the temperature. It is the only scale where you can say that it is twice as warm when the value doubles. Though Kelvin is the base SI unit, this textbook uses SI-derived units such as Celsius as SI units. The only exception is when energy must be calculated, where Kelvin is necessary to use.

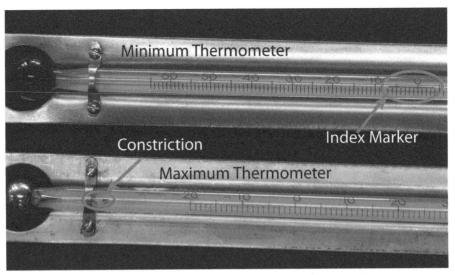

Figure 1.4 Minimum thermometer (top) shown with the index showing a minimum temperature of 4 °C and a maximum thermometer shown with a constriction in the inner tube near the metal mounting band.

A number of other useful thermometers exist. The maximum thermometer has a constriction immediately above the bulb preventing the liquid from returning to the bulb when the measured substance cools (Figure 1.4). This feature allows the thermometer to "remember" the maximum temperature since the last time the thermometer was reset. Holding the top of the thermometer and shaking it forces the liquid past the restriction and resets a maximum thermometer. If you have seen anybody shake a glass thermometer prior to taking somebody's temperature, you have seen the resetting of a maximum thermometer. The minimum thermometer utilizes an index marker that has a diameter similar to the inside of the inner glass tube. The liquid pulls down the index marker during cooling, but remains in place when the liquid expands. This feature allows the minimum temperature to be "remembered." Simply tipping the minimum thermometer resets it by allowing the index to rise to the top of the liquid. These thermometers allow us to record the high and low temperatures over a 24-hour period without the need to sit and watch the thermometers for the entire day. That would be a boring job.

Thermistors are electrical circuits that measure the changing resistance in an electrical circuit that occurs with a changing temperature. This relationship determines the temperature scale. They have no glass and are typically smaller and faster than a liquid-in-glass thermometer. Most digital thermometers that you purchase these days to monitor if you have a fever use thermistors.

Radiometers measure the amount of radiation coming from the direction it is pointing. We will learn later that everything emits radiation (yes, you are radiant) and radiometers measure this emission. Radiometers can be used as thermometers because the amount of radiation matter emits is proportional to its temperature. If you have seen somebody measure their temperature by pointing a thermometer to their head, you have seen a radiometer. An advantage of these radiometers is that they can measure temperature without physically touching the object. Radiometers can be attached to a satellite orbiting Earth to measure the temperature of the Earth's surface around the world. However, because the air between the surface and the radiometer can affect the measurement, obtaining the Earth's surface temperature requires a complex calculation.

An interesting and important observation (as we will see later) is an atmospheric profile of atmospheric temperature from the ground up. To measure the temperature at different vertical levels, the thermometer can be attached to a balloon filled with Hydrogen or Helium (both lighter than air), allowing it to rise. In order to obtain the measurements, a radio transmitter accompanies the balloon and sends the data to a surface station. This balloon is called a weather balloon and the instrument package it carries is called a radio-sonde or rawinsonde if the balloon is tracked to measure winds.

Figure 1.5 shows the vertical temperature profile averaged from all over the world at all times of the year for several years from the surface to about 130 km (81 miles) altitude. The temperatures on this image are the annual-global-mean temperature. The surface temperature is the annual-global-mean surface temperature and the increase in this value would be global warming. Notice that the temperature near the surface decreases from the surface up. The rate at which the temperature increases or decreases is called the

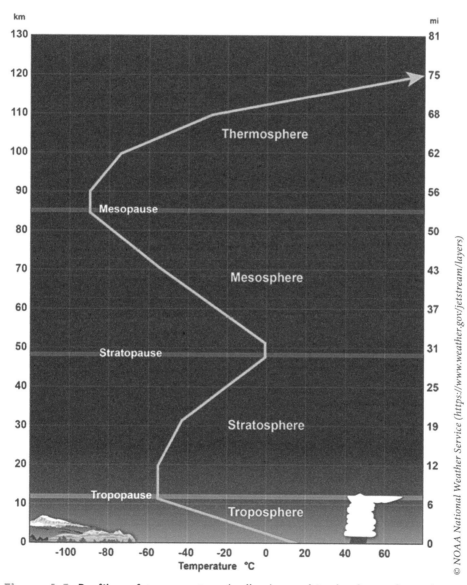

© NOAA National Weather Service (https://www.weather.gov/jetstream/layers)

Figure 1.5 Profiles of temperature (yellow) vs. altitude shown from the surface to 130 km (81 miles) altitude.

environmental lapse rate. Because we call it a lapse rate, the value is positive when the temperature is decreasing (or lapsing) as you go up. The symbol for environmental lapse rate, Γ_e is calculated as follows,

$$\Gamma_e = \frac{\Delta T}{\Delta z} = \frac{T_2 - T_1}{z_2 - z_1}$$

where T is temperature, z is altitude, and Δ represents a change in the adjacent variable (e.g., ΔT is the change in temperature). The last expression, right of the last equal sign, defines ΔT and Δz, respectively, as the difference of each parameter at two different altitudes. The subscripts provide additional details about the variables. The "e" subscript denotes that the lapse rate is for the environment and the "2" and "1" represents two different altitudes above the surface. When the temperature of the higher altitude (subscript 2) is less than the temperature of the lower altitude (subscript 1), the fraction will be negative. In this case, multiplying the negative sign in front of the fraction results in a positive environment lapse rate, Γ_e. Therefore, when the temperature decreases from the surface up, the lapse rate is positive.

This mathematical symbology is important to understand and is an example of the mathematical expressions used throughout the book. The final expression in the above mathematical expression can be calculated by observing the temperature at two altitudes and substituting them in for T_1 and T_2. The altitudes of the observations would then be substituted for z_1 and z_2 where z_1 is the altitude where temperature T_1 is observed and z_2 is the altitude where temperature T_2 is observed.

Notice in Figure 1.5 that the near-surface temperature lapse rate is positive (temperature decreasing from the surface up). In later chapters, it will be shown that the sun heats the surface of the Earth, which then heats the atmosphere from the bottom up. That is why the lowest 10 km (6 miles) of the atmosphere has a positive temperature lapse rate. The layer exhibiting this temperature pattern is called the **troposphere**. Above this layer, the temperature stops changing (tropopause) at around 10 km (6 miles) and then the lapse rate becomes negative. The reason the temperature increases as you go above about 10 km (6 miles) is that there is a lot of ultraviolet light from the sun absorbed by ozone in this part of the atmosphere. This layer above the tropopause, with a negative lapse rate, is called the **stratosphere**. Above the ozone layer, the temperature stops changing (stratopause) and then the lapse rate becomes positive again. The temperature decreases as you continue up to about 85 km (53 miles). This layer above the stratopause with a positive lapse rate is called the **mesosphere**. At the top of the mesosphere, the temperature once again stops decreasing and the coldest temperatures in the atmosphere are found in the mesopause. Above this point, there is very little air and the absorbed sunlight is strong enough to break apart air molecules. The absorption causes the air to warm and the lapse rate becomes negative again. This top layer is the **thermosphere**. Satellites and the space station orbit in the thermosphere. Although most people associate where the satellites orbit as outer space, there is enough air at these altitudes to cause the satellites to slow and eventually fall back to Earth. Where the atmosphere ends and outer space begins is somewhat ambiguous.

Much of the heating and cooling of the atmosphere occurs near the surface of the Earth. Near the surface is the most important location to forecast weather because it is the area that we most notice the weather. Surface weather stations observe all weather parameters within 10 m (32 feet) and 1.5-2 m (5-7 feet) above the Earth's surface. The benefit of measuring at these altitudes is twofold. First, most people's heads (our personal primary

Patterns

Patterns are everywhere and humans are quite adept at finding them. Noticing patterns is an important precursor to asking scientific questions, or hypotheses, about the patterns. Classifying patterns based on features or functions helps scientists to make hypotheses and determine relationships. They also allow scientists to develop mathematical expressions for them, which helps to understand the patterns. Patterns require careful observation and are a unifying concept because all scientists in every branch of science engage in pattern recognition.

In this chapter, we use the pattern of temperatures in the vertical to classify different layers of the atmosphere. The classification of layers leads to the observation of the composition and energy transfer from the sun and Earth within and between each layer. Mathematical representations, such as the lapse rate, help scientists understand the important features and functions of each layer. Throughout this book, patterns such as clouds, pressure, storm tracks, winds, horizontal and vertical temperature distribution, etc., lead to questioning why these patterns exist. Observing, measuring, and documenting these patterns is the first step in the scientific method.

sensing instrument) are located in this range. Second, the lapse rate below the temperature observing altitude is large and varies dramatically from day to night and from cloudy to sunny periods. During clear daytime conditions, the lapse rate within this altitude can be as large as 10 °C/m (5.5 °F/foot). This means that in the day your feet can experience a 10 °C (18 °F) hotter temperature than your abdomen. At night, when the ground cools, the surface air lapse rate can be as low as −3 C/m (or −1.6 °F/foot).

Wind

Winds come about from air in motion. When you feel the wind, what you are feeling is air moving from one location to another. Mean and instantaneous wind velocities are reported to the public. The averaging time is typically two minutes and the SI unit is m/s. The traditional units of measure are the mile per hour (mph) and the nautical mile per hour or knot. A nautical mile is 1/60 of a degree of latitude when moving along a line of longitude or north to-south. The purpose of this unit of measurement is to make naval navigation simpler, but it remains the traditional meteorological unit of measurement. There are 1.15 statute miles in a nautical mile so the difference is small. The textbook will mostly use the SI unit and the knot.

Velocity is one of several special quantities used in weather called a vector quantity. Vector quantities require both a magnitude and a direction. For wind, speed is the magnitude. When you are driving in a car, your speed-o-meter tells you how fast you are going, but does not tell you your direction. Direction is either given using compass directions (i.e., north, south, east, and west) or a 360 degree measurement of a circle where north is 0°, east is 90°, south is 180°, and west is 270° (Figure 1.6). Wind direction always refers to where the air is coming from. Winds are reported with both speed and direction, such as north at 5 m/s (10 knots). In this case, the speed is 5 m/s (10 knots) and the direction is north (i.e., the air is coming from the north and moving toward the south).

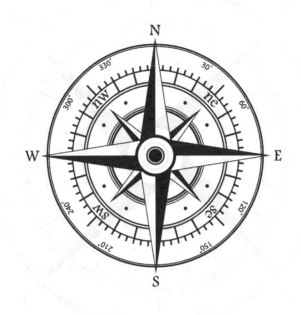

Figure 1.6 Picture showing a compass with four compass points: north (N), east (E), south (S), and West (W). Directions not exactly on the four compass points are subdivided (e.g., SW for southwest) as shown or can be given as a direction in degrees shown on the outer edge.

Figure 1.7 An aerovane outside of Eastern Michigan University.

A few different instruments measure wind. **Anemometers** measure the wind speed. The most common type of anemometer is the cup anemometer, consisting of three cups extending from a central pole that captures the moving air and causes the pole to turn. The rotational rate of the turning pole provides a measure of the wind speed. Another kind of anemometer uses a propeller instead of cups. The wind causes the propeller to spin, much like when you blow on to a fan to make it spin. The speed the propeller spins is proportional to the wind speed.

Wind vanes measure the wind direction. Wind vanes consist of a flat metal plate on one side of a rotating pole and a counterweight on the opposite side. Unlike the anemometer this pole does not spin, but rotates to align with the wind direction. An aerovane, shown in Figure 1.7, typically consists of a wind vane where the counterweight is a propeller. Therefore, the metal plate aligns the instrument in the direction of the wind and the wind then turns the propeller. In later chapters, radars are discussed, which can also be used to measure wind velocity.

Understanding forces is necessary to understand what causes wind. Forces also help us understand how air moves in the vertical, which is critical in understanding how clouds, precipitation, and thunderstorms form.

Force and Acceleration

A force is anything that causes matter to change its velocity and, like velocity, is a vector. The SI unit of measure for force is the Newton, N, and the traditional unit is the pound, lb. Acceleration is a measure of the change in velocity that forces cause and the SI unit, m/s², which is also the traditional unit. Acceleration is also a vector quantity. Automobiles are a familiar example to help describe the difference between acceleration, velocity, and speed. Automobiles have three accelerators (bet you did not know that). One pedal (usually all the way to the right), commonly called the accelerator pedal, is used to change the velocity in the forward direction. Another pedal, commonly called the brake or de-accelerator pedal, changes velocity in the backward direction. A third device, known as a steering wheel, changes the direction of the car (which is also a change in velocity because of the directional change). The change in velocity can be a change in magnitude, direction, or both. Sir Isaac Newton provided us with the relationship between force, mass, and acceleration in his second law of motion: Force, F, is equal to the product of mass, m, and acceleration, a.

$$F = ma$$

Newton's name is applied to both this law and the unit of measure (come up with a scientific law and your name can be used).

Notice that the traditional unit is the pound. Most people recognize pounds as a measure of weight. Weight is the downward force caused by your body on the Earth. It comes about from the product of your mass (i.e., how much matter you contain), and the acceleration of your mass. On Earth, that acceleration comes about from gravity. On the surface, you accelerate toward the center of Earth at 9.8 m/s². If you were to take a rocket ship to the moon and you did not lose any matter on the trip (such as losing body parts), your mass would be the same. However, because you would be accelerating toward the center of the moon at a smaller rate (1.6 m/s²), your weight on the moon would be about 1/6 of your weight on Earth.

Air consists of matter and has mass. The combination of this mixture of gases is heavier than you probably think. The entire Earth's atmosphere weighs approximately 11,619 quadrillion pounds! However, for weather forecasting, the total weight of air is not as important as how it is distributed, which is represented by pressure.

Pressure

It is important to realize that air has mass in order to understand how winds blow in the horizontal. However, it is not important for us to know the weight of the entire Earth's atmosphere, just how it is distributed. The weight of the atmosphere over some small area, usually a square meter, provides this distribution. The weight, or force, per square meter of air is its pressure. The unit of measurement is the Newton per square meter, N/m², also known as the Pascal. The traditional unit in meteorology is the millibar, but many may have heard of the pound per square inch. We will learn the details later, but the larger the pressure difference across two locations, the larger the force that causes air to move (i.e., wind).

Barometers measure pressure and there are two main types. Mercury barometers consist of an evacuated tube (zero pressure) placed upside down in a bowl of mercury that is open to the atmosphere (Figure 1.8). As previously stated, a pressure difference across two locations will cause air to move, it will also cause mercury to move. Therefore, the higher pressure of the atmosphere surrounding the bowl of mercury forces the mercury

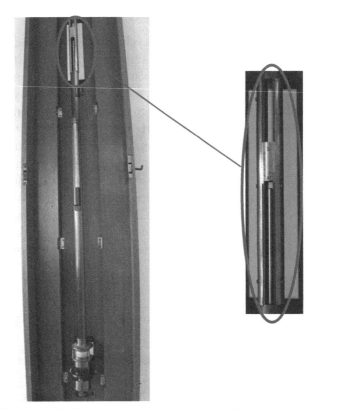

© Tom Kovacs

Figure 1.8 Picture showing a mercurial barometer with inset showing the top of the mercury column. The tube of mercury is upside down in a bowl of mercury that is open to the atmosphere and is at the bottom of the figure.

up the evacuated tube. The same thing happens when you put a straw in a beverage. In order to get the liquid up the straw, you need to reduce the pressure inside the straw. You do this by sucking out the air in the straw. This causes the beverage to rise up in the straw and eventually into your mouth. If you had a thick enough straw, you would not be able to suck enough air out of the straw to cause the beverage to rise. Try sucking a beverage up a cardboard paper towel holder. You will not be able to do it (and you would look somewhat funny trying).

The difference in pressure between inside and outside of the tube directly relates to the level the mercury rises. The pressure outside the tube is the atmospheric pressure. Because there is zero pressure inside the tube, the amount the mercury rises is directly related to the atmospheric pressure. Being a metal, the mercury in the evacuated tube is called a bar and this became a unit of measure for pressure. This is why the millibar (or thousandth of a bar) is traditionally used, but the numerically equal hectopascal (hPa; or hundred Pascals) is increasingly used. The Pascal is the SI unit for pressure. The mercury will typically rise between 28 and 32 inches at sea level (inches of mercury is another unit often used for pressure). Therefore, mercury barometers are typically about 3 feet (36 inches) tall.

The aneroid (meaning without liquid) barometer is another type of pressure instrument (Figure 1.9). It consists of an aneroid cell, which is a thin and compressible metal enclosure with no inside pressure. The atmospheric pressure then increasingly compresses the aneroid cell so that the displacement is directly related to the atmospheric pressure.

People often use aneroid barometers in their homes because the aneroid cell is only an inch or two and does not contain mercury, so it is smaller and safer (though not as accurate). If you have a barometer with "sunny," "fair," and "stormy" written on it, it is an aneroid barometer. It communicates the usual weather that comes with low and high pressure. The reason for this relationship is discussed later. Digital barometers on home weather stations work somewhat similar to aneroid barometers.

Figure 1.10 shows the mean pressure of the atmosphere from the ground to 16,200 m above ground. The figure illustrates that pressure always decreases as you go up in the atmosphere. The highest pressures are always at the surface. Going up and finding a higher pressure almost never happens in weather forecasting applications. The highest commercial aircraft flies at around 200 hPa (200 mb), which is about 20% of the surface pressure and contains 20% of the surface oxygen. Aircraft are pressurized because passengers and crew could not survive in such a low-pressure environment.

Figure 1.9 Picture of an aneroid barometer showing the recording drum on the left and the aneroid cell on the right, which is a small flexible metal container that expands and contracts with changing pressure. The needle records the change in the anaroid cell onto the drum.

Figure 1.10 An Illustration showing the decrease in pressure (left) with height (right) along with the highest mountain in North America and commercial jet cruising altitude for reference.

Density

Density largely determines the vertical winds as will be discussed later. Density is a measure of how much matter is contained in some volume. For example, envision two dice that were exactly the same size in length, width, and depth (the product of these three spatial dimensions is the volume). If one was made of wood and the other steel, the steel one will be much heavier (Figure 1.11). The reason is there is much more matter in the steel die (and therefore more mass) than the wood die. Density is a measure of the ratio of an object's mass to its volume:

$$density = \frac{mass}{volume},$$

The unit is kg/m³. If you put the two dice in a bowl of water, the wood die would float and the steel die would sink. The reason for this is that the steel die has a higher density than water and the wood one has a lower density. Temperature also affects density. Warm water is less dense than colder water and warm air is less dense than colder air. You can actually heat water and make it float on top of colder water. If the cold and warm water were colored differently, you would be able to see this.

Some people falsely think that things that float are lighter. However, the observation that battleships float and sand grains sink would be hard to explain if you think this way. The reason battleships float is that density, not the mass or weight, determines whether something will float. If you measured the mass of the part of the ship under water, it would be equal to the mass of that same volume of water. Since we know steel is quite dense, how can that be? The answer is that battleships are not solid steel. They have air in them (fortunately for the occupants). With the right mixture of air and steel, you can get a mass equal to the mass of the volume of water that the battleship displaces (i.e., the volume of the ship that is below the water). If the ship fills with water, displacing the air in the ship, then this mass will increase and the ship will sink.

DENSITY

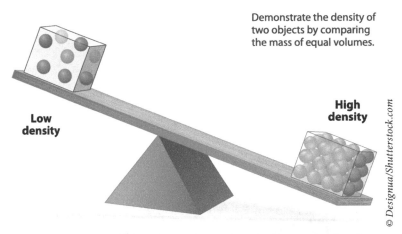

Demonstrate the density of two objects by comparing the mass of equal volumes.

Low density

High density

© Designua/Shutterstock.com

Figure 1.11 An illustration showing that for two equal volumes, the mass can be different depending on the amount of matter (e.g., steel is more dense than wood because there is more matter within the same volume).

The relative density of air largely determines what air will rise and what air will sink. Later chapters will show that rising air causes clouds and thunderstorms to form. Therefore, density is critical to the forecasting of weather and this textbook will spend much time on it.

Water

All these parameters bring us back to one of the most important constituents of the atmosphere, water. Water is important to forecasting weather because it exists in all three phases at normal atmospheric pressures and temperatures. This fact leads to water forming visible liquid, solid clouds, falling liquid, and solid precipitation in an atmosphere with invisible gaseous water. No other compound on Earth does this in the atmosphere. On other planets and moons with different pressures and temperatures, other elements

---

Digging Deeper

Why are there so many absolute humidity units of measurements?

The SI unit for measuring the amount of water in the gas phase of the atmosphere is kg/m^3, which is a density. Absolute humidity is also called vapor density. Most calculations will require humidity measurements with these units because they are the SI units. Instruments cannot easily measure this number directly, and a technique to measure absolute humidity with thermometers will be covered shortly. Vapor pressure is not an SI unit, but is more traditional because of its relationship to measuring air pressure. Mixing ratio is not and SI unit, but has an important function that simplifies forecasting. Mixing ratio does not change when air moves vertically whereas the other units of measurement do. An example will help illustrate this function.

Rising air expands in the lower pressure environment that exists higher up. The expansion causes only the denominator (i.e., volume in m^3) in absolute humidity to change. However, this causes the absolute humidity as a whole to change. It also causes the pressure of the rising air to change and therefore the vapor pressure of the rising air to change. However, the mass of rising air and the mass of its water vapor does not change unless there is a phase change. Therefore, mixing ratio does not change when air rises, and this makes it easier to understand the characteristics of rising air as we will see later (Table 1.1). The existence of so many scientific units are confusing, but multiple units have different uses depending on the application. However, it arguably makes learning science more difficult.

Table 1.1 Calculation of absolute humidity and mixing ratio for air moving from higher to lower pressure values (i.e., different heights) assuming a surface air density of 1.2 kg/m^3 at 1000 hPa (1000 mb) and 1.2 g of water vapor in the rising air

	Near sea level (1000 mb)	At 500 mb
Mass of water	1.2 g	1.2 g
Mass of air	1.2 kg	1.2 kg
Volume of air	1 m^3	2 m^3
Absolute humidity	1.2 g/m^3	0.6 g/m^3
Mixing ratio	1 g/kg	1 g/kg

work in this way. For example, on Saturn's moon Titan, methane and ethane behave in a similar way to water with methane and ethane clouds, precipitation, rivers, and lakes.

Water in the gas phase is known as water vapor. There are a number of ways to express the abundance of water vapor in the atmosphere, which is a parameter called humidity. Humidity can be expressed both as an absolute and relative number. Absolute humidity tells us how much water vapor is actually in the air and its standard unit is a density, kg/m³. Traditionally, absolute humidity is expressed as a mixing ratio of grams of water per kilogram of air, g/kg, and as a vapor pressure, mb. Vapor pressure is the amount of pressure in the atmosphere due to water (also known as the partial pressure). This textbook mostly uses kg/m³ and mb, but will also use g/kg when it is more traditionally used.

Relative humidity is a helpful parameter because it tells us how close the atmosphere is to forming clouds. Clouds form when the amount of water vapor in the atmosphere reaches its capacity, also known as saturation. The capacity is related to temperature and, when the atmosphere reaches this capacity, the air is saturated at that temperature. The capacity increases at higher temperatures. For a given temperature, we can calculate the vapor pressure or mixing ratio at this capacity. This parameter is called the saturation vapor pressure or saturation mixing ratio. The highest the saturation vapor pressure can reach in the atmosphere is the atmospheric pressure. When the temperature reaches the boiling point, the saturation vapor pressure is equal to the atmospheric pressure. This is why the boiling point will be lower at a higher altitude where the atmospheric pressure is lower. The boiling point is lower because a lower temperature is needed for the saturation vapor pressure to match the lowered atmospheric pressure.

The actual measured vapor pressure or mixing ratio (i.e., the amount of water vapor in the air) is not always at capacity, or at its saturation vapor pressure or saturation mixing ratio. The ratio of the measured vapor pressure and mixing ratio to the capacity (the amount of water vapor in the air when the air is saturated) is the parameter known as relative humidity (RH):

$$RH = \frac{vapour\ pressure}{saturation\ vapour\ pressure} = \frac{mixing\ ratio}{saturation\ mixing\ ratio}$$

Relative humidity is expressed as a percentage by multiplying the ratio by 100%. Therefore, when the vapor pressure is equal to the saturation vapor pressure, the air is saturated. At saturation the above ratios equals one, the relative humidity is 100%, and clouds form. If the relative humidity is less than 100%, then the air is not saturated and clouds will not form. In essence, the relative humidity tells you how close the atmosphere is to forming clouds. People mistakenly think that you can feel relative humidity, but you can only feel relative humidity when it is near 100%, when water begins to condense causing things to feel damp. People mostly feel absolute humidity when they say things like, "it is humid today" and "the air is making my hair frizzy".

The problem with the parameters for absolute humidity is that they are not directly measured. Therefore, directly measured parameters are observed and then related to absolute humidity. One way to measure absolute humidity is to cool the air down until the saturation vapor pressure drops to the vapor pressure (i.e., saturation occurs) and water condenses. The temperature that this condensation forms is called the dewpoint temperature. If the air has more water vapor in it, saturation occurs at higher temperatures. Therefore, the more water vapor in the air, the higher the dewpoint temperature.

Dewpoint temperature is measured with a device known as a dewpoint hygrometer. A crude dewpoint hygrometer is a cold beverage (Figure 1.12). You may have noticed that when you bring a cold beverage out on a humid day condensation forms on the surface of the beverage container. This condensation forms because the beverage is cooling the air down to its dewpoint temperature. If there is not enough water vapor in the air (vapor pressure or mixing ratio is too low), or the beverage does not cool the air to a low enough temperature (saturation vapor pressure is too high), the relative humidity will not reach 100% and condensation will not form on the beverage. When the beverage's temperature causes the air's saturation vapor pressure to be equal to the air's vapor pressure, the beverage temperature equals the air's dewpoint temperature. This is exactly how a dewpoint hygrometer works. Dewpoint hygrometers simply cool air down until condensation forms, then measures the temperature of the air, which is the dewpoint temperature.

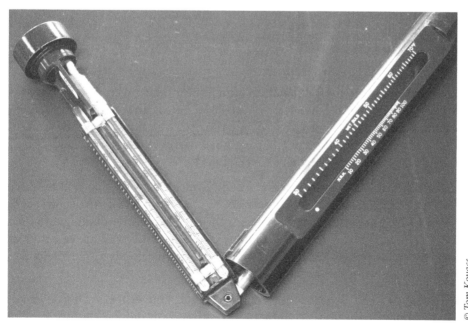

© Patchra Suttivirat/Shutterstock.com

Figure 1.12 Condensation occurs on a cold beverage when the air in contact with the glass is colder than the dewpoint temperature of the air.

A second way to measure absolute humidity is evaporate water into the air causing the temperature of the remaining liquid water to lower. The lowered temperature will lower the saturation vapor pressure of the air in contact with this remaining liquid water. Eventually, the temperature and saturation vapor pressure will lower to the vapor pressure of the air. The temperature this occurs at is then directly proportional to the vapor pressure you are measuring. An instrument called the sling psychrometer is used to measure this lowered temperature (Figure 1.13). The sling psychrometer has two liquid-in-glass thermometers mounted side-by-side. The mount can be spun to allow water to evaporate off a wet "sock" on the bulb of one of the thermometers. The temperature that the sock on the "wet-bulb" lowers down to is the wet-bulb temperature. You can then derive the absolute humidity values from the

© Tom Kovacs

Figure 1.13 A picture showing a sling psychrometer with the dry bulb thermometer (left) and the wet bulb thermometer (right) with a sock on the wet bulb.

Figure 1.14 Standard rain gauge (left) and weighing rain gauge (right).

© Tom Kovacs

measurements of these two thermometers. You can also derive the relative humidity with a sling psychrometer. The wet-bulb thermometer is directly proportional to the absolute humidity, vapor pressure, or mixing ratio. The dry bulb thermometer simply gives you the air temperature, which is directly proportional to saturation vapor pressure or the saturation mixing ratio. The ratio of the two derived values gives the relative humidity.

A **Rain gauge** measures precipitation at the Earth's surface and a radar measures precipitation when the water is in the cloud. Radar is discussed later. Standard rain gauges are two concentric tubes of different opening cross-sectional areas topped off by a funnel to a small opening (Figure 1.14). The ratio of the opening cross-sectional areas of the two tubes is 10:1. Therefore, if a hundredth of an inch of rain falls on the outer collector tube, the inner measurement tube will collect a funneled amount equal to a tenth of an inch. A ruler is then placed in the measurement tube. A tenth of an inch is measurable with a ruler, but a hundredth of an inch is not. When a hundredth of an inch of precipitation falls, it funnels to a tenth of an inch in the collection tube. A special ruler is used that already has this 10:1 conversion of measured to actual precipitation accumulation so the correct precipitation amount is observed.

When frozen precipitation falls, the observer removes the funnel and measurement tube prior to the event. The collector tube then collects the frozen precipitation. The observer then brings the collector tube inside, melting and measuring the precipitation. This melted precipitation is the liquid-equivalent precipitation accumulation.

Actual snowfall is measured on a white board, which is simply a flat white board. The white color prevents the sun from melting the snow. The observer then measures multiple locations of the snow accumulation and averages these observations for the final mean value.

Clouds

Clouds are reported as the fractional amount of sky they cover. The observer stands where the entire sky is visible and determines the amount of the sky, in eighths, is covered with clouds. This is often reported as follows: clear (zero eighths), few clouds (one or two eighths), scattered clouds (three or four eighths), partly cloudy or broken (five, six, or seven eighths), or cloudy or overcast (eight eighths).

Cloud classifications are also reported and have significance that will be discussed later. There are three main types of clouds: **stratus**, **cumulus**, and **cirrus**. Stratus clouds are layered and featureless. Featureless means that they have little shading differences or contrast over a large part of the sky. Cumulus clouds are puffy and are often the clouds people try to see as physical shapes (e.g., bunnies). Cirrus clouds are high clouds composed of ice giving them a wispy, feathery shape.

Cloud classification also employs various prefixes and suffixes. Stratus clouds use the prefix "nimbo-". Cumulus clouds use the suffix "-nimbus", meaning the cloud is producing precipitation that is reaching the ground. Mid-level clouds use the prefix "alto-", meaning the clouds are neither low nor high clouds. Upper troposphere

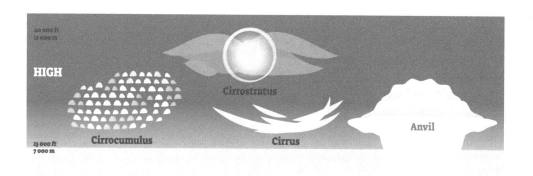

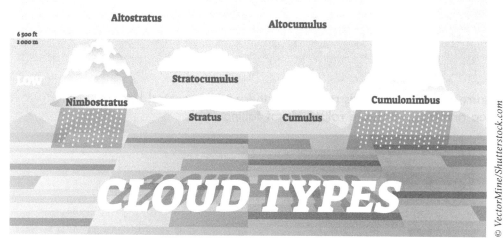

© VectorMine/Shutterstock.com

Figure 1.15 Cloud types and their approximate altitudes for midlatitudes are shown.

clouds use the prefix "cirro-". Layered clouds with little vertical extent use "strato-" as a prefix (Figure 1.15).

High-Level Clouds

High clouds are typically above 7 km (23000 feet) in the midlatitudes and are composed of ice crystals. They are all cirrus or cirro- clouds. Cirrus clouds look feathery or wispy and are high clouds with snow falling (called fallstreaks) from them (Figure 1.16). The feathery part is actually snow. Observing the orientation of the wisps relative to the main cloud can give you an idea of upper-level wind direction. Cirrocumulus clouds are high cumulus clouds (Figure 1.17). They are actually of similar size to the low puffy-looking cumulus clouds, but are over 7 km (4.4 miles) away from the observer so they look smaller than the tip of your finger with your arm extended. Cirrostratus clouds are difficult to see because they simply make the sky look whiter, much like haze. However, haze is typically near the Earth's surface and composed of liquid, whereas cirrostratus are near the top of the troposphere and composed of ice crystals. Cirrostratus also cause halos (Figure 1.18) or sun dogs to form around the sky or moon. Light refracts through ice crystals in high altitude cirrostratus clouds producing halos, which often form ahead of warm fronts and can predict precipitation within 24 hours. A warm front did bring precipitation about 8 hours after the picture in Figure 1.18.

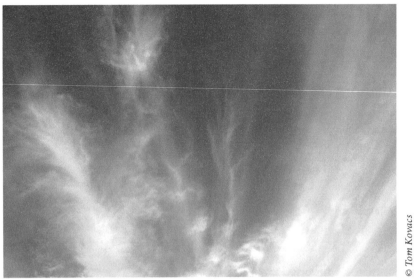

Figure 1.16 Cirrus clouds appear feathery with a central bright area and tails, which are fallstreaks of falling snow.

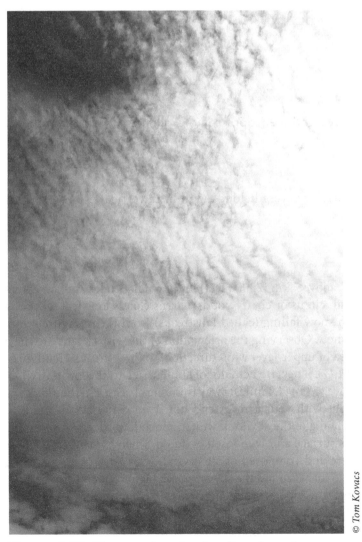

Figure 1.17 Cirrocumulus clouds often form in curvy lines, which are actually waves.

© Tom Kovacs

Figure 1.18 A halo around the sun in a cirrostratus cloud often predicts precipitation within 24 hours.

© Tom Kovacs

Figure 1.19 Altocumulus clouds are cloud puffs that appear larger than cirrocumulus because they are closer to the ground and observer.

Mid-Level Clouds

Mid-level clouds are typically between 2 km (6500 feet) and 7 km (28000 feet) in the midlatitudes and are often liquid clouds, but may contain a mixture of liquid water and ice clouds in winter and colder climates. All mid-level clouds have the prefix *alto-* in their naming conventions. The two main types of mid-level clouds are altocumulus and altostratus. Altocumulus clouds look like larger cirrocumulus clouds. They are larger than the tip of your finger, but smaller than a fist from an extended arm. Altocumulus clouds are larger because they are not as far away from a ground observer (Figure 1.19). Altostratus clouds, like cirrostratus clouds, allow the sun through and can predict precipitation because they form ahead of warm fronts (Figure 1.20). The difference in appearance is that there are no halos; instead the sun appears distorted (not circular). Expect precipitation within several hours because the warm front and precipitation are closer than when observing altostratus.

Figure 1.20 Altostratus clouds are composed of supercooled liquid water, which produces no haloes like cirrostratus, but the sun can be seen as a distorted disk through the clouds unlike stratus.

Figure 1.21 Stratus clouds are uniformly gray with virtually no shading differences or cloud edges.

Low-Level Clouds

Low-level clouds are typically within 2 km of the surface in the midlatitudes and are most likely to be liquid. Most low-clouds form from air rising from the surface with the bottom of the cloud forming at nearly the same altitude, giving the appearance of flat bottoms. For stratus clouds where edges are not seen, the clouds are uniformly gray with little shading differences in the cloud (Figure 1.21). For cumulus (Figure 1.22) and **stratocumulus** (Figure 1.23) clouds, the edges of the cloud will be thinner, allowing more sunlight through and giving the clouds a "silver lining". The difference between cumulus and stratocumulus is that you cannot see much, if any, white puffy cloud over the darker

Figure 1.22 Cumulus cloud have a darker flat base and vertical extension of white and puffy cloud.

Figure 1.23 Stratocumulus clouds are cumulus clouds that have flattened and spread out into a layer. They are different from stratus in that you can see darker and lighter parts of the clouds. The lighter parts are the thinner edges.

base in stratocumulus because they are a layered cumulus cloud. All low clouds can precipitate to the ground. For cumulus and stratus clouds, precipitating clouds would have the nimbus suffix or the *nimbo-* prefix added, respectively, producing cumulonimbus and nimbostratus clouds.

Fog forms when the base of stratus clouds are at the Earth's surface, which occurs with a surface relative humidity near 100%. The term, "the fog is burning off", comes from the sun heating the ground and lowering the relative humidity causing the fog to evaporate. Because fog evaporates from the bottom up it also appears that the fog lifts, but that is not what is actually happening.

Figure 1.24 Cumulonimbus clouds have a flat top where rising air reaches a layer that prevents further rising so the cloud spreads out giving the cloud an anvil appearance.

Multi-Level Clouds

Sometimes clouds can exist at multiple levels on top of each other with clear areas in between levels. Although surface observers often only see the lowest layer of clouds, this multi-layering is important to pilots, in satellite remote sensing, and for weather models. Oftentimes it is difficult for a surface observer to see the different layers, but satellites give the weather observer a view from the top-down perspective. Satellite analysis techniques observe multi-layer clouds and are covered in Chapter 3.

Cumulus clouds can grow to several kilometers in altitude and there are multiple names for the different types of cumulus clouds. In this text, we will only cover cumulonimbus clouds. Cumulonimbus clouds typically grow vertically until some layer above prevents it from growing further (Figure 1.24). Once it hits this layer, the cloud will stop growing vertically and will begin to grow horizontally. This horizontal growth at the top of a cumulonimbus cloud gives it the appearance of an anvil.

Weather Observing

Weather observations are highly organized internationally by the World Meteorological Organization (WMO), a special agency under the United Nations. The WMO facilitates worldwide cooperation in establishing observing networks, exchanging information, standardizing observations, and applying this information to support human activities and natural resources. The WMO standardizes the times of observations, the instruments used, the units of measurement, the observation technique, and the calibration standards. This standardization provides confidence that differences between the values of weather parameters are because of differences in the parameters themselves and not from instrumentation differences.

The agency in the U.S. responsible for meeting the WMO specifications is the National Oceanic and Atmospheric Administration (NOAA) under the Department of Commerce.

NOAA then funds a number of agencies related to weather and climate forecasting. These agencies include the National Weather Service (NWS), National Ocean Service (NOS), National Ocean and Atmospheric Research (OAR) and the National Environmental Satellite, Data, and Information Service (NESDIS).

Observing Times

Observation times are highly coordinated. Weather stations observe on the hour every hour and release weather balloons at least two times a day. Sounds simple, but this is more complex than it sounds. For example, weather balloons are sent up at noon and midnight every day, but noon in the U.S. can be three hours different in New York (Eastern time zone) as it is in California (Pacific time zone). Furthermore, some locations observe daylight savings time and others do not. To time balloons to go up at the exact same time, you would need to agree on a time zone to define when noon and midnight actually occur.

The WMO and all member nations agree that all weather observations use the time zone of the prime meridian, which runs through the town of Greenwich, England. Because the prime meridian is located at zero degrees longitude, this time is labeled with the capital letter, Z, so that noon in this time zone would be labeled 12 Z. Alternatively, this time zone is also labeled Greenwich Meridian Time (GMT) and Universal Time Coordinated (UTC). Therefore, when looking at weather data, the time stamp for midnight will often look like one of these: 00 Z, 00 GMT, or 00 UTC (four digits are sometimes used when minutes are also included).

To convert to local time one must add or subtract the time difference between their time zone and the time zone at the prime meridian. For example, the Eastern Standard Time (EST) zone is 5 hours behind, so you would subtract 5 hours from the reported time. 12 Z is 7 EST. During daylight savings time, clocks spring ahead 1 hour and the Eastern Time zones are only 4 hours behind, so you would subtract 4 hours from the reported time. Time is based on the 24-hour clock with no AM or PM. For example, 18 Z is 1 PM EST.

Instrumentation, Calibration, and Uncertainties

The WMO standardizes the calibration of instruments traceable to an international standard. Most calibration standards are based on invariant constants of nature. For example, for temperature there are a number of specific points, called triple points, where a substance can exist in all three phases in equilibrium at the same time. The triple point of water is 0.01 °C (32.018 °F). By international agreement, the international standard for temperature are triple points of a large number of substances that span a large range of temperatures.

Standardizing the instrument and calibrating off a standard helps to make the measurements accurate. An official thermometer in Africa, for example, should be able to be brought to Australia and measure the same temperature within the uncertainties of the instrument. The standardized instrument should accurately measure the temperature when averaged over many measurements, but individual measurements may differ. The spread of measurement by an instrument is the precision of that instrument, which determines the uncertainty of that instrument. No instrument is perfect, but it will measure the same value for the same conditions within some level of uncertainty. By standardizing the instruments, the uncertainties of the instruments are known (yes, uncertainties are known, it is the measured value that is not) and the same for all instruments measuring that parameter. The WMO member nations select instruments that have relatively small uncertainties, but those uncertainties are never zero.

Siting and Instrument Placement at a Weather Station

The placement of instruments adheres to requirements to standardize the measurements and to remove local effects that can bias the data (i.e., make artificially high or low). For example, the official height for temperature measurements is 1.5-2 m (5-6 ft). The thermometer must be in a radiation shield, which is usually a white enclosure with openings to allow airflow. Thermometers should avoid placement near sources of heat like vents, air conditioners, etc. and should not be placed over irrigated surfaces, cement, asphalt, rock, or dark colored surfaces. Grassy surfaces are best. Placement of thermometers should be two times away from an object as that object is high. For a 20 foot building thermometers should be 40 feet from the building. Placing a thermometer too close to the building causes the heating from the building to bias the air temperature too high when winds blow from the building. Other weather parameters have different citing requirements. Most weather parameters are measured at 1.5 m (5 ft) above the ground except winds, which are reported at 10 m (32 ft) altitude.

Summary

Weather forecasting is an excellent topic for learning and applying the scientific method. At the foundation of the scientific method are observations and data. All weather forecasts are based on observations and data. Weather forecasting is not unique in how scientists use observations and data. One unifying concept that all scientists use when considering observations and data is to pick out patterns that help us understand the world we live in.

Each data type or parameter has its own units of measurement, which provides a standard magnitude to compare. All scientists follow an international system of units of measure (SI units). The base unit of measurement that all other units are derived includes the kilogram, second, meter, Kelvin, and Ampere. This textbook attempts to use SI derived units and traditional units together to help the reader appreciate the magnitude of measurements.

The chapter began with a discussion of what makes up everything in the known universe: matter. Nitrogen, oxygen, and water, is the gaseous matter that makes up most of the atmosphere. However, in the case of water, all three states of matter typically exist and the changes between states, or phase changes, were discussed. Because the atmosphere is composed of gaseous matter, it has mass, which is a measure of the amount of matter.

This chapter explored all of the basic weather data parameters including temperature, wind, pressure, density, humidity, precipitation, cloud cover, and cloud type. Instruments have been created to observe each parameter. Instruments are not perfect measurements and the spread of observations for a constant parameter provides a measure of their uncertainty. The World Meteorological Organization (WMO) standardizes measurements with these instruments so that uncertainties, measuring times, and measuring locations are all standardized.

Key Terms

Matter

Mass

SI Units

Phases of Matter

States of Matter

Condensation

Freezing

Deposition

Melting

Evaporation

Sublimation

Temperature

Thermometer

Radiometers

Radiosonde

Environmental Lapse Rate

Troposphere

Stratosphere

Mesosphere

Thermosphere

Velocity

Vectors

Anemometers

Wind Vane

Force

Acceleration

Pressure

Barometer

Density

Water Vapor

Humidity

Absolute Humidity

Mixing Ratio

Vapor Pressure

Relative Humidity

Saturation Vapor Pressure

Saturation Mixing Ratio

Dewpoint Temperature

Sling Psychrometer

Wet-Bulb Temperature

Rain Gauges

Stratus

Cumulus

Cirrus

Cirrocumulus

Cirrostratus

Altocumulus

Altostratus

Stratocumulus

Cumulonimbus

Nimbostratus

Universal Time Coordinated

Calibration

Accurate

Uncertainties

Precision

Questions and Problems

1. What is the difference between a solid, liquid, and gas?

2. What phase change occurs with the development or formation of the following:

   a) shrinking ice cubes in your freezer

   b) frost

   c) fog

   d) clouds

   e) hail

3. Why does temperature decrease as you go up in the troposphere? What is the parameter that is positive in the layer that expresses this temperature behavior?

4. Describe how the temperature lapse rate is used to define the different layers of the atmosphere.

5. If a weather balloon measures a temperature of 10 °C at 1 km and 18 °C at 1.5 km, what is the temperature lapse rate of this air? Show your work.

6. If you were facing east and the wind was blowing in your face at 10 knots, how would the wind be officially reported? Give the direction in both compass direction and degrees.

7. What is the net force on 1 kg of air that is moving at constant velocity? Show your work.

8. If you have a mass of 30 kg, what is your mass and weight on the Earth and moon? (Hint: calculate the force and use the conversions in the appendices and text)

9. Find the elevation of the top of Mt. Everest and use Figure 1.10 to determine the approximate percentage of oxygen compared to sea level (approximately 1000 mb).

10. Using the equation for density, provide the proportion of mass, volume, and density of a half stick of butter to a full stick of butter.

11. How does relative humidity typically change throughout the day? Use the equation for relative humidity to justify your description.

12. Using the equation for relative humidity, describe the two ways that the relative humidity can increase.

13. What will happen to the dewpoint temperature for air that has a temperature increase with no addition of water vapor? Explain.

14. Which of the following weather parameters always decrease as we climb upwards in the atmosphere? Explain your choice.

    a) Temperature

    b) Pressure

    c) Wind speed

    d) Humidity

15. Which clouds forecast that precipitation will occur at least a few hours into the future and why are they good forecasters of precipitation?

16. How do you convert from universal time coordinated (UTC) to your local time during standard and daylight savings time? How can UTC and your local time be on different days?

17. If you created a robot arm to throw darts at a dart board and it aims to make a bulls-eye, but hits the outer ring scoring double 20 every time is the arm accurate? Is it precise? Explain the difference.

Other Resources

https://www.emich.edu/geography-geology/weather for links to useful weather data to go along with this textbook and updates to any broken links in the textbook.

Chapter 2

Climate Data

Introduction

Climate is a difficult word to define and differentiate from weather. A good explanation of the difference is that weather determines what clothes you wear whereas climate determines what clothes you own. Alternatively, climate is what you expect whereas weather is what you get. Although these explanations help to understand the difference between climate and weather, they are neither precisely measurable nor definitions. A popular statistical definition of climate is that it is the long-term average of weather in a particular location. Likewise, climate change is a change in the long-term average of weather in a particular location.

Climate is important to define and measure because it determines what organisms can survive in an area. Not only do you want to know what to have in your wardrobe, but you also want to know what plants can grow on your property. It is also important to define in order to know if it is changing. A changing climate requires plants and animals to adapt or move to an area that has a climate survivable for them. Objectively defining climate allows us to assess whether the speed at which climate changes makes adaptation and survivability possible. If climate changes too rapidly, some plants and animals will not be able to adapt fast enough and will become extinct.

Most weather parameters have daily and seasonal cycles based on orbital parameters and location on Earth. Daily means are a part of climate data averaged over daily cycles. These cycles need to be well-sampled and consistently measured in order to be valid and without bias. For this reason, most weather parameters are sampled at least twice daily for upper-air data and hourly for surface data. Chapter 1 discussed how the WMO standardizes these measurements. If data were observed at one part of the day for a number of years and then another part of the day thereafter, changes would appear for reasons that are unrelated to a changing climate. If the observer were allowed to choose when to observe, then the data may become biased. For example, if the observer only observed when it was comfortable, then the data may have a warm, cold, or dry bias depending on the observers, comfort. Some description of the daily fluctuations are usually included in climate data like daily maximums and minimums. Annual means are also a part of climate data. Annual means average over the seasonal cycles so that they should not change from year-to-year. Annual means are usually an average of the daily means. Monthly and seasonal means are calculated similarly and provide information about the nature of the subannual fluctuations.

An important consideration is how many measurements and over what period determines a long-term mean. Because measurements are not perfect and weather parameters have random fluctuations, it is not satisfactory to use a single daily or annual mean to define a climate. Likewise, it is not satisfactory to compare a single measurement for two different years to determine if the climate is changing. The WMO sets the standard that 30 different measurements are satisfactory to give a mean that is representative and still allows for a determination of climate change. Effectively, this means that 30 years of data must be averaged to obtain climate means. Because of the statistical nature of climate, this chapter first discusses climate statistics before discussing the various climate data sets available.

Climate Statistics

Climate means and standard deviations are the most fundamental climate statistics. These climate statistics are defined like any mean and standard deviation. A **sample mean**, $\bar{x}$, is equal to the sum of the data values divided by the number of data values where n is the number of data points:

$$\bar{x} = \frac{x_1 + x_2 + \ldots x_n}{n},$$

For example if we have n = 3 temperatures, x_1 = 2 °C, x_2 = 3 °C , and x_3 = 7 °C then:

$$\bar{x} = \frac{2 + 3 + 7}{3} = \frac{12}{3} = 4 \ °C.$$

Most climate data are given as a mean, maximum, and minimum. In the previous example, the maximum is 7 °C, minimum is 2 °C, and the mean is 4 °C. Oftentimes, data is just a sample of all the possible temperatures. For example, the monthly mean temperature in Philadelphia, Pennsylvania for the month of September is 72.5 °F. This monthly mean is based on a sample of one location with data observed hourly. Philadelphia is a large city with temperatures that vary from downtown to the suburbs and close to bodies of water vs. far from bodies of water. A cold front can come through and drop the temperature from 25 °C (77 °F) to 15 °C (59 °F) within an hour, but the only data points averaged will be on the hours. Therefore, it is important to consider how representative any data are.

As mentioned in Chapter 1, the World Meteorological Organization (WMO) standardizes instruments and siting of observations. Nonetheless, a true mean is an ideal while a sample mean that is representative of the true mean is the goal. Furthermore, weather stations must sometimes be moved and instruments must sometimes be replaced. These events are documented and the data statistics must be tested to see if the instruments are causing any inaccuracies or biases. A bias would be if a new instrument was reading higher than an older instrument or if a new station had higher precipitation than an old station. In scientific measurements, a bias occurs when observation sampling design causes a parameter to be higher or lower than the actual value. Random sampling is an important way to avoid bias, but with climate, data sampling is done in one location at uniformly spaced times. Nonetheless, bias can be tested.

Weather and climate are complex and it is important to have an idea of how much we know, which we can do statistically. For example, when considering one component of climate change, whether Earth is getting warmer, or **global warming** is occuring, we want to be sure that the change is significant and not a normal fluctuation. In these cases, it is helpful to calculate the statistic known as the **sample variance**, s^2, and its square root, the **sample standard deviation**, s (Figure 2.1), which provides the variability of the data. We can check if the current global annual mean temperature is significantly different using the sample mean and sample standard deviation.

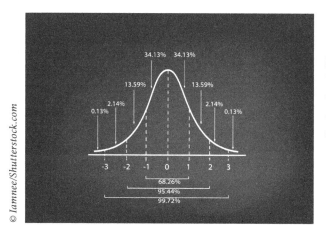

Figure 2.1 Randomly distributed data plotted around an expected mean value. Many students know this as a bell curve. The zero on the x-axis is the mean and the numbers 1, 2, and 3 are the number of standard deviations from the mean along with the percentage of values within each standard deviation.

Digging Deeper

Variance and Significance of Change

Variance is a measure of how much data varies from its mean. It is essentially the mean of the squared differences between every value and the sample mean. For the sample variance one less than the number of values, n, divides the sum of the squared differences. Therefore, variance is calculated as:

$$s^2 = \frac{1}{n-1} \sum_{i=1}^{n} (x_i - \overline{x})^2$$

$$= \frac{1}{n-1} [(x_1 - \overline{x})^2 + (x_2 - \overline{x})^2 + \dots + (x_i - \overline{x})^2].$$

For our previous example this would be calculated as follows:

$$s^2 = \frac{1}{3-1} [(2-4)^2 + (3-4)^2 + (7-4)^2]$$

$$= \frac{1}{2} [(-2)^2 + (-1)^2 + (3)^2]$$

$$= \frac{1}{2} [4+1+9] = \frac{14}{2} = 7.$$

Then, the sample standard deviation is just the square root of the sample variance:

$$s = \sqrt{s^2} = \sqrt{7} = 2.65.$$

For a normally distributed set of data (i.e., a bell curve), 68.3% of the data should be within the standard deviation of the data set (Figure 2.1). In our case, 66.7% of the data is within the range of the mean (i.e., between 4-2.65 and 4+2.65).

In order to know if the Earth is warming, we must know if the present global mean temperature is significantly higher than in the past. It could be that today's temperatures are part of the normal fluctuation of the entire history of global mean temperature data. To test if two sample means are significantly different an estimate of the standard error, $s_{\overline{x}}$, of the sample mean temperatures must be made. If the sample mean plus or minus its standard error does not fall within the past sample mean plus or minus its standard error, then the means are significantly different. Tests of a level of significance in this difference are also available and can provide us with a percentage level of confidence that the two values are different. An estimate of the standard error of a sample mean is calculated as follows:

$$s_{\overline{x}} = \frac{s}{\sqrt{n}}.$$

From this equation, if we have an infinite number of random samples, then the standard error would be zero, meaning that we know the mean of the entire population exactly. However, we do not always have that much data. We can increase the likelihood of determining if there is a change by reducing the standard error with more data. Increasing our sample size by a factor of 100 decreases our standard error by a factor of the square root of 100 or 10. This increases our chances of establishing that a change in the two means is not due to a random fluctuation.

The more data we have, the more confident we can be in our conclusions. More data temporally and spatially means that we have more of a representation of what we are trying to represent. When scientist state that the globe is definitely warming, they usually mean they are at least 95% confident. With more data and an increase in the change, confidence grows and can be quantified based on the data. By 2013, confidence was well over 99% that the Earth is warming[1].

The amount of warming is calculated in a similar way. The more data we have, the smaller the range we can apply to the value of the warming. The amount of warming is more precisely known than the actual values of the past and present global temperature means. For example, a 1 °C change in global temperatures is more precisely known than knowing that the global annual mean temperature changed from 15 °C to 16 °C. For this reason, most climate data is reported as an anomaly to or difference from a mean and not as an actual value. Therefore, when viewing climate trend plots, the y-axis is given in terms of an anomaly to a predetermined mean period. The WMO standardizes the predetermined mean to be over a 30-year period.

Determining a cause of a climate change is different from determining if the climate is changing. Causes require correlation and causation. Correlation is a measure of how much the change in two temporally or spatially varying quantities are similar. Two different parameters are correlated if they vary similarly.

For example, your age and your weight in the first 12 years of life are almost exactly correlated. However, factors other than age determines a person's weight. By analyzing the variances in weight and the variances in other factors, it is possible to get an idea of which factors are most important. The same is true in climate data.

Analysis of variances allows us to know which factors are most important in determining the change in a climate parameter. The concentration of greenhouse gases are highly correlated with temperature change, but it does not explain all of the change nor all of the variance. Furthermore, the correlation does not imply causation. For example, a person's weight and height are correlated, but a person's weight does not cause a person's height. Getting heavier does not mean that you will become taller. In fact, a person's height in the first 12 years of life correlates with the Earth's global mean temperature, but there is no causation between the two.

Causation is a much more difficult problem to prove. In the example of global warming, the proof that humans are causing global warming is a much more difficult problem. Correlation and causation must be shown. Greenhouse gases, as we shall see in Chapter 4, can cause the Earth to warm, but warming can also cause the greenhouse gases to increase. In both cases, correlation and causation can be proven, but do greenhouse gases cause global warming or does global warming cause an increase in greenhouse gases? Furthermore, an increase in greenhouse gases may only explain a minor part of the variance in global mean temperatures.

Causation is usually shown in laboratory experiments. It is easy to show that increasing temperatures occur when you add greenhouse gases to an enclosed space. However, the Earth is much more complicated and this only proves that greenhouse gases can be a cause. The best way to prove that greenhouse gas concentration leads to global warming is to use mathematical models, incorporating all the known processes to replicate the changes. Climate models are discussed in Chapter 15.

---

[1] IPCC, 2013: *Climate Change 2013: The Physical Science Basis. Contribution of Working Group I to the Fifth Assessment Report of the Intergovernmental Panel on Climate Change* [Stocker, T.F., D. Qin, G.-K. Plattner, M. Tignor, S.K. Allen, J. Boschung, A. Nauels, Y. Xia, V. Bex and P.M. Midgley (eds.)]. Cambridge University Press, Cambridge, United Kingdom and New York, NY, USA, 1535 pp.

Ask Questions and Define Problems

Observations and data may be the foundation of the scientific method, but asking questions is a necessary scientific practice in proceeding with the scientific method. Asking well-defined questions is a scientific practice, but it extends well beyond science. The process of observing, stimulating curiosity, experiencing, reading, and doing anything that can inspire questions and then formulating a well-defined question requires a habit of mind. A well-defined scientific question is one that can be answered empirically, meaning that it can be answered by observation or experience. The question is well defined if the answer to the question answers what the person really wanted to know and is sufficient in detail. It is sufficient in detail if somebody that has the knowledge to answer can answer, or an observation or experiment can be designed to answer.

A well-defined question often asked regarding climate change is how do we know what is causing climate change? This question relates to the question of how we know that humans and not an unknown natural fluctuation cause the changes we observe. After all, we know that climate has changed much more in our geologic past. The dinosaur period was much warmer than our current climate and humans were not around to cause this. Based on this knowledge, the question should be asked. It is defined well enough that somebody could design an experiment or find observations that can answer this question.

The change in the observed means and variances are largely modeled by the climate models discussed in Chapter 11, and greenhouse gases are a major part of that cause. Therefore, statistically unknown factors would only explain a small part of observed changes. However, unknown natural processes can cause the increase in greenhouse gases, so this still does not prove that humans cause the increase in greenhouse gases. Chapter 15 discusses how we know that a large majority of the increase in greenhouse gases is human-caused.

Climate Data Sets

The National Center for Environmental Information (NCEI; ncei.noaa.gov) is the main climate data repository for the U.S. The NCEI works with a large network of international organizations to share climate data generated worldwide. The archive at NCEI and at the many World Data Centers include instrument and proxy data. Instrumental climate data are data measured by climate or weather instruments. Many of the networks of instrumental data have global data records that extend back to the mid-19th century. Some instrumental records extend back to the 17th century, but are not global. Prior to this period, no direct instrumental measurements of climate data exist. Yet, it is important to have an idea of how climate changed prior to this period. Proxy data are methods to recover climate data before this period by observing physical characteristics of past environments that are preserved today.

Historical documents that include climate data are a type of proxy data set. Examples include farmer and mariner logs, newspaper articles, diaries, and other written documents that can give information used to reconstruct yearly climate. An example would be farmer logs of first and last frost dates. Along with other growing season data it is possible to reconstruct how much colder or warmer it was in the past. Multiple proxies are used to ensure consistency. The information from historical documents are more complete in the

Figure 2.2 Picture showing a cross-section of a tree with tree rings. Tree rings are created when a tree is in an actively growing season (light rings) and a dormant season (dark rings) with the rings along the outer edge formed in the last years of the tree's life.

recent past and give us information on the order of the past 1000 years. On the order of the past 1000 years means roughly several hundred years to a few thousand years ago.

Tree rings are another source of proxy data (Figure 2.2). In areas where there is a distinct growing season trees grow in diameter rapidly compared to the dormant season when trees grow little. Different color rings will be apparent in a cross-section of a tree. The growing season produces the lighter rings and the dormant season produces the darker rings. The number of light or dark rings determines the age of a tree when it died. The width of the light rings varies depending on the condition of the growing season. Recovering past yearly temperature and precipitation data requires a comparison of growth rings from similar tree species in the area to known temperature and precipitation data. Finding trees dead long ago allows this proxy to provide climate data on the order of 10,000 years.

Glacial ice over 4000 m (2.5 miles) deep in Antarctica form in layers with each successively deeper layer older than the last. The cold and warm season layers are distinct when observed under a microscope so that ice can be analyzed each year. Ice cores are drilled in the ice and a core is pulled out of the hole (Figure 2.3). Inside the ice within each layer, tiny bubbles preserve the well-mixed atmospheric air when the bubbles formed. This air is sampled to provide information on the concentrations of greenhouse gases. Greenhouse gases are atmospheric components that warm the Earth in a process discussed in Chapter 4.

The water itself gives us information on the atmospheric temperature when the ice formed based on the amount of heavy isotopes of oxygen present. Isotopes of oxygen are oxygen atoms of different molecular weights because of additional neutrons in the

Figure 2.3 Pictures of glacial ice after removal of a core of ice with a special drill.

nucleus. Water molecules contain two hydrogen atoms and one oxygen atom. The oxygen atoms in different water molecules are naturally composed of different oxygen isotopes. Colder atmospheres in which the glacial ice forms contain smaller concentrations of heavy oxygen isotopes. Ice core analysis provides climate data on the order of a million years because no glacial ice existed on Earth more than a couple million years ago.

Sediments in oceans and lakes also provide proxy data not on a yearly basis, but closer to a decadal resolution. The sediment at the bottom of oceans and lake have built up over time with each successively deeper layer older than the last. Different sediment layers within an ocean or lakebed contain different seeds, pollens, fossils, and other chemicals from which to infer climate. Shelled animals within the sediments can also provide us with temperature data when those animals died based on oxygen isotope analysis. The oxygen isotopes in shelled animals has a reversed correlation between climate temperatures and oxygen isotopes from that in glacial ice. Glacial ice comes from water in the atmosphere whereas oxygen in the calcium carbonate in shelled animals comes from water that has not evaporated into the atmosphere. Therefore, in colder climates, heavy isotopes of oxygen are higher in concentration in oceans and lake water and thus in the shells of these animals. Lake sediment provides information on the order of hundreds of thousands of years because no lakes present today are older than that. Ocean sediment can possibly provide us with climate information on the order of millions of years.

Many other proxy data exists with varying periods and resolutions for which they provide climate data. Fossils provide some of the oldest climate proxy data. Fossils can contain traces of past atmospheres whereas the fossils themselves tell us the type of plant and animal life that existed. With knowledge of the climate this life needed to survive, it is possible to infer climate conditions during that time. Fossils have provided us with climate information for the past billion years, but time is less resolved.

Climate Parameters

Climate parameters can be over different spatial and time scales. For example, consider planning a trip in a few months and you want to know whether to plan outdoor or indoor activities. You would need to know the mean daily temperature and monthly precipitation of your destination. That is a shorter time scale than if you wanted to know how much the Earth has warmed or will warm over 3 decades. Data for your trip is also more localized than the warming of the entire planet. Climate data are global, regional, and local with different averaging methods. The climate parameters of interest may be different for these scales too. Globally, mean temperatures, extreme temperatures, sea level rise, and sea-surface temperature help describe changing global climate parameters and their global effects. Regional changes respond to global changes, but they may not be uniform. Mean temperatures, precipitation extremes, and coastal flooding respond differently in different regions to global climate changes. Recording these parameters are part of the climate datasets. Locally, maximum temperatures, minimum temperatures, and precipitation are climate data that people use to make lifestyle decisions and plan travel. This section will discuss global climate data first and then move to regional and local climate data.

Proxy Data

Reconstructions of temperature data for the past 500 million years and greenhouse gas data for the past 0.8 million years exist. Figure 2.4 shows temperature data for the past 500 million years from multiple proxy sources. It is important to understand that the proxy data is not as resolved as the instrumental data. For example, the rapid rise and drops in temperature in the past probably occur over tens of millions of years.

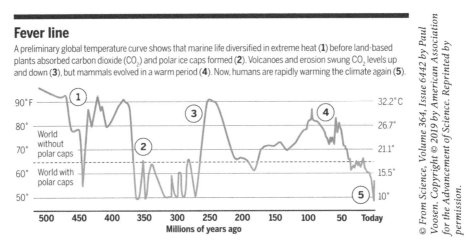

Fever line

A preliminary global temperature curve shows that marine life diversified in extreme heat (**1**) before land-based plants absorbed carbon dioxide (CO_2) and polar ice caps formed (**2**). Volcanoes and erosion swung CO_2 levels up and down (**3**), but mammals evolved in a warm period (**4**). Now, humans are rapidly warming the climate again (**5**).

© From Science, Volume 364, Issue 6442 by Paul Voosen. Copyright © 2019 by American Association for the Advancement of Science. Reprinted by permission.

Figure 2.4 Temperature reconstructed from proxy data is shown.

Because of the long timeline, the current global warming is difficult to spot at the very right of Figure 2.4. This temperature reconstruction brings up a number of important points. First, temperatures in our distant past were both much higher and lower than present temperatures. The lower temperatures were **ice ages**, which are periods where glacial ice existed on Earth. The higher temperatures were substantially higher. Second, the speed of the temperature change is more important than the magnitude of the change. Many organisms certainly adapted to the climate changes in the past even though the changes were much larger than present warming. However, concerns of the effects of our present global warming is less about the magnitude and more about the speed of the warming, which is not clear in Figure 2.4.

Another important feature in Figure 2.4 is that the most recent ice age started over two million years ago and defines the period known as the **Pleistocene**. An oscillation in temperature over the last one million years is apparent with a period of about 100,000 years. Temperatures swing between colder (ice age) and warmer (**interglacial period**) than present (Figure 2.5). We are currently within an interglacial period, which started over 10-20 thousand years ago and defines the period known as the **Holocene**.

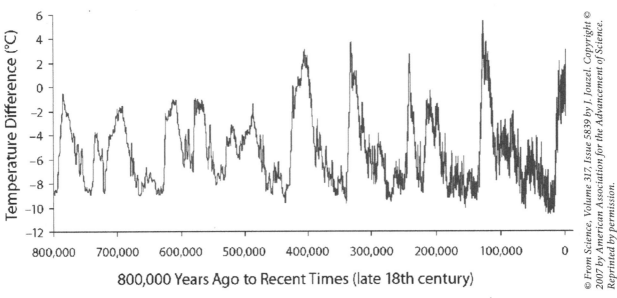

© From Science, Volume 317, Issue 5839 by J. Jouzel. Copyright © 2007 by American Association for the Advancement of Science. Reprinted by permission.

Figure 2.5 Temperature difference from the mean temperatures of the late 18th century from ice core data are shown for the last 800,000 years.

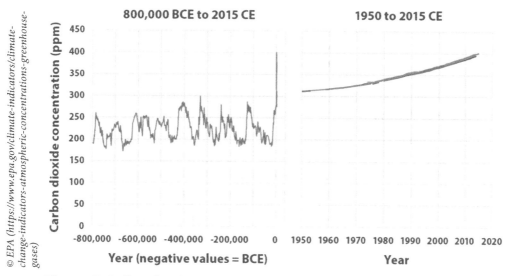

© EPA (https://www.epa.gov/climate-indicators/climate-change-indicators-atmospheric-concentrations-greenhouse-gases)

Figure 2.6 Graphs showing carbon dioxide concentration over the past 800,000 years from ice core data (blue) and instrumentation (orange). The instrument data are expanded in the right panel.

These oscillations correlate well with a time series of the greenhouse gas carbon dioxide (Figure 2.6). Carbon dioxide warms the climate, but it also increases in a warmer climate. Evidence suggests that the changing temperatures cause the changes in greenhouse gases during these ice ages. Nonetheless, these cycles suggest an important feedback mechanism where increasing global temperatures cause an increase in greenhouse gases and increasing greenhouse gases causes increasing global temperatures.

Instrumental Data

In the U.S., the NCEI manages archival and access to global instrumental climate data. The data is freely available to anybody. Some of the data goes through other national and international data centers. International groups and data centers manage and share data readily.

Global mean annual temperatures provides the data that people reference when talking about global warming. Figure 2.7 shows the yearly global mean from 1880-2018 as an anomaly to the 1901-2000 mean. The global mean annual temperature in 2018 was

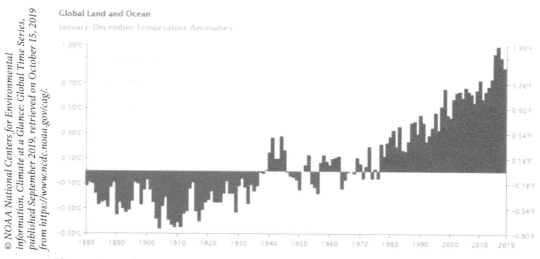

© NOAA National Centers for Environmental information, Climate at a Glance: Global Time Series, published September 2019, retrieved on October 15, 2019 from https://www.ncdc.noaa.gov/cag/.

Figure 2.7 Global mean annual temperatures from 1880-2018 plotted as an anomaly to the 1901-2000 mean.

0.83 °C (1.43 °F) above the 1901-2000 mean. The highest global annual mean during this period was in 2016 and was 1 °C (1.8 °F) above the mean. Although these temperatures fluctuate, the trend is upward with a confidence greater than 99% based on a statistical analysis discussed in the previous section. It is also possible to plot this seasonally to see how different seasons have changed. For example, northern hemisphere winter is warming even faster with a global mean temperature in 2018 of 1.03 °C (1.85 °F) above the 1901-2000 mean (not shown).

Similar to what occurs during interglacial periods, glaciers melt and the sea level rises. Figure 2.8 shows the mean level of the oceans and their increase from 1880. Sea level has been rising since the last glacial period more than 10000 years ago. However, the speed at which the sea is rising has accelerated due to global warming.

Sea surface temperature is also increasing at a rate similar to the atmosphere. Figure 2.9 shows the sea surface temperatures from 1880-2015 mostly matching the atmospheric temperature rise. When materials warm, they expand, so the expansion of the ocean partially causes the increase in sea level.

Extreme weather is another climate parameter that communicates the effects of the global climate change. For example, **extreme temperatures** are the percentage of days in the year that experience temperatures higher and lower than 90% of the 1961-1990 daily means. Prior to this period, hot and cold extremes were both the same at 10% of days. However, in 2018 extreme hot days were at 18% of days whereas extreme cold days were at 6%[2]. These observations communicate that extremely hot days are increasing and extremely cold days are decreasing, but still occur.

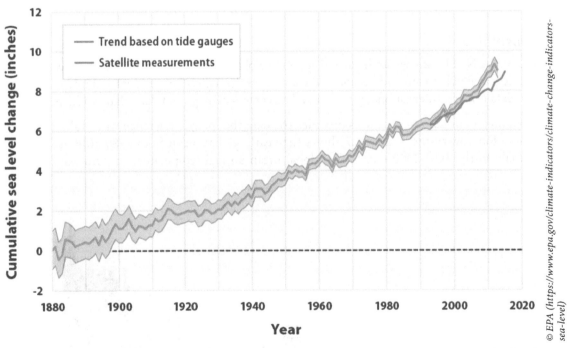

© EPA (https://www.epa.gov/climate-indicators/climate-change-indicators-sea-level)

Figure 2.8 Cumulative sea level increase since 1880 observed by tidal gauges (yellow) and satellite measurements (blue). The gray envelope around the tidal gauge data are uncertainties (estimates of standard error of the mean) in the measurement.

---

[2] Blunden, J. and D. S. Arndt, Eds., 2019: State of the Climate in 2018. Bull. Amer. Meteor. Soc., 100 (9), Si–S305, doi:10.1175/2019BAMSStateoftheClimate.1.

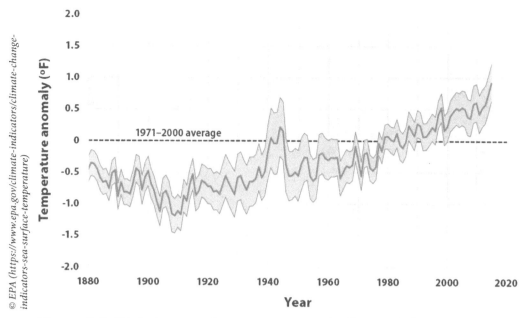

Figure 2.9 Global sea surface temperature (yellow line) from 1880-2015 reported as an anomaly to the 1971-2000 mean. The grayed area surrounding the yellow line represents uncertainties (estimates of standard error of the mean) to the measurement.

Regional scale changes respond to the global changes in varying ways. In the U.S., the change in temperatures are not uniform across the U.S. Figure 2.10 shows how temperatures have changed across the U.S. with the greatest warming in the northern states, including Alaska. Notably, some states in the south have shown little to no change.

Precipitation is another climate parameter that has shown some notable changes regionally. Global and U.S. total precipitation has not changed much in response to global warming. However, 1-day extreme precipitation events have increased in the U.S. Figure 2.11 shows the percentage of land mass in the U.S. that has experienced extreme precipitation events from 1901-2015. Extreme precipitation events have increased significantly starting in the 1980s.

Sea level rise is also not uniform globally. Some parts of the U.S. coastline have experienced significantly more sea level rise than the global mean. This increase has led to more coastal flooding events. Figure 2.12 shows how coastal flooding events have dramatically increased in the 60-year period from the 1950s. Some areas that were land in the 20th century are now considered ocean. Figure 2.13 shows the amount of land that has been lost to the ocean since 1996 on the U.S. east coast. Although there is currently more flooding in the Mid-Atlantic States, the southern states are flatter in elevation and are expected to be lost to the ocean more rapidly.

Locally, the National Weather Service (NWS; www.weather.gov) provides preliminary access to daily and monthly means of temperature at each climate station. These climate stations are the official reporting stations for describing local climate. Following the link and clicking on a location in the map will take you to the local NWS office. From here, you can click on 'climate and past weather' to obtain 'local' data. Under the 'local data/records' tab and 'climate records by month' link you can find daily means of maximum, minimum, and mean temperatures and monthly mean precipitation for each climate station. In addition, you can find extremes for temperature and precipitation. Under the

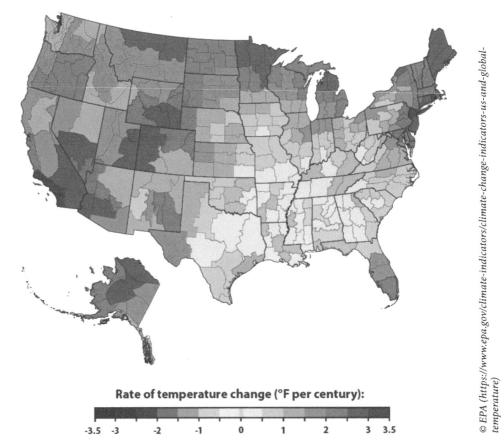

Rate of temperature change (°F per century):

-3.5 -3   -2   -1   0   1   2   3 3.5

© EPA (https://www.epa.gov/climate-indicators/climate-change-indicators-us-and-global-temperature)

Figure 2.10 Rate of temperature change in oF per decade for NOAA climate divisions in the U.S. from 1901-2015. The color scale representing the rate of temperature change is shown at the bottom.

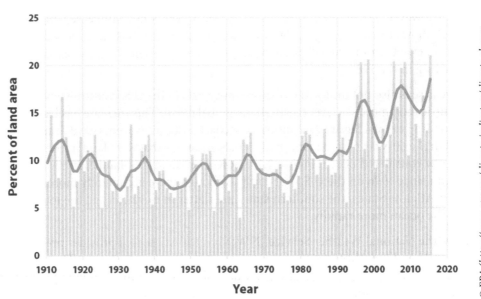

© EPA (https://www.epa.gov/climate-indicators/climate-change-indicators-heavy-precipitation)

Figure 2.11 The percent of land area experiencing extreme precipitation events is shown each year from 1910-2015 (bars) along with the 9-year moving average (yellow line). Extreme precipitation events are those that are far above the mean 1-day precipitation amount for each area.

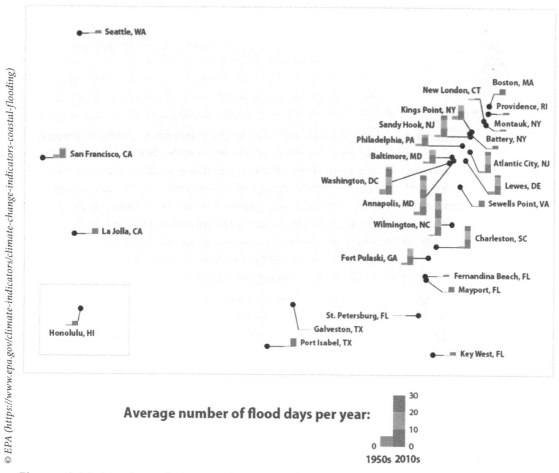

Average number of flood days per year:

Figure 2.12 Number of days with coastal flooding in select cities of the U.S. for the 1950s (yellow bar) and 2010-2015 (blue bar) is shown. Each 10 flood days alternate in shades of these colors.

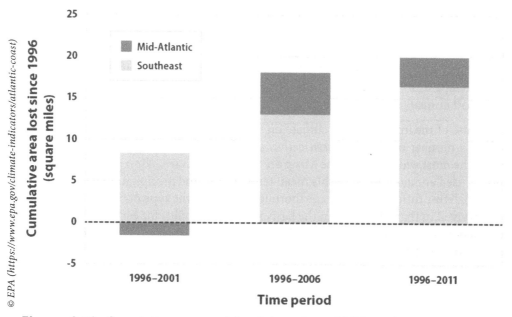

Figure 2.13 Cumulative area of land lost since 1996 is shown for southeast states (yellow bar) and Mid-Atlantic States (orange bar). Ocean area converted to land if the bar is under zero.

'observed weather' tab, the "preliminary monthly climate data" product provides observed daily and monthly means reported for temperature, precipitation, wind, cloud cover, and snow cover for the past few years. Observed temperature and precipitation monthly data are also compared to climatological means.

Archived Climate Data Sets

Different science groups reconstruct instrument and proxy climate data. The instrument global mean temperature data are particularly well-established. A number of groups analyze these temperature time series to ensure that any changes are climatic and not artifacts. An artifact is a change in the time series that is not natural, but caused by flaws in the measurement. For example, the change may be due to a change in instrumentation or a relocation of a weather station. Areas may be oversampled with weather stations more densely covering populated areas and lacking coverage in mountainous and ocean areas. Having independent groups of scientists produce these quality checked datasets and provide them for comparison gives more confidence that any changes are real.

The temperature data shown in Figure 2.7 comes from the Global Historical Climatology Network – Monthly (GHCN-M) and the International Comprehensive Ocean-Atmosphere Data Set (ICOADS) data sets. These datasets are quality checked by NCEI. Several others data sets exist and although they are not exactly the same, using different land and ocean coverage, they show similar results.

Classifying Climate

Climate is a significant factor in determining the organisms that can survive on a planet. The key climate parameters affecting survivability are temperature and precipitation throughout the year. Annual mean temperatures do not provide enough information on survivability. Despite similar annual mean temperatures, continental and marine locations may have very different annual temperature ranges. Continental locations receive most of their weather from land areas whereas marine locations receive most of their weather from water-covered areas. Even though Boston, MA is on the U.S. east coast, most of Boston's weather comes from the west, which is mostly land. Therefore, the proximity to water sources does not determine the type (continental or marine) of climate. It is the type of surface upstream of a location that does. Continental climates have large annual temperature ranges that support different organisms than marine climates, which have small annual temperature ranges.

Because of the importance of climate on the type of organisms that you would expect to find, a number of climate classification schemes were developed in the 20th century. One of the most widely used is the Köppen climate classification scheme. Wladimer Köppen used annually and monthly mean temperature and precipitation data throughout a year to define different climates. A thorough survey of the type of organisms or biomes that survived in that climate form the basis for the thresholds for each climate classification. Rudolph Geiger completed modifications to the Köppen classification system later in the 20th century.

The Köppen-Geiger climate classification system consists of five major classifications. The major classifications, their letter designation, and their characteristics are as follows:

A (Tropical)—Every monthly mean > 18 °C (64 °F) with significant precipitation.

B (Dry)—Annual precipitation is below a threshold that is higher for a higher mean annual temperature and a higher proportion of spring and summer precipitation.

C (Temperate)—Coldest monthly mean temperature is between 0 °C (32 °F) and 18 °C (64 °F) and warmest monthly mean temperature > 18 °C (64 °F)

D (Continental)—Coldest monthly mean temperature is < 0 °C (32 °F) and warmest monthly mean temperature > 10 °C (50 °F)

E (Polar)—Every monthly mean temperature < 10 °C (50 °F)

Major classifications are further subdivided based on the seasonal distribution of precipitation and the level of heat. The seasonal distribution of precipitation is the second letter designation for all but polar climates. The letters and their classifications are as follows:

f (rainforest)—All months > 60 mm (2.4 in)

m (monsoon)—A month < 60 mm (2.4 in) with a minimum depending on annual precipitation

w (dry winter)—threshold depends on major classification and winter includes fall and winter

s (dry summer)—threshold depends on major classification and summer includes spring and summer

The level of heat is the third letter designation for only the C and D climates. Tropical climates (A) do not have a level of heat designation. Dry climates (B) use h for hot (coldest monthly mean > 0 °C or 32 °F) and k for cold (coldest month < 0 °C or 32 °F). Polar climates (E) use T for tundra (warmest monthly mean temperature > 0 °C or 32 °F) and F for eternal winter (warmest monthly mean < 0 °C or 32 °F). The third letter designation for Temperate (C) and Continental (D) and their classification are as follows:

a (hot summer)—warmest month > 22 °C (72 °F)

b (warm summer)—warmest month < 22 °C (72 °F), warmest 4 months > 10 °C (50 °F)

c (cold summer)—warmest month < 22 °C (72 °F), warmest 1-3 months > 10 °C (50 °F)

d (very cold winter)—coldest month < −38 °C (−38 F), warmest 1-3 months > 10 °C (50 °F)

Classifications are determined by major classification first and then subclassifications, starting at A and working down to E. Figure 2.14 shows the Köppen-Geiger climate classification system based on the GHCN version 2 station data (circa 2007). These climate designations change as climate changes. Following the change in these climate designations is one way to follow how climate change affects organisms.

Local and Microclimate

The Köppen-Geiger climate classification system is more of a regional classification system. Smaller-scale climate differences can be dramatic and affects organisms, industries, and weather and climate observations. The previous chapter discussed siting weather instruments because of the effects of surface type, buildings, etc. nearby. These effects represent variations in local and microclimates. Siting weather stations avoids local and microclimates that are not representative of a large area as described in Chapter 1. Nonetheless, climate data sets are tested for biases that these local and microclimates can have on studies of global climate change. Local climates are on the order of the size of large cities and their metropolitan areas. Microclimates are on the order of the size of single buildings.

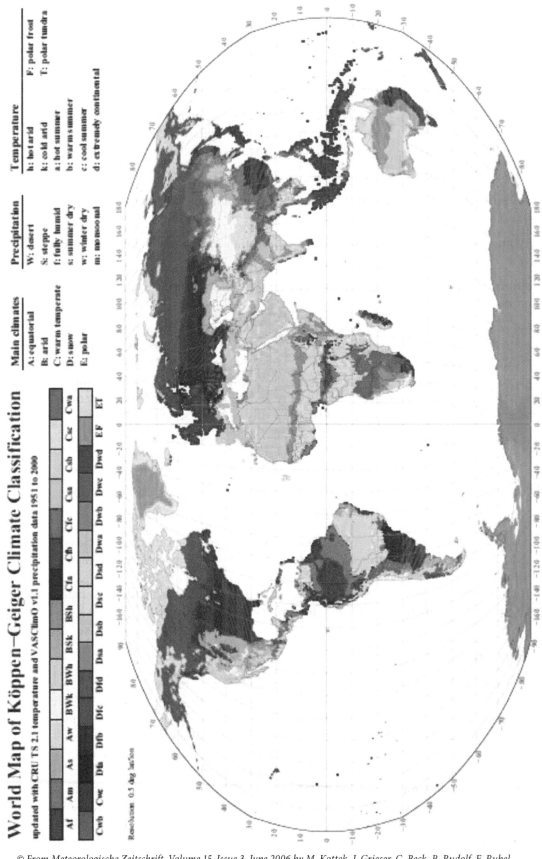

Figure 2.14 Updated world map of the Köppen-Geiger climate classification

A major impact to local climates are hills and valleys. In the northern hemisphere, hills block the sun on the north side for much of the year. Mountains do the same thing and alter the precipitation pattern. The windward sides of mountains receive much more rain than the opposite side of the mountain from where the winds come from, also known as the lee side (Figure 2.15). When plotting the horizontal distribution of precipitation, mountains produce a rain shadow. The rain shadow is an absence of precipitation on the lee side of the mountain. Rain shadow deserts are local- and regional-scale features found on the lee side of the Sierra Nevada and Rocky Mountains in Figure 2.14.

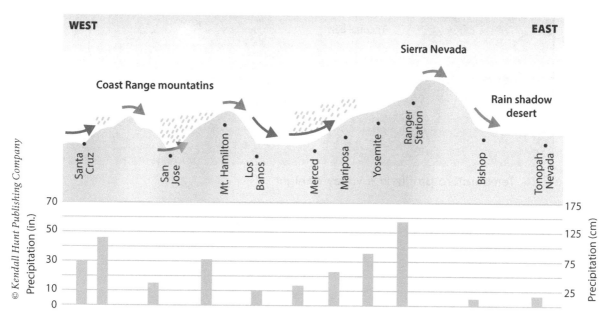

Figure 2.15 Precipitation versus distance from the Pacific Ocean (bottom) along with an illustration of topography (top) are shown. The Pacific Ocean is on the left (west) side.

Valleys also affect the temperature distribution. At night, the surface air cools and becomes denser. This dense cold air drains down the valley walls into the valley floor. Temperature profiles in valleys at night capture this effect with the coldest air found at the valley bottom and warmer air found along the valley walls and above the valley floor (Figure 2.16). Camping on valley walls and not valley floors is best for keeping warm.

Urban developed areas play a major role on local climate because of the heat generation of industrial areas, impervious materials replacing vegetation, and heat absorption of asphalt and concrete. Figure 2.17 shows the surface temperature in Providence, RI and the surrounding suburbs and rural areas. Temperatures within Providence, RI on July 31, 2002 are at least 12 °C (22 °F) warmer than surrounding rural areas. The differences are usually greatest in winter and evenings when energy absorbed by concrete and asphalt continue to emit into the urban environment. Evaporation and transpiration of water into the air in rural areas also reduces temperatures. This effect is called the urban heat island. Because climate stations are located in urban and rural areas, it is important to consider the effects of global warming in relation to the urban heat island. Nevertheless, local climate effects and land developmental changes are a significant factor in local and regional climate change.

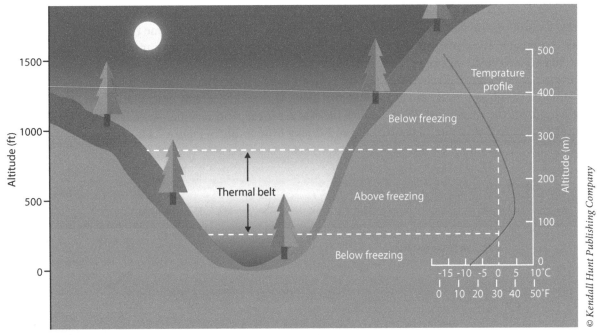

Figure 2.16 Temperature profile in a valley at night

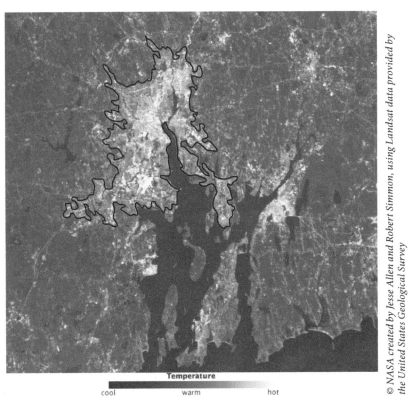

Figure 2.17 Image from the Enhanced Thematic Imager (ETI) onboard NASA LandSat 7 satellite showing the surface temperature of providence, RI (outlined in black) on July 31, 2002. The difference in temperature between the city and rural areas is about 12 °C (22 °F).

Summary

The difference between weather and climate is statistical. Weather is based on the various weather parameters measured at a single time. Climate is a long-term (at least 30 year) average in those weather parameters at a particular location. The importance of climate is that it largely determines the survivability of plants and animals. From a human perspective, it largely determines comfort, crop production, recreation, and wardrobe choices. However, if the climate changes, it may also affect natural hazards, living conditions, outdoor working conditions, food and water availability, and a number of other social, economic, and health concerns.

Statistical analysis of climate data helps to understand if climate is changing and by how much. Climate means such as daily and annual means may change locally, regionally, or globally. Climate change is the term used for changes to any of the climate parameters. Global warming is the specific term for the increase in global annual average temperature.

Climates have changed throughout Earth's geologic history and we use proxy data to infer those changes. Proxy data is data that is not a direct measurement of the climate data. An example of a climate proxy discussed is using the width of tree rings to infer the climate for the species of that specific tree in a specific year in the past.

Because of the importance of climate, several classification schemes exist to classify the climates of the world. The Köppen-Geiger climate classification system is one of the most often used. It uses temperature and precipitation averages and annual patterns to classify climates into six major climates and several subclimates. These classifications were created based on an analysis of the types of plant and animal life found within each classified climate. These climate classification schemes classify regional climates, but mountains, coastlines, and urban centers can affect local and microclimates.

Key Terms

Climate

Climate Change

Daily Mean

Global Warming

Sample Mean

Sample Variance

Standard Deviation

Anomaly

Correlation

Causation

Analysis of Variance

Proxy Data

Tree Rings

Ice Cores

Isotopes of Oxygen

Sediments in Oceans and Lakes

Fossils

Ice ages

Pleistocene

Interglacial Period

Holocene

Extreme Weather

Extreme Temperatures

1-Day Extreme Precipitation

Artifacts

Köppen Climate Classification System

Microclimates

Windward Side

Lee Side

Rain Shadow

Urban Heat Island

Questions and Problems

1. What is the difference between weather and climate?

2. Which of the following describes the weather and which describes the climate of a location?

    a) Today's high is 25 °C (77 °F)

    b) This month has been warm

    c) The average high this month is 10 °C (50 °F)

    d) Each day this week the high temperature has increased.

    e) Over the last 50 years the average high in January has increased by 1 °C (2 °F).

3. If the average high in July is 85 °F can the following temperatures for the week at a station in July be considered an average week: 90 °F, 94 °F, 95 °F, 92 °F, 71 °F, 75 °F 78 °F? Explain.

4. For the temperature data in the previous question, would the 10 °F standard deviation be considered an average week if the average standard deviation of the temperatures at this station for July is 3 °F? What does this mean about these temperatures compared to average?

5. How do scientists know that the Earth's global mean temperature after the dinosaurs went extinct were some of the warmest in the last 500 million years even though no humans were present to observe the temperature that far back?

6. What are some of the tools that scientists use to determine how climate varied in the past? Name three of them. For each give what they can tell us and how they do so.

7. In Figure 2.2, what would you look for in the tree rings to find the warmest wettest years if this were a species of tree that grew best in warm and wet climates?

8. In Figure 2.5, temperatures varied widely over the past 400,000 years causing glacial and interglacial periods. Describe this fluctuation with relevant years including when you would expect glaciers to be retreated and when you expect they would be advanced. Also, provide what you expect to find in your analysis of ice cores at these times.

9. Using Figure 2.8, calculate and compare 1900-1910 and 2000-2012 for the approximate rate in inches per decade that the global oceans are rising. Given the acceleration in the rise of the global oceans, how long do you estimate that Miami, FL (elevation 6 feet) will be completely under water and would you expect it to be unlivable prior to when the city is completely under water?

10. Climate change has occurred throughout our planet's history, but why is the current warming so alarming and significant to our civilization?

11. Use the National Weather Service site to document the average high and low for the day that your homework assignment is due for your location and a location with a much warmer or colder climate. Also, provide the high and low temperature for this date in the previous year.

12. What data would you need for your city to use the Köppen classification scheme to classify its climate?

13. Using Figure 2.14, what is the Köppen classification for your city? In a warming world if the Köppen classification zones moved north, what would the classification for your city change to and what would be the biggest change to expect to your climate?

14. Using Figure 2.14, what is the biggest difference in climate conditions that you would expect between western Washington (green shaded) and eastern Washington (orange shaded). What feature of Washington State would explain the difference in the climate over such a small, regional area?

15. On a winter evening, why are suburbs usually colder than the inner-cities? For a major metropolitan area like Chicago, Illinois how much colder would you expect winter evening temperatures to be in the suburbs?

Other Resources

https://www.emich.edu/geography-geology/weather for links to useful weather data to go along with this textbook and updates to any broken links in the textbook.

Chapter 3

Weather Maps, Radar, and Satellite

Introduction

It is helpful to scientists to organize and visualize the data we get from the various instruments discussed in Chapter 1. For example, looking at a table of pressures from various weather stations does not readily show us how air will move. However, if we were to organize these numbers onto a map, we can see their spatial relationships to reveal how air will move. The movement of this air is what causes our weather to change and is important for forecasting the weather.

Most people are interested in the weather at the surface of where we live. The surface weather is certainly important, but what happens above the surface affects much of what happens at the surface. This three dimensionality of weather is unexpected to most people learning weather and it takes time to appreciate the complexity inherent in this geometry. To standardize the terminology of the vertical dimension, this textbook will use the following definitions (ref Figure 3.1):

- Surface or Earth's surface is the actual land or ocean surface of the Earth.
- Surface air is the layer of air that surface weather stations observe (i.e. lowest 10 m).
- Mean sea level is the mean elevation of the ocean's surface (at least the recent average).

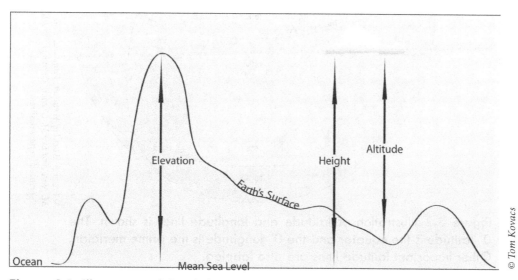

Figure 3.1 Illustration of the definitions used in this textbook is shown.

- **Height** is the distance to a point above the Earth from mean sea level.
- **Elevation** is the distance between mean sea level and the Earth's surface. Not all land surfaces are at mean sea level. Denver, CO, for example, has an elevation of 1.6 km (1 mile).
- **Altitude** is the distance to a point above the Earth from the Earth's surface.

Most people use altitude and height synonymously, but this textbook will use the convention that meteorologists use to define height as referenced from mean sea level. Altitude can also have this definition, but this textbook will define altitude only from the Earth's surface to avoid confusion.

Reading Maps

Reading maps is an important skill to learn for weather and climate. First, there is a standard way to describe locations on a map. A grid of **latitude** and **longitude** lines are used to describe any location on the globe (Figure 3.2). The 0° latitude line runs east-west and is called the **equator**. Moving north from the equator, the latitude lines increase to 90° N or just 90°. Moving south from the equator, the latitude lines increase to 90° S or just −90°.

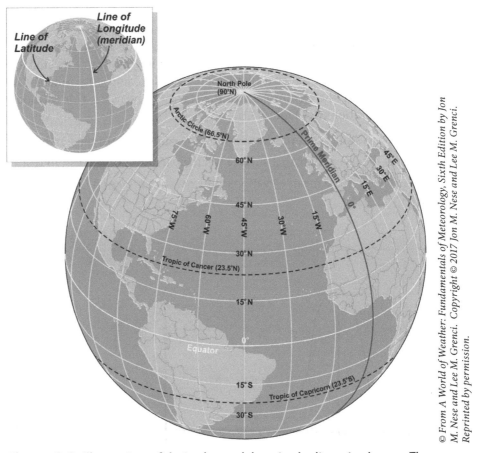

Figure 3.2 Illustration of latitude and longitude lines is shown. The 0° latitude is the equator and the 0° longitude is the prime meridian. Other important latitude lines are also labeled.

The 0° longitude or meridian line runs north-south and is called the prime meridian. Moving east from the prime meridian, the longitude lines increase to 180° E or just 180°. Moving west from the prime meridian, the longitude lines increase to 180° W or just −180°. Referring to north, on a map, will never be referred to as up, because of the three-dimensionality of weather, which causes confusion.

Maps are two-dimensional representations of a three-dimensional surface. For this reason, no matter how you spread out the three-dimensional surface in two-dimensions, there are distortions. Attempts to convert the three-dimensional surface to two-dimensions are called map projections. The most common map projections used in weather maps are mercator and polar stereographic. Mercator maps have longitude lines running parallel from south to north. The problem with this projection is that it makes land near the North and South Poles appear larger than they actually are. Most maps in this textbook are polar stereographic (e.g. Figure 3.2). Polar Stereographic maps have longitude lines that converge at the poles. The problem with Polar Stereographic is that east and west are not left-to-right on the map, but curve in an arc. By looking at the border between the U.S. and Canada along 49 °N latitude, the type of map can be determined. If the line is straight left-to-right it is likely mercator, if it is curved it is likely polar stereographic (cf. Figure 3.2).

Surface Weather Data

Pressure has a central role in moving the air in the Earth's atmosphere. After all, the movement of air is wind, which also causes changes in our weather. Because of its importance, surface weather maps usually highlights some form of pressure representation. Television weather broadcasts usually show large L's and H's that move across a weather map. These L's and H's represent centers of low and high pressure, respectively. Their importance is discussed later.

Surface Maps

When pressure is observed from a station barometer, the value is called the station pressure. Plotting station pressures on a weather map would cause the L's to be on top of mountains and the H's to be near coasts. This distribution is because pressure decreases with increasing height. Because stations higher in elevation have surfaces that are higher than stations that are lower in elevation, the higher station pressures will be lower.

In order to compare the pressure differences at a single height, to analyze their effect on winds, a reference height is chosen. All station pressures are adjusted to the pressure they would have, if they were measured at this reference height. The reference height chosen is the mean sea level. Stations on the ocean coast are at an elevation of mean sea level, but most stations are not. For stations 2000 m (6600 feet) above sea level, we can dig a 2000 m (6600 feet) hole in the ground and lower a barometer to get the pressure at mean sea level. However, this technique would be absurd and quite a safety hazard.

Luckily, we know exactly how pressure changes in the vertical. Near the surface, pressure decreases approximately 1 hPa (1 mb) for every 10 m (33 feet) above mean sea level and pressure always decreases as you go up. Millibars and meters are the traditional units used in weather and will be used in converting station pressure to sea-level adjusted pressure. An example, using the land cross-section in Figure 3.3, illustrates this conversion.

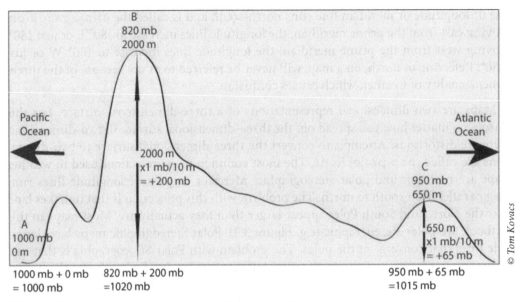

Figure 3.3 Sample calculations adjusting station pressure to sea-level pressure for three different stations.

A station (station B) that has an elevation of 2000 m must have its pressure adjusted by a factor of 1 mb/10 m times the elevation in meters above sea level. The adjustment would be 2000 m × 1 mb/10 m = 200 mb. Because the station is above sea level, the adjustment to sea level would be a positive increase on the station pressure. Therefore, we would add 200 mb to the station pressure of 820 mb giving a sea-level adjusted pressure of 820 mb + 200 mb = 1020 mb.

Once all pressures have been adjusted to sea level, they are plotted on a map. To facilitate easy reading, contours, called isopleths, are drawn on the map. Isopleths are lines of equal value. For pressure, the lines of equal values are called isobars.

Isoplething starts by selecting a base value and a contour interval. For sea-level-adjusted pressures, the base value is typically 1000 mb and the contour interval is 4 mb. Starting with 1000 mb, isobars are drawn such that all pressures higher than 1000 mb are on one side and all pressures lower than 1000 mb are on the other side of the isobar. Stations, with a value of 1000 mb, would fall on the isobar. Sometimes, you may need to draw more than one 1000 mb isobar. Next, a 996 mb and a 1004 mb isobar are drawn following the same procedure as the 1000 mb isobar. Isoplething continues until there are no reported sea-level-adjusted pressures more than 4 mb higher or lower than the highest or lowest value isobar, respectively. Sometimes 1000 mb is not on the map like Figure 3.4, but you still follow the same procedure, drawing all the necessary isobars.

Once the surface weather map has been isoplethed, the map will have transformed from a complex map of numbers, to only a few isobars like Figure 3.5. You can be confident that all stations between the 1020 mb and 1024 mb isobars have sea-level-adjusted pressures between these values. In addition, it is straightforward to find the local high and low pressure values. The highest values are on the high side of the highest value isobars and marked with an 'H'. The lowest values are on the low side of the lowest isobar and marked with an 'L'. Often, there are multiple H's and L's on a surface map because there are multiple peaks and valleys of pressure just like there are multiple peaks and valleys in mountainous terrain.

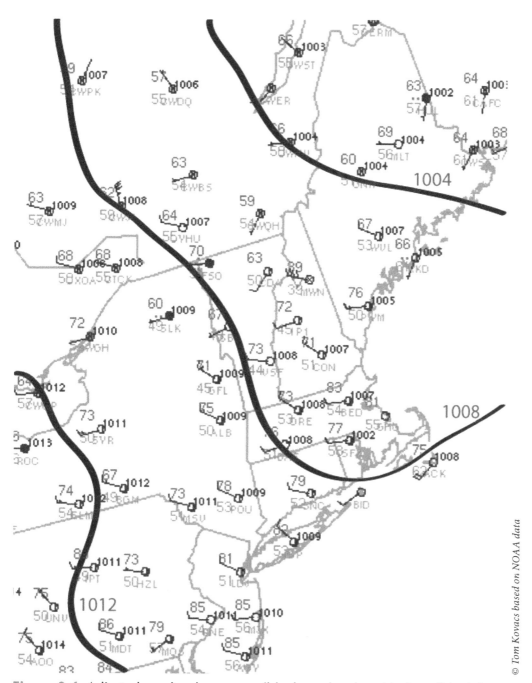

Figure 3.4 Adjusted sea-level pressures (black numbers) and isobars (black lines with blue labels) for the northeast of the U.S. on 1900 UTC August 10, 2019 are shown.

Typically, weather broadcasters will show the fronts and add other information to these surface maps, to present to the public, but isobars are rarely included. Weather forecasters will often add different information to their maps, rarely excluding isobars. Typically, fronts and station models are included with the isobars on maps forecasters use. Fronts are discussed shortly, but station models are a shorthand way of including all the other surface weather data recorded at each station and were included in Figure 3.4.

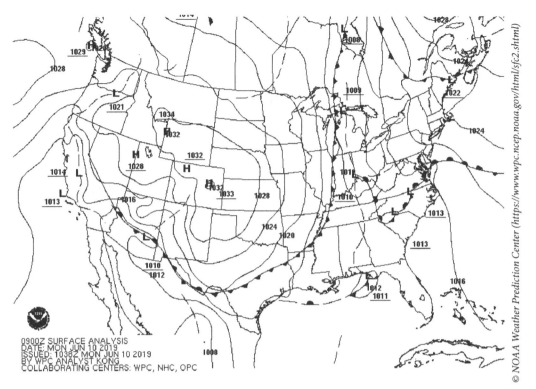

Figure 3.5 Surface weather map with isobars, high and low pressure centers, and fronts.

Scientific Practices

Analyzing and Interpreting Data

Data, directly from instruments, also called raw data, are not necessarily available in a form that provides easy analysis and interpretation. Collecting and presenting data to provide easy analysis to reveal patterns and relationships is an important scientific practice. It is also often necessary to present the data in a way that is easy to communicate to others. Tabulating, graphing, imaging, applying false color to represent signal levels in an image, contouring, and statistical analysis are all techniques used to analyze data. Once analyzed, the presented data must be interpreted. Practice in data interpretation in all these forms is engaging in a scientific practice.

The way data is presented depends on what you are trying to communicate. Weather broadcasters attempt to present complex science information to the public so they know how to prepare for any outdoor activities. Broadcasters and the National Weather Service attempt to warn people of impending hazardous weather with location, description, and safety preparation for the impacts. Weather forecasters attempt to prepare data in a way that patterns and important relationships become clear when analyzing the data. Forecasters then interpret the data to make forecasts and to prepare the forecast for presentation to other forecasters or the public.

This chapter describes the ways that forecasters organize data through weather maps, vertical profiles, cross-sections, satellite images, and radar images. All the data in this book are available on the Internet and the reader should make an effort to obtain this data and analyze it using the techniques described in the book. Professional forecasters use many of these maps, profiles, and images and are not as simple as what you see on television. They all require time to analyze; the information will not be immediately apparent.

Figure 3.6 shows a typical surface station model and has the following components:

- A central circle where the station is located. The circle is increasingly shaded to represent the number of eighths of the sky covered with clouds. An open circle represents a completely clear sky and a completely filled circle represents an overcast sky. Sometimes an x will be found in the circle which means that the sky is obscured (e.g. by smoke from a nearby fire).

- A **wind barb** extending from the circle. The wind barb provides both the direction with the staff of the barb and the speed with the 'feathers' on the end of the staff. You can think of the barb as an arrow with the arrowhead missing. Mentally adding an arrowhead on the side opposite of the 'feathers' gives the wind direction. The wind direction is reported as where the air is coming from. Therefore, a barb extending straight up from the circle would be coming from the north. There are three different kind of 'feathers'. A half line representing 2.5 m/s (5 knots), a full line representing 5 m/s (10 knots) and a pennant representing 25 m/s (50 knots). To determine the wind speed you would simply add the feathers on the wind barb.

- The surface air temperature in °F located to the upper-left of the center circle.

- The surface dewpoint temperature in °F located to the lower-left of the center circle.

- A code for the present weather located between the temperatures and decoded in Figure 3.7.

- A coded pressure located to the upper-right of the center circle. The code is three digits, which is the tens, unit, and tenths place value of pressure in both hPa and mb. A number '10' is appended to the front of the three digits if they are in the range of 000-499 and the number '9' is appended if they are in the range of 500-999 (e.g. 107 would be equal to a surface pressure of 1010.7 mb).

- The pressure trend located to the right of the center circle. The sign of the change and the number of tenths of hPa and mb is often given. Sometimes there will also be a trace showing the general behavior of the pressure change (i.e. continuously falling, steady, and rising-then-falling, etc.).

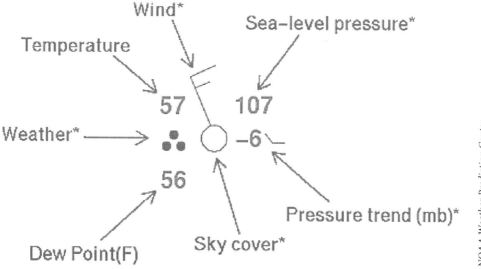

Figure 3.6 Surface station model is shown with the standard location of weather data.* The wind, sea-level pressure, pressure trend, and sky cover are described in the text. The possible weather codes are described in Figure 3.7.

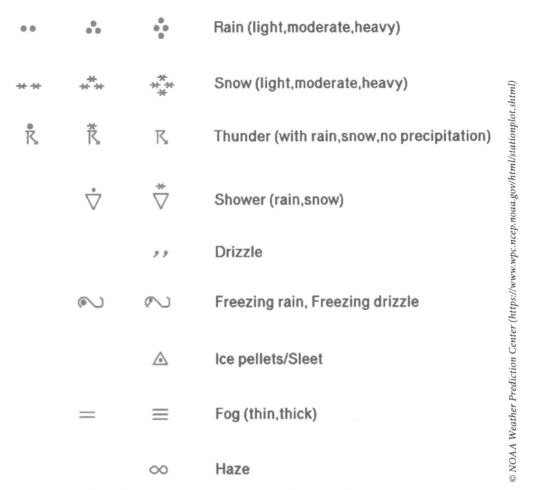

© NOAA Weather Prediction Center (https://www.wpc.ncep.noaa.gov/html/stationplot.shtml)

Figure 3.7 Significant weather codes on surface weather maps.

For example, Figure 3.8 shows a surface map of the western U.S. on 1500 UTC July 10, 2019 with station models. The map initially appears complex because a lot of information is included, but with practice, these maps become simpler to read. Figure 3.8 is a zoomed in version and you can zoom into these maps online to focus on a smaller area. The conditions in central Kansas (the station circled in red) at this time using the techniques to decode the station model described previously are temperatures of 77 °F, Dewpoint 66 °F, Pressure 1019.4 hPa (1019.4 mb), pressure trend is rising by 21 tenths hPa (2.1 mb), winds are from the northeast at 10 knots, and the sky cover is clear.

Air Masses

Simply looking at the location of high and low pressure centers and weather models for the reported stations is not analyzing the surface maps. Weather forecasters initially analyze surface weather maps to identify **air masses** and the transitions between air masses. It is the movement of these air masses and their transitions that help forecast the weather. Air masses are a mass of air with uniform temperature and humidity between the size of Texas and the size of the entire U.S. Because an air mass can extend from the northernmost to the southernmost states, the temperatures and humidity values are uniform relative to the location. For example, in January, a temperature of 5° C (41 °F) would be cold for residents of Miami, FL, but not for residents of Minneapolis, MN. A temperature of –25 °C (–13 °F), however, would be considered cold for residents of Minneapolis, MN.

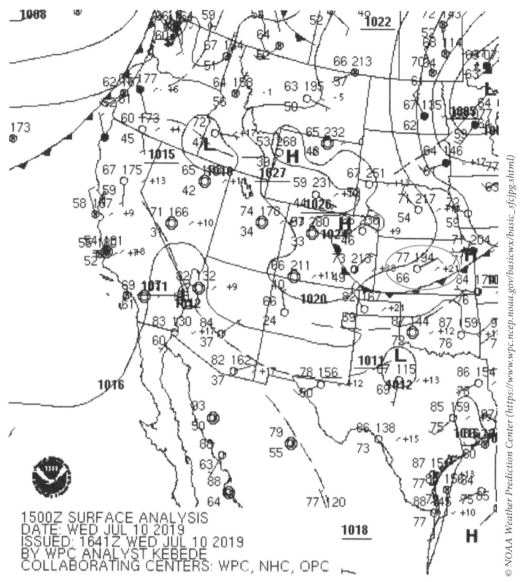

Figure 3.8 Surface map from 1500 UTC July 10, 2019 with station models is shown. The station circled in red is decoded in the text.

Although these two temperatures are 30 °C (54 °F) apart, residents would call 5° C (41 °F) in Miami and –25 °C (–13 °F) in Minneapolis cold. If equally perceived cold temperatures existed throughout the eastern half of the U.S., then this is a cold air mass. This cold air mass originated from some cold location.

For the U.S., cold polar (P) air masses originate from locations north of the U.S. Air masses are defined by where they originate. Air, that spends time in latitudes north of the U.S., will invariably become relatively cold by U.S. standards because the sun at these latitudes is less strong. Likewise, warm tropical (T) air masses originate from locations south of the U.S. The air mass, in our example, likely spent time in Canada, Alaska, Siberia, or Greenland before moving into the U.S. Sometimes, Arctic (A) air masses originate north of the Arctic Circle and bring near record-breaking cold air masses to areas south of the Artic.

Maritime (m) air masses originate from over bodies of water and continental (c) air masses originate over land. Maritime air masses are relatively humid and continental air

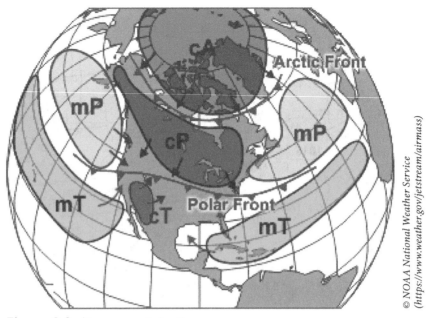

Figure 3.9 Air mass origination areas.

masses are relatively dry. These air masses gain these characteristics over the surface they originate. Like the polar and tropical air masses, these air masses move.

Air masses are completely defined by combining the temperature and humidity characteristics. For example, an air mass originating over Canada would be classified as cP or continental-polar. cT, mP, mT, and cA are other possible air masses. See Figure 3.9 for the origination location of the various types of air masses.

Air masses move from their origination points, which gives us our variations in weather. For example, the central U.S. may be experiencing maritime tropical air that moved in from the Gulf of Mexico one day and then continental polar air from Canada the next. Oftentimes, as a continental polar air mass moves into an area from the north it is associated with northerly winds. These northerly winds are the air mass moving into the area. If you have ever experienced a cold winter day with howling north winds, you are simply experiencing a cold air mass rapidly moving in from the north.

Air masses do eventually change to match the characteristics expected of the area of the world over which they reside. The ocean will eventually moisten a dry air mass and the tropics will eventually warm a cold air mass. The length of time this occurs depends on several factors including the season and the topography, but typically takes 2-5 days. Cold air masses will warm faster in summer than in winter. Humid air masses will dry faster when they move over mountain ranges because the mountains generally cause air to lose its humidity in the form of precipitation. This process is discussed in later chapters.

Surface Fronts

Typically, on surface weather maps there are places where it is difficult to determine whether an air mass is relatively cold or warm and therefore tropical or polar. The same can be true about continental or maritime. These areas often have rapidly changing conditions over a small distance. Looking back at Figure 3.4, the temperatures range from 60 °F in the north to 78 °F in the south of New York State. In an August afternoon 60 °F is somewhat cooler than normal whereas 78 °F is normal. These areas of rapid change are

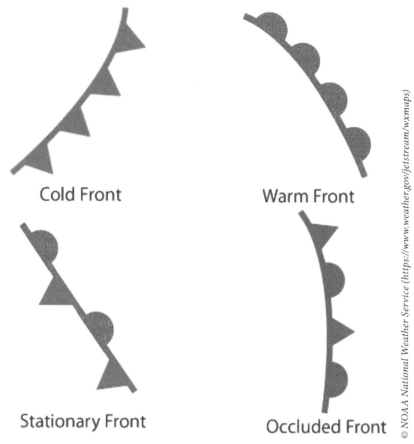

Figure 3.10 Common frontal symbols.

transition zones between two air masses. Forecasters often mark the warm or dry end of these transition zones with a line called a front. There are four different kind of surface fronts depending on the movement of the transition zone (Figure 3.10).

When a colder air mass is advancing into areas that are currently relatively warm, the transition zone is a cold front marked with the cold front symbols. Think of war zone front where the cold air mass is winning the battle with the warm air mass and moving into areas previously occupied by the warm air mass. The cold front symbol is a line on the leading edge of the transition zone with triangles drawn on the side opposite of the cold air mass. The triangles should appear to be pointing in the direction that the cold air mass is advancing.

When the warm air mass is advancing, the transition zone is a warm front marked with the warm front symbols. The warm front symbol is a line on the trailing edge of the transition zone with semicircles drawn on the side opposite of the warm air mass. The semicircles should appear to be pointing in the direction that the warm air mass is advancing. The frontal lines are drawn such that if a cold front were suddenly to stop advancing and then reverse direction it would become a warm front without needing to draw the line in a different location. Only the symbols would change.

When neither air mass is advancing, the transition zone is a stationary front marked with the stationary front symbols. The stationary front is a line of alternating cold and warm front symbols drawn at the warm end of the transition zone. The stationary front is drawn with the cold front symbols (triangles) on the side opposite of the cold air mass and the warm front symbols (semicircles) on the side opposite of the warm air mass.

In the special case where a cold front appears to overtake a warm front, the transition zone between the cold and warm air masses disappears at the surface. Warm fronts never appear to overtake cold fronts for reasons we will discuss later. An **occluded front** is drawn in the location where this apparent overtaking takes place. The occluded front is drawn between the cold air mass behind the cold front and the cold air mass ahead of the warm front. These two air masses do not have much of a transition between them and eventually the differences are so small that no front is drawn. The occluded front is marked with alternating cold and warm front symbols on the same side of the front.

Air masses do not only exist at the surface, but also extend upward from the surface. Vertical cross-sections of fronts help demonstrate the type of weather to expect with the passage of cold, warm, and occluded fronts. The leading edge of the transition zone between air masses (i.e. the front) does not extend perpendicular from the surface, but slopes upward over the cold air. This sloping behavior over the cold air exists at all fronts, but the steepness of the sloping is very different for each front. The biggest contrast in slope steepness is between the cold and warm fronts and the slope explains much of the differences in weather experienced at these two fronts.

Figure 3.11 illustrates the slope of a cold and warm front and the expected weather on either side of the front. Where a cold front exists, there is an advancing cold air mass and a retreating warm air mass (right side of Figure 3.11). The air in contact with the ground typically moves slower (impeded by friction) than the air above. The advancing cold air slows at the surface causing a steep frontal slope between the two air masses. The consequence of this is that the cold air mass forces the warm air up at a rapid rate. This leads to cumulus-type clouds and potentially cumulonimbus clouds. Cumulonimbus clouds produce showers and thunderstorms, which is the typical type of precipitation at cold fronts.

Where a warm front exists, there is an advancing warm air mass and a retreating cold air mass (left side of Figure 3.11). The retreating cold air slows at the surface causing a shallow frontal slope between the two air masses. The consequence of this is that the cold air mass forces the warm air up at a slow rate. This leads to stratus-type clouds and potentially nimbostratus clouds. Nimbostratus clouds produce a steady rain that is rarely heavy with no thunderstorms, which is the typical type of precipitation at warm fronts.

In fact, the gentle slope of warm air over a warm front produces a specific pattern of clouds and precipitation as you move from the surface front to the colder air. At the front,

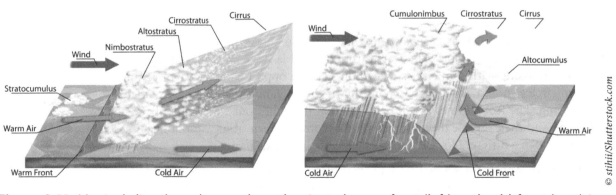

Figure 3.11 Vertical slice through a north-south oriented warm front (left) and cold front (east) is shown with clouds and typical weather conditions from west (left side) to east (right side).

clouds form very near to the surface producing fog. Farther into the cold air, the front is progressively higher off the ground producing progressively higher stratus clouds. The progression of clouds is stratus near the surface front, altostratus farther away from the front, and cirrostratus farthest away from the front. Beneath the cirrostratus (which often produces a halo around the sun or moon), you are in an area of an approaching warm front and can expect precipitation in around 24 hours. This forecast works most of the time if the front continues in your direction and there is enough humidity. Beneath altostratus, you are closer to the surface front and can expect precipitation within the next several hours. If there is enough humidity, the stratus clouds will be nimbostratus (i.e. it will be precipitating).

In winter, when frozen precipitation is possible, warm fronts produce a specific pattern of precipitation. Starting again, near the warm front where the air is the warmest, rain is likely (as long as the warmest air is above freezing beneath the frontal surface). The progression of precipitation is then freezing rain, sleet and eventually snow farthest away from the front.

There are a few other patterns to expect as cold and warm fronts pass. All fronts exist in pressure troughs so frontal passage marks the lowest pressure. As a front approaches the pressure will decrease, hit a minimum when the front arrives, and then rise after it passes a station. The surface winds will shift. Typically, the winds are more southerly on the warm side of a front and more northerly on the cold side of a front. Therefore, if a cold front passes your area the winds will shift from a southerly direction to a northerly direction. This shift makes sense since the cold air in the northern hemisphere is in the north so when cold air is moving into an area, it will likely come from the north.

Stationary fronts also tend to produce rising air. Because all fronts exist in pressure troughs, air tends to move toward the low pressure at the surface. Therefore, warm air will move toward, up, and over the cold air at the front. Remember that a stationary front means the boundary between cold and warm air does not move, but the warm air itself still moves toward the front. Because the front does not move, clouds and precipitation tend to form over the same geographic area. Flooding rains are more likely to form at stationary fronts for this reason.

Occluded fronts mark an area where an increasingly deeper layer of cold air at the surface lifts a substantial amount of warm humid air. In the winter, this can produce substantial wintery precipitation. Eventually, the rising air will weaken because occluded fronts typically mark the transition of the end of the imbalances that initially caused these fronts. The significance of these fronts will become more apparent in Chapter 7 where midlatitude cyclones are covered.

Upper-Air Weather Data

The upper troposphere often determines the development of surface weather. For this reason, forecasters release weather balloons (they use satellite and commercial aircraft data too) to probe the upper-air above the surface layer (Figure 3.12). They create upper-air maps by selecting data from every weather balloon launched at 00 Z or 12 Z at a specific pressure level to create a map at that upper-air level. The combination of several different standard upper-air maps creates a vertical cross-section of the atmosphere. A graph of data from individual weather balloons are called soundings. Soundings provide detailed information over the local area of the weather balloon. The upper-air maps and soundings are discussed in this section.

Figure 3.12 Weather balloon and radiosonde prior to release by a forecaster at a National Weather Service site.

© NOAA National Weather Service (https://www.weather.gov/bmx/kidscorner_weatherballoons)

Upper-Air Maps

Upper-air maps are made for different levels above the ground. Because the elevation of the ground varies greatly in some parts of the world, altitude is not the parameter used to define the map levels. Pressure, which decreases with increasing height, defines levels of upper-air maps.

As a weather balloon rises, it radio transmits data to the ground. Weather balloons record data at two types of levels, significant and mandatory. Weather balloons record any significant data such as a rapid change in a weather parameter at what are called significant levels. Upper-air maps require weather data only at the mandatory pressure levels. The mandatory pressure levels in the troposphere are 1000 mb, 925, mb, 850 mb, 700 mb, 500 mb, 400 mb, 300 mb, 250 mb, and 200 mb. Remember, the lower the pressure the higher the height.

Like surface maps, station models contain all the weather data on each upper-air map. The upper-air station models are like the models on the surface maps with a few differences. First, the air temperature and dewpoint temperature are reported in Celsius instead of Fahrenheit. Second, no cloud cover information is reported because there is nobody stationed up there to look up at how much of the sky is covered with clouds (somebody would have to float at these levels to do so). Third, pressure and pressure tendency are not reported because the pressure at every station on a 500 mb map would always be 500 mb. Instead, the height of the pressure level is reported. Therefore, instead of isobars, upper-air maps have lines of constant height known as height contours.

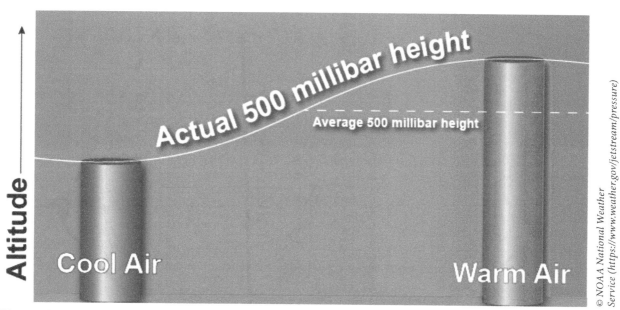

Figure 3.13 The height of the 500 mb level is shown at different locations. Warmer air beneath upper-air pressure levels tend to cause them to be found at higher heights.

Figure 3.13 illustrates what the 500 mb upper-air level would actually look like. Everywhere on the 500 mb level is the exact height where a weather balloon launched from different surface locations would record a pressure of 500 mb. Notice that the pressure level is lower on the left and higher on the right. That means the weather balloon had to rise higher on the right in order to get to a pressure of 500 mb. The reason for this is due to the temperature of the air beneath this pressure level. When the air is warmer, it expands and the 500 mb surface is higher. In the northern hemisphere, the air in the south is typically warmer and 500 mb heights are higher than in the north.

Figure 3.14 shows an actual 500 mb map. Typically, upper-air maps have two sets of different plotted contours depending on the parameter's importance for that pressure level. For the 500 mb map, the two contours are isotherms or lines of equal temperature (red dashed contours) and height contours (solid thin black contours). The contour interval for the height contours on the 500 mb map is typically 60 m. As expected, the highest value contours are in the south and they decrease to lower values in the north (black ovals in Figure 3.14).

Another feature, typical of these upper-air maps, is the waviness of the height contours. These ubiquitous atmospheric waves are an important feature in the development of surface weather systems and are covered in Chapter 7. Nonetheless, it is important to be able to identify the waves and their features. Each wave, like the more familiar water wave, has a trough or low point and a ridge or high point. On the map in Figure 3.14, a trough sags south (which you should not think of as down) and represents relatively low heights at that latitude. In contrast, ridges bend north and represents relatively high heights at that latitude. In order to identify a trough or ridge, you should identify at least three adjacent height contours containing the wave. The distance from one trough to the next or one ridge to the next is the wavelength.

Each upper-air map has different contoured parameters and different coded heights on them. The 1000 mb map is the upper-air map closest to the surface and is often representative of the surface weather. In mountainous regions, surface pressures are less than 1000 mb so the 1000 mb level would be below the ground. The 1000 mb map is not often used

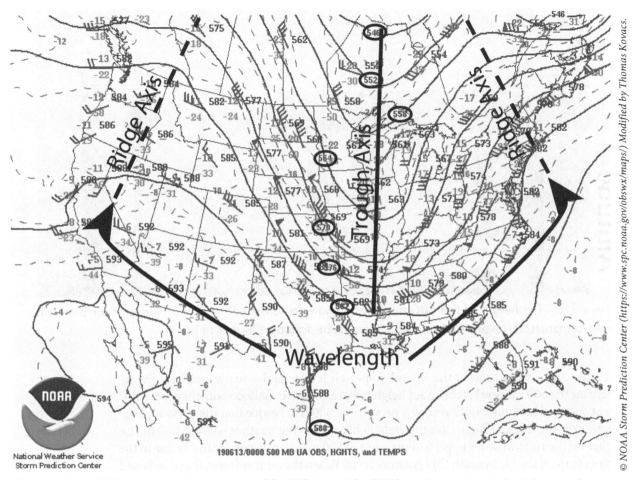

Figure 3.14 500 mb map observed at 00 UTC June 13, 2019 is shown. A dashed line is drawn through ridge axes and a solid line is drawn through a trough axis in the height contours (thin solid lines). Height contour labels are circled and would need to be multiplied by 10 to get meters.

except to calculate the thickness between the 500 mb and 1000 mb map. Thickness is calculated as the height of the 1000 mb level minus the height of the 500 mb level. Thickness provides an idea of the temperature of the entire lower troposphere because the warmer the layer the farther these surfaces will spread out and the larger the thickness. This relationship with the temperature of an entire layer makes thickness an excellent parameter for identifying fronts.

On the 925 mb, 850 mb, and 700 mb upper-air maps, the air temperature, dewpoint temperature, and height contours are contoured (See Figure 3.15 for the 925 mb map). The height contours are coded with three digits and the last digit dropped because it is always zero. The first digit is usually omitted in the station model except for the 925 mb map where the heights are always less than 1000 m and therefore just three digits.

On the 500 mb, 300 mb, 250 mb, and 200 mb upper-air maps, the humidity is not as important and usually not contoured. The 500 mb map usually just has height and temperature contours. For the three uppermost maps, the winds are much more important than temperatures and height contours so **isotachs** (lines of equal wind speed) and streamlines (lines parallel to wind direction) are often contoured instead (See Figure 3.16 for 300 mb map). **Divergence** values may also appear on 300 mb maps. Divergence is a measure of the spreading out of winds. Higher values become increasingly important to the development of surface weather systems. Later chapters discuss the importance of upper-air divergence.

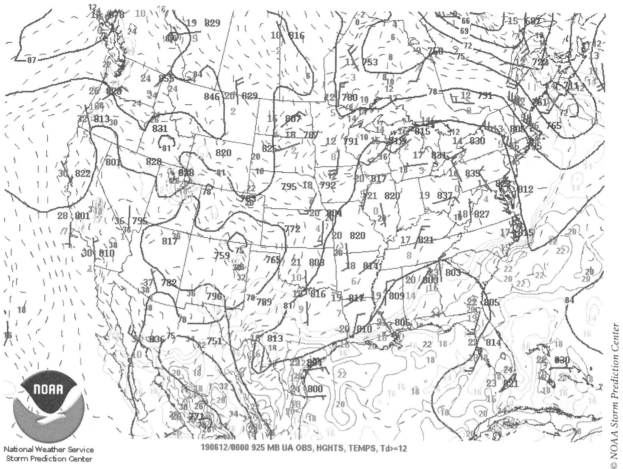

National Weather Service
Storm Prediction Center

190612/0000 925 MB UA OBS, HGHTS, TEMPS, Td>=12

Figure 3.15 925 mb map observed at 00 UTC June 12, 2019 is shown with contours of height (black lines), temperature (red dashed lines), and dewpoint temperature (green lines only for values greater than 12° C).

Digging Deeper

Divergence

Divergence is calculated as a change in wind speed, v, divided by change in position, x, as follows:

$$\text{Divergense} = \frac{\Delta v}{\Delta x} = \frac{v_2 - v_1}{x_2 - x_1}$$

For example, if the wind speed from the west in Pittsburgh, PA (x_1) is 10 m/s (v_1) and the wind speed 400 km to the east in Philadelphia, PA (x_2) is from the west at 20 m/s (v_2) then the divergence is:

$$\text{Divergense} = \frac{v_2 - v_1}{x_2 - x_1} = \frac{20\frac{m}{s} - 10\frac{m}{s}}{400,000\,m} = \frac{10\frac{m}{s}}{400,000\,m}$$

$$= 0.000025\frac{1}{s} = 2.5 \times 10^{-5}\frac{1}{s}$$

If the values of the wind in the stations were reversed, the resulting negative sign means convergence whereas a positive sign, like in the example, is divergence. It makes sense that this example area is experiencing divergence because the winds are increasing as you follow them from west to east. This increase in the winds would cause the air to spread apart or diverge. The values are typically less than 20 × 10^{-5} s^{-1} and are contoured without the 10^{-5} s^{-1}.

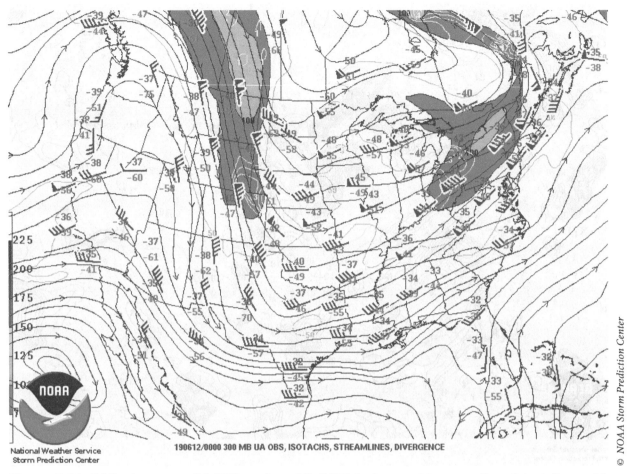

National Weather Service
Storm Prediction Center

190612/0000 300 MB UA OBS, ISOTACHS, STREAMLINES, DIVERGENCE

Figure 3.16 300 mb map at 00 UTC on June 12, 2019 is shown with streamlines (black lines with arrows) and divergence (yellow lines).

Soundings

Data from a single weather balloon is called a sounding. These data are plotted on a **Skew-T diagram**. The Skew-T diagram has temperature as the x-axis and pressure as the y-axis. Although the pressure grid is horizontal, the temperature grid is not vertical, but skewed diagonally from left-to-right (Figure 3.17). The observed air and dewpoint temperatures are plotted on this diagram. Along the right side, the wind barbs are plotted at their corresponding pressure-levels providing the wind speed and direction just like on the weather maps. Along the left, the height is recorded.

Soundings are used for numerous reasons but are most important in precipitation-type and thunderstorm forecasting. The heights, where the air and dewpoint temperatures nearly equal, is where cloud formation is likely. Looking at the temperatures at these heights gives you a clue to the type of precipitation that would form in these clouds. Then, looking at the temperature beneath this level helps forecast melting or freezing as the precipitation falls from the cloud. Snow may form at some heights whereas rain may form at others. This complexity in precipitation formation is why you can sometimes get snow and rain from the same cloud. The pattern of temperature and winds, across the different heights, are largely responsible for determining whether you can expect rain or severe thunderstorms in a location. The Skew-T diagram in Figure 3.17 was observed during one of the largest tornado outbreaks in U.S. history (292 tornadoes on that day). Specific analyses of soundings for these applications are discussed in later chapters.

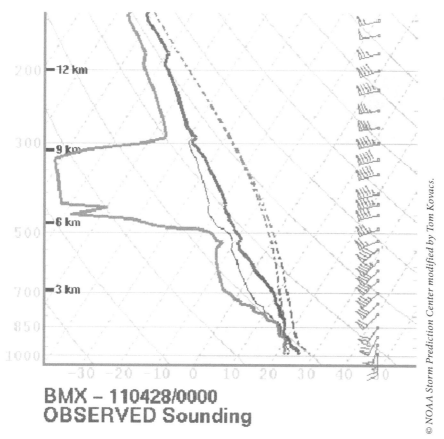

BMX – 110428/0000
OBSERVED Sounding

© NOAA Storm Prediction Center modified by Tom Kovacs.

Figure 3.17 Skew-T diagram from Birmingham Alabama at 00 UTC April 28, 2011 on a day of a 292-tornado outbreak is shown. Observed air temperature (red) and dewpoint temperature (green) are plotted along with wind barbs along the right side. Temperature is on the x-axis, but the grid does not run straight up, but instead is skewed and follows the dashed lines. To illustrate all temperatures greater than 0 C are shaded red and all temperatures less than 0 °C are shaded blue with the 0 °C line as the dividing line. Pressure is on the y-axis and the grid does run straight across following the solid lines. Other lines are described in later chapters.

Satellite Images

Satellites provide a platform for mounting weather instrumentation to observe weather from space. Their height, inclination angle (angle the orbit makes with the equator), and orbital shape determines the characteristics of the orbit. The satellite's height requires a specific velocity in order to maintain orbit. If a satellite in orbit accelerates, then the satellite will speed off into outer space and if it decelerates, it will fall back to the ground. The importance of the different types of orbits and the instrumentation used in weather forecasting are discussed in this section.

Geostationary Orbiting Satellites

The geostationary orbit follows the equator (0° inclination angle) with a height of 35,786 km (22,240 miles). The velocity of the satellite needed to maintain this orbit is equal to the angular velocity of the Earth (i.e. geosynchronous). This synchrony leads to

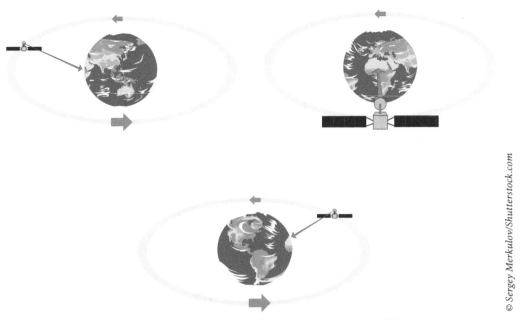

Figure 3.18 Satellite in geostationary orbit shown at three different times in its orbit. Notice that the satellite is always over equatorial Africa.

the satellite always positioned above the same point on Earth (Figure 3.18). Satellites, in this orbit, allow instrumentation to observe the same scene on Earth at all times. This height has advantages and disadvantages. The advantage is that it is far enough from the surface of the Earth that instruments can see and observe half of the entire Earth at all times. The disadvantage is that the features it can resolve are limited by the large distance the satellite is from the Earth.

One of the simplest and most important instruments on satellites is the visible imager. Most cameras we use on our phones have a device that records the intensity of visible light within millions of tiny squares called **pixels**. Assembling these pixels into a two-dimensional grid gives us an image (i.e. a picture). The visible image is just a camera in space taking pictures of half the Earth (Figure 3.19). The current version of the weather image is called the **Advanced Baseline Imager**. It has a pixel size as small as 0.5 km (.31 mi) and can take a full image every five minutes (and over smaller areas every 30-60 s). From these data, you can see where clouds are located. By looping several images together, you can see how clouds are moving and developing. Of course, with the sun as the light source, these images show clouds only with sufficient daylight. Later, other instruments on the satellites that can observe clouds at night are discussed.

There are several of these satellites around the world because one satellite can only see half the Earth and with poor resolution near the horizon. The U.S. have two geostationary satellites called **Geostationary Orbiting Environmental Satellite** (GOES 16 and GOES 17). GOES 16 (above 75.2° W) is positioned above the equatorial Atlantic Ocean, GOES 17 (above 137° W) is positioned above the equatorial Pacific Ocean. These two satellites allow for maximum resolution over the entire U.S and much of the Atlantic and Pacific Oceans.

Polar Orbiting Satellites

Another important orbit is the low (200 – 2000 km above the Earth's surface) **polar or inclined orbiting satellites**. The word, inclined, means that it orbits with an angle to

2019-12-15 17:00:18 UTC

Figure 3.19 Full disk view from GOES 16 observed at 17 UTC December 15, 2019

the equator. Geostationary orbits have a 0° inclination and orbits over the poles have a 90° inclination. Satellites in low Earth orbit move at a rotational velocity much faster than the Earth's rotation and can make one complete orbit in less than two hours! These satellites do not stay above the same point on Earth. From space, the orbit traces out a repeating circle around the Earth. However, because the Earth rotates under this repeating circle the surface over which the orbit travels is continually farther to the west. When a low Earth orbiting satellite make a second pass over any latitude, it will be west of its previous orbit. This allows low Earth orbiting satellites to observe the entire globe, but it moves over the same location only twice a day (once in the AM and once in the PM). Many weather satellites are in low earth orbit of varying inclinations and have instrumentation useful for weather forecasting that are discussed in later chapters.

Radar Images

Radar is an acronym for Radio Detection and Ranging. Most radar images the public sees are from radars on the ground. The main components of a radar are a transmitter and a receiver. The transmitter (or sender in Figure 3.20) sends out a radio frequency wave (a pulsed beam of light that you cannot see). The transmitted pulse reflects off different size objects in the atmosphere. Most radars that forecasters use are optimized to reflect off raindrops; this is the detection part of the acronym. Raindrops reflect a portion of the beam (i.e. echo) back to the radar where a sensor (Figure 3.20) receives it. Because we know the speed of the radio frequency wave (i.e. speed of light) and the time the echo took to make a round trip from a rain drop, we can calculate how far the rain drop is from the radar. This calculation is the ranging part of the acronym.

Most radars today can also determine how fast the raindrop is moving toward or away from the radar using the **Doppler effect**. The Doppler effect is the effect to sounds that you hear when an object like an automobile is moving past you (Figure 3.21). Sound travels in waves. An object moving toward you compresses the sound waves so they arrive at your ear with higher frequency. When an object is moving away from you, the sound

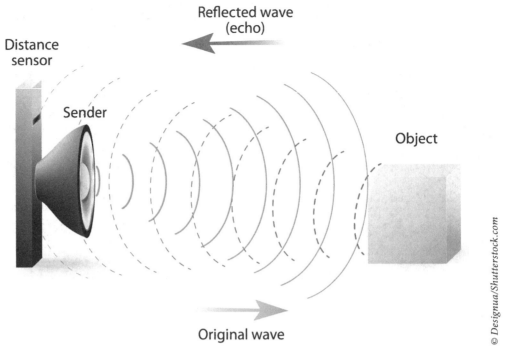

Figure 3.20 An object reflects a portion of the pulsed radio-frequency waves sent by radar producing an echo that a sensor at the radar observes.

Doppler Effect

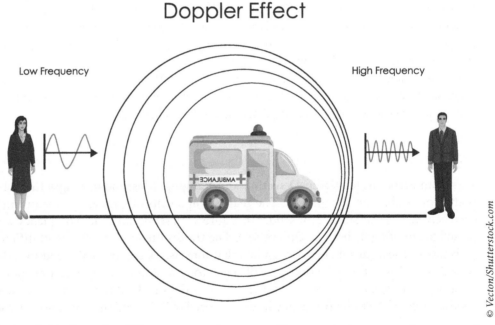

Figure 3.21 Doppler Effect on sound waves off an ambulance moving toward and away from a person

waves spread apart so they arrive at your ear with lower frequency. Listen to a car or train pass by you and you will hear this frequency shift. Wind-blown raindrops shift the frequency of radar waves just the same. Therefore, if the raindrop is moving toward the radar, the frequency will increase and if it is moving away from the radar, the frequency will decrease. **Doppler radars** can operate in precipitation mode where it detects and ranges precipitation or it can run in velocity mode where it measures the shift of the reflected radio frequency wave. The larger the shift, the faster the raindrop is moving and therefore the faster the winds.

Radars pulse their transmitted beams so that they can collect all of the reflectivity of the first pulse and then turn a little bit before sending out another pulse. This allows radars to observe precipitation all around the radar. Figure 3.22 shows a sample of a radar image. The radar is geographically located in the center of the image at the end of the large black arrow. The radius of the radar range is around 140-180 miles. The scale on the right side is color coded for the reflection that the radar observes, commonly called reflectivity. The amount of reflectivity can vary over many orders of magnitude so that the units are given logarithmically. The unit dBZ are decibels (dB) of reflectivity (Z). Because the unit is logarithmic, you cannot say that a reflectivity of 40 dBZ will produce twice the precipitation rate of a reflectivity of 20 dBZ. In fact, the precipitation rate in this case would be more than 10 times greater. Typically, blue is assigned to reflectivities less than 20 dBZ. The blue areas in Figure 3.22 are probably receiving light rain, but it may not make it all the way to the ground. There are two important things to consider when interpreting a radar image. First, raindrops reflecting the radio frequency waves are in the clouds and may evaporate before reaching the ground. Second, different kinds of objects reflect radio frequency waves differently. For example, snow does not reflect as effectively as rain so a 20 dBZ snowfall is a fairly moderate snow whereas a 20 dBZ rainfall may not even be reaching the ground and if it does it would be very light.

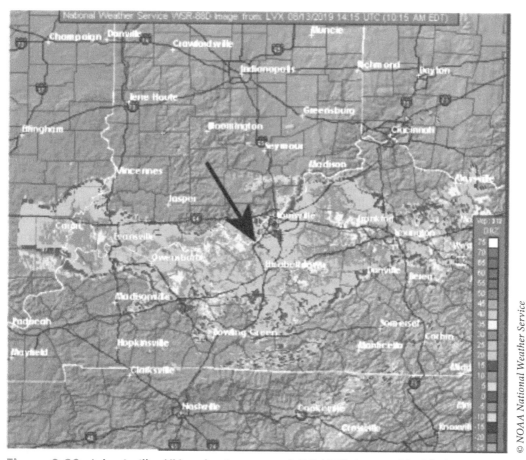

Figure 3.22 A Louisville, KY radar image at 1415 UTC August 13, 2019 is shown. Black arrow points to the surface location of the radar.

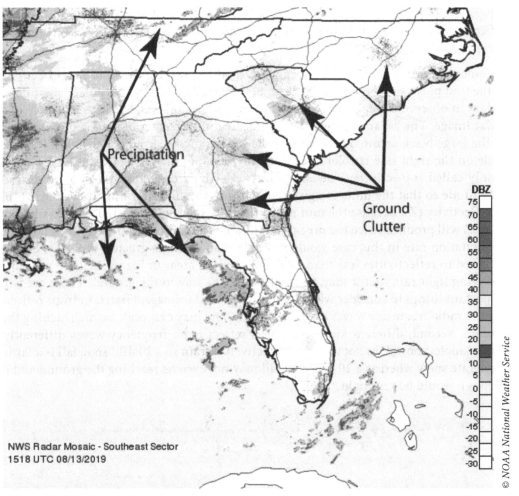

Figure 3.23 Composite or mosaic of radar reflectivity for the southeast U.S. at 1518 UTC on August 13, 2019 is shown.

Radars sometimes have a problem where the vertical temperature distribution can cause the transmitted radar beam to propagate anomalously (not follow its expected path). Often at night, the radar beam will bend toward the ground. When this happens objects on the ground will tend to reflect the radar beam back to the receiver. **Ground clutter** produces a roundish reflectivity pattern. Figure 3.23 shows a composite of 20-30 radar images stitched together for the southeast U.S. The circular speckled pattern of ground clutter is easy to pick out from actual precipitation echoes. Looping the images into a video reveals that the roundish pattern does not move and appears to speckle due to the anomalous propagation.

Summary

Data and observations are the foundation of the scientific method, but analyzing that data is more effective when presented well. This chapter explored the various ways that weather data are presented for analysis. Examples of presentation methods used in weather forecasting include maps, soundings, images, and cross-sections.

Surface and upper-air weather maps are produced to get a full cross-section of various observed weather parameters in the atmosphere. The standard weather maps include those weather parameters most important at those levels for forecasting. At the surface, pressure and pressure centers along with boundaries between the air masses called fronts are most important. Symbols are used to characterize fronts as cold, warm, stationary, or occluded depending on the direction the air masses are moving. Upper air maps are plotted on pressure levels and the height of that pressure level is contoured on these maps. In the lower troposphere, temperature and humidity are of greatest importance while in the upper troposphere wind speed and direction are most important.

Data from a single weather balloon launch are plotted on a Skew T diagram and called a sounding. Skew T diagrams plot the air and dewpoint temperatures on a graph with pressure on the y-axis and temperature on the x-axis. The grid lines for temperature are skewed thus the name of the diagram. Wind barbs are also plotted.

Weather satellites orbit the Earth in different orbits with instruments mounted on them. These instruments provides a mobile weather station that can view large parts of the Earth at once and observe many different weather parameters at many different levels in the atmosphere. Radars are mostly ground-based instruments that observe raindrops in clouds, but Doppler radars use the Doppler effect to measure winds within precipitating clouds.

Key Terms

Mean Sea Level	Wind Barb	Divergence
Height	Air Masses	Skew-T Diagram
Elevation	Front	Geostationary Orbit
Altitude	Warm Front	Pixels
Latitude	Cold Front	Advanced Baseline Imager
Longitude	Stationary Front	
Equator	Occluded Front	Geostationary Orbiting Environmental Satellite (GOES)
Prime Meridian	Upper-Air Maps	
Map Projection	Soundings	Polar or Inclined Orbit Satellites
Station Pressure	Mandatory Pressure Levels	
Sea-Level Adjusted Pressure		Radar
	Isotherms	Doppler Effect
Isopleths	Trough	Doppler Radar
Isobars	Ridge	Reflectivity
Station Models	Isotachs	Ground Clutter

Questions and Problems

1. If you look at your mercury barometer and get a station pressure reading of 960 mb at a station elevation of 500 m, what is the sea level adjusted pressure?

2. What are the primary air mass source regions in North America (give location and type of air mass)?

3. What are the primary weather parameters used to define an air mass?

4. Describe some of the changes in weather conditions (winds, temperature, clouds, precipitation, pressure changes) you would expect to observe as a cold front approaches and passes through your location. (Note: be specific about which changes occur before the cold front reaches your area and which changes occur after the cold front passes your area.)

5. Describe some of the changes in weather conditions (winds, temperature, clouds, precipitation, pressure changes) you would expect to observe as a warm front approaches and passes through your location. (Note: be specific about which changes occur before the warm front reaches your area and which changes occur after the warm front passes your area.)

6. What are two differences and one similarity between a cold and warm front passing your location?

7. How would clouds and the type of precipitation change if you were to drive southward in the cold air north of a warm front during winter?

8. Use the websites in the textbook or the online resources below to find surface low- and high-pressure centers. What is the value of pressure for the highest high-pressure centers and the lowest low-pressure centers? Do an Internet search, compare the lowest pressures to some of the strongest hurricanes, and provide the hurricane name, year, and lowest central pressure in your comparison.

9. Draw a vertical cross-section through a cold front and label the cold and warm air masses and the direction the cold air mass is moving. Also, draw an arrow for air rising over the front.

10. Draw a vertical cross-section through a warm front and label the cold and warm air masses and the direction the cold air mass is moving. Also, draw an arrow for air rising over the front.

11. Use the websites in the textbook or the online resources below to zoom in on a surface map station model for a station and decode it. Accompany your decoding with a zoomed in copy of the station model.

12. Use the websites in the textbook or the online resources below to zoom in on an upper-air map station model for a station and decode it. Accompany your decoding with a zoomed in copy of the station model.

13. What are the mandatory upper level maps and their approximate heights above the ground? You may need to look at each map to get an idea of their approximate height.

14. How can a change in wind speed along the path that air moves lead to divergence or convergence?

15. Describe the orbit of a geostationary orbiting satellite and the benefits of this orbit.

16. Describe separately how a radar detects and ranges precipitation.

17. What information can you get from radar reflectivity?

18. Sometimes radar images show reflectivity erroneously. Describe an example of how this can happen and how you can spot this.

Other Resources

https://www.emich.edu/geography-geology/weather for links to useful weather data to go along with this textbook and updates to any broken links in the textbook.

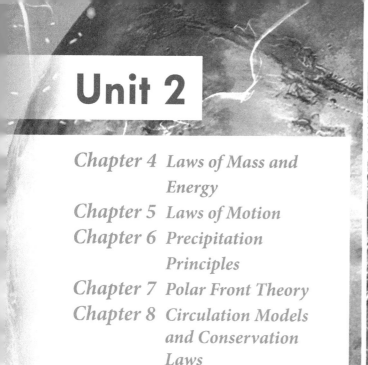

Unit 2

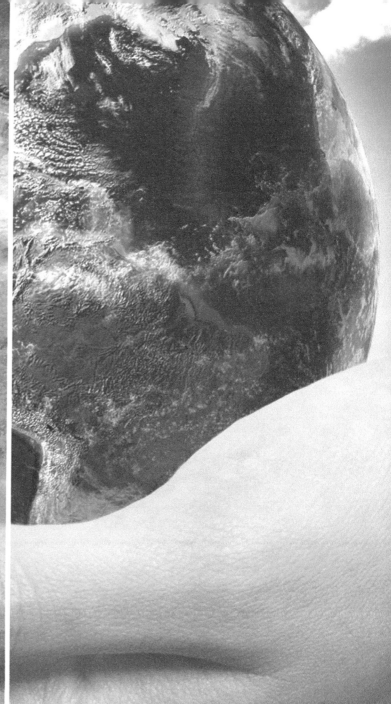

Physical Laws, Theories, and Principles

Chapter 4

Laws of Mass and Energy

Introduction

This chapter begins a higher level of the scientific method. The chapters prior to this were all about the foundation of the scientific method: observations and data. The next few chapters will discuss how scientists use observations to attempt to understand nature. Physical scientists formulate questions called hypotheses that they can test. For example, do objects move in the direction pushed and does the rate at which they accelerate depend on how hard I push? These are not only questions, but they are testable questions. Experiments can be designed to gather data to answer these questions. For each question, several scientists will set up a number of experiments over a long time and report their results publicly. After many different tests of a hypothesis by different scientists results in the same answer to that hypothesis then a scientific theory, principle, or law is established. Therefore, the questions not only need to be testable, but the results must be repeatable.

This is very different from how people use the word theory in conversation. For example, I have often heard a student say something like, "I have a theory as to why my instructor is so mean". If the use of the term, theory, here referred to the physical scientific meaning, the statement would be absurd. First, there is no objective measure of meanness. There is no mean-o-meter. You would have to define meanness in some objectively measurable way. It would be difficult to set up an experiment to test a level of meanness, and until then, you could not publish your results so that others could repeat the experiment. Students would need to publish their conclusions and others would need to repeat the experiments over a long period under different conditions. I suspect these students did not follow this procedure. In this case, the student's statement was not a theory, but just an opinion. The danger here is that people start thinking that scientific theories are just like opinions from scientists. In the next few chapters, we will explore some of the scientific laws, theories, and principles that forecasters use to forecast the weather. These all followed the rigorous scientific method described here.

First Law of Thermodynamics

The first law of thermodynamics provides a way to describe how energy, heating, and temperatures are related. We can all observe that on most days, around noon, when the sun is unobstructed, the air gets warmer, and on most nights, the air gets colder.

It is simple observations such as these that begs the question, what determines how much the temperature changes in a location.

First, science has jargon that must be learned, and thermodynamics is loaded with jargon. Some of the jargon, unfortunately, is familiar to most people, but not in the way used in thermodynamics. A good example is energy and heating. Energy is the capacity to do work and has the SI units of the calorie (C) or Joule (J). In order to do work, and if you are reading this you are doing work, you need to use energy. You need to constantly replenish your energy or you will no longer be able to do work (this is important to you because your heartbeat counts as work). The unit of measure gives you a clue to how you replenish your energy. All nutritional labels provide a measure, in calories, of how much energy you are putting into your body.

It is also important to note that using energy does not mean that the energy no longer exists. The First Laws of Thermodynamics is based on the Law of Conservation of Energy, which states that energy is neither created nor destroyed. Therefore, when energy is used by something, it is either converted to a different form or transferred to something else. The First Law of Thermodynamics relates to the conversion or transfer of energy. After all, the word thermodynamics is made up of thermo (meaning heat) and dynamics (meaning motion), so the word means the movement of heat or energy.

There are two main types of energy, kinetic and potential. Kinetic energy is the amount of energy contained in motion given by its mass and velocity. Potential energy is the energy of position relative to some energy field. For example, an object sitting on a desk has some potential energy relative to the gravitational field of the Earth. Pushing the book off the desk allows it to convert that potential energy to kinetic energy as the book falls to the floor. Other examples of potential energy is the potential energy relative to an electric field (electrical energy), magnetic field (magnetic energy), nuclear field (nuclear energy), etc.

Heat or heating is simply a measure of the amount of energy transferred, but it can also refer to energy in transfer or the process of transferring energy. In the distant past, it was thought that there was an actual mass transfer, but we now know that is not true. Nonetheless, the idea has stuck, and it leads to confusing statements such as heat rising. In reality, warm air rises because there is no mass that is heat. There are three mechanisms to transfer energy: conduction, convection, and radiation, which are discussed later in this chapter.

To keep track of how much energy is contained in matter, internal energy, U, is used. Internal energy is a measure of the potential and kinetic energy within the constituent molecules of matter. Internal energy can be increased by increasing the kinetic energy of the internal molecules. This increase means that the molecules within matter actually move faster, which can be measured as a temperature increase. You can visualize this as molecules move around in space, but also vibrate and rotate around the chemical bonds that hold molecules together.

Internal energy can also change through the chemical bonds themselves, which often happens during a phase change. When matter changes phase, the change in the internal energy depends on the direction of the phase change. For phase changes toward gases, (i.e. solid to liquid, liquid to gas, and solid to gas) the internal energy increases. Figure 4.1 shows an example of this change as ice initially at −30 °C eventually rises to over 100 °C. In regions I, III, and V, the temperature is increasing. However, the phase changes occurs in regions II and IV with no temperature change. Energy is still going into the water and internal energy is increasing, but that internal energy is not changing the temperature,

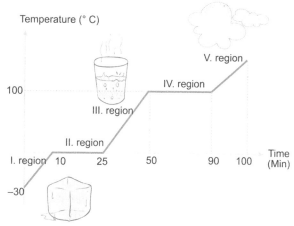

Figure 4.1 Water consistently heated is shown starting at 0 minutes as ice at a temperature of −30 °C and ending at 100 minutes as steam at a temperature of greater than 100 °C. Region I: added energy goes into increasing the temperature of ice from −30 °C to 0 °C. Region II: added energy goes into changing the ice to liquid water. Region III: added energy goes into increasing the temperature of water from 0 °C to 100 °C. Region IV: added energy goes into changing the liquid water to steam. Region V: added energy goes into raising the temperature of the steam.

it is energizing the intermolecular bonds to cause a phase change. The energy comes from the environment, surrounding the matter undergoing the phase change. For phase changes toward solids, (i.e. gas to liquid, liquid to solid, and gas to solid) the internal energy decreases. The energy is released to the environment surrounding the matter undergoing the phase change.

The heating involved in this phase change is called latent heat because phase changes do not change the internal kinetic energy. Therefore, the matter undergoing the phase change does not change temperature. An example of this energy exchange is apparent to anyone that has sweat. Sweat cools us because the liquid on our body evaporates (liquid to gas phase change). The energy that goes into increasing the internal energy in the sweat to execute this phase change comes from the surrounding environment of the sweat, which is largely our skin. The loss of internal energy from our skin lowers its temperature, but the sweat does not change temperature, it only changes phase.

The first law of thermodynamics is essentially the mathematical expression of the Law of Conservation of Energy. It is expressed by a simple looking formula:

$$U = q - w,$$

where ΔU is the change in internal energy of matter, q is the amount of heating, and w is the work that matter does. Like in Chapter 1, the Greek symbol, Δ, is used to represent the change in internal energy. By heating matter, the internal energy increases, and by doing work, the internal energy of matter decreases. Heating the object can cause the internal molecules to increase their kinetic energy (i.e. increase in temperature) or cause a phase change (i.e. latent heat), but both do not occur. Internal energy changes involving work is discussed later.

Mass and Energy: Flows, Cycles, and Conservation

Two of the most fundamental and unifying laws in all of science are the Laws of Conservation of Mass and Energy. These two laws constrain what can occur in any system because the amount of mass and energy can change only through transferring into or out of the system. Identifying and budgeting mass and energy is an important scientific practice. Later, Chapter 8 will cover the hydrologic cycle, which budgets the flow of mass, in this case the mass of water, through the Earth's systems. Water changes phases and moves into and out of the atmosphere and Earth. Chemical change can convert water to other compounds through chemical change, but the total mass must stay the same. Determining how mass transfers is consistent in biology, chemistry, geology, hydrology, meteorology, and any other science that considers water. Conservation of energy must also be considered in these changes. Phase changes and chemical reactions often come with a transfer of energy, but the total energy must stay the same.

In this chapter, the focus is on the first Law of Thermodynamics, which comes from the Law of Conversation of Energy. This unifying equation budgets the transfer of energy within matter through a transfer of energy into or out of that matter or work done on or by that matter. Within matter, internal energy, U, accounts for this energy, which physically is a combination of the molecular motions, measured by temperature, and the potential energy states of that matter. Energy states of the matter can be the arrangement of bonds leading to the different phases or the different locations of electrons within an element or compound. From this viewpoint, one can visualize the increase or decrease of internal energy caused by a change of temperature or a change of phase. The energy input or output then comes from heating, q, or work, w. Heating comes from conduction, convection, or radiation (called diabatic processes). Work comes from expansion or contraction (i.e. change in volume).

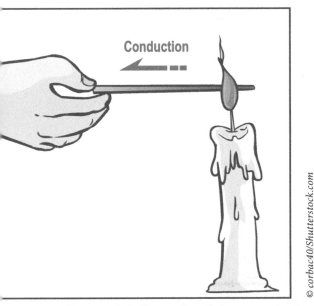

Figure 4.2 Example of how conduction transfers energy. The stick is touching the fire and transferring energy from the tip that is in the fire to the person's fingers. Energy always transfers from hot to cold.

© corbac40/Shutterstock.com

Conduction

The first of the three heating mechanisms is known as conduction. Conduction is a transfer of energy when two objects are in contact. Energy always flows from the object with higher temperature to the object with lower temperature (Figure 4.2).

The **heat conductivity** of an object is the rate at which energy transfers by conduction and mostly depends on the type of substance. Energy transfers through matter faster in substances with a higher heat conductivity. Air has one of the lowest known heat conductivities. Table 4.1 provides some common heat conductivities in relation to the conductivity of air. Interestingly, the experiment that first determined some of the heat conductivities involved coating different materials in wax and heating one end of the object and timing how long it took the melting wax to move across the object.

Table 4.1 Heat Conductivity scaled to air (i.e. 2× would be double) between 0 and 20 °C. Values are approximate because there is a range of values for most substances.

Substance	Heat Conductivity relative to air (at 0-20 °C)
Fiberglass insulation	2×
Wood (pine)	4×
Dry soil	8×
Water	23×
Glass	43×
Concrete	49×
Wet soil	80×
Ice	85×
Stainless Steel	635×
Aluminum	3846×

Fingers are sensitive instruments used to feel hot and cold. However, we do not actually feel the temperature of the objects we touch; we feel the loss or gain of energy from our fingers. If the loss or gain of energy were rapid, it would rapidly change our finger's temperature. If we were to touch two objects that are at the same temperature, but have two very different heat conductivities, they would feel like different temperatures to us.

For example, on a cold day when the air temperature is near the freezing point, steel and wood fences would be at the same freezing temperature, but would feel different. Steel has a much higher heat conductivity than wood (over 150× more conductive according to Table 4.1). When our fingers touch the fences, energy would transfer via conduction from our finger to the fence because our fingers are (hopefully) warmer. However, energy would transfer away from our fingers faster when touching the steel fence and our finger temperature would decrease faster. Most would think the metal fence is colder, but the two fences are at the same temperature.

Convection

The second of the three heating mechanisms is **convection**. Convection is a transfer of energy by the mass movement of a **fluid**. Fluids are gases and liquids, so the atmosphere and ocean are fluids. In the atmosphere, convection, in the horizontal, (i.e. north, south, east, or west) is performed by wind. If air is blown from a cold location, like a lake in summer, to a warmer location, that is convection. In the horizontal, convection is sometimes called **advection** and meteorologists often use convection solely for a vertical transfer of energy. When air heats and expands, its density decreases (Figure 4.3). Relatively less dense air rises (i.e. warm air rises). The rising air transfers both mass and energy upward. Convection is the primary way energy is transferred up in the troposphere. This transfer

How Thermals Form

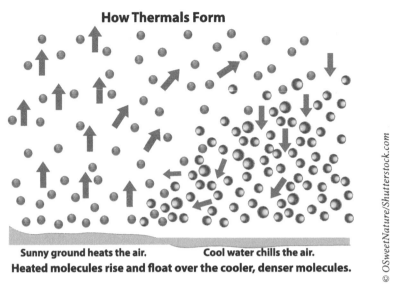

Sunny ground heats the air.   Cool water chills the air.
Heated molecules rise and float over the cooler, denser molecules.

© OSweetNature/Shutterstock.com

Figure 4.3 Example convection with heated molecules (red) expanding and rising and cooled molecules (blue) contracting and sinking.

of energy is how the upper troposphere is heated, not by the sun. Why the sun does not effectively heat the upper atmosphere is discussed shortly.

Radiation

The third of the three heating mechanisms is **radiation**. Radiation should not be confused with radioactivity, which expels particles and is nearly always harmful to living organisms. Radiation can be harmful, but is often not. In fact, everything emits radiation at all times.

Radiation is the transfer of energy via **electromagnetic (EM) waves** (Figure 4.4). These waves are similar to water waves in that they have crests and troughs. The distance from one crest to the next is the wavelength (SI unit is the meter). The Greek letter, λ,

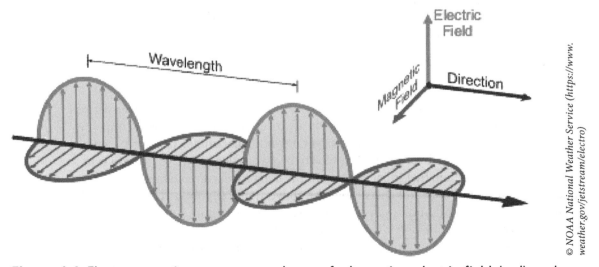

© NOAA National Weather Service (https://www. weather.gov/jetstream/electro)

Figure 4.4 Electromagnetic waves are made up of alternating electric field (red) and magnetic field (blue) waves that share a wavelength between adjacent crests or troughs.

represents **wavelength**. Electric and magnetic fields produce EM waves. Electric fields induce magnetic fields and magnetic fields induce electric fields. For this reason, either type of field will induce alternating electric and magnetic fields, which are EM waves.

EM waves transfer energy away from the emitter. The amount of energy transferred is inversely proportional to the wavelength of the EM wave. That means that smaller wavelength EM waves, carry larger amounts of energy.

The entire range of wavelengths of EM waves is called the **EM spectrum**. The spectrum of wavelengths starts at very small wavelengths on the order of 0.00000000000000001 m and continues all the way to 10000 m. Because of the large range, alternative ways are used to express wavelength to avoid writing so many zeros. First, **scientific notation** is used so that instead of writing all the zeroes, the wavelength is expressed as a number multiplying some power of 10. Positive exponents are the number of places needed to move the decimal point to the right so that 1.1234×10^4 is 11234. Negative exponents are the number of places needed to move the decimal point to the left so that 1.234×10^{-1} is 0.1234 and 1.234×10^{-5} is 0.00001234. Because of the importance of wavelengths with a value near 10^{-6} m, sometimes micrometer (μm) is used as the unit so that instead of using 1.2×10^{-5} m (which is the same as 12×10^{-6} m), 12 μm is used. Similarly, for smaller wavelengths, we substitute nanometer (nm) for 10^{-9} m. For example, 12×10^{-9} m is 12 nm.

The EM spectrum is described in ranges of wavelengths called **radiation bands** (Figure 4.5). Starting with the longest EM waves equal to 1000 m, the band between 0.1 m (10 cm) and 1000 m is the **radio frequency band**. You may be aware of these EM waves if you have ever listened to the radio (or antenna TV or cellphone), which are transmitted via radio-frequency EM waves. These waves were also mentioned in the last chapter when radars were discussed. The first 'r' in radar, which stands for radio, is a description of the wavelength of the transmitted waves in the EM spectrum. However, some radars also transmit in the next smallest radiation band discussed next.

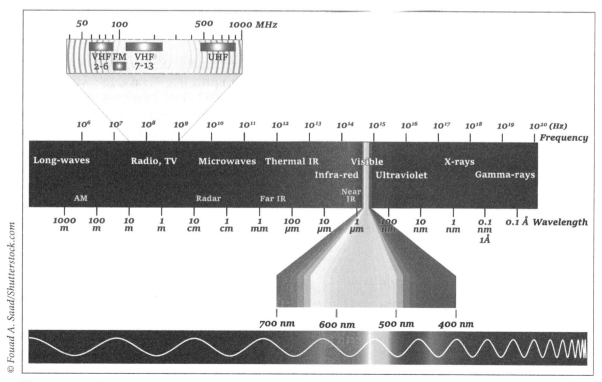

© Fouad A. Saad/Shutterstock.com

Figure 4.5 EM spectrum with expanded views of the radio, TV frequency bands and the visible wavelength bands.

The band between 0.1 cm (1 mm) and 10 cm is the microwave band of the EM spectrum. These waves have smaller wavelength and therefore each wave carries more energy. It carries so much energy that we can use a box that transmits microwaves to heat up our food. The way microwaves heats our food is that molecules in the food, mostly water, absorb microwaves and that energy raises the temperature of the food. Because of a lack of water, microwaves do not directly heat the plate the food is on, but the food will eventually heat the plate through conduction.

The band with wavelengths between 1 mm and 0.001 mm (1 µm) is the infrared (IR) band. The IR band is often divided into thermal IR and near IR. Thermal IR is the longer IR wavelengths and near IR is the shorter IR wavelengths near the visible wavelengths that we can see. Longer IR wavelengths are called thermal IR because emitted wavelengths depends on temperature of the emitter and most things on Earth emit at these wavelengths. Therefore, you can observe these wavelengths to get their temperature (thermal imagers work this way). However, much colder and much hotter objects emit or radiate at different wavelengths than thermal IR. The sun for example emits in the near IR, visible, and ultraviolet (UV), which is why you can see when it is in the sky (it emits visible) and it causes you to tan or burn (it emits UV). The band with wavelengths between 0.1 µm and 0.001 µm (1 nm) is the ultraviolet band.

In between the IR and UV bands lies the most familiar visible band. The reason the band is called visible is that humans can see these EM waves because they give us the sensation of vision and color. All other wavelengths are invisible to us.

Two things determine the energy within radiation, the wavelength and the amount or amplitude of the waves. Visible and longer wavelengths carry a relatively small amount of energy per wave, but some emitters produce a large amount of radiation (i.e. large amplitude). Microwave ovens, for example, send out low energy microwaves, but at high amplitudes enough energy is emitted to heat and possibly burn our foods. For smaller wavelengths, the energy, carried by a single wave, can cause major impacts to molecules. Absorbing these energetic EM waves can break apart molecules and atoms. This radiation is commonly referred to ionizing radiation.

Starting at the ultraviolet band, these waves can break apart the DNA in our skin potentially causing cancer. At smaller wavelengths, like X-rays, the wavelengths are small enough to penetrate your skin and reflect off bones. That is why we use X-rays to take a picture of our internal skeletal structure. Nevertheless, this radiation can cause damage, which is why X-ray technicians expose you to a small dose (small amplitudes). X-rays are largely safe because your body can usually correct any damage if the doses are small.

Up to now, the term emission has been used when EM waves come from an object. Emission is just that and causes the object to lose energy proportional to the amount and wavelength of the radiation. A few physical laws dictate the emission of radiation from an object.

Stefan-Boltzmann Law

The Stefan-Boltzmann Law relates the energy emitted by an object to its temperature. Hot objects emit more radiation than cold objects. In fact, the emission energy depends on temperature to the fourth power:

$$E = \sigma T^4$$

where E is the emission energy, T is the temperature of the emitter, and σ is the Stefan-Boltzmann constant (σ = 5.67 × 10^{-8} W/m^2·K^4). Multiplying the Stefan-Boltzmann constant by the fourth power of temperature in Kelvin gives a value with the unit W/m^2.

$$\frac{W}{m^2 K^4} \times K^4 = \frac{W}{m^2}$$

Multiplying the Stefan-Boltzmann constant by the fourth power of temperature in Celsius, causes the units and the answer to be incorrect. The units of the constant shows you the units of temperature you must use.

The units of W/m^2 are not a unit of energy. The unit is an energy divided by 1 s and 1 m^2. Therefore, 5.67 W/m^2 is the same as 5.67 Joules emitted in 1 s and across an area of 1 m^2. The emission of Earth, at a global mean temperature of 288 K emits

$$E = 5.67 \times 10^{-8} \frac{W}{m^2 K^4} \times (288\,K)^4 = 390 \frac{W}{m^2}.$$

The sun on the other hand at a surface temperature of 6000 K emits 73,483,200 W/m^2. The sun is also a lot larger (many more m^2 larger) so in total it emits many orders of magnitude more energy than the Earth.

The specific wavelengths of EM waves emitted by an object, called the emission spectrum, depends on the temperature and atomic composition of the object doing the emitting. Objects composed of many different atoms emit energy in a wide band of wavelengths. Individual molecules composed of few atoms like the individual gases that make up 99% of our atmosphere emits specific wavelengths over a small band of wavelengths. A different law, Wien's Law, dictates the amount of energy emitted at each wavelength by an object with many different atoms.

Wien's Law

Wien's Law relates temperature to the wavelength at which matter emits the largest amount of energy. As stated earlier, large objects with many different molecules emit over a wide range of wavelengths, but not equally at all wavelengths. In fact, if you were to graph the energy emitted versus wavelength you would get a curve called the Planck function (shape shown in Figure 4.6) with a peak wavelength (λ_{max}) given by Wien's Law.

The peak emission wavelength, λ_{max}, is inversely proportional to temperature

$$\lambda_{max} = \frac{2897 \quad m \cdot K}{T},$$

where T is the temperature of the emitter. Plugging in the Earth's global mean temperature of 288 K gives the peak wavelength of emission at 10 μm. Referring to Figure 4.5, 10 μm is in the thermal IR, which is why you do not see light radiating from Earth. Plugging in the sun's surface temperature of 6000 K gives the peak wavelength of emission at 0.5 μm. Again, referring to Figure 4.5, 0.5 μm is in the visible, specifically green. The sun does not look green because it only peaks at this wavelength. The sun emits strongly at all visible wavelengths so it appears white, which contains all the visible colors. You may have noticed that the sun appears yellow, orange, or even red at sunrise or sunset. This appearance is due to the filtering of the atmosphere, which we will shortly discuss. Nonetheless, if you looked at the sun while above the atmosphere the sun would appear white (though you would burn your eyes looking).

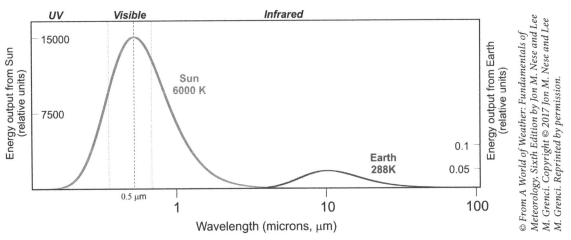

Figure 4.6 Energy output from the sun (left y-axis) and Earth (right y-axis) plotted against wavelength (μm) with the UV, Visible, and Infrared parts of the spectrum denoted along the top. Wien's law gives the peak energy output for the sun and Earth (peak of each curve).

Radiative Transfer

A good way to visualize how EM waves travel out from an emitter is to see yourself and a few of your friends riding along with a number of different waves. In this visualization, the sun is the emitter of the waves and the Earth's atmosphere, Earth's surface, or space is the endpoint. Figure 4.7 labeled the four different waves your group is riding along as wave 1, wave 2, wave 3, and wave 4. The sun emits all four waves, which travel a path that takes them toward Earth. With nothing in space, nothing will happen to these waves until they get in the Earth's atmosphere.

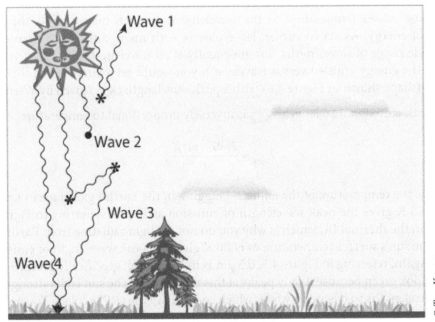

Figure 4.7 Four solar radiation EM waves entering the Earth's atmosphere. The asterisk represents a scattering event, a dark circle represents absorption, and an arrowhead represents transmission to an observer or to space.

Upon entering the Earth's atmosphere, wave 1 will be the first wave to interact with an atmospheric molecule. Most atmospheric molecules do not absorb sunlight and that is the case here. However, it does get scattered. Scattering is similar to reflection except scattering redirects light in any direction whereas reflection redirects light toward one specific angle (like a mirror). In this case, wave 1 is scattered back towards space and leaves the Earth's atmosphere, never to return. Perhaps, it makes it to the International Space Station, which is how astronauts would see the glow of our atmosphere.

Farther in, a molecule absorbs wave 2. As stated in the previous paragraph, this is not common but does happen. Ozone in particular will absorb part of the solar emission spectrum. That wave no longer exists. It has increased the internal kinetic energy of the molecule doing the absorbing and, therefore, increased its temperature. Absorption of radiation is how we feel warmer when standing in sunlight. Our skin is absorbing some of the sun's radiation. Our skin is also scattering a part of the sun's radiation. The scattered light does not warm us, but it does allow us to be seen. Without visible light scattering off an object, it would appear black.

As wave 3 and 4 continue on their journey, wave 3 gets scattered like wave 1, however this time wave 3 is scattered a second time and directed back toward the Earth's surface. Some of the sunlight that makes it to the Earth's surface is scattered prior to reaching the surface. Because scattering occurs in all directions, there is a probability that scatterers will redirect some light out into space (like wave 1) and some back to the surface (like wave 3). Once getting to the surface, the surface can absorb that light, causing it to warm much like wave 2 warmed the atmosphere. It can also be scattered by the surface back into the atmosphere again. A person's eye can also absorb it so that they see whatever scattered it last. In this case, the last scatterer was a molecule that makes up the blue sky. Scattering by the sky is called sky light and is why the sky is also bright on sunny days. Without this kind of sky light, we would only see the white sun and the sky would appear black.

Finally, wave 4 made it all the way to the ground without being scattered or absorbed. In that case, the wave transmitted through space and the atmosphere. The ultimate fate of wave 4 could then be any of the possibilities of wave 3. The difference is that this wave was not scattered by the sky so this wave would cause a person's eye to see the solar disk. When a thick cloud moves in front of the sun, no waves transmit from the sun to the ground and you do not see the solar disk, but you still see the sky and clouds.

Now, in reality there are not just 4 waves within sunlight, but a number that would be difficult to write without scientific notation on a single line of text (trillions wouldn't even come close). A percentage of waves from the sun is scattered back out into space. That percentage defines the parameter albedo. Surfaces that are more reflective have high albedos like freshly fallen snow. That light allows astronauts to see the Earth. Similarly, the moon scatters sunlight back into space and some of that is directed to our eyes on Earth allowing us to see it.

The blue sky is actually scattered sunlight. The reason that it is blue is that the atmosphere selectively scatters shorter wavelengths of light more efficiently so the blue side of the visible EM spectrum is scattered much more than the red part. This is the filtering, mentioned earlier, that makes the sun appear yellow, orange, or red at sunrise and sunset. The atmosphere scatters out the blue part of the spectrum to an increasing amount when the sun is low on the horizon. When the sun is low on the horizon its light goes through an increasing amount of the atmosphere before making it to the ground. What is left of the non-scattered sunlight (wave 4's from Figure 4.7) is increasingly on the yellow, orange and red part of the sun's spectrum.

When the sky is full of clouds, thick enough to prevent us from seeing the solar disk, then all the light we see on Earth is scattered (all the wave 3's and no wave 4's from Figure 4.7). Clouds do not absorb much light, which is why it does not get completely dark on overcast days. However, thicker clouds will cause an increasing amount of sunlight to be scattered back to space preventing that light from making it to the Earth's surface. These thick clouds (think tornadic thunderstorm clouds) cause it to be dark at the surface. These same clouds are bright when viewed from above because a large percentage of the sunlight is redirected back up and out into space (high albedo).

Scattering does not occur with equal probability in all directions and how clouds scatter depends on the composition of the clouds. Liquid water clouds tend to be more uniformly scattering than ice clouds, which scatter more in the forward direction. That is why the base of lower clouds is darker than high cirrus clouds. Cirrus clouds, being composed of ice, scatters a larger proportion of light in the forward direction. When flying above cirrus clouds they are not very bright, but a lower liquid water cloud will be much brighter because of the larger proportion of light scattered backwards. This scattering behavior affects how clouds appear on satellite and is one way we can tell the altitude of clouds when looking on satellite. The different scattering behaviors also affects how these different clouds influences our climate.

Radiation Balance

The temperature and its changeable behavior depends strongly on the balance of absorbed radiation minus emitted radiation. Much like the balance in any money account, it depends on deposited money minus spent money. This balance not only determines how temperature changes from minute-to-minute, but also from day-to-day, season-to-season, and year-to-year. In this section, we will start with year-to-year changes.

Solar Energy

The amount of radiation from the sun coming into the Earth is mostly a constant, S_o, and is equal to 1367 W/m². Multiplying this by the cross-sectional area of the Earth, πr_E^2, gives the total energy per second or Watts intercepted by and hitting the Earth's surface,

$$E = S_O \pi r_E^2,$$

where r_E is the radius of the Earth.

Radiation Balance with no Atmosphere

Radiation balance is simpler when you disregard the atmosphere. Of course, you cannot disregard the Earth's atmosphere, but by doing so we can later find out the effect of the atmosphere. With no atmosphere, the sun's radiation is partially absorbed or scattered at the surface depending on the surface albedo. The Earth has an albedo, α, of about 30% so that $(1-\alpha)$ or 70% of the sun's 1367 W/m² is absorbed.

When the IR emission by the Earth (if it had no atmosphere) balances the absorbed solar radiation, it results (See digging deeper for the calculation) in a **global mean temperature** of 255 K (0 °F). If this were Earth's actual global mean temperature, the oceans would freeze and Earth would be an ice planet. However, this balance (steps 1–3 in Figure 4.8) occurs with no atmosphere because the effect of the atmosphere was ignored.

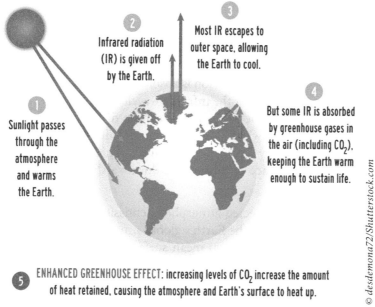

① Sunlight passes through the atmosphere and warms the Earth.

② Infrared radiation (IR) is given off by the Earth.

③ Most IR escapes to outer space, allowing the Earth to cool.

④ But some IR is absorbed by greenhouse gases in the air (including CO_2), keeping the Earth warm enough to sustain life.

⑤ ENHANCED GREENHOUSE EFFECT: increasing levels of CO_2 increase the amount of heat retained, causing the atmosphere and Earth's surface to heat up.

© desdemona72/Shutterstock.com

Figure 4.8 Radiation balance without an atmosphere (1-3) and with an atmosphere (1-4).

Digging Deeper

Calculating Radiation Balance

The amount of energy absorbed by the Earth's surface if it had no atmosphere is,

$$E_{in} = (1-\alpha)S_0\pi r_E^2$$

The absorbed energy warms the Earth. If the Earth had no way of removing the absorbed energy, it would burn up. However, all matter radiates an amount, σT^4, given by Stefan-Boltzmann's Law. Multiplying this by the spherical surface area of the Earth, $4\pi r^2$ gives the total energy per second or Watts leaving the Earth's surface if it had no atmosphere. Notice that the Earth absorbs an amount equal to the cross-sectional area, πr_E^2, but emits over its entire spherical surface area, $4\pi r_E^2$, which is 4 times greater. The amount of energy emitted by the Earth's surface is,

$$E_{out} = (1-\alpha)4\pi r_E^2 \sigma T^4$$

On an annual basis, the amount coming in is balanced, and therefore equal, to the amount leaving. Equating E_{in} to E_{out},

$$(1-\alpha)S_0\pi r_E^2 = 4\pi r_E^2 \sigma T^4$$

The πr_E^2 on both the left-hand and right-hand sides divide out so that,

$$(1-\alpha)S_0 = 4\sigma T^4$$

Solving for T and substituting $\alpha = 0.3$, $S_0 = 1367$ W/m², $\sigma = 5.67 \times 10^{-8}$ W/m² K⁴, gives

$$T = \sqrt[4]{\frac{(1-\alpha)S_0}{4\sigma}} = \sqrt[4]{\frac{(1-0.3)1367\,W/m^2}{4\times 5.67\times 10^{-8}\,W/m^2K^4}} = 255\,K$$

Radiation Balance with an Atmosphere

Fortunately, Earth has an atmosphere with constituent gases that disproportionately absorb the Earth's emission, compared to the sun's radiation. These gases, known as **greenhouse gases**, have an absorption spectrum where the visible light from the sun is not absorbed while the Earth's emission is absorbed. The main atmospheric gases, nitrogen and oxygen, do not absorb at the infrared wavelengths of Earth's emission. However, the more complex atmospheric gases such as carbon dioxide, water vapor, methane, and others do. This absorption warms the atmosphere, but like all matter, the atmosphere also emits radiation given by Stefan-Boltzmann law. This emission changes the radiation balance at the Earth's surface by adding the downward directed atmospheric emission (Figure 4.8 step 4).

Adding the downward directed atmospheric emission is a more complicated calculation. However, when doing so the Earth's global annual mean temperature becomes 288 K (59 °F). The Earth's global annual mean surface temperature is about 33 K (59.4 °F) warmer than it would be without an atmosphere. This difference is produced by the greenhouse effect of the atmosphere (Figure 4.8 number 4).

This calculation is remarkably close to what we observe when averaging all of the world's surface thermometers over an entire year. The calculation of Earth's global annual mean temperature is relatively simple. It largely depends on the amount of sunlight coming in, the Earth's albedo, and the greenhouse effect. This simplicity is one reason that it is possible to forecast the Earth's global annual mean temperature over a century into the future. Of course, this means that an increase in the atmospheric greenhouse effect would necessarily lead to an increase in the global annual mean temperature. An increase in the global annual mean temperature is the definition of global warming.

Distribution of Temperature on Earth

The temperatures on Earth vary largely with latitude due to the spherical geometry of the Earth. For example, Figure 4.9 shows that the amount of energy in each ray of light from the sun is equal, but when that ray hits the top of the atmosphere of the Earth, it spreads

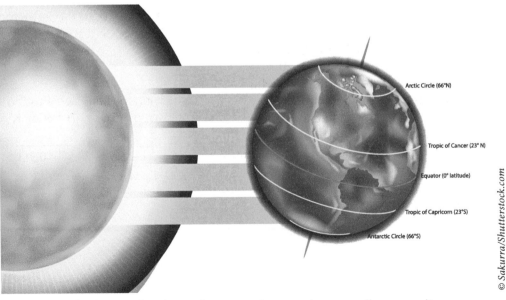

© Sakurra/Shutterstock.com

Figure 4.9 Sun's rays (each ray has equal energy) unequally spreading across the Earth's surface at different latitudes.

out along the curvature of the atmosphere so that the amount of energy at any one location is different. Where the sun's rays come in perpendicular (often called direct radiation), the amount of energy per square meter on the top of the atmosphere of the Earth is the same as it is in space. In this situation, the sun is directly overhead and you would cast no shadow. However, as you move toward the Earth's poles the same size ray distributes over a larger area of the top of the atmosphere of the Earth. The same energy over a larger area causes less energy per square meter on the Earth's surface. These non-perpendicular rays are called indirect radiation. In this situation, the sun is not directly overhead and you cast a larger shadow like when sunset approaches. This increasingly indirect sunlight toward the poles is why the tropics tend to be much warmer than the poles.

The Reason for the Seasons

The seasons occur because the spread of solar energy on the Earth's surface changes with the angle of the sun in the sky and the duration of daylight. Both of these change throughout the year because of the tilt of the Earth's rotation axis relative to its orbital plane around the sun (Figure 4.10). The Earth's orbital plane is simply the filled in ellipse (not quite a circle) you would get if you traced the Earth's revolution around the sun. The Earth's rotation axis tilts 23.5° relative to this ellipse, but the direction that the North Pole faces does not change much from year-to-year. The North Pole always faces the star Polaris (the North Star). Therefore, as the Earth revolves around the sun, direct radiation occurs at different latitudes between 23.5° N and 23.5° S.

Starting at the northern hemisphere winter solstice (December 20–22), the North Pole faces away from the sun (Figure 4.10 leftmost Earth position). At this time, the most direct radiation and energy from the sun shines on 23.5° S latitude. The energy drops as you move either north or south from this latitude. The southern hemisphere receives

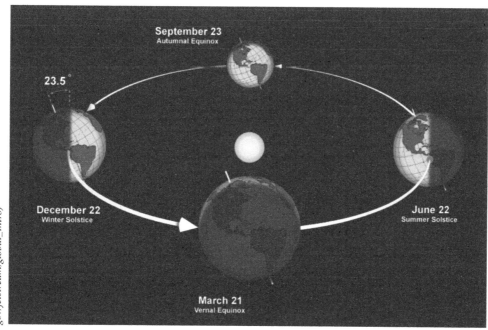

© NOAA National Weather Service (https://www.weather. gov/jetstream/global_intro)

Figure 4.10 Earth location at the beginning of four different seasons on its journey around the sun is shown. The white arrows trace out the path of the Earth around the sun and defines the orbital plane. The Earth's rotation axis is tilted at a 23.5° angle to the orbital plane.

most of the sun's energy, which is why the southern hemisphere is experiencing summer at this time while the northern hemisphere is experiencing winter.

The Earth moves counterclockwise to the northern hemisphere vernal equinox (March 19–21; bottommost Earth position). At this time, the most direct radiation and energy from the sun shines at the equator (0° latitude). The energy drops as you move either north or south from this latitude. An equal amount of energy is directed in the northern and southern hemispheres, which is why this season is called an equinox. The Earth then comes to the rightmost position in Figure 4.10, the northern hemisphere summer solstice (June 20–21). The most direct radiation shines on 23.5° N latitude. The northern hemisphere now receives most of the sun's energy, which is why the northern hemisphere is experiencing summer. The energy distribution once again becomes equal in each hemisphere at the autumnal equinox (September 20–22).

To emphasize that the distance between the sun and Earth has little to do with the seasons, the northern hemisphere winter solstice is also the time that the Earth makes the closest approach to the sun. Because the Earth is closer to the sun and moves more quickly around the sun between northern hemisphere fall and winter, these seasons are about four days shorter than spring and summer (go ahead and count the days).

The duration of sunlight also changes throughout the year because the path that the sun makes across the sky changes (Figure 4.11). Many think that the sun always rises in the east and sets in the west, but that is only strictly true on the equinoxes (blue path in Figure 4.11). During the summer solstice (red path in Figure 4.11), the sun rises in the northeast and sets in the northwest in the northern hemisphere. This path of the sun across the sky is longer causing longer daylight. The closer to the poles you are as the summer solstice approaches, the longer the day. In fact, if you are close enough to the poles, the sun is actually up all 24 hours (no sunset). The reverse of this is that the closer to the poles you are as the winter solstice approaches, the shorter the day and if you are close enough to the poles the sun is set for all 24 hours (no sunrise).

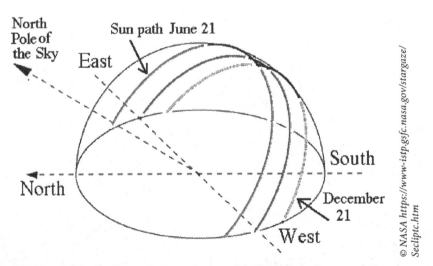

© NASA *https://www-istp.gsfc.nasa.gov/stargaze/ Secliptc.htm*

Figure 4.11 Sun's path across the sky for the winter solstice (green), summer solstice (red) and the equinoxes (blue) in the northern hemisphere midlatitudes. A person subjected to these sun paths would be standing in the center of the circle. The black curve from north to south represents the sun's position at solar noon.

The combination of how direct the radiation is and the length of the day determines how much energy from the sun you receive. Understanding this geometry is important to people and industries that depend on the energy from the sun such as the agriculture and solar power industries. From an energetics standpoint, how direct the radiation is, is the most important factor. The latitudes receiving the most direct radiation, receives much more energy from the sun then the latitudes receiving 24 hours of sun.

The Diurnal Cycle

Daylight occurs where the Earth's surface is facing into the sun while night occurs where the Earth's shadow is in the way of the sun. These changes within a 24-hour period defines the diurnal cycle. The most energy coming in occurs during the day for that reason. However, because of the greenhouse effect, the Earth does not lose energy very quickly keeping the day and night relatively close in temperature (around 10 °C or 18 °F daily of diurnal variation, but varies due to a number of factors). With a much smaller greenhouse effect, but a similar duration of daylight, Mars has a 40 °C or 72 °F diurnal variation in temperature.

Figure 4.12 shows the change in temperature throughout a day without wind or clouds. The energy balance depends on the amount of solar radiation gained minus the amount of Earth radiation lost. When the sun is below the horizon, the amount of solar radiation is zero so the temperature change depends on the amount of Earth radiation gained or lost. On nights without clouds, the Earth radiation is nearly always negative, meaning the surface is losing energy, and the temperature will decrease. This situation occurs from after sunset to before sunrise.

At sunrise, the solar radiation begins to increase; however, until the amount of solar radiation absorbed at the ground becomes greater than the Earth radiation lost, the

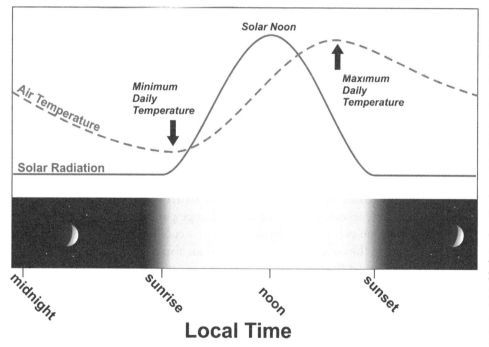

Figure 4.12 Temperature (top, red line), the outgoing Earth energy rate (bottom, blue line) and incoming solar energy rate (bottom, yellow line) for a 24-hour period starting and ending at midnight.

temperature will decrease. It is not until the absorbed solar radiation is greater than the Earth radiation lost that the minimum temperature is reached; typically less than a half hour after sunrise. The solar radiation continues to increase until solar noon when the solar radiation absorbed is the greatest. The difference between the solar radiation and the Earth's radiation is greatest at this time too. Therefore, this is the time that the temperature increase should be the fastest, not the time of the maximum temperature. That does not happen for another few hours while the energy from solar radiation is greater than the Earth radiation lost. As the temperature of the Earth's surface increases, the Earth radiation increases because of Stefan-Boltzmann's law. Once the energy from the solar radiation, which is decreasing in the afternoon, becomes equal to the Earth radiation, which is increasing in the afternoon, then the maximum temperature is reached; usually around 3-4 hours after solar noon depending on the season. After then, the Earth's surface is losing more energy than gaining and the temperature begins to decrease.

Other Factors Affecting the Diurnal Cycle

Radiation is one of the strongest influences on temperature, but conduction, convection and latent heating also play an important role in achieving energy balance and climate over the entire Earth. Examples include the jet stream, ocean circulation, Hadley cells, etc. Many of these processes will be discussed in later chapters. Here other factors are presented that become more significant locally.

Clouds

Clouds can have a significant effect on surface temperatures because of their effect on solar and Earth's radiation. Clouds reduce the amount of solar radiation reaching the surface by scattering some of the solar radiation back to space. Most people probably notice that when a cloud moves overhead and the sun is out that the surface becomes colder, but this effect only occurs during the day when the sun is over the horizon. However, less obvious is the effect that clouds have on the Earth radiation, which occurs all 24 hours. Clouds are strong absorbers of Earth's radiation. During the day, the scattering effect of clouds is greater, but cooling would be much larger if clouds did not also absorb Earth's radiation so strongly. At night, the absorption no longer competes with the scattering effect and clouds can actually warm the surface. Low clouds and the layer it is in can be warmer than the surface at night and so the Earth radiation at the surface in this case would be positive and the Earth's surface would warm. Cloudy evenings tend to be warmer than clear evenings (Figure 4.13).

Advection

Sometimes warmer or colder air can be moving in to an area from any horizontal direction and reduce or even reverse the temperature change pattern expected on clear and calm days. This advection can be a local effect such as a cool breeze off a lake or a warm breeze from the south in the northern hemisphere. It can also be much larger in scale such as with the passage of a cold front.

Conduction and Convection

When radiation is absorbed at the surface, conduction warms the air above and convection moves it vertically. Earth's radiation will also warm the air, but the air is also radiating. One misconception is that the Earth's surface holds the radiation from the day and warms the air at night when it releases it. However, remember that when radiation is absorbed it ceases to exist and goes in to increasing the energy and, therefore, the

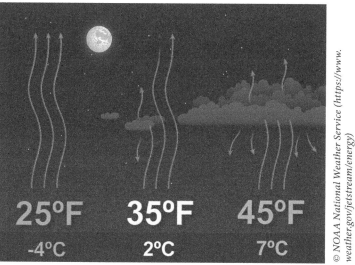

Figure 4.13 Effect of absorption of Earth's radiation by clouds on the nighttime surface temperatures.

temperature. In addition, everything is always emitting radiation, the amount of which depends on its temperature (Stefan-Boltzmann law). Although the ground is radiating and cooling the Earth's surface, conduction and convection often transfer this temperature change to increasingly higher layers. At night, this transfer only occurs in the lowest few hundred meters or lowest 100 mb. This layer is called the nocturnal boundary layer and is thinner on calm and clear evenings. When this layer is thin, the temperatures at the surface will drop rapidly in the early evening and rise rapidly during the morning because conduction and convection have only a small layer to cool or warm.

Summary

Data and observations, the foundation of the scientific method, sets the stage for scientists to ask questions about what we observe. When those questions are testable, also known as hypotheses, experiments can be formulated to establish a set of laws, theories, and principles that explain the natural and physical world. This chapter begins to discuss those laws, theories, and principles that apply to all physical sciences and specifically to weather and climate forecasting.

The Laws of the Conservation of Mass and Energy states that matter and energy cannot be created or destroyed and sets the stage for the First Law of Thermodynamics. The First Law of Thermodynamics states that the change in internal energy of matter is the difference between the amount of heating on that matter minus the work that matter does. Internal energy is the sum of molecular kinetic energy, measured by temperature, and the potential energy of molecular chemical bonds. When energy is added to matter, the temperature can increase, or the intermolecular bonds can change in a way to cause a phase change. Melting, evaporation, and sublimation require energy to break bonds and make matter move more freely. In contrast, freezing, condensation, and deposition require energy to form bonds and make matter move less freely. The energy is added to or removed from the environment and is called latent heat.

Heating, or the transfer of energy, can occur through conduction (molecule-to-molecule), convection (mass movement of a fluid), or radiation (transfer of electromagnetic (EM) waves. The wavelength of these waves determines many of their properties; most importantly, that shorter wavelength waves have higher energy. The spectrum of EM waves is classified within radiation bands including from longest to shortest wavelengths: radio, microwave, infrared, visible, ultraviolet, and x rays. EM waves are emitted by all matter. The amount of energy emitted by matter depends on temperature as given by Stefan Boltzmann's Law. The distribution of emission energy as a function of the wavelength is a specific shape with a peak wavelength inversely proportional to temperature given by Wien's Law. The sun with a much higher temperature emits much more energy per square meter and at a shorter wavelength than the Earth.

Radiation balance occurs when the amount of absorbed sunlight is equal to the amount of emission of the Earth. This balance changes seasonally as the Earth revolves around the sun because of the tilt of the Earth's rotation axis. It also changes within a day as the Earth rotates on its axis. Because the atmosphere consists of gases that absorb more in the Earth's emission spectrum than the sun's emission spectrum, this greenhouse effect increases the amount of radiation emitted toward the Earth's surface. The greenhouse effect of the atmosphere makes the Earth warmer and increasing the amount of greenhouse gases in the atmosphere should cause the Earth to warm (global warming). Clouds also have a strong greenhouse effect that counteracts the shading effect during the day and may warm the Earth's surface at night.

Key Terms

Hypotheses	Fluid	Stefan-Boltzmann Law
Theory	Advection	Wien's Law
First Law of Thermodynamics	Radiation	Scattering
Energy	Emission	Absorption
Work	Electromagnetic (EM) Waves	Transmission
Heat	Wavelength	Albedo
Law of Conservation of Energy	EM Spectrum	Global Mean Temperature
Kinetic Energy	Scientific Notation	Greenhouse Gases
Potential Energy	Radiation Bands	Direct Radiation
Internal Energy	Radio Frequency Bands	Indirect Radiation
Latent Heat	Infrared (IR) Bands	Tilt of the Earth's Rotation Axis
Conduction	Thermal infrared (IR)	Diurnal Cycle
Heat Conductivity	Near infrared (IR)	Solar Noon
Convection	Ultraviolet Band	Nocturnal Boundary Layer
	Visible Band	

Questions and Problems

1. Describe an example of how you have actually felt latent heat. Include the phase change and why that phase change had the perceived effect.

2. Which phase changes to water would heat the surrounding air?

3. Which type of fence would feel the coldest if you touched it in winter with your bare hands and why?

4. Most people consider an air temperature of 25 °C (77 °F), even on a cloudy day, to feel rather comfortable. However, if you were to walk into a lake with a water temperature of 25 °C (77 °F) on that same day, it would feel rather cold. Explain why.

5. Most people consider an air temperature of 25 °C (78 °F) comfortable when they are not wet. However, if they come out of a lake (no matter the temperature of the water) they will feel a chill in that same air. Explain why.

6. What color clothing is best to wear on a hot sunny day? Why does this color keep you cooler than any other color?

7. If most of the energy that heats the Earth comes from the sun then why are the hottest temperatures in the atmosphere found at the Earth's surface and not higher in the atmosphere?

8. If cumulus clouds scatter all of the light from the solar disk then why does it not get dark when a cumulus cloud covers the sun?

9. If grass and trees are green then what can you say about the importance of the green part of the sun's emission spectrum to participating in photosynthesis in these plants?

10. What is the atmospheric greenhouse effect?

11. What is the important characteristic of a gas that makes it a greenhouse gas?

12. Which property of electromagnetic radiation is inversely proportional to temperature and what does inversely proportional mean in this context?

13. An object is absorbing 3 W of visible light, has a temperature of 25 °C (77 °F), and is in radiative equilibrium. What type of and how much radiation is it emitting?

14. What is the source of visible light that allows us to see the moon? Use each of the terms: emission, absorption, scattering, and transmission to describe completely the path of light from this source to your eyes that allows you to see the moon.

15. Why are temperatures warmest around the equator even though the amount of energy in a beam of sunlight is the same everywhere on the sun-side of a polar orbiting satellite?

16. How would the seasons on Earth be different if the Earth's axis was not tilted?

17. Why don't the day's high temperatures occur at noon when the sun is highest in the sky and the radiation from the sun is the greatest?

18. If the clouds unexpectedly cleared (i.e. this was not forecasted) on a calm winter evening, how would the evening's low temperatures likely compare to the forecasted low temperatures and why?

Other Resources

https://www.emich.edu/geography-geology/weather for links to useful weather data to go along with this textbook and updates to any broken links in the textbook.

Chapter 5

Laws of Motion

Introduction

This chapter focuses on the causes of moving air. Moving air is wind so this chapter focuses on what causes wind. The chapter starts with wind in the horizontal and concludes with wind in the vertical. Winds in the horizontal moves large weather systems. Vertical winds are referred to as rising/sinking air on a large scale and updrafts/downdrafts in thunderstorms. Horizontal winds affect vertical winds, which cause clouds and precipitation, leading to the topic of the next chapter.

Newton's Laws of Motion

Named after Sir Isaac Newton, the three laws of motion constrains the motions of the atmosphere. Newton's first law states that an object will stay at rest or at constant velocity unless acted upon by a force. This behavior is called inertia and it helped to define forces.

NEWTON'S 2nd LAW

$$\vec{F} = m\vec{a}$$

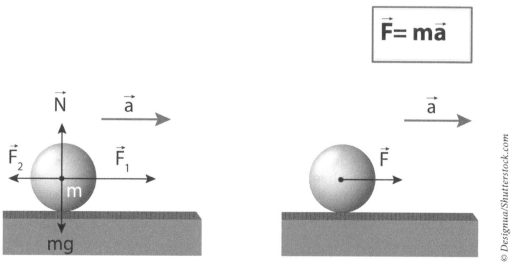

Figure 5.1 Newton's second law shows how the sum of forces is related to the change in movement of a mass. In this case, the forces in the vertical are balanced, but in the horizontal, they are not. $F = F_2 - F_1 = ma$.

© Designua/Shutterstock.com

Newton's second law of motion quantitatively relates a force to a change in velocity (i.e. acceleration). It equates the net sum of applied forces to the product of the objects mass and the resulting acceleration (Figure 5.1). This second law will be used throughout this chapter to describe quantitatively how air moves in the atmosphere. Newton's third law is a reminder that there are no isolated forces and for every applied force there is an equal and opposite force.

Newton's second law completely describes wind and its change. Although numerous forces act on the wind leading to complex motions, a few major forces describe most of this motion. The following subsections discuss these forces individually. Then, the chapter ends with Newton's second law applied to describe how these forces balance to create much of the observed winds.

Pressure Gradient Force

The first major force is the **pressure gradient force** (PGF). A **gradient** is a change in a parameter across some distance and is expressed mathematically as follows:

$$gradient = \frac{\Delta parameter}{\Delta x}$$

Here, Δ represents a change in a parameter and x represents a coordinate or location. Typically, x and y represent coordinates in the east-west and north-south direction, respectively. The pressure gradient is expressed mathematically as follows:

$$pressure\ gradient = \frac{\Delta p}{\Delta x}$$

where P represents pressure. To actually calculate it in the east-west direction you would need to know two pressure values (P_1, P_2) at two different locations with east-west coordinates (x_1, x_2) and then calculate,

$$pressure\ gradient = \frac{\Delta p}{\Delta x} = \frac{p_2 - p_1}{x_2 - x_1}$$

The denominator would simply be the east-west distance between the two coordinates or locations. A pressure gradient causes a force called the pressure gradient force (PGF). The pressure gradient force pushes fluids (including air) from high pressure to low pressure (Figure 5.2).

As the pressure gradient increases (i.e. a larger change in pressure over the same distance), the force on the air between two locations increases. When plotting isobars on weather maps, uniform contour intervals of 4 mb are used. Therefore, on these maps the ΔP is always 4 mb so the pressure gradient force is inversely proportional to the distance between the isobars. As the distance between isobars increases, the PGF decreases, which results in slower winds. This relationship is one reason why isobars are so important.

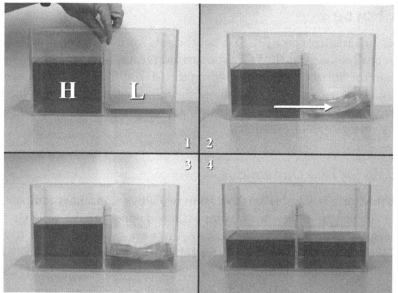

Figure 5.2 Demonstration of the pressure gradient force (PGF) is shown. In quadrant 1, fluids filled at different levels have a central barrier lifted a short distance. The difference in fluid height creates high pressure (H) on the left side and low pressure (L) on the right. In quadrants 2 and 3, the PGF pushes the liquid from high to low. In quadrant 4, the levels of liquid are the same so the PGF is zero and the liquid is at rest again.

Digging Deeper

Deriving the Pressure Gradient Fore

Remember that pressure is the force of air divided by the area of that force. In the case of the PGF in the east-west direction, x, the area is equal to the north-south distance (Δy) times the up-down distance (Δz). Therefore, the pressure gradient is

$$\frac{\Delta P}{\Delta x} = -\frac{1}{\Delta x}\frac{PGF}{area} - \frac{PGF}{\Delta x \Delta y \Delta z}$$

Here the pressure, P, was substituted with the force (in this case the PGF) divided by the area ($\Delta y \Delta z$). The negative sign is because the direction of the PGF is from high to low pressure or opposite to the direction that the pressure is increasing. Because Volume (V) is equal to $\Delta x \Delta y \Delta z$, the equation for PGF comes from multiplying both sides by V to get

$$PGF = -V\frac{\Delta P}{\Delta x}.$$

To get this equation into the more familiar form of Newton's second law (i.e. F=ma), substitute the definition of density (ρ) equal to the mass (m) divided by the Volume (V) of air to get

$$PGF = ma = -\frac{m}{\rho}\frac{\Delta P}{\Delta x}$$

Typically, in weather these forces are considered per unit mass by dividing both sides by mass and setting mass equal to 1 kg (all forces in this textbook will be described this way),

$$PGF\ per\ 1kg\ of\ air = -\frac{1}{\rho}\frac{\Delta P}{\Delta x}.$$

Likewise, if the pressure gradient is in the north-south direction the equation is

$$PGF\ per\ 1kg\ of\ air = -\frac{1}{\rho}\frac{\Delta P}{\Delta y}.$$

Technically, the units of this equation is m/s^2, which is an acceleration, but we are multiplying a unit mass to get a force with the unit of Newton.

Coriolis Force

Often the pressure gradient force (PGF) is not the only force acting on air. The **Coriolis force** (CF) is equally as large as the PGF. The two forces must be considered to know how air will move in the horizontal. Understanding the CF is difficult because of the geometry. Luckily, it is not necessary to understand the full geometry in order to understand this force. Here, the CF is simplified by explaining its origins in two dimensions and then its applications on the three-dimensional Earth.

Coriolis Force on Two Dimensions

To appreciate the Coriolis, CF, it is best to start in two dimensions. Envisioning a rotating platform found on playgrounds with two kids sitting on opposite sides will help illustrate the idea of perspective and the CF. In this case, there are two perspectives to consider. Perspective 1 is a "birds-eye" view or view from above the platform (Figure 5.3). Perspective 2 is that of the kids on the platform.

If the platform does not rotate and a kid throws the ball to the other, both perspectives will see the ball move in a straight-line path. If the platform is rotating counterclockwise as viewed from above and a kid throws the ball to the other, the two perspectives will see different paths. Perspective 1 (birds-eye) will still see the ball move in a straight line (labeled true path). However, because the platform will rotate while the ball is in the air, the ball will miss the receiver to their left. Even though the kid threw the ball in a straight line, the kids (perspective 2) will see the ball curve to the right (labeled apparent path).

In perspective 2 there is no actual force causing the ball to curve to the right. According to Newton's laws, the ball will continue to move at constant velocity until a force acts on the ball. However, if the kids were to describe the movement of the ball they would need to invent an unknown force to account for the curvature. This unknown force is the apparent force called the Coriolis force.

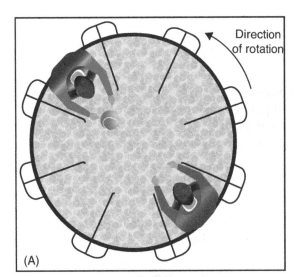
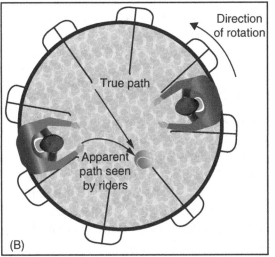

Figure 5.3 Birds-eye perspective of kids on a rotating platform is shown. If a kid throws a ball on a rotating platform, a viewer flying above the platform will see the ball move in a straight path (labeled true path). However, the platform will rotate under the ball while in flight and the receiving kid will move away from the true path of the ball such that the ball will miss the kid to the left. To the kids, the ball will appear to curve to the right (labeled apparent path).

Coriolis Force on Earth

On Earth, we are standing on a rotating platform (i.e, the Earth) and objects in motion above the rotating Earth appear to curve in transit. In order to account for this acceleration we must invent an apparent force. Of course, we know the curvature is because we are on a rotating reference frame. Nonetheless, creating this apparent force, called the Coriolis force (CF), accounts for this deflection whenever we consider motion on Earth. On the three-dimensional spherical Earth, there are three things that the magnitude and direction of the CF is proportional to: latitude, rotation rate, and velocity of the object.

Latitude

The CF is proportional to latitude because the amount and direction that you are rotating depends on latitude. You are rotating if your head rotates as the Earth rotates. When you are standing at the North Pole (90° N), your head is rotating counterclockwise. However, when you are standing at the South Pole (90^0 S) your head is rotating clockwise. This fact seems counterintuitive. However, if you were to videotape the stars throughout the evening at the North and South Poles, you would see the stars rotate in opposite directions. The stars would rotate counterclockwise at the North Pole and clockwise at the South Pole.

You can see this with a globe too. If you spin the globe with your hand from left-to right, you will get the direction that the Earth spins. If you look down at the North Pole while it is spinning you will see it rotate counterclockwise. If you hold the globe above your head and look at the South Pole while it is spinning you will see that it rotates clockwise.

When standing at the equator (0^0 latitude), your head does not rotate at all. If you were to videotape the stars throughout the evening at the equator, you would see the stars move in a straight line across the sky. The Earth does not go from no rotation to maximum rotation as you step north or south from the equator. It actually changes gradually, though in opposite directions, from zero at the equator to a maximum at the poles.

Rotation Rate

Remember the example of the kids on the rotating platform. If you ever watched kids on these vomit-inducing play structures, you would see them make one complete rotation in about 10 seconds. Rotation rate is measured in rotations per second. In this case, the rotation rate is about one rotation per 10 seconds or 0.1 revolutions/s. The Earth rotates once per day or one time every 86400 s. In this case the rotation rate is 0.0000116 revolutions/s or 1.16×10^{-5} revolutions/s.

The Earth's rotation rate is much slower. Therefore, the apparent force that makes a noticeable curve in a ball over the rotating platform will have a negligible effect on a ball thrown over the Earth's surface. Because of this, air coming out of a balloon or water flushed down a toilet will have no noticeable curvature due to CF. This lack of curvature is obvious to anyone that has thrown a ball, but many think that the CF influences water going down the drain. Although this influence is true, it is imperceptible. Water going down a drain in a sink or down a toilet does so because of other factors such as the shape of the bowl or any initial rotation of the water. You can confirm this by filling a stoppered sink and letting the water come to rest. After several minutes, swirl the water with your finger clockwise or counterclockwise and watch the water go down the sink, after removing the stopper, in that direction.

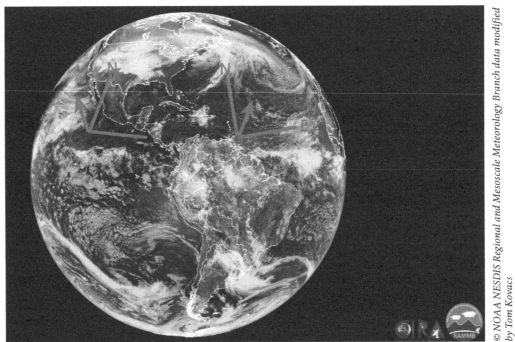

© NOAA NESDIS Regional and Mesoscale Meteorology Branch data modified by Tom Kovacs

Figure 5.4 Illustration of how the north (red line labeled N), east (red line labeled E), up (red arrow) coordinate system on the spherical Earth changes as you move from location to location. Even if you move straight east, from the birds-eye view from space, the direction of east is changing.

Velocity

The reason that the Coriolis force is proportional to the velocity of the moving object is more difficult to understand. To people on Earth, north, south, east, west, up, and down are always the same. However, from a "birds-eye" view from space that coordinate system is constantly changing (Figure 5.4). Therefore, objects moving east, for example, in different locations on Earth have different velocities as seen from space. Therefore, the faster the object moves from one location to another the faster its velocity changes and the larger the CF.

Coriolis Force Equation

Given that the rotation rate of the Earth is a constant, at each latitude the magnitude of the local rotation rate is expressed as a constant, f, called the **Coriolis parameter** (Table 5.1). Then, Coriolis force (CF) is expressed as the product of a constant (f) times the velocity perpendicular and to the right of the CF (in the northern hemisphere). In the east-west direction, the CF is the product of the Coriolis parameter times the velocity, v, positive is from the south.

$$CF \text{ (in the east-west direction)} = fv$$

In the north-south direction, the CF is the product of the Coriolis parameter times the east-west velocity, u, positive is from the west.

$$CF \text{ (in the north-south direction)} = -fv$$

The Coriolis parameter is positive in the northern hemisphere and negative in the southern hemisphere. The effect of the CF is to cause moving objects to bend to the right in

Table 5.1 Shown is the magnitude of the Coriolis parameter (f) in revolutions/s for selected latitudes in the northern hemisphere. For the southern hemisphere, the values would be the negative of all the given magnitudes.

Latitude	Coriolis Parameter (revolutions/s)
0	0
5	1×10^{-5}
23.5	6×10^{-5}
45	10×10^{-5}
66.5	13×10^{-5}
90	15×10^{-5}

© Tom Kovacs

the northern hemisphere and to the left in the southern hemisphere (the sign of the result ensures the proper directions). For example, in the northern hemisphere, a wind from the west (positive u) would cause a negative CF in the north-south direction (i.e. from the north or toward the south). The effect is negligible within 5° latitude of the equator. It is not noticeable over short distances but must be taken into account for long-range motion and affects long-range ballistic missiles, airplane routes, and even long range-gunnery. The effect is significant in large-scale atmospheric motions. For smaller-scale motions such as tornadoes, the effect is not significant.

Friction

Friction is a force that opposes motion. Friction often entails a number of forces that, in sum, oppose motion. This complexity often causes friction to be difficult to quantify and to understand its behavior. In most atmospheric applications, friction comes about from molecular viscosity and eddy viscosity.

Random motions of molecules bumping into one another causes molecular viscosity. For a flat surface like the ocean or flat land, molecular viscosity is rather simple to understand, but if the surface is rough (rocks, trees, buildings, etc.) then this viscosity becomes more complex and can lead to eddy viscosity.

Turbulent whirls or eddys cause Eddy viscosity. Obstructions increase these whirls and surface heating from the sun can make them larger. Eddys lead to variable winds called gusts. Gusty winds are typically larger in the afternoon when the sun is out because the surface heating makes the eddys larger. Larger eddys makes the winds more variable. These eddys can also pull down stronger winds from higher layers of the atmosphere.

The effects of friction are most noticeable near the ground because most of the sources of friction are related to the ground. In fact, most objects have a measurable layer where friction is significant. This layer transitions rapidly to a smoother layer above. In the atmosphere, this layer is known as the planetary boundary layer.

Centripetal and Centrifugal Forces

When air circulates around a center, such as low- and high-pressure centers, a centrifugal force must be overcome to keep air circulating. You can feel the centrifugal

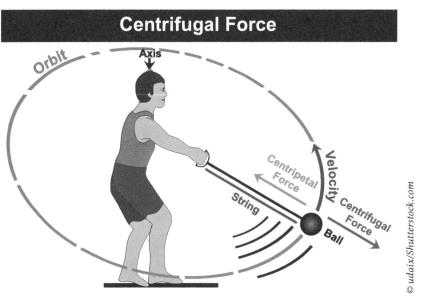

Centrifugal Force

Figure 5.5 An object orbiting around a central rotation axis has a centrifugal force due to the inertia of the ball wanting to move in a straight line, which it would if the athlete let go of the string. An equal and opposite centripetal force, the athlete's hold on the string, must be applied to counter the inertial force.

force when swinging an object attached by rope around one's body (Figure 5.5). In that case, you and the tension in the rope are supplying a **centripetal force** keeping the object in circular motion. From the object's perspective, it feels the outward centrifugal force due to inertia (i.e. the tendency for the object to move in a straight line). Similar to when you turn a sharp corner in a car, your inertia causes you to feel a centrifugal force pushing you in the opposite direction of the turn. In the atmosphere, the centripetal force must overcome inertia in order to turn the winds around the low- and high-pressure centers.

Law of Gravity

Gravity is a force that attracts two masses together. The magnitude of the gravitational force is proportional to the mass and the distance between the masses. The Earth's mass is extremely large compared to the atmosphere so air accelerates to the center of the Earth. This acceleration is called the gravitation acceleration and is numerically equal to 9.81 m/s^2. As you move away from the surface, gravity decreases. Where the Earth is thicker, like mountains or glaciers, the gravitational acceleration is measurably different and scientists have used this to monitor the changing size of glaciers and volcanoes.

Balance of Forces in the Horizontal

No single force determines the acceleration of a mass. Newton's second law states that the sum of forces determines the acceleration of a mass. It is rare for a single dominating force to determine the direction that air will move. Some forces, including those not mentioned in this chapter, play an insignificant role in the movement of air. Each section below demonstrates, quantitatively and graphically, how each of the significant forces balance to determine how air moves.

Above the planetary boundary layer where friction is not significant, the only two forces that need be considered in most cases are the pressure gradient force (PGF) and the Coriolis force (CF). The balance of these two forces is called **geostrophic balance**. The PGF requires a pressure gradient and the CF requires air to be moving. The PGF will cause stationary air to accelerate from high to low pressure. Once moving, the CF is directed at a right angle (90°) to the right of the motion in the northern hemisphere and to the left of the motion in the southern hemisphere.

The best way to demonstrate this graphically is by using vectors. Forces are vector quantities. An arrow graphically represents the direction of the vector while the length of that arrow represents the magnitude of that vector (Figure 5.6). Throughout most of the atmosphere, geostrophic balance is maintained. The magnitude and direction of the pressure gradient determines the length and direction of the PGF vector. The magnitude is determined by how far apart the isobars or height contours are. The PGF vector points perpendicular to the isobars or height contours toward lower values. With geostrophic balance, the CF must be equal and opposite, but should point 90 degrees to the right of the velocity vector. The velocity vector in Figure 5.6 is east so the CF vector should be pointing 90 degrees to the right or south. In this case, there is no net force on this air so that the force parameter in Newton's second law would be zero:

$$F = ma = 0 = CF + PGF,$$

$$CF = -PGF$$

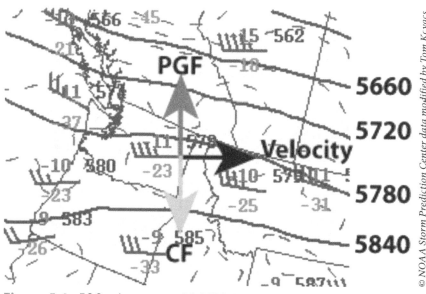

Figure 5.6 500 mb map on 12 UTC August 19, 2019 with velocity vector (black arrow), PGF vector (red arrow), and CF vector (green arrow). The velocity vector is pointing parallel to the observed wind and the PGF is pointing perpendicular to the height contours toward lower height contours (i.e. lower pressure). The CF is pointing at a right angle to the right of the velocity vector. The length of the CF and PGF are equal and opposite (i.e. balanced).

In order for the product of mass and acceleration to be zero, the acceleration must be zero. Therefore, this air is not accelerating and the CF is equal and opposite of the PGF. That does not mean air is not moving, but it is moving at a constant velocity. Notice the movement is parallel to the height contours at the end of the wind barb (where all the vectors originate from) with lower pressure on the left side of the moving air.

On an upper-level map, air is nearly always in geostrophic balance so that winds (blue wind barbs on Figure 5.6) are parallel to height contours (black lines in Figure 5.6). When viewing this map, it is incorrect to think that air will curve to the right because this would be considering only one of the forces. Air at this level moves in response to a balance of forces. Therefore, air will actually move parallel to the height contours throughout the domain of this map. Interestingly, when you are looking at an upper level map you essentially have a map of how air will move! Unfortunately, these maps change more often than road maps and we will later discuss how these maps change.

These two forces are rarely not in balance or when they are, they are not in balance for very long. Imbalances will not be perceptible on a continental-scale 300 mb map such as shown in Figure 5.7. The winds here always appear to be in geostrophic balance with the winds parallel to height contours. However, there are often small locations where the distance between the height contours are rapidly separating or getting closer together. In these cases, there will be a brief time where the PGF will be larger or smaller than the CF. Therefore, the air will briefly be out of geostrophic balance ($F \neq 0$) and the air will accelerate by turning into the larger force. Later chapters will discuss these instances because they have significant local effects.

Notice that streamlines (black lines in Figure 5.7) on a 300 mb map are somewhat wavy. These waves, mentioned in Chapter 3, are significant and a common feature in

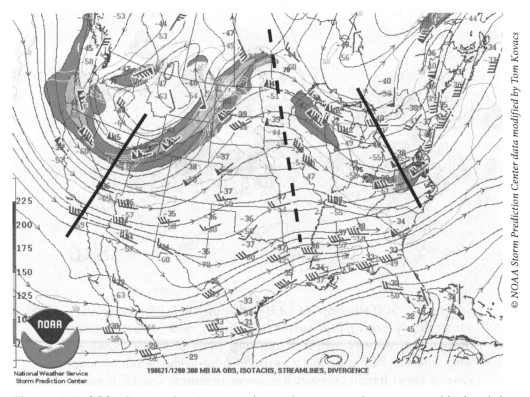

© NOAA Storm Prediction Center data modified by Tom Kovacs

Figure 5.7 300 mb map showing troughs on the west and east coasts (thick solid black lines along trough axes) and a ridge (thick dashed black lines along ridge axis) in the middle of the U.S.

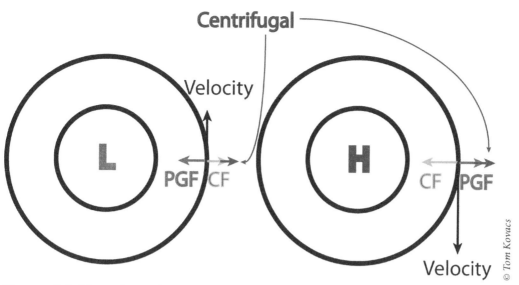

Figure 5.8 Three-force balance around centers of low and high pressure is shown. The pressure gradient force (red), Coriolis force (green), and Centrifugal force (blue) sum to balance producing the shown wind velocity at the location where all the arrows originate (black).

disturbed fluid flow like water waves disturbed by the winds. Airflow disturbed by mountains and temperature gradients produce waves. In the northern hemisphere, due to the force balance, air always moves counterclockwise around a trough (thick solid black lines in Figure 5.7) and clockwise around a ridge (thin dashed black lines in Figure 5.7). Air often slows coming into a trough and then accelerates and diverges after moving through a trough. Looking closely in Figure 5.7, you can see that divergence contours (yellow lines) are more numerous, east of the trough axes.

If the curvature is large, another force becomes important. In Figure 5.8, air is flowing around low- and high-pressure centers. This highly curved flow causes a force imbalance because the air is always turning, which is an acceleration. A force is required to cause this acceleration inward and balance the tendency to move in a straight line (i.e. inertia). Around low pressure, the centrifugal force adds to the CF to balance the excess PGF needed to turn the wind. Around high pressure, the centrifugal force adds to the PGF to balance the excess CF needed to turn the wind. The PGF, in both cases, is the same in Figure 5.8 and is dependent on the distance between the isobars. However, the CF must adjust or the air would fly off in a straight line away from the center of circulations. The CF is dependent on the wind velocity. Therefore, for the same pressure gradient the velocity of the winds must be larger around high-pressure than around low-pressure centers. In reality, pressure gradients are usually greater around low-pressure centers counteracting this effect.

Within the Planetary Boundary Layer

Within the planetary boundary layer, friction is significant and must be included in the force balance. With the pressure gradient force (PGF) and the Coriolis force (CF), adding friction produces a three-force balance. The simplest way to describe the effect of friction is to consider air in balance between PGF and CF above the boundary layer. Then, envision the wind coming down to the surface. Friction will cause the winds to slow down. If the pressure gradient does not change, then the reduced velocity will reduce the CF and the air will briefly be out of balance. The air will turn into the larger PGF until the sum

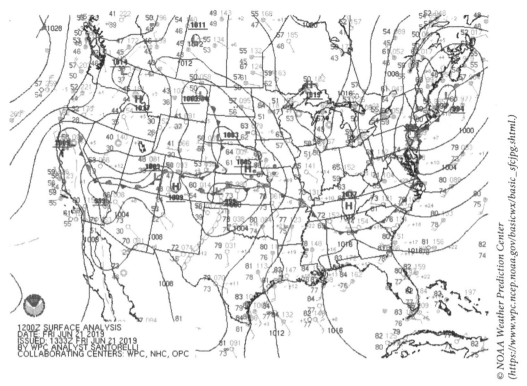

Figure 5.9 Shown is a surface map at 1200 Z June 21, 2019. Notice how the wind barbs at the surface are mostly turned in towards lower pressure.

of CF and friction balance the PGF. On average, this occurs when the winds turn at a 30° angle to the isobars toward lower pressure.

Figure 5.9 is a surface map with an example of winds in this balance. Most of the wind barbs turn by approximately a 30° angle across isobars into lower pressure or out of higher pressure. You may notice in Figure 5.9 that not all winds turn into lower pressure by the average 30°. Local effects overwhelm this force balance. For example, mountain breezes that flow downhill as a mountain cools and valley breezes that flow uphill as a mountain warms dominates in mountainous areas.

One of the most important observations to take from Figure 5.9 is that as air circulates around a low-pressure center the air spirals into the center of low pressure. The same thing happens as water goes down the drain in a bathtub. It also happens in tornadoes and causes the suction and characteristic roar. All of these examples have centers of intense low pressure. This spiral of air into low pressure at the center is a source of convergence, which causes air to rise (tornadoes suck air, soil, cars, houses, and cows upward). Upcoming chapters will highlight the significance of this surface convergence effect to clouds, precipitation, and thunderstorms.

Vertical Motion of Air

As alluded to at the end of the last section, rising air is significant to weather and identifying these areas is significant to weather forecasting. In the vertical (up-down direction), air is nearly always in a two-force balance like air horizontally above the planetary boundary layer. The two forces in balance are the vertical pressure gradient force (PGF) and gravity. Because pressure is highest at the surface, the vertical PGF is directed upward and gravity, g, is directed downward. This balance is called hydrostatic balance and exists in all fluids including the atmosphere and ocean. Hydrostatic balance largely determines how rapidly pressure drops as you go up. In hydrostatic balance, there is no net force on this air so that the force parameter in Newton's second law is zero and all of the following equations are equivalent:

$$F = ma = PGF + g = 0,$$

$$PGF = -g,$$

$$\frac{1}{\rho}\frac{\Delta P}{\Delta z} = -g.$$

$$\Delta P = -\rho g \Delta z.$$

This last equation means that as you go to higher altitudes (Δz is positive), the change in pressure (Δp) is negative meaning pressure is decreasing. However, there are cases where air is accelerated upwards, like the convergence into surface low pressure. The following sections discuss this and other upward forcing mechanisms.

Topographical Forcing

As air moves toward an obstacle such as a building or mountain, it is forced upward over the obstacle. This mechanism for producing rising air is called topographic or orographic lifting. With enough humidity, clouds form. Because these obstacles do not move, the clouds continually form in the same area and are called orographic clouds (Figure 5.10). Often these obstacles produce waves in the air and with each wave crest orographic clouds may form downstream of the obstacle.

© JoannaPerchaluk/Shutterstock.com

Figure 5.10 Orographic clouds shown forming over a mountain in Spitsbergen.

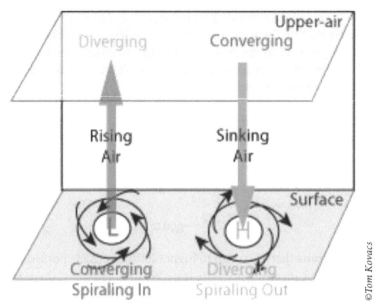

Figure 5.11 Diagram of convergence and divergence that occurs at the surface and in the upper air of developing surface low- and high-pressure centers.

Convergence/Divergence

As discussed previously in this chapter, air spirals and converges into a surface low-pressure center (Figure 5.11). This convergence causes a compensating vertical motion, which must be up from the surface because the ground blocks downward moving air. Likewise, the spiraling and diverging of air out of a high causes a compensating downward movement of air.

A similar motion, but opposite in direction, occurs at the top of the troposphere. For reasons discussed shortly, the stratosphere acts as a barrier similar to the ground. Therefore, convergence at the top of the troposphere will cause compensating downward moving air. In contrast, divergence at the top of the troposphere will cause compensating upward moving air. Because the winds tend to be stronger at the top of the troposphere the convergence and divergence at these levels are critically important to identify. The upper-air winds often dominate the rising of air and the development of surface high- and low-pressure centers. This effect will be detailed in Chapter 7.

Convection

Convection was discussed in the last chapter as the transfer of energy by the vertical movement of air (advection is the horizontal movement of air). Therefore, convection relates to both the transfer of energy and the mechanism to cause air to rise. Rising air occurs because of a buoyancy force described by the **Archimedes Principle**. The Archimedes Principle states that any object immersed in a fluid is buoyed by a force equal to the weight of the fluid displaced by the object. Remember that weight is a force, in this case the **buoyancy force**, which is proportional to the density difference between an object and the fluid in which it is submerged.

In the atmosphere, the two fluids with different densities that are relevant are both air. Often air of different densities is produced by different temperatures because of uneven heating. For example, surrounding a parking lot is usually some type of vegetation. When exposed to the sun the parking lot and the grass surfaces do not increase in temperature at the same rate. The uneven temperature change causes the air above the different surfaces to be different densities. Buoyancy forces warmer, less dense air upward. For this reason, sunlight often causes convection and produces cumulus clouds, which are often called convective clouds. Thunderstorms often form this way, although the other mechanisms for causing rising air also aid in the formation of thunderstorms.

Frontal Lifting

Because fronts typically reside in pressure troughs (local areas of low-pressure) air typically converges toward a front from both sides of the front. Convergence typically causes rising air at the surface and, because the warm side of a front is less dense, warm air will always rise up and over cold air at all fronts. This mechanism is called frontal lifting. Due to the steepness of cold fronts, they force air upward faster than along warm, stationary, and occluded fronts. The rapid rising of air at cold fronts tend to form thunderstorms.

Static Stability

Once air is forced upward by one of the four mechanisms previously discussed, the behavior of the rising air depends on the temperature lapse rates. For example, although cold fronts are more likely to cause thunderstorms, if the temperature lapse rates are large, any front can form thunderstorms. The lapse rates have threshold values that impede or accelerate rising air. Static stability determines these thresholds.

Science Unifying Concept

Stability and Change

An important unifying concept is how change happens. Typically, this change is in relation to a state of equilibrium. However, an important consideration for static, or non-moving systems, is that forces are still acting on the system even if they are not moving. It is important to understand those forces. A book lying on the table is still subject to gravity. In this case gravity is opposed by a normal force, which is essentially the table maintaining a continuous solid surface. If the table were aging or rotting, the book would eventually fall through the table. A more difficult concept is recognizing a system in dynamic equilibrium. A car moving at constant velocity is in dynamic equilibrium. It is moving, but if the velocity is constant then the car is in equilibrium.

This chapter discussed air in motion and the balance of forces that led to its movement. These forces can change, but often the time to reach equilibrium with these forces is fast enough that air is often in equilibrium and at constant velocity. Winds on weather maps are often in equilibrium and it is not necessary to consider the individual forces in determining the movement of air on weather maps. Air across the maps will simply follow the local wind observations and height contours. Nevertheless, changes in the forces do cause accelerations and these accelerations have important effects. In addition, if the equilibrium is unstable, a change away from equilibrium can be accelerated. Usually this is done through feedback processes. For example, a stable ladder can move a little increasing the gravitational force back to its original position. This is a negative feedback because the movement in one direction is increasing the force in the opposite direction like standing on a ladder propped at a large angle to a wall (Figure 5.12). An unstable ladder would increase the gravitational force in the direction of movement. This is a positive feedback because the movement in one direction is increasing the force in that same direction like standing on a ladder propped at a small angle to a wall.

Figure 5.12 Picture of a ladder that is too upright to be stable. If a person were to pull back on this ladder, gravity would cause it to continue backwards. Placing the ladder at a larger angle is more stable so that if the ladder were pulled back gravity would return it forward.

Static stability relates to an equilibrium state in general. The behavior of a system moved slightly away from equilibrium determines the different types of stability. For example, if air moves at a constant height and is in complete balance with all forces, then this air is in equilibrium. Encountering a small hill forces the air up and over the hill. This air has moved a little out of equilibrium. If the air were to fall back down to its original height after ascending the hill it would have done so because the air was originally in a **stable equilibrium**. If the air were to continue to rise after ascending the hill it would have done so because the equilibrium the air was originally in was an **unstable equilibrium**.

The static stability of the environment is determined by how the density, and therefore the temperature of the atmosphere, changes with height. Larger decreases in the density and temperature with increasing height (i.e. larger environmental lapse rate) means a more unstable atmosphere (Figure 5.13). In an unstable atmosphere, rising air becomes increasingly buoyant. Even rising air that is initially not buoyant can become buoyant if the environmental lapse rate is large enough. To determine static stability, we need to know how much rising air cools and compare it to the environmental lapse rate.

The previous chapter stated that expanding air is an example of how internal energy changes without heating. Expanding air is doing work to push the atmosphere out of its way. When air rises and the pressure of its environment decreases, the higher pressure

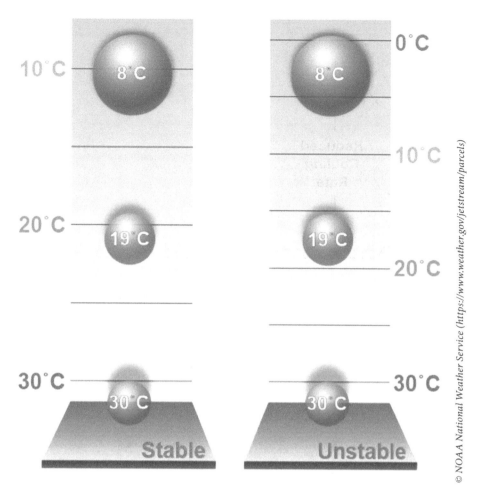

Figure 5.13 A rising air parcel (blue sphere) decreases in temperature with height at a constant rate. If the environmental temperature (vertical axis) cools slower with height than a rising air parcel then the environment is stable and the parcel will eventually stop rising (left column). If the environmental temperature (vertical axis) cools faster with height than a rising parcel then the environment is unstable and the parcel will keep rising because it will never lose buoyancy (right column).

rising air pushes the environment out of its way so that it may expand. The expansion is work and decreases the internal energy as required by the First Law of Thermodynamics. The decrease in internal energy manifests in a decreasing temperature or a change in phase. If the air does not change phase, the decrease in temperature is a constant known as the **unsaturated (or dry) adiabatic lapse rate**. This is a lapse rate because the temperature of rising air is decreasing or lapsing at a specific rate. The rate is relative to the height change not on time. It is **adiabatic** (meaning without heat) because the change in temperature occurs because of work and not heating (e.g. conduction, convection, or radiation). The unsaturated lapse rate, Γ_u, is the same no matter where in the atmosphere the rising air occurs and its value is approximately 10 °C/km (5.5 °F/1000 feet). Figure 5.14 shows air rising, expanding, and cooling at this rate below a cloud (dashed line) or in unsaturated air.

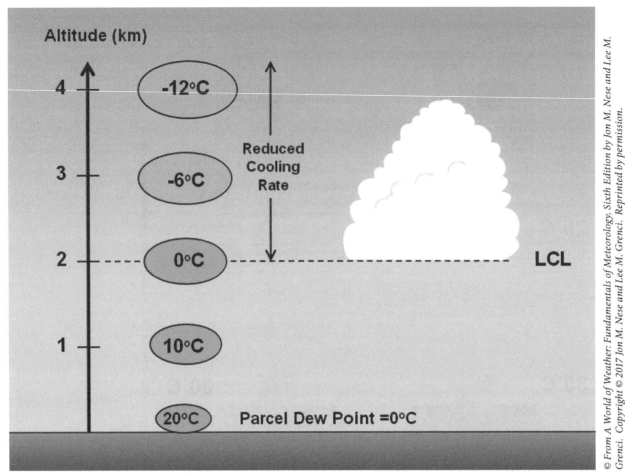

Figure 5.14 Diagram shows how air that is unsaturated (red ovals) would rise to different heights, expand, and cool at the unsaturated adiabatic lapse rate. Once the air temperature and dewpoint within the air parcel becomes equal, the air has reached the lifting condensation level (LCL). Any further rising (purple ovals) would cause condensation, latent heating, and a cloud will form. The latent heating reduces the adiabatic lapse rate to the saturated adiabatic lapse rate above the LCL.

The change in internal energy can also cause a phase change instead of a temperature change. If the temperature of rising air decreases to its dewpoint temperature and the air saturates then some of the loss of energy will be latent heating, not temperature decrease, as water condenses. Therefore, rising and expanding air that is saturated will not lose temperature as rapidly. Rising saturated air has a smaller lapse rate called the **saturated adiabatic lapse rate**. The saturated adiabatic lapse rate is not the same everywhere like the unsaturated adiabatic lapse rate because it depends on how much water is in the rising air. As saturated air rises, a larger water content causes more condensation, more latent heating, and less cooling. The saturated (or moist) adiabatic lapse rate, Γ_s, has a variable value, but always less than Γ_u (10 °C/km). For saturated air at the surface, Γ_s averages around 6 °C/km and approaches 10 °C/km for very dry air. Figure 5.14 shows air rising, expanding, and cooling at this rate within a cloud (above the dashed line).

The temperature of the rising air's new environment may also change. Weather balloons observe this change in temperature; it cannot be calculated like the change in the rising air's temperature. This observation of the environmental temperature change leads to a third parameter called the environmental lapse rate, Γ_e, discussed in Chapter 1.

With the knowledge of the lapse rate of the rising air (Γ_u or Γ_s) and the observation of the environmental lapse rate (Γ_e) it is possible to define the environment's stability. The environment can be in one of three different stability regimes: absolutely stable, absolutely unstable, and conditionally unstable.

Absolutely Stable

Absolutely stable environments are environments where the environmental lapse rate *is less than* both the adiabatic lapse rates, $\Gamma_e < \Gamma_u$ and Γ_s. These environments have lapse rates so small that any rising air will *cool at a faster rate than the environment* and become negatively buoyant. Therefore, rising air is impeded in these environments whether unsaturated or saturated. If the initial mechanism for rising air (e.g. convection) is strong enough and there is enough humidity, clouds and precipitation can still form. However, the clouds will not be very thick and the precipitation will not be very heavy because of the unfavorable environment for rising air.

Absolutely Unstable

Absolutely unstable environments are environments where the environmental lapse rate *is greater than* both the adiabatic lapse rates, $\Gamma_e > \Gamma_u$ and Γ_s. These environments have lapse rates so large that any rising air will *cool at a slower rate than the environment* and become positively buoyant. Therefore, rising air is accelerated in these environments whether unsaturated or saturated. These environments typically occur only very near the Earth's surface (lowest 10 m or so) during intense heating from the sun. Absolutely unstable environments support convection of energy from the solar-heated surfaces to layers higher in the atmosphere. If this layer becomes thick, it can help produce intense vortices such as dust devils.

Conditionally Unstable

Conditionally unstable atmospheres are environments where the environmental lapse rate is less than the unsaturated adiabatic lapse rate, $\Gamma_e < \Gamma_u$, but greater than the saturated adiabatic lapse rate, $\Gamma_e > \Gamma_s$. These environments have lapse rates such that rising unsaturated air will cool faster than the environment, but rising saturated air will cool slower than the environment. This stability condition supports clouds and thunderstorms when some other mechanism lifts air to a point that the air saturates. Often, this occurs in the afternoon during the warmer seasons when the sun has heated the surface to support convection high enough that air cools to its dewpoint temperature. This process is why most thunderstorms form in the afternoon.

Skew-T Diagrams

The typical diagram for assessing static stability is the Skew-T diagram (Figure 5.14). Skew-T diagrams, first discussed in Chapter 3, have reference lines for how the air and dewpoint temperatures within rising air will change. The grid of the Skew-T diagram includes horizontal lines representing pressure and skewed lines for the temperature. The −30 °C isotherm is labeled, but these isotherms are available every 10 °C for reference. The diagram also includes three other reference lines.

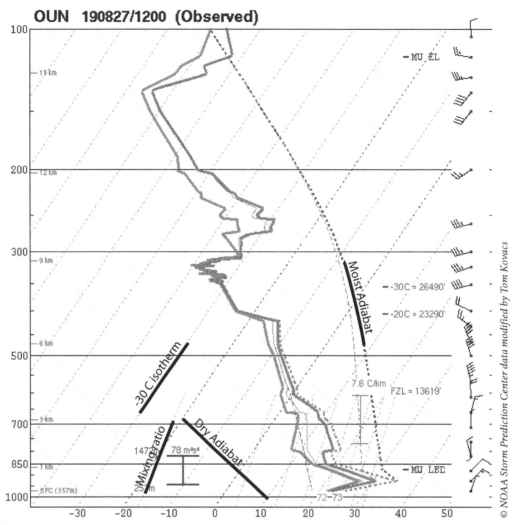

Figure 5.15 Skew-T diagram shown for Oklahoma City, OK at 12 UTC August 27, 2019 is shown. Black lines highlight reference lines explained in the text.

An unsaturated or **dry adiabat** is labeled in Figure 5.15 (see the thick black line from 0 km to 3 km height spanning the 10 °C to –20 °C isotherms). This line represents a change of 30 °C over a vertical distance of 3 km. Dividing the two values gives the unsaturated of dry adiabatic lapse rate, 10 °C/km.

A saturated or **moist adiabat** is labeled in Figure 5.15 (see the thick black line from 6 km to 9 km height spanning the 9 °C to –9 °C isotherms). This line represents a change of 18 °C over a vertical distance of 3 km. Dividing the two values gives the mean saturated or moist lapse rate, 6 °C/km. For saturated air, the humidity increases at higher temperatures so moist adiabats have smaller lapse rates here. This relationship causes moist adiabats to be curved on Skew-T diagrams. They are more vertical (smaller lapse rate or loss of temperature with height) at higher temperatures and pressures (or lower heights). They approach dry adiabat slopes at lower temperatures and pressures (higher heights) where there is little water vapor in the rising air.

The final reference line labeled in Figure 5.15 is the mixing ratio (see the thick black line from 0 km to 3 km height spanning the –17 °C to –23 °C isotherms). This line represents a change of 6 °C over a vertical distance of 3 km. Dividing the two gives the dewpoint temperature lapse rate, 2 °C/km. Rising air maintains a constant mixing ratio as described in Chapter 1. Therefore, the dewpoint temperature of air rising from the surface can be calculated by drawing a line parallel to the mixing ratio line nearest the surface dewpoint temperature.

Interestingly, a line parallel to a dry adiabat through the surface temperature and a line parallel to a mixing ratio line through the surface dewpoint temperature meet at the height that rising air becomes saturated. This level is called the Lifted Condensation Level (LCL) and is a way to calculate the height of the cloud base of low clouds. Because air temperature and dewpoint temperature at the surface change little in the horizontal, the LCL is nearly the same horizontally throughout a cumulus cloud. This uniformity causes these clouds to have flat bases.

Finally, you can also compare the slopes of the observed air temperature (red line in Figure 5.15) and the dry and moist adiabats for a quick graphical way to determine static stability. If the environmental temperature is more negatively sloped (a shallower slope from right-to-left) than both dry and moist adiabats, then the environment is absolutely unstable. The atmosphere in Figure 5.15 is absolutely unstable from about 925 mb to about 850 mb. If the slope of the environmental temperature is less negatively sloped (a steeper slope from right-to-left) or even positively sloped, then the environment is absolutely stable. The atmosphere in Figure 5.15 is absolutely stable from the surface to about 925 mb. If the slope of the environmental temperature is between the slopes of the dry and moist adiabats then the atmosphere is conditionally unstable. The atmosphere in Figure 5.15 is conditionally unstable from about 850 mb to about 800 mb. The more negatively sloped the environmental temperature line the more unstable the air is.

Summary

Three laws of motion govern the movement of matter, including air, and are named after Sir Isaac Newton. Newton's First Law states that an object will stay at rest or at constant velocity unless acted upon by a force. The second law quantitatively relates a force to acceleration. The third law states that there are no isolated forces and for every applied force there is an equal and opposite force. It is Newton's second law that this chapter uses to show how air moves in all directions in the atmosphere. Moving air is wind.

The pressure gradient force (PGF) and the Coriolis force (CF) govern wind in most of the atmosphere. The PGF occurs when there is a difference in pressure (i.e. gradient of pressure) over some distance. The PGF is directed from higher to lower pressure. The CF is an apparent force that only exists to those on a rotating platform, like a spinning Earth. It depends on the rotation rate of the Earth, latitude, and the velocity of an object moving above the Earth's surface. CF is directed toward the right of the moving wind in the northern hemisphere. The geostrophic balance of the PGF and CF causes wind to move parallel to isobars and height contours with low pressure to the left of the moving air. Near the surface, friction is a third force that becomes significant and is directed in the opposite direction of wind. Air in geostrophic balance that sinks to the surface adjusts to the three-force balance in a way that turns the wind on average by 30° into low pressure.

Vertical winds are important to the formation of clouds, precipitation, and thunderstorms. Four mechanisms for causing rising air include topographical forcing, convergence/divergence, convection, and frontal lifting. Once rising, static stability will determine if the air will continue to rise or fall back down. Static stability depends on the comparison of the environmental lapse rate measured by a weather balloon and the saturated and unsaturated adiabatic lapse rates that governs rising air. When the environmental lapse rate is larger than the lapse rate of rising air, the environment is unstable and air will continue to rise. Skew-T diagrams are a tool used by weather forecasters to plot weather balloon data and rapidly analyze static stability.

Key Terms

Wind

Rising/Sinking Air

Updrafts/Downdrafts

Laws of Motion

Inertia

Pressure Gradient Force

Gradient

Coriolis Force

Coriolis Parameter

Friction

Molecular Viscosity

Eddy Viscosity

Planetary Boundary Layer

Centrifugal Force

Centripetal Force

Gravity

Geostrophic Balance

Hydrostatic Balance

Topographic of Orographic Lifting

Archimedes Principle

Buoyancy Force

Frontal Lifting

Static Stability

Stable Equilibrium

Unstable Equilibrium

Unsaturated (or Dry) Adiabatic Lapse Rate

Adiabatic

Saturated Adiabatic Lapse Rate

Absolutely Stable

Absolutely Unstable

Conditionally Unstable

Dry Adiabat

Moist Adiabat

Lifting Condensation Level (LCL

Questions and Problems

1. How are the pressure gradient force and actual wind speed related in terms of both magnitude and direction?

2. Which has a larger pressure gradient force (PGF), the PGF through a 1 cm balloon nozzle with an added 10 mb pressure inside the balloon or the PGF in a strong hurricane with a pressure gradient of 10 mb over a 10 km distance? Explain.

3. Using the websites from Chapter 3, obtain a surface weather map, identify a strong pressure and temperature gradient, and circle them on the map. Make sure you include a copy of the marked up map in your answer.

4. A planet similar in size to Earth is discovered with a rotation rate that is twice that of Earth, but in the opposite direction. Name two differences in the Coriolis force between this planet and Earth.

5. Why don't winds blow in the same direction as the pressure gradient force?

6. For horizontal motion of the wind, what forces must be considered at 5 km above the surface? What additional force must be considered at the surface?

7. What is the effect that friction has on the winds and which map can this effect be seen?

8. Provide a scenario where the air would not be in geostrophic balance. Why would it not be in balance in this case?

9. Would you expect more rising air on a sunny or cloudy day and why?

10. Why does air rise in low-pressure systems and sink in high-pressure systems?

11. Because the pressure decreases from the surface up, the vertical pressure gradient force is directed upward. Why, then, doesn't air rush out into space?

12. What does it mean for the atmosphere to be unstable? Give the technical definition and an interpretation of what this means for the weather.

13. Why does warming air rise, but rising air cools?

14. Describe the three different named temperature lapse rates. Which of these are measured, and which are calculated? In addition, which one of them is a constant?

15. Why is the saturated adiabatic lapse rate less than the unsaturated adiabatic lapse rate?

16. On a clear sunny day how do you expect the static stability to change and why?

17. If there are low-level cumulus clouds out, what part of the cloud is the lifting condensation level (LCL)? Explain.

18. Why would you expect cumulonimbus clouds to be less common in winter?

19. The temperature inside a large, expandable, but weightless, hot-air balloon is 30 °C, the temperature outside is 10 °C, and the environment lapse rate is 5 °C/km. How high will the balloon rise before it is no longer buoyant?

Other Resources

https://www.emich.edu/geography-geology/weather for links to useful weather data to go along with this textbook and updates to any broken links in the textbook.

Chapter 6

Precipitation Principles

Introduction

The previous chapter provided a description of the scientific laws, theories, and principles for how air moves over a very large scale (i.e. several hundred kilometers or miles). One of the things that makes weather so difficult to forecast is the extensive range of sizes of atmospheric phenomenon. In this chapter, the governing laws are on the opposite side of the scale. To understand cloud formation and the growth of the various types of precipitation, a molecular description is required.

Cloud Formation

Relative humidity is a key parameter for determining cloud formation and it is important to review its equation in Chapter 1. Relative humidity measures how close the air is to saturation with water vapor in terms of a percentage. At 100% relative humidity, the air is saturated, and water will begin condensing more than it evaporates. To achieve 100% relative humidity, the amount of water in the air would need to increase (numerator in relative humidity equation) or the air's capacity for water vapor would have to decrease (denominator in relative humidity equation). Normally, it is the capacity that decreases in cooling air (Figure 6.1). In the atmosphere, air can cool at night or by rising and expanding as we learned in Chapter 5. The former usually results in fog while the latter is how clouds typically form. Therefore, rising air normally leads to air saturating. However, in the air a relative humidity of 100% is not the only ingredient to form clouds.

This saturation point (i.e. relative humidity equal to 100%) will cause water to begin condensing on to the ground, cars, airplanes, grass (dew), etc. However, relative humidity is defined relative to a large flat surface of pure water onto which water can easily condense. In the atmosphere, water molecules would need to stick together to form a drop. Unfortunately, the evaporation rate for such small drops is so large that the relative humidity would need to be well over 100% for water molecules to stick together fast enough to overcome evaporation.

© Tom Kovacs

Compressed and warmed   Expanded and cooled

Figure 6.1 Demonstration of a cloud forming in a jar is shown. When cloud condensation nuclei (smoke in the left picture) is added to a humid jar sealed with an elastic band, a cloud forms when pulling up on the band, which expands, and cools the air adiabatically (right picture).

Kohler's Theory

Fortunately, there are surfaces in the atmosphere for water to condense, but they are microscopic. Tiny particles in large numbers serve as cloud condensation nuclei (CCN). CCN can come from dust, smoke, sea salt, soot, etc. and have natural and anthropogenic (human-created) sources. According to Kohler's theory, when water condenses onto CCN they create a solution drop that is no longer pure water. The resulting solution drop allows condensation at a relative humidity of 100%. Furthermore, the CCN come in a wide variety of sizes producing cloud drops of various sizes with the larger ones more likely to produce a cloud drop. However, the smaller CCN outnumber the larger by several orders of magnitude. The mean size of CCN is 0.0001 mm (0.1 µm or 0.00001 inch). If you look at a meter stick with millimeter markings, you will see that a millimeter is quite small. If you further divide those by 10,000, you can appreciate the size of a CCN. You would not be able to see this. The human eye can see down to about 0.1 mm.

Once the air saturates, water condenses on these CCN to produce spherical drops of water that quickly grow in diameter by a factor of 100 to 0.01 mm (10 µm or 0.001 inch; Figure 6.2). This size is still too small to see with the human eye, but the combined effect of millions of these drops per cubic meter produces a visible white cloud. Although the individual drops are invisible to the eye, the drops are large enough to scatter sunlight equally at all wavelengths, which is why clouds appear white.

Stokes' Law – Why Clouds Float

Clouds are also small enough that they fall at a velocity that is not perceptible to the eye, which is why clouds appear to float. Stokes' Law provides the physical basis for determining how fast spherical objects, such as cloud drops fall within a fluid such as the atmosphere. Essentially, objects accelerate downward until gravitational acceleration balances air resistance at a velocity called the terminal velocity.

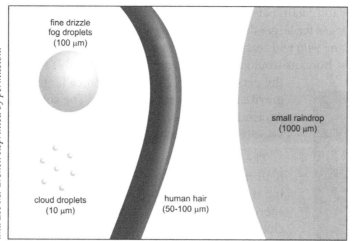

Figure 6.2 Relative sizes of cloud droplets, fog drops, and raindrops as compared to the width of a human hair

Digging Deeper

Stokes Law and Terminal Velocity

Gravity forces cloud drops downward. The gravitational force depends on mass, which depends on the third power of the radius of the cloud drop. However, the atmosphere provides a resistance (air resistance) or drag to falling drops, which depends on the product of the radius and the velocity of the cloud drop. It also depends on the viscosity, or resistance to movement, of the atmosphere, which can be considered constant for a falling drop. As cloud drops accelerate downward, they obtain an increasingly large drag that counters the gravitational force. Eventually, these two forces will come into balance (equal and opposite) at a velocity known as the terminal velocity as shown in the force balance in Figure 6.3.

The gravitational force grows proportional to the third power of the radius and air resistance grows proportional to the first power of the radius. Therefore, larger drops end up falling faster than smaller drops because the downward gravitational force grows much faster as the drops become larger. You can calculate the terminal velocity for different size drops by setting the two forces equal,

$$6\pi\eta rv = \frac{4}{3}\pi r^3 \rho g,$$

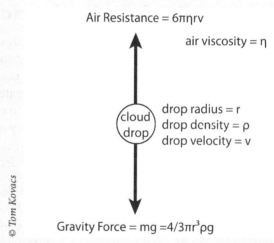

Figure 6.3 Force balance in the vertical for a cloud drop is shown. The air resistance upward balances the gravity force downward when the falling drop is in equilibrium and falling at a constant velocity known as the terminal velocity. The drop is falling through an atmosphere with a viscosity, η.

And solving for v (and cancelling the π on both sides),

$$v = \frac{2}{9}\frac{r^2 \rho g}{\eta},$$

The density of water, ρ; Earth's gravitational acceleration, g; and air viscosity, η values can all be found in Appendix B.

In order to remain balanced between air resistance and gravity, the terminal velocity becomes larger for larger drops. A somewhat related example is of a person jumping out of an airplane who will reach a terminal velocity of around 200 km/hr (120 mph). At that speed, most humans would die on impact with the ground. To prevent death on impact, the person must make air resistance larger without increasing the gravitational force (your weight). The solution is to deploy a large parachute that does not weigh that much to reduce the terminal velocity enough that the impact is not deadly.

The terminal velocity, for cloud drops, is around 5 mm/s (0.01 mph). Once below, the cloud base the air is unsaturated causing these small drops to evaporate. This combination of slow fall speed and decreasing relative humidity below the cloud is why clouds never appear to fall out of the sky (again they appear to float). In order to maintain a cloud, it must continue to rise or have a substantial amount of water vapor injected into their environment. **Mammatus clouds**, which form underneath some cumulonimbus anvils, appear to bulge downward (Figure 6.4). Downward forming clouds are quite rare and requires a substantial amount of water vapor. Otherwise, rising air is essential for nearly all clouds.

Figure 6.4 Mammatus clouds shown above a farm field from an approaching thunderstorm.

Precipitation Formation

Precipitation forms from cloud drops, but not all clouds precipitate to the ground. As cloud drops grow larger, they will fall faster. Precipitation that reaches the ground are simply cloud drops that have grown large enough, so they fall fast enough to make it to the ground before they evaporate. Cloud drops must grow to at least 0.1 mm (0.01 inch; Figure 6.2) or by a factor of 10 to make it to the ground before evaporating. However, these clouds would need to form very near the ground in order for drops of this size to make it to the ground before evaporating. These drops are known as **drizzle** (or mist) and form in fog or very low clouds. The drops are barely visible.

Condensation is not fast enough to grow drops to this size. The volume of water needed to increase the diameter 10-fold is 1000 times more than the amount of the cloud drop. Condensation alone would take days to produce a drop that can precipitate. Yet, clouds can form and begin precipitating within 20 minutes. Therefore, other faster mechanisms are necessary to help grow cloud drops to produce precipitation. Without these mechanisms in place, clouds will not precipitate, which is why not all clouds precipitate.

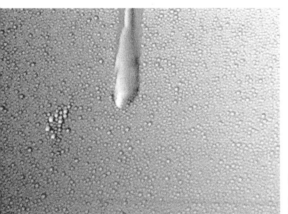

Figure 6.5 Picture demonstrating collision-coalescence on a glass shower wall. Large drops fall through smaller drops colliding and merging with them to make an even larger drop.

Collision-Coalescence Theory

At heights where clouds are near or above the freezing point, precipitation forms by the warm cloud precipitation process also known as the **collision-coalescence** process. Cloud drops grow by colliding together and coalescing into a single drop instantly doubling the size of the drop (Figure 6.5). These drops will then fall faster. In order for cloud drops to collide at appreciable rates the cloud drops need to be at different sizes, so they fall at different rates.

132 Physical Laws, Theories, and Principles

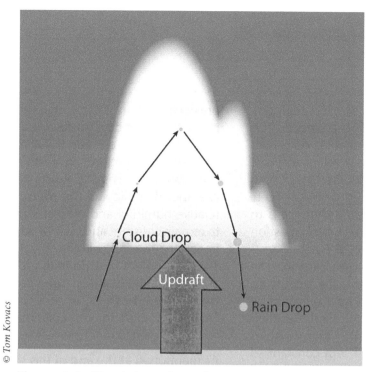

Figure 6.6 Cloud drop shown forming in a cumulus cloud with an updraft. Once the cloud drop attains a terminal velocity greater than the updraft speed (which it does at the top of its trajectory) it will begin to fall. All the while, the drop is in the saturated cloud environment the drop continues to grow by collecting smaller drops.

Once the drop grows large enough that its terminal velocity is larger than the updraft (rising air) velocity, then the drop will fall (Figure 6.6). However, it is not until the drop falls out of the cloud that it will begin evaporating. Stratus clouds tend to have smaller updraft velocities, which produces smaller, but more uniformly sized drops than cumulus clouds. Because of the smaller uniformly sized drops, stratus clouds tend to produce lighter and more uniform precipitation rates than cumulus clouds. Cumulus clouds produce heavier, but shorter periods of precipitation known as showers.

The warm cloud precipitation process is not very effective because the surface tension of spherical drops is large and drops tend to bounce off one another and not coalesce. Furthermore, small drops tend to flow around one another not even colliding unless they come together almost "head-on". Glancing blows tend not to produce coalescence. Because of this, clouds that do not reach a temperature well below the freezing point (warm clouds) tend to produce only drizzle. The inefficiency of the warm cloud process is another reason why not all clouds precipitate. Clouds are more effective at producing precipitation with larger updraft velocities and/or cloud temperatures that are significantly below the freezing point.

Bergeron Theory

With temperatures sufficiently below the freezing point, precipitation grows by the cold cloud precipitation process (Bergeron process). Similar to condensation, water will not deposit from the vapor phase directly to the solid phase without a surface to do so.

Planning and Carrying Out Investigations

The first three chapters of this textbook described the importance of observing, recording, and presenting data. Scientists do this to describe the world and to develop and test theories of how the world works. Developing and testing theories is the topic of Chapters 4-8. The first step to producing theories is to develop a hypothesis or testable question based on observation. Then, the actual testing requires careful planning to carry out an investigation. This process starts by identifying the important variables and how they can be observed, measured, and controlled. Deciding on the dependent and independent variables is next. Control variables are kept constant so that only experimental variables are allowed to vary. Finally, a control experiment where no variables vary is planned so that the effects of the experimentally varying variables are determined by comparing them to the control experiment.

For example, in the case of precipitation, scientists observed that precipitation could develop as early as 20 minutes after the formation of a cloud. However, the condensation process that forms clouds, discussed in the previous section of this chapter would take many hours or days to form a drop capable of growing large enough to fall to the ground without evaporating. To test the collision-coalescence process, scientists had to build a chamber that allowed the control variables of relative humidity and droplet size distribution to remain constant and controlled. In the experiment, they varied collision velocity and angle. This experiment was done in a chamber with an electrical field and charged drops, allowing the charged drops to fall at a controlled rate. From this experiment, collision efficiencies were observed to determine drop growth rates.

As mentioned at the end of this section, scientists observed that collision coalescence would only produce drizzle. This shortcoming is not a failure and is often how science works. Other scientists took the results of this study and the observation that cumulonimbus clouds produce heavy rain in as little as 20 minutes. This observation led to the hypothesis that heavy precipitation often comes from mixed phase clouds and led to the investigation that formulated the cold cloud precipitation process.

In addition, small drops of suspended water will not freeze at the freezing point. Like saturation, freezing temperatures are defined over a flat surface of ice on the ground, not a spherical drop or ice crystal suspended in the atmosphere. Like condensation, freezing and deposition require nuclei, in this case, ice nuclei (IN). However, not all Cloud Condensation Nuclei (CCN) are IN. In order for something to be an IN, it needs to look something like an ice crystal (i.e. six sided). Some desert dust, bacteria, pollen, and volcanic ash can act as IN. Because IN are less available, water suspended in air typically remains liquid down to −5 °C (23 °F) and can remain liquid as low as approximately −37 °C (−33 °F). Liquid drops at temperatures below the freezing point are known as supercooled drops.

The Bergeron process is effective at growing precipitation because when a drop freezes or an ice crystal forms, the saturation vapor pressure or saturated mixing ratio drops over the ice. The saturation vapor pressure over ice is smaller than over a supercooled liquid drop at the same temperature. Ice crystals that form in these supersaturated environments grow rapidly. Deposition will rapidly drop the vapor pressure within the cloud, but in the presence of many supercooled liquid drops there is an enormous supply of water (i.e. the evaporating liquid drops). Therefore, the relatively few ice crystals grow rapidly at the expense of the far larger number of supercooled drops (Figure 6.7). The effect is to produce large precipitation sized ice crystals in a short time.

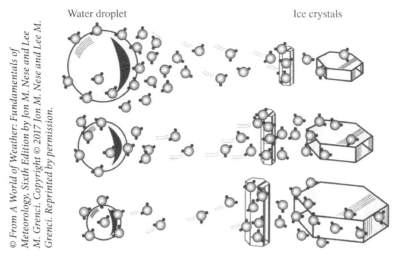

Water droplet   Ice crystals

Figure 6.7 When liquid drops and ice crystals form in the same location, the environment becomes supersaturated over ice and unsaturated over liquid. The ice crystals grow rapidly while the liquid drops shrink.

Furthermore, once these ice crystals form and fall to warmer parts of the cloud they can nucleate other supercooled drops. This nucleation is especially effective if the ice crystals shatter on their way down, which they often do. The shattering produces a large number of IN. If the IN fall through the atmosphere where the temperature is above freezing, they will begin to melt and can produce wet snow at the surface, or if the temperatures are warm enough, large rain drops.

Precipitation Type

Precipitation can fall as a number of different types. In this section, the type of precipitation that makes it to the ground will be the focus. However, what makes it to the ground may not be the same type of precipitation that formed in the cloud. The type of precipitation that makes it to the ground depends on the temperature profile, updraft velocity, and cloud height.

Warm Season Precipitation

Warm season precipitation is the precipitation that excludes those types that requires near freezing surface temperatures. Drizzle, rain, and hail are warm season precipitation.

Drizzle

Drizzle was mentioned previously and is the lower end of the size range for liquid precipitation (between 0.1 and 0.5 mm). Drizzle requires a low cloud height and typically forms by the warm cloud precipitation process. If the clouds are too high, the drizzle will evaporate before it hits the ground. Any precipitation that evaporates before it hits the ground is called virga.

Rain

Rain covers the rest of the size range for liquid precipitation typically no larger than 6 mm. Raindrops are largely spherical until they reach the upper end of their size range where they begin to flatten out as they fall. They do not look like teardrops as they are often pictured.

© Tom Kovacs

Figure 6.8 Raindrops (red arrows pointing out the clearest drops) shown falling in some foliage. The raindrops are the circular spots, not teardrops as often depicted.

The teardrop shape comes from water falling from a faucet. The water drop sticks to the faucet and elongates it into the teardrop shape most people are accustomed to seeing. However, once the drop detaches from the faucet it eventually settles to its spherical shape (Figure 6.8).

Even if you were to throw a bucket of water high over your head, the water would leave the bucket as one giant sheet but would hit the ground as small spherical drops. You can try this experiment and listen as it sounds like rain drops when it hits the ground. The reason raindrops are smaller than 6 mm is because they become unstable due to turbulent fluctuations and begin to break apart producing multiple smaller drops. It is reassuring that you will not drown under a one-foot diameter raindrop.

Rain forms by both the collision-coalescence and Bergeron process. The temperature profile must be above freezing over a large enough vertical distance to melt precipitation created by the Bergeron process before it hits the ground. If not, you would get wet snow even if the surface temperature were above freezing. It may be surprising to know that even in summer much of the rain that falls started out as snow. In addition, in winter you can get snow even if the temperature at the surface is above freezing.

Hail

Hail requires strong updrafts in a cloud that extends high enough that both liquid and solid precipitation can form. It is also necessary that the highest height where the temperature remains above freezing (called the **freezing level**) is not more than about 1.1 km (3600 feet). Otherwise, the hailstone may not make it to the ground without melting. Hail initially forms when raindrops rise high enough into a cloud that they freeze, which occurs in most thunderstorms. However, if the updrafts are not strong enough, hail will not grow large enough to make it to the ground as ice[1].

Cross-sections of hail show a layered structure of alternating white and translucent layers. This layering is due to the various environments that the hailstone encounters during its growth. When hailstones encounter large amounts of supercooled water that freezes slowly, a translucent layer forms. Otherwise, water freezes rapidly and traps air bubbles giving it an opaque white layer (See https://www.youtube.com/watch?v=AN-XFCKYdew for a video of this process from the University of Illinois extension). Hail typically has a layer of liquid on its surface that makes it sticky and can coalesce with other hailstones giving them a lumpy appearance. **Accretion** is the term given to hailstones, or any ice, that stick together. In order to grow large hail, the updrafts need to be large enough to support the hailstone in the air while it grows. Forecasting hail size is discussed in Chapter 14.

Sometimes thunderstorms turn the sky green. These so-called **green thunderstorms** were thought to be due to hail in the storm, but recent research has found green thunderstorms without hail. It is likely that green thunderstorms contain large amounts of liquid water that filter the sunlight.[2] Nonetheless, high water content thunderstorms often have the ingredients to be severe and are often associated with hail and tornadoes.

---

[1] Nelson, S. P., 1983: The influence of storm flow structure on hail growth. *J. Atmos. Sci.*, **40**, 1965–1983.
[2] Gallagher, F, 2000: Distant Green Thunderstorms – Fraser's theory revisited. *J. Appl. Meteorology and Climatology*, **39**, 1754-1761.

Cold Season Precipitation

Cold season precipitation includes snow, wet snow, sleet, ice pellets, freezing rain, and freezing drizzle. Each type has its own characteristics and effects, particularly on transportation, but also power outages and shoveling.

Snow and Wet Snow

Snow is the most familiar of cold-season precipitation. Snow forms by deposition and ice crystal growth. Like any crystal, it grows through a specific habit or shape. Because of the shape of the water molecule and its 120° bond angle, nearly all ice we see on Earth grows six-sided. Depending on temperature and humidity, numerous shapes are possible including needles, dendrites, plates, and columns (Figure 6.9). Needles form at the warmest temperatures and look like little needles that would be six-sided columns if seen under a microscope. Dendrites are what most people associate with snowflake shape and are always six-sided. The exact shape of dendrites depends on their own unique trajectory through the cloud. The nearly infinite growth pathways of dendrites give rise to the saying that, "no two snowflakes are ever alike". Dendrites form in the optimum temperature to produce the heaviest snows. Plates tend to form at colder temperatures and gives the ground a sparkly appearance when walking in a lit area or in sunshine. The sparkle comes from light reflecting off the flat side of the

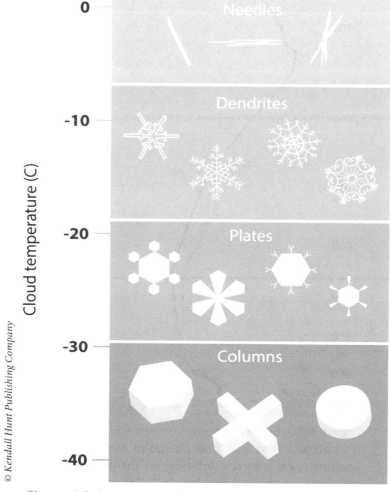

Figure 6.9 Ice crystal habits at different temperature ranges

plate. Because they hit the ground in random directions, you only see the bright plates that direct light to your eyes. The bright plates you see change as you walk causing the sparkle.

Snow requires a sufficiently thick layer of below freezing temperatures to form (Figure 6.10). If snow encounters above-freezing temperatures on their way down, they can partially melt producing **wet snow**. Wet snow is sticky and accretion of dendrites, in particular, can produce large aggregates of snowflakes, which can also accumulate quite rapidly.

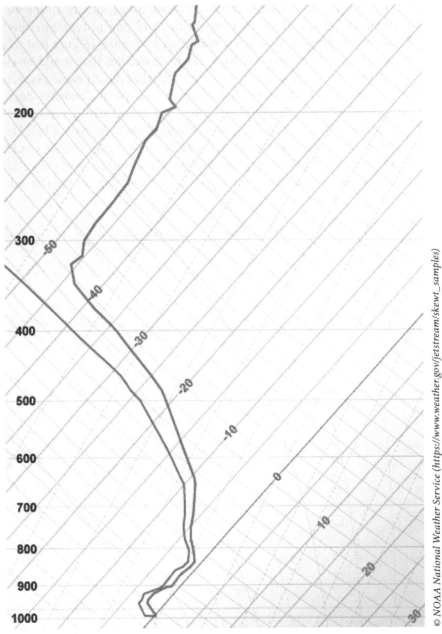

Figure 6.10 Skew-T diagram for snow is shown with measured air temperature (red line) and dewpoint temperature (blue line). The pressure axis lines are labeled on the left and the temperature axis lines are skewed and labeled diagonally from left to right. All temperatures above the freezing point of water (0 °C) are shaded red and those below the freezing point (0 °C) are shaded blue.

Sleet and Ice Pellets

The terms **sleet** and **ice pellets** are not universally accepted. In the U.S., they are the same and are raindrops that freeze as they fall to the Earth's surface (Figure 6.11) They are distinguished from **snow pellets or graupel**, which forms when supercooled water freezes to snowflakes and are softer than sleet or hail. In Canada, the term sleet is not used as it is in the U.S., so this section covers the precipitation known as sleet in the U.S. and ice pellets in Canada [from Glossary of Meteorology].

Sleet or ice pellets form from the freezing of raindrops or the refreezing of partially melted snowflakes. They require a temperature at or below the height of formation that alternates between above- and below-freezing. Sleet or ice pellets start out as rain drops in a layer that is above freezing and then fall through a below freezing layer that is thick enough to freeze the drops <u>before</u> they hit the ground (Figure 6.12). The emphasis on the word "before" is to separate them from freezing rain.

© NOAA National Weather Service (https://www.weather.gov/jetstream/skewt_samples)

Figure 6.11 Sleet on a piece of wood.

Sleet or ice pellets feel like little pinches on exposed skin and bounce off most objects before settling on some object near or on the ground. They rarely build up and weigh down objects, but they can be heavy to shovel. They are not particularly slippery to walk or travel on but are not pleasant to walk in while it is precipitating. Despite the unpleasant feel, they are probably the least problematic of all types of winter precipitation.

Freezing Rain and Freezing Drizzle

Freezing rain and **freezing drizzle** are perhaps the most problematic and damaging of the winter precipitation types. The storms that produce freezing rain and freezing drizzle are referred to as ice storms. Freezing rain is indistinguishable from rain as it is falling and feels like rain if you are outside, in contrast to sleet, which feels like ice cubes are falling from the sky. The distinguishing feature of freezing rain and drizzle is the fact that they freeze <u>after</u> they reach the Earth's surface. The importance of this is that they coat the surface they hit and freeze to it. This process produces what is commonly referred to as **black ice**, a term that comes about from the fact that freezing rain is often translucent and invisible when freezing on black asphalt roads. On the surface, freezing rain can be slippery and untreated sidewalks and roads are extremely hazardous. If it snows or sleets prior to the freezing rain, a frozen shell will form on a crustier layer beneath making it less hazardous if you can break through the shell when walking. Freezing rain will build ice on power lines and trees potentially causing both to fall over in winds creating power outages (Figure 6.13).

© C. Lee Parrish/Shutterstock.com

Figure 6.13 Damage caused by an ice storm

Freezing rain requires a temperature profile that has an above-freezing-temperature-layer to produce liquid precipitation or completely melting any ice falling from above (Figure 6.14). A shallow or thin below-freezing-temperature-layer at the surface is required. This layer must be shallow enough in the vertical for the raindrops not to freeze in the air, but <u>after</u> they reach the Earth's surface. Freezing rain cannot exist unless the

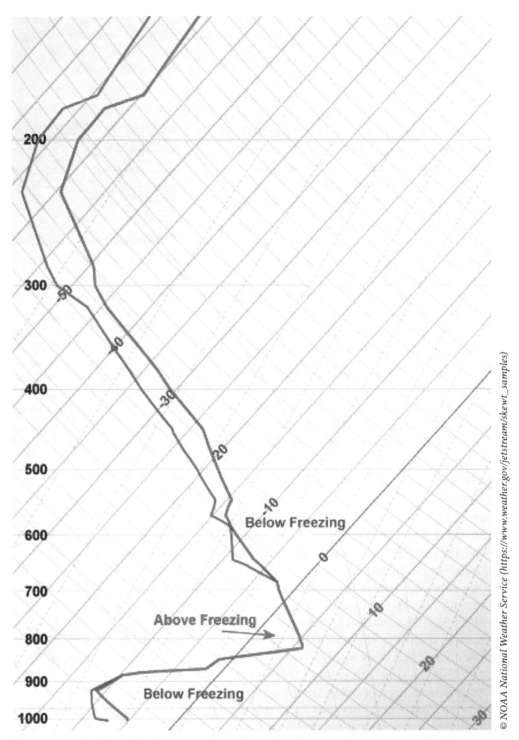

Figure 6.12 Skew-T diagram for sleet is shown with measured air temperature (red line) and dewpoint temperature (blue line). The pressure axis lines are labeled on the left and the temperature axis lines are skewed and labeled diagonally from left to right. All temperatures above the freezing point of water (0 °C) are shaded red and those below the freezing point (0 °C) are shaded blue. The layers of above and below freezing temperatures are also labeled.

© NOAA National Weather Service (https://www.weather.gov/jetstream/skewt_samples)

surface temperature is at or below freezing because the rain must reach the Earth's surface in the liquid state and then freeze to it. If the surface temperature were above freezing in the Skew-T diagram in Figure 6.14 then you would get rain.

Freezing drizzle forms similar to freezing rain except by the collision-coalescence process. The environment for freezing drizzle that makes it different from drizzle is that the cloud layer is shallow and entirely contains supercooled liquid drops. The top of the cloud must remain below freezing but above a temperature (usually around –10 °C) where ice nuclei will not cause freezing of the supercooled drops. This type of precipitation has some of the same hazards as freezing rain but is much more hazardous to airplanes. Because the cloud layer contains no ice, but only supercooled raindrops, the airplane will serve as

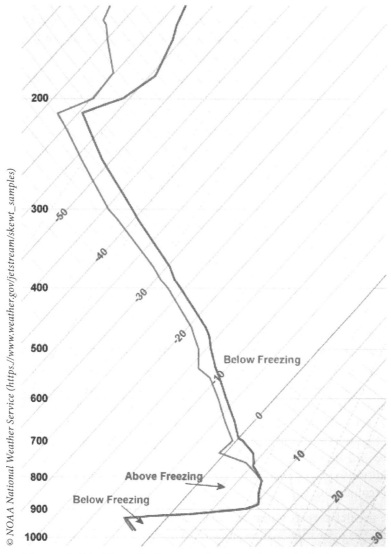

Figure 6.14 Skew-T diagram for freezing rain is shown with measured air temperature (red) and dewpoint temperature (blue). The pressure axis lines are labeled on the left and the temperature axis lines are skewed and labeled diagonally from left to right. All temperatures above the freezing point of water (0 °C) are shaded red and those below the freezing point (0 °C) are shaded blue. The layers of above and below freezing temperatures are also labeled.

© NOAA National Weather Service (https://www.weather.gov/jetstream/skewt_samples)

the only ice nuclei in the cloud. All the supercooled raindrops will freeze to the plane, ice the wings, and can cause the plane to lose lift. If the plane does not navigate above this cloud layer in time, it may never succeed and eventually can become too heavy to remain airborne. This type of condition is why planes will be de-iced prior to takeoff to prevent or delay water from freezing to the airplane.

Liquid Water Content of Frozen Precipitation

Forecasting precipitation type and frozen precipitation accumulations are extremely difficult for numerous reasons. First, there are the same difficulties as for forecasting liquid precipitation. That includes forecasting the total amount of liquid falling from the sky, which depends on the humidity, temperature, location of convective clouds, and the speed of the individual clouds. It also includes the forecast track of the larger system (e.g. fronts, low-pressure centers). Sometimes a difference in 40 km (25 miles) in the forecast track of a front can mean the difference between flooding rain and no rain.

Second, are the difficulties in forecasting precipitation type. The type of precipitation depends on where the clouds that are producing the precipitation lies within the forecasted temperature profile. Different precipitation types can form at different heights within the cloud. Therefore, what makes it to the ground may be a multitude of precipitation types. This complexity is why you will sometimes here a forecast of a mixture of rain, freezing rain, sleet, and snow. The forecast can mean that the different precipitation types will fall at different times, but they can also fall at the same time.

Finally, in forecasting accumulations it is important to know the average snow accumulation to liquid precipitation ratio, commonly known as the snow ratio (Figure 6.15). If you have overcome the difficulties in forecasting the amount of water precipitation and precipitation type, you still need to know how quickly it will accumulate on the ground. Freezing rain has a snow ratio of 1:1 because freezing rain falls as rain. However, once some sleet and wet snow become mixed, the ratios begin to increase to 2:1 and 3:1. Therefore, if the equivalent of one inch of rain fell as sleet and wet snow, that would accumulate to two or three inches of heavy wet snow or slush.

If the precipitation is all snow, with temperatures at the surface below the freezing point, the snow ratio is typically around 10:1. Now, if the equivalent of 1 inch of rain fell as snow the snowfall accumulation would be ten inches. However, not all snow has the same liquid water content, which largely depends on temperature throughout the profile. Just a few degrees colder, –7 °C to –3 °C (20 °F to 27 °F), and the ratio is 15:1. Some snows such as the powdery snow that makes skiing popular in the Rocky and Alps mountains have a snow ratio of 20:1 or 30:1 because of the cold temperatures, typically –12 °C to –8 °C (10 °F to 19 °F). Humidity also plays a role in the snow ratio causing the snow ratios to stop rising in much colder temperatures.

If you were able to predict correctly that one inch of liquid precipitation will fall on your city and you expect regular snow with a snow ratio of 10:1. You would be off by ten inches of snow accumulation if you actually receive a powdery snow with a snow ratio of 20:1. Even though to a person shoveling the snow, the two snowfalls would weigh the same, the actual accumulations would be very different and your forecast would be considered a failure. Forecasting precipitation amount or accumulations are not easy and, yet, are often how the public judges' forecasters.

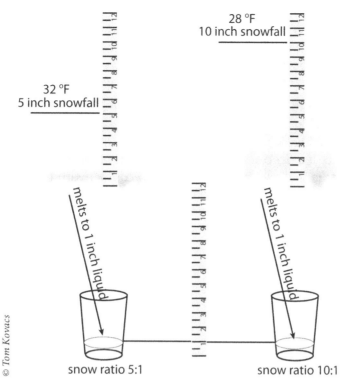

28 °F
10 inch snowfall

32 °F
5 inch snowfall

melts to 1 inch liquid

melts to 1 inch liquid

© Tom Kovacs

snow ratio 5:1   snow ratio 10:1

Figure 6.15 Demonstration of snow ratios are shown for two different snowfalls with the same amount of liquid water after removing a core of snow with the same diameter as the glass and melting it. Warmer snow accumulates more slowly than colder snow.

Summary

Clouds form when the relative humidity reaches 100% in the presence of cloud condensation nuclei (CCN). CCN are microscopic particles in the air that provide water surfaces on which to condense. Without CCN, water would have difficulty merging because the evaporation rate is too large for very small droplets. Kohler theory states that when water condenses onto CCN they create a solution drop that is no longer pure water. The resulting solution drop allows condensation in the atmosphere at a relative humidity of 100%. This overcomes the rapid evaporation of very small drops and allows cloud drops to form.

Precipitation drops are simply cloud drops that have grown large enough to fall fast enough to make it to the ground without completely evaporating. Cloud drops fall very slowly and when they grow, they fall faster. If an updraft is present in the cloud, cloud drops can grow larger before they are large enough to fall and overcome the updraft. Growth occurs through a process of colliding and coalescing with smaller drops in warm clouds (above freezing). The warm cloud growth process is inefficient and generally leads to drizzle. Heavier precipitation requires below-freezing temperatures so that ice forms. Raindrops do not freeze at temperatures slightly below freezing producing supercooled drops. Ice nuclei must be present to freeze suspended liquid at temperatures near, but below freezing. The saturation vapor pressure over ice is smaller than that over liquid so an environment that is saturated over liquid is supersaturated over ice. Ice grows rapidly in this environment and heavy rain typically grows through this process.

Warm season precipitation depends on cloud height, updraft speed, and the height of the freezing level. Low clouds and fog with small updrafts produce drizzle, which are small raindrops. Large updrafts with a low freezing level will produce hail, which are frozen raindrops supported by the updraft. Hail collects supercooled raindrops and can grow by merging with other hailstones in a process called accretion.

Cold season precipitation type is forecasted with the aid of a Skew-T diagram. Snow grows by deposition in a temperature profile that is near or below freezing throughout the atmosphere. When liquid water is present in warmer layers it can freeze on the way to the surface if a deep subfreezing layer is present near the Earth's surface. If the subfreezing layer is shallow, the drops freeze on contact with the ground producing freezing rain. Larger liquid water contents are present in frozen precipitation when the ground temperatures are warmer causing the snow ratio to be smaller. Snow ratios are the ratio of accumulation of frozen precipitation to liquid water accumulation.

Key Terms

Cloud Condensation Nuclei (CCN)	Ice Nuclei (IN)	Dendrites
Kohler's Theory	Supercooled Drops	Plates
Cloud Drops	Virga	Wet Snow
Stoke's Law	Raindrops	Sleet
Air Resistance	Hail	Ice Pellets
Terminal Velocity	Freezing Level	Snow Pellets or Graupel
Mammatus Clouds	Accretion	Freezing Rain
Drizzle	Green Thunderstorms	Freezing Drizzle
Collision-Coalescence	Snow	Black Ice
Bergeron Process	Needles	Snow Ratio

Questions and Problems

1. How do clouds form? Make sure you include all the processes and ingredients that leads to cloud formation.

2. What is the main difference between cloud drops and raindrops?

3. Why do clouds appear to float?

4. Why can drizzle only fall from cloud bases that are very close to the ground?

5. What is the difference between cumulus and stratus precipitation? What is the main characteristic of the environments that these clouds form that causes this difference?

6. How does the Bergeron process lead to rapid growth of precipitation particle sizes?

7. Describe the differences between sleet and freezing rain specifically in relation to the types of phase changes and temperature profile.

8. Hail is often layered and lumpy, what causes this strange appearance?

9. If you held out your hand while it is precipitating how would freezing rain feel differently than sleet?

10. What type of precipitation are possible for the following observations:

    a) 850 mb (1500 m) temperature = 1°C, surface temperature = 2°C

    b) 850 mb (1500 m) temperature = 1°C, surface temperature = −1°C

    c) 850 mb (1500 m) temperature = −3°C, surface temperature = −1°C

11. Ice nuclei play many different roles in the formation of winter precipitation. Name two different roles that leads to the formation of two different cold season precipitation via different phase changes.

12. How are the clouds that produce freezing rain different from those that produce freezing drizzle?

13. What type of winter precipitation is the most dangerous to aircraft? What does the airline industry do to address this hazard?

14. How can the uncertainty of water content in snowfall lead to large uncertainties in snowfall accumulation forecasts?

Other Resources

https://www.emich.edu/geography-geology/weather for links to useful weather data to go along with this textbook and updates to any broken links in the textbook.

https://www.youtube.com/watch?v=AN-XFCKYdew for a video of hail formation from the University of Illinois extension

Chapter 7

Polar Front Theory

Introduction

The previous chapter covered the laws, theories, and principles governing precipitation in all its forms. This chapter covers the laws, theories and principles that govern large-scale storm systems bringing the midlatitudes most of its precipitation, the low-pressure system. Atmospheric circulation, around a center of low pressure, is called a cyclone and those that generally form and develop in the midlatitudes are called midlatitude cyclones. Midlatitude cyclones form on a virtually permanent feature of the atmospheric circulation called the polar front. Polar front theory provides a framework for understanding the progression of cyclogenesis (initial formation of a cyclone), development, and dissipation of these midlatitude systems. The semipermanent nature of the polar front is part of the Earth's general circulation, which is discussed in the next chapter. Smaller cyclones that do not necessarily form on the polar front do not conform to this theory, such as tornadoes and tropical cyclones (i.e. tropical storms, hurricanes, typhoons, etc.).

Polar Front Theory and the Lifecycle of the Midlatitude Cyclone

The Polar Front Theory is based on observations that midlatitude cyclones tend to develop on the polar front (usually found in the midlatitudes) where temperature gradients already exist. The theory provides an idealized progression of the midlatitude cyclone through its lifecycle based on the observation of many previous cyclones.[1]

The lifecycle starts with an initial low-pressure center forming on the polar front (Figure 7.1 upper left). Where they form geographically, and why they develop, is discussed in following sections. Once formed, counterclockwise circulation at the surface causes warm air to advance northward ahead of the low and cold air to advance southward behind the low. This circulation produces a wave on the polar front during the genesis stage. With adequate humidity, clouds and precipitation will form around the surface low-pressure center and along the fronts. Because the rising air is gentler along the warm front, the clouds extend over a wider area. Clouds, produced by convergence around low pressure, combines with the warm front clouds, causing the head of the comma shape of a well-developed midlatitude cyclone. The cold front clouds produce the tail.

---

[1] Bjerknes, J., 1919: On the structure of moving cyclones. Geofys. Publ., 1 (2), 1–8.

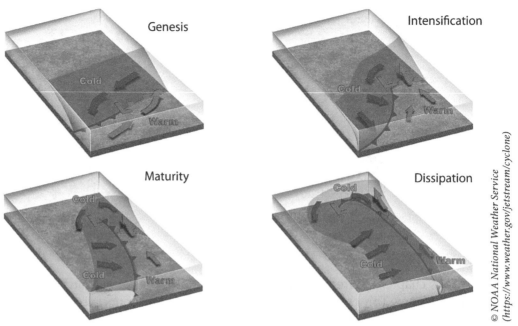

Genesis   Intensification

Maturity   Dissipation

Figure 7.1 Idealized lifecycle of a midlatitude cyclone with cold wind (blue arrows) and warm wind (red arrows) provided. The fronts extend in the vertical with the warm air (red shading) moving up and over the cold air (blue shading). North is at the top of each figure.

Science Unifying Concept

Structure and Function

Recognizing structure, function, and their relationship are important concepts throughout all sciences. When picking up something unfamiliar, it is human nature to wonder what an interesting part does. When trying to fix something, you first observe its structure and then determine how each part functions. For example, trying to sleep with a leaky toilet will drive many to want to fix it immediately. When looking at a toilet, all you see is porcelain, water, and some sort of handle. Determining what the handle does is important to the function of the toilet, but the tank hides the clues. Opening the tank reveals a lever attached to the handle, which is also attached to something plugging a hole that leads to the toilet bowl. Activating the flusher usually unplugs the hole and water then drains into the toilet bowl. Prior to activating the handle, some sort of gasket prevents water from leaking into the toilet bowl.

The gasket often fails causing the toilet bowl to leak. Observing structure and paying attention to function can help you easily fix an annoying leaking toilet.

Jacob Bjerknes did the same thing with midlatitude cyclones. Using coastal observation sites during World War I in Norway, Bjerknes observed the structure of the midlatitude cyclone that led to the Polar Front Theory. He observed convergence lines ahead of and behind the center of low pressure, which became the warm and cold fronts. He also observed the nature of clouds along these convergence lines, which helped him to explain the main inflows of the midlatitude cyclone. He did all this using surface-based observations because upper-air observations and satellites did not exist at the time. This functioning at the surface led to a three-dimensional description once upper-air observations became available.

Because warm air advances ahead of a low, the polar front becomes a warm front at this location. Likewise, because cold air is advancing behind the low, this front becomes a cold front. During intensification, cold fronts circulate around the low-pressure center with warm fronts moving with the low-pressure center (Figure 7.1 upper right). Throughout this period, the central pressure is decreasing, causing the pressure gradient to increase between the center of the cyclone and the outer edge. This produces more isobars on a surface map. The resulting pressure gradient force increases the wind speed. At this stage, winds and precipitation increase around the cyclone. However, the area of surface warm air, called the warm sector between the cold and warm fronts is getting smaller. The center of low pressure increasingly backs into the cold air. For the health of a midlatitude cyclone, moving into the cold air is a problem because the separation of cold and warm air provides the energy for the cyclone.

Eventually, cold air surrounds the low as it separates from the polar front (Figure 7.1 lower left). The warm sector lifts off the surface beginning at the apex of the wave, which is the intersection of the cold and warm fronts. This begins the mature and most intense stage of the midlatitude cyclone. An occluded front attaches the low to the intersection of the fronts. The occluded front typically has a weak temperature gradient across it at the surface, but the warm sector still exists above the surface. A trough of warm air aloft (TROWAL) will form from the occluded front and wrap counterclockwise around the low-pressure center. The TROWAL is an area where warm humid air produces a significant amount of precipitation around low pressure. In the winter, the warmer air transports a large amount of humidity and precipitation that can maintain its frozen form in the cold surface layer of air below. The heaviest snow accumulation is found in the path of this TROWAL.

Some midlatitude cyclones can last in its mature stage for days with lows reforming on the polar front if upper air divergence is available. However, the primary source of the cyclones' energy (separation between cold and warm air) is gone for the original low, which dissipates causing the midlatitude cyclone to enter its final stage, the dissipation or spin down stage (Figure 7.1 lower right). The low continues to cause air to spiral into it and fills with air, like a hole that is dug fills with dirt, the depression will eventually disappear. That is what happens to a decaying midlatitude cyclone, it fills with air. Filling with air raises the central pressure until it is nearly equal with the surrounding pressure. At that point, there is no longer a central low pressure, and like a filled hole, it disappears.

During the dissipation stage, the midlatitude cyclone will continue to produce precipitation, but gradually this will decrease. If the low becomes "cut-off" from the strong upper level winds, it can become relatively stationary. With a strong source of humidity, the cut-off low can produce significant rain beneath the area that it occupies for several days, although cut-off lows are not common.

Cyclogenesis and Baroclinic Instability Theory

Midlatitude cyclones need three main ingredients to form (i.e. cyclogenesis). The first ingredient is the rotation from the rotating Earth. The second ingredient is a strong temperature gradient, which naturally occurs on Earth because of the difference in solar heating from the equator to the poles. A large temperature gradient provides air of two different densities adjacent to one another. This situation is not stable because of Archimedes Principle. The less dense warm air will tend to rise up and over the denser cold air. This movement is a conversion of potential energy to kinetic energy from air in motion. The third ingredient is wavy flow that occurs naturally from the previous two ingredients or from disturbances such as mountains. This natural occurrence of wavy flow and cyclones will be demonstrated below. We have seen that the Earth's atmosphere has an abundance of wavy flow in previous chapters.

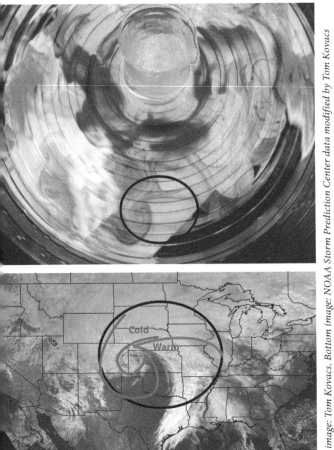

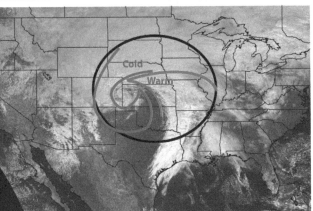

Figure 7.2 A homemade rotating table (top image) recreates a midlatitude cyclone shown in a visible satellite image from 17 UTC March 13, 2019 (bottom image). The table is rotating counterclockwise so the beaker with ice represents the North Pole. Blud dye is cooled by the ice and red dye is warmer. Analogous air masses with the same color scheme are shown in the bottom image.

© Top image: Tom Kovacs. Bottom image: NOAA Storm Prediction Center data modified by Tom Kovacs

These three ingredients produce a spinning cyclone due to a type of instability not covered yet. Chapter 5 discussed static stability. Static instability causes rising air to become more buoyant and to continue to rise. A different type of instability, called **baroclinic**[2] **instability**, relates to winds crossing isotherms, which causes advection (i.e. horizontal convection). Waves cause air to cross isotherms if a temperature gradient is present such as across the polar front. When air crosses isotherms, it deepens the waves and causes more air to cross isotherms, which deepens the waves, and so on. A deeper wave on a rotating planet causes a spinning cyclone to spin faster for reasons discussed later.

It is possible to recreate these midlatitude cyclones in the laboratory using the aforementioned necessary ingredients. In Figure 7.2 (top image) is a fluid rotation tank rotating counterclockwise and made with a rotating tray, water, red and blue dye, a beaker of ice, and a Lego motor.[3] The beaker of ice in the middle acts as the North Pole because the rotation of the tank is the same as the northern hemisphere. Blue food coloring dropped near the beaker of ice represents cold air with a well-formed Arctic region and red food coloring elsewhere represents warm air. Waves and cyclones naturally occur. In the bottom Figure 7.2, the large comma-shaped cloud mass circled in this visible satellite image is a midlatitude cyclone. Both the lab and actual midlatitude cyclones have the same weather features. Where the blue and red dyes come together in the tail is a cold front and in the head of the comma-shape cyclone is a warm front. These features do not form if the water does not rotate or the beaker of ice is not present.

Coastal Midlatitude Cyclones and Nor'easters

Temperature gradients exist on the polar front but are particularly strong in late fall and winter in certain geographical locations. At this time, the temperature gradient between the water and land are greatest. The temperature gradients are large here because water has a significantly higher **heat capacity** than land. Heat capacity is the amount of energy needed to raise or lower the temperature of 1 g of matter by 1 °C. Because water has a higher heat capacity, as fall approaches, the temperatures begin to fall faster on land than in water. By late fall, the land temperatures are considerably colder than the water temperatures.

Cyclogenesis is favored in areas where this temperature gradient is greatest as shown in Figure 7.3. In fact, each of these areas have names such as the North and South Pacific, Gulf, and Atlantic or Hatteras Lows. We attach names to them because midlatitude cyclones

---

[2] From the Greek word *baro*, which relates to pressure and *klines*, which relates to inclining or intersecting

[3] Hill, S., J. Lora, N. Khoo, S. Faulk, J. Aurnou, 2018: Affordable rotating fluid demonstrations for geoscience education, The DIYnamics project. *Bulleting of the AMS*, **99**, 2529-2537.

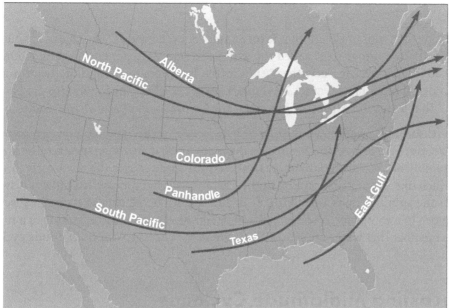

Figure 7.3 Areas of cyclogenesis shown with arrows representing the usual direction of movement.

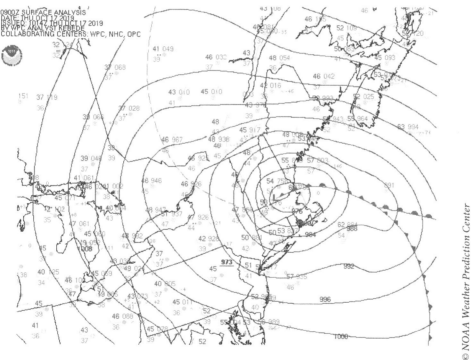

Figure 7.4 Nor'easter moves onshore along the east coast of the U.S on October 17, 2019.

continuously form in these areas. However, once formed, not all of these cyclones develop for reasons discussed later. The largest temperature gradient forms off the coast of North Carolina because of the proximity of the warm Gulf Stream to the cold land. This area is the birthplace of **Nor'easters**, which are particularly strong midlatitude cyclones in the Northeast. The term Nor'easter comes from the strong northeasterly winds these storms produce. The counterclockwise flow around a Hatteras low produces the northeast winds when it is offshore of the U.S. east coast (Figure 7.4).

Lee Cyclogenesis

The lee side of mountains is another favored area for cyclogenesis. The side of a mountain that air initially approaches is called the windward side and after cresting the mountain, it descends on the lee side. As with coastal storms, low pressure is continually forming on the lee sides of mountains. Figure 7.3 shows a few areas where the mountains are particularly tall that forms the Alberta Clipper and the Colorado, Panhandle, and Texas Lows.

The reason that cyclones tend to form here is due to the law of conversation of angular momentum. As the air crosses the ridge, from the air's perspective, the ground drops rapidly away. This rapidly increasing vertical space causes the air to stretch vertically. Much like an ice skater pulling in their arms or a jump rope pulled tight as it swings around, the spin increases when stretched. In the horizontal, this stretching causes the air to move in a wavy (north-south) pattern, forming a trough on the lee side of a mountain. Remember that waves are one of the ingredients necessary for midlatitude cyclones to form.

Forecasting Midlatitude Cyclones

Midlatitude cyclones cause air to spiral and converge into the low at the surface. The converging air at the surface causes the total amount of air in the center of the low to increase. More air increases the weight of the air here, raising the pressure on the surface. Therefore, lows, once formed, tend to fill with air causing the cyclone to disappear.

In order for a midlatitude cyclone to continue to develop, something must remove air from the column of air above the center of the surface low. The mechanism for this removal happens in the upper troposphere. Chapter 5 introduced how divergence occurs in the upper troposphere downstream of upper level troughs. Divergence near the top of the troposphere removes the air that surface convergence provides. If the divergence in the upper troposphere is greater than the convergence at the surface, then the midlatitude cyclone can continue to develop.

One of the weaknesses of Polar Front Theory is that it does not describe how midlatitude cyclones develop and strengthen. A stronger midlatitude cyclone can be defined in a number of ways. One way to define the strength of a midlatitude cyclone, is based on its central pressure. The cyclone is stronger when its central pressure is lower because this determines the pressure gradient force, which increases the circulation of air around the low. With a faster circulation, the winds observed at the surface are stronger; top wind speed can also define strength. A faster circulation also causes greater convergence into the low and air will rise over the fronts faster. The latter two effects help to produce clouds and precipitation in the cyclone. A final way to define the strength of a midlatitude cyclone is with the amount of precipitation it produces in any one location. The amount of precipitation depends on the central pressure but is also dependent on the speed the low is moving and the amount of humidity available to the cyclone. All the factors that lead to a stronger cyclone such as central pressure, surface wind speed, precipitation, movement speed, and access to humidity must be forecasted.

Upper Tropospheric Divergence and the Jet Stream

One of the ramifications of the equator-to-pole temperature gradient, geostrophic balance, and hydrostatic balance is the existence of jet streams. A strong temperature gradient requires a strong pressure gradient and the winds must become increasingly

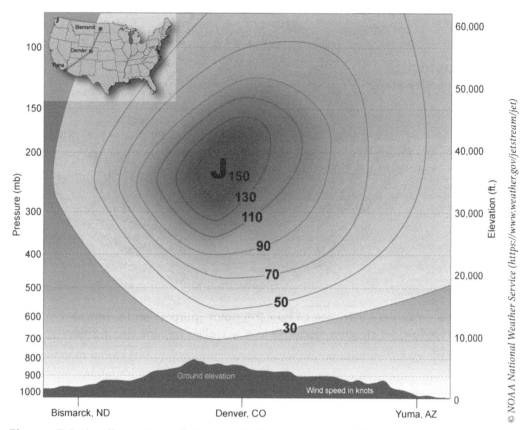

© NOAA National Weather Service (https://www.weather.gov/jetstream/jet)

Figure 7.5 An illustration of the vertical cross-section of a jet stream showing wind speeds in knots.

westerly with increasing height to maintain the various force balances. This leads to a rather confined area of the atmosphere near the top of the troposphere (about 1-2 km in the vertical) where winds are the strongest (Figure 7.5). These streams of air, called jet streams, are linked with strong surface temperature gradients. Therefore, jet streams and fronts are related and have similar sizes in the horizontal of about 200-400 km wide. Winds in jet streams are typically greater than 35 m/s (70 knots) and can exceed 75 m/s (150 knots).

Two westerly upper troposphere jet streams: the **polar jet** (typically 40°-60° latitude) and the **subtropical jet** (typically 20°-40° latitude) exist in both northern and southern hemispheres (Figure 7.6). The subtropical jet stream is a little higher in the atmosphere, typically found on the 200 hPa (200 mb) or 250 hPa (250 mb) maps, while the polar jet stream is lower, typically found on the 250 hPa (250 mb) or 300 hPa (300 mb) maps. Details of the location and number of upper troposphere jet streams are discussed in the next chapter.

Because jet streams exist at an altitude of 8-12 km (26,000-39,000 feet), commercial jets fly in them to get a tail wind when flying east. Commercial jets fly outside the jet stream when flying west. Unfortunately, for most flyers, turbulence is often present on the edges of jet streams.

Baroclinic instability and obstructions at the surface like mountains cause jet streams to be wavy with troughs and ridges. As air moves through these waves, it often

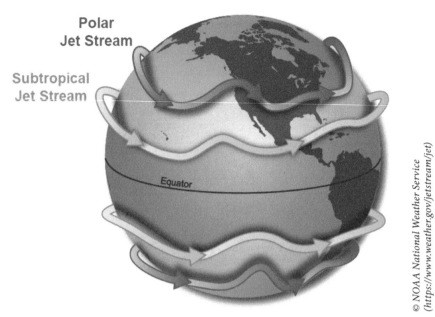

Figure 7.6 An illustration of how the polar (purple) and subtropical (yellow) jet streams meander in a wavelike fashion around the world.

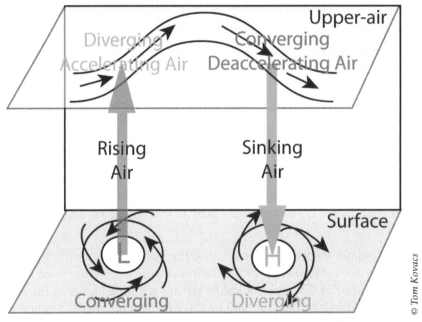

Figure 7.7 Diagram of divergence and convergence of air in the upper troposphere and its relation to developing surface low- and high-pressure centers.

accelerates causing areas of convergence and divergence in different parts of the wave. Air converges coming into a trough and diverges coming out of a trough (Figure 7.7). When air converges into the trough, air piles up like a traffic jam on a highway that occurs when drivers spot a police officer on the side of the road ahead. This jam causes the weight of the air upstream of the trough axis to increase, which increases the

Observing Vorticity to Identify Upper-Air Divergence/Convergence

The actual locations of upper-air divergence are somewhat vague in the descriptions in this chapter. Calculating divergence was discussed in the "Digging Deeper Box" in Chapter 3 as a small difference (order of 10^{-5} revs/s) of two large terms (order of 10 m/s). Because of the large errors in this value, a better way to find upper-air divergence is by computing vorticity. Vorticity is the spin of air and divergence is equal to the change in vorticity of the airflow. Typically, vorticity is plotted on the 500 hPa (500 mb) level.

This relationship can be understood if you consider a spinning ice skater. When they bring their hands and legs inward (convergence) they begin to spin faster. For this reason, as air converges it spins faster (increased vorticity). In contrast, when ice skaters spread their arms and legs outward (divergence), they begin to spin slower. For this reason, as air diverges, it spins slower (decreased vorticity).

Vorticity comes about from three sources: shear, curvature, and planetary. The planetary source is simply the Coriolis parameter, f, given in Table 5.1 and is due to the magnitude of the spin of the Earth at each latitude. The curvature and shear combined are called relative vorticity being relative to the planet's spin. Curvature vorticity is illustrated in Figure 7.8a. Air going around a ridge is doing so in a clockwise manner. This clockwise movement is negative spin or negative vorticity. In contrast, air going around a trough is doing so in a counterclockwise manner. This counterclockwise movement is positive spin or positive vorticity. Shear vorticity is illustrated in Figure 7.8b. Air going around a ridge or trough is usually moving fastest at the top of the ridge and bottom of the trough. If you were to envision a fan in this flow, the faster air would spin the fan so that the fan would spin clockwise in the ridge and counterclockwise in the trough. The shear and curvature often produce negative relative vorticity in the ridge and positive relative vorticity in the trough.

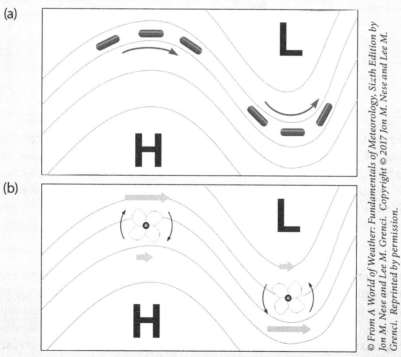

(a)

(b)

© From A World of Weather: Fundamentals of Meteorology, Sixth Edition by Jon M. Nese and Lee M. Grenci. Copyright © 2017 Jon M. Nese and Lee M. Grenci. Reprinted by permission.

Figure 7.8 Illustration showing a) curvature and b) shear contributions to relative vorticity.

Vorticity has a magnitude and units similar to divergence, 10^{-5} revs/s. Vorticity is plotted in these vorticity units. The values are usually positive in the northern hemisphere because the planetary vorticity is positive (counterclockwise looking down on Earth) and large in the midlatitudes. The top of ridges is the location of the lowest vorticity or vort miN (N). The bottom of troughs is the location of the highest vorticity or vort maX (X) (Figure 7.9).

The largest vorticities are found in troughs (high counterclockwise curvature) and poleward of jet streams (high counterclockwise shear). Because the change in vorticity of air flowing through a vorticity field is proportional to divergence, air flowing from a center of maximum vorticity (X in Figure 7.7 and Figure 7.9a) is divergent. Forecasters frequently use analysis of vorticity maximums to diagnose upper-air divergence, rising air, and surface midlatitude cyclone development.

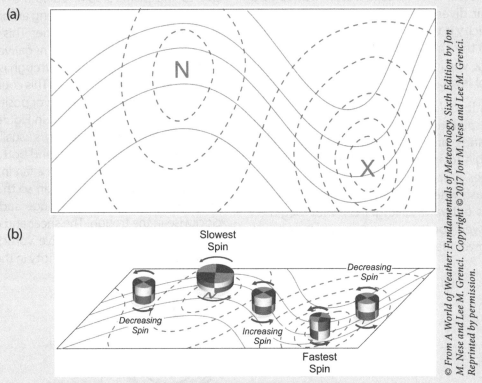

Figure 7.9 a) The top of ridges are the location of the lowest vorticity or vort miN (N). The bottom of troughs are the location of the highest vorticity or vort maX (X). b) Vort mins are associated with the slowest spin because the relative vorticity is negative here whereas vort maxes are associated with the fastest spin because the relative vorticity is positive.

surface pressure. Increased weight maintains high pressure below areas of upper-air convergence even as air is diverging out of the high at the surface. Conversely, when air diverges out of the trough, air spreads apart like when people pass a police officer on the side of the road. This spreading apart causes the weight of the air downstream of the trough axis to decrease, which decreases the surface pressure. Decreased weight maintains low pressure below areas of upper-air divergence even as air is converging into the low at the surface. Therefore, wavier jet streams increase the strength of midlatitude cyclones in specific areas of the jet stream.

The higher jet stream speeds often lead to higher upper-air divergence compared to the surface convergence leading to lower surface pressure. Acceleration and deceleration of the winds in different parts of the jet stream occur for reasons other than troughs/ridges. Acceleration leads to a pattern of convergence and divergence due to the force imbalances causing the accelerations. These force imbalances are particularly large in areas where the jet stream winds are large called jet streaks.

Jet streams and streaks are found on 250 or 300 mb maps. Jet streaks are within jet streams where the winds are larger than 35 m s^{-1} (70 knots) in the summer and 45 m s^{-1} (90 knots) in the winter. Jet stream winds are generally stronger in winter because the temperature gradients are larger in that season. As air enters the jet streak, it is accelerating because the speed is increasing. Often, jet streaks are found in pressure troughs. When they are exiting the trough, the acceleration from the trough to the jet streak is particularly large. The pressure gradient force (PGF), which causes the acceleration in these areas are out of balance with the Coriolis force (CF). The PGF will be larger as air enters a jet streak and the winds will turn slightly into low pressure (north of a westerly wind in the northern hemisphere). This causes convergence on the left (relative to the wind direction) entrance region (Figure 7.10) and divergence on the right entrance region of a jet streak. The reverse pattern occurs as the air exits the jet streak and the PGF decreases. The PGF will be smaller than CF and the winds will turn slight into high pressure. This causes divergence on the left exit region (Figure 7.10) and convergence on the right exit region of a jet streak.

Some situations produce exceptionally strong upper air divergence and rising air, which can lead to rapidly dropping pressures at the surface and strong thunderstorms. When an upper-air trough tilts along a line from northwest to southeast, the slope of the trough axis is negative and are called negatively tilted troughs (Figure 7.11). The significance of a negatively tilted trough is that it produces extreme upper-air divergence. The strong jet stream winds have to make a very sharp turn through the negatively tilted axis, which produces this divergence.

Another scenario of strong upper-air divergence occurs when two jet streams split. In that case, the patterns of divergence of the two jet streams become collocated and the divergence becomes large. Split stream, negatively tilted troughs, and exceptionally strong jet streaks can cause the divergence to be large enough for a rapidly developing

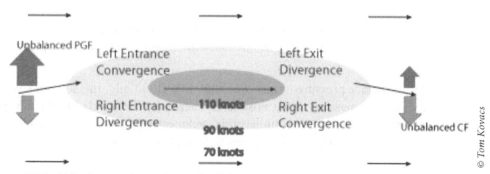

Figure 7.10 Wind speeds or isotachs (blue shading, knots) for air entering and exiting a jet streak are shown with the pattern of convergence/divergence generated by the jet streak. In the entrance region the pressure gradient force (PGF) has increased and is temporarily unbalanced turning the winds (black lines) toward lower pressure. In the exit region the PGF has decreased and the Coriolis Force (CF) is temporarily unbalanced turning the winds toward high pressure.

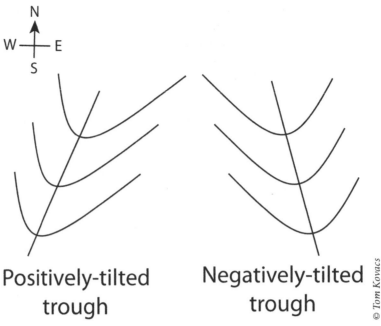

Figure 7.11 Examples of positively- and negatively-tilted troughs in height contours.

© Tom Kovacs

midlatitude cyclone called a **bomb cyclone** to form. Bomb cyclones are simply a special name given for midlatitude cyclones that decrease in surface pressure by at least 24 hPa (24 mb) in 24 hours.

Longwaves and Shortwaves

Oftentimes, people talk about being stuck in a weather pattern. Although there is a number of things this can mean, typically they are referring to the longwave pattern. **Longwaves** have wavelengths about the entire length of the U.S. They are related to the path that the jet stream follows and can be easily found at the 500 mb or 300 mb level. A hemispheric 500 mb level map (Figure 7.12) allows observation of the longwave pattern of ridges and troughs that meander around the world. These waves are called **planetary waves or Rossby waves** named after the scientist that studied and described them. Typically, there are anywhere between two and seven wavelengths of waves around the world. These longwaves do not move with the upper-level winds, the winds move through them. For this reason, they can stay in one place for weeks at a time causing consistent weather at a location.

With a mean surface pressure of just over 1000 hPa (1000 mb), the 500 mb level represents the center of mass of the atmosphere. Therefore, the winds at 500 mb guide large atmospheric features such as midlatitude cyclones and fronts. In fact, midlatitude cyclones typically move in the same direction with approximately half the speed of winds at this level. For this reason, longwaves are useful for predicting movement of these large systems. Sometimes a low- or high-pressure center can be stuck in an area of slow or no guiding winds. In this case, movement can slow or cease and if it is a low-pressure system, large precipitation amounts can fall. Hurricane Harvey in 2018, was an example of a

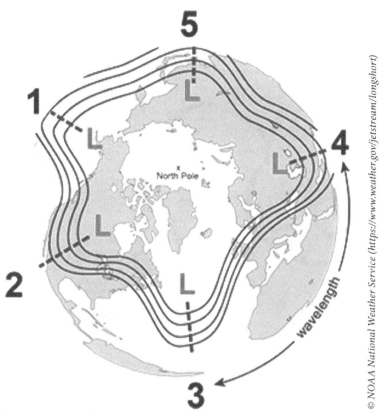

Figure 7.12 500 mb hemispheric map is shown with a 5-wave pattern. 500 mb height contours are centered on the North Pole. Trough axes are marked with dashed lines and the wavelengths (numbered) counted.

low-pressure center that was stuck in an area of no guiding winds and dropped nearly 1.5 m (5 feet) of rain in the Houston, TX area.

Because upper-air divergence occurs downstream of a longwave trough, those areas can expect wetter than normal conditions. Likewise, upper-air convergence occurs upstream of a longwave trough and those areas can expect drier than normal conditions. Troughs form in layers of cooler air so areas located in a trough can expect cooler than average weather. Likewise, ridges form in layers of warmer air. Depending on where you are located relative to a stationary longwave pattern you can predict whether the weather will be cooler/warmer than average or wetter/dryer than average. Looking at the movement of the longwave pattern gives you an idea of how long this period might last. Oftentimes, when the longwave has a large amplitude ridge downstream, the longwave pattern will not move anytime soon. These patterns are called omega blocks because the ridge makes the Greek letter Omega shape (Figure 7.13).

In addition, the amplitude of the waves effect the weather. If the waves are zonal or aligned with the latitude lines so that troughs and ridges are small, then upper air divergence is small and the development of midlatitude cyclones are unlikely. If the waves have large amplitude ridges and trough then midlatitude cyclones are more likely.

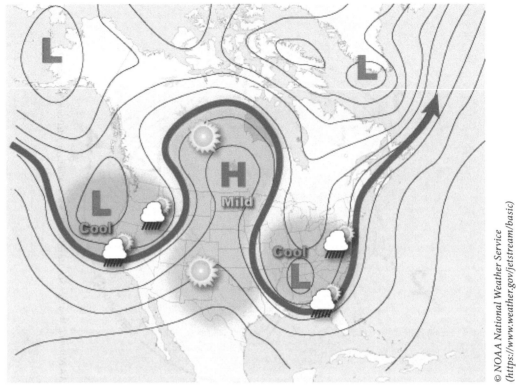

Figure 7.13 Upper-air map with height contours (black lines) showing winds (blue arrow) in the shape of the Greek letter omega, indicative of an omega blocking pattern.

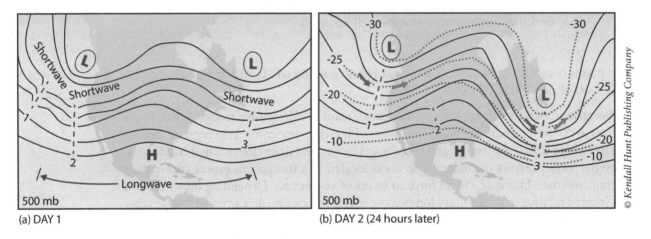

Figure 7.14 Diagram of three shortwaves (dashed lines) moving through a longwave trough in the height contours (black lines) shown on two different days. Shortwaves 1 and 3 are moving through a longwave trough and amplifying it whereas shortwave 2 is moving through a longwave ridge and weakening it.

Occasionally, **shortwaves** can be found riding along within the longwaves. These waves do move along with the wind at 700 mb and, therefore, move through the longwave pattern. They are best seen in the lower to middle troposphere particularly on the 500 or 700 mb map (Figure 7.14). Shortwaves are important because they tend to give longwave troughs an extra shot of energy when the trough of the shortwave moves through the

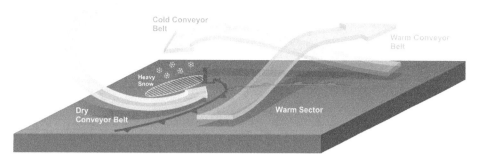

Figure 7.15 Diagram of the conveyor belt model of the midlatitude cyclone is shown. The three different conveyor belts of air: warm (thick yellow arrow), cold (blue arrow), and dry (thin yellow arrow) are shown.

longwave trough. The effect is a much deeper trough and an increase in upper-air divergence downstream of the trough. Longer range forecasting requires not only interpreting the weather expected through the longwave, but also understanding when to expect the longwaves to change and move.

Atmospheric Rivers

The previous sections established the movement speed and central pressure of midlatitude cyclones as one factor for the amount of precipitation an area will receive. However, the amount of humidity that feeds into the system is extremely important. These systems obtain humidity from the major humidity sources, which are mostly maritime tropical air, but can also be maritime polar air. In order to understand the access that midlatitude cyclones have to humidity, it is important to discuss an alternative model to polar front theory known as the conveyor belt model.

The conveyor belt model of midlatitude cyclones looks at the currents of air more than the structure of fronts that the polar front theory does. It employs three important conveyor belts within the structure of the midlatitude cyclone (Figure 7.15). The first conveyor belt is known as the warm conveyor belt and is essentially the trajectory air takes within the warm sector of the cyclone. It starts out at the surface and rises over the warm front. This conveyor belt transports warm humid air that also rises over both the warm and cold fronts. The air that rises over the cold front makes up the tail of the comma shape of well-developed midlatitude cyclones.

When the system occludes, the warm conveyor belt can split and create a TROWAL ahead of the occluded front. In the winter, this is the area of the heaviest snows. If this conveyor belt has access to a large body of warm water, then the cyclone can produce a lot of precipitation. A quick way to determine this is to look at radar and see if precipitation is falling along the cold front all the way to a maritime tropical air mass source region. Another way is to look at the 850 mb map and see if winds are strong and in the correct direction to direct humidity from a maritime tropical air mass. These low-level jets of humidity are called atmospheric rivers. Their strength is related to the total cross-sectional area (width and vertical distance) of high humidity air, and the wind speeds in this humid air. If there is no humidity source or it is weak with weak winds, even a strong midlatitude cyclone will have a small amount of precipitation.

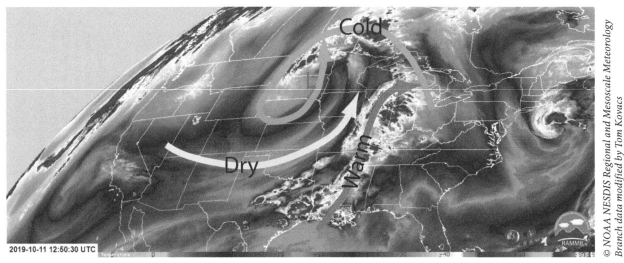

Figure 7.16 Upper water vapor image (GOES 16 band 8) showing a midlatitude cyclone with the dry (yellow), warm (red), and cold (blue) conveyor belts around a midlatitude cyclone (L).

A second conveyor belt is known as the **dry conveyor belt**. It forms in the upper atmosphere behind the cold front and sinks toward the ground as it approaches the surface low. This conveyor belt originates from the jet stream and follows the converging side of a jet streak with sinking cold air behind the cold front. Satellite imagery that is sensitive to upper troposphere water vapor shows this conveyor belt best (Figure 7.16). The dry conveyor belt has two dramatic effects on midlatitude cyclones. First, it transports dry air behind the cold front that can wrap up around the surface low as it occludes. This "dry slot" can cut off precipitation and its timing is important for knowing when precipitation will end in a cyclone event. Second, it can transport strong upper level winds to the surface creating the strongest winds in a midlatitude cyclone near the surface low behind the cold or occluded front.

The third conveyor belt is known as the **cold conveyor belt**. It carries air ahead of the warm front at the surface and spirals into the low as it rises. This makes up the head of the comma shape of the midlatitude cyclone. Precipitation around the comma head is typically light (unless a TROWAL forms) because the cold conveyor belt does not transport as much humidity as the warm conveyor belt. The air is more stable, so the clouds are typically lower.

Summary

Midlatitude cyclones bring a significant amount of precipitation to the midlatitudes, especially in the winter season. Cyclones are circulation systems around low pressure that also include tropical cyclones and tornadoes. Midlatitude cyclones form naturally on our rotating planet with a temperature gradient from north to south. Sharp temperature gradients or disturbances to the flow such as mountains cause the flow to be wavy. The wavy flow can cause temperature advection, which leads to a wavier flow and so on. This type of feedback where a disturbance leads to an initial wave to grow is called baroclinic instability.

Polar front theory is based on observations of hundreds of midlatitude cyclones and describes their structural life cycle. In the genesis stage, a low-pressure center forms on the polar front and transports cold air north ahead of the low (cold front) and warm air south behind the low (warm front). In the intensification stage, the pressure decreases, which increases the circulation, and the cold front rotates counterclockwise around the low pressure. In the mature stage, the low is increasingly surrounded by cold air, cutting off its main energy source, which is the temperature gradient. Finally, in the dissipation stage, cold air surrounds the low, which begins to spin down and fill with air, causing the low-pressure center to disappear.

Midlatitude cyclones develop if there is an area of upper-air divergence above the surface low that can remove air and lower pressures at the surface. Upper-air divergence is found downstream of upper air pressure troughs axes and in the left exit and right entrance region of jet streaks. Jet streaks are areas within a jet stream where winds have accelerated. Upper-air pressure troughs may strengthen if shortwaves move through them.

An alternative model, known as the conveyor belt model, helps to understand the movement of air through a midlatitude cyclone. In this model, dry, cold, and warm

Key Terms

Cyclone

Midlatitude Cyclones

Polar Front

Cyclogenesis

Baroclinic Instability

Heat Capacity

Nor'easter

Law of Conservation of Angular Momentum

Warm Sector

Trough of Warm Air Aloft (TROWAL)

Jet Streams

Polar Jet

Subtropical Jet

Jet Streaks

Negatively-Tilted Troughs

Bomb Cyclone

Long Waves

Planetary or Rossby Waves

Omega Block

Zonal

Shortwaves

Conveyor Belt Model

Warm Conveyor Belt

Atmospheric River

Dry Conveyor Belt

Cold Conveyor Belt

conveyor belts of air move through the cyclone. The warm conveyor belt is the current of air within the warm sector that transports warm humid air into the cyclone. This humidity transport is also known as atmospheric rivers and with a robust source of humidity can cause substantial precipitation within the cyclone. The cold conveyor belt is a current of cold humid air ahead of the warm front that circulates around the low-pressure center. The dry conveyor belt descends from the jet stream and can end precipitation at a location when it moves in and cause high winds.

Questions and Problems

1. What are the three ingredients needed for cyclogenesis?

2. Describe how two of the ingredients needed for cyclogenesis is recreated in the rotating table experiment in Figure 7.2.

3. Baroclinic instability, like static stability, happens when a small perturbation grows through some amplification process. For baroclinic instability, what is the perturbation and the amplification process?

4. All the predominant locations for cyclogenesis can be categorized into two different types. What are these two types and what is a key factor of each that leads to cyclogenesis?

5. What happens to the position of the cold front and warm front as a midlatitude cyclone matures. Use a diagram to illustrate your description for at least three stages in its life cycle.

6. Prior to a severe cold-air outbreak, a strong surface cyclone moves across the central and eastern U.S. What is the role of the surface cyclone in the development of the cold wave?

7. In front of which front can the warm sector be found in a midlatitude cyclone?

8. Why are clouds and precipitation associated with low-pressure systems?

9. What type of weather would you experience if the TROWAL of a cyclone were overhead in winter? How about summer?

10. What is a cutoff low? What is it cut-off from and how can it affect the weather for locations under the cutoff low?

11. If upper level divergence exceeds low-level convergence is the surface system a high or low pressure and is it getting stronger? What would change and in what direction for it to be strengthening?

12. Would a midlatitude cyclone intensify or dissipate if the axis of an upper-air trough were located to the east of a surface low? Include a diagram that illustrates this situation and includes the relative position of the trough axis on the upper-air map and the center of low pressure on the surface map.

13. If upper-air divergence were no longer above the center of a midlatitude cyclone why would it dissipate?

14. Why does the track of a midlatitude cyclone typically curve to the northeast? Hint: Consider the location of the surface low within a favorable location for upper-air divergence.

15. What is a jet streak? What upper-air map would you go to find them and what would you look for on that map?

16. Why are jet streams found above surface temperature gradients?

17. Air moving around an upper-level trough deaccelerates. Why is this and what weather feature does this have a forecastable impact?

18. Draw three or four 300 mb contours and three or four isotachs showing how a jet streak would appear on this upper-level map. Where would upper-air divergence be expected on your diagram?

19. Draw three or four 300 mb contours and three or four isotachs showing how a jet streak would appear on this upper-level map. Where is the entrance and exit region of the jet streak? In which of these regions is the pressure gradient force likely greater than the Coriolis force?

20. How do jet streams and jet streaks cause the development of a surface cyclone?

21. When people talk about being stuck in a warm weather pattern, what map can you use to confirm this and what are you looking for on this map?

22. What feature can weather forecasters use the 700 mb map to identify to determine whether a midlatitude cyclone may get an extra shot of energy and strengthen? How does this feature strengthen midlatitude cyclones?

23. What is the best way to identify atmospheric rivers to forecast whether a midlatitude cyclone will have a significant amount of humidity to produce large amounts of precipitation?

Other Resources

https://www.emich.edu/geography-geology/weather for links to useful weather data to go along with this textbook and updates to any broken links in the textbook.

Chapter 8

Circulation Models and Conservation Laws

Introduction

Last chapter provided a conceptual model of midlatitude cyclones that is an idealization of real midlatitude cyclones. Scientists often use the laws, theories, and principles to put together conceptual models of major processes. Scientists consider creating models an important part of the scientific method.

Scientific Practices

Developing and Using Models

Scientists create models in order to have a mental, graphical, or mathematical simplification of a complex concept. In the last chapter, we learned how scientists first gathered data on midlatitude cyclones, which are a complex atmospheric feature, and distilled the essential features into a simplified graphical representation. Both the polar front theory and the conveyor belt models are conceptual models with the presented diagrams representing the model. Later, mathematical models will be used that are based on mathematical representations of scientific laws. Graphical representations can also be developed from these mathematical models and the two different representations provide the scientist different perspectives and have different uses. Graphical

models usually help to develop a mental understanding of the concept to make forecasts or develop experiments.

Although models work in general to understand complex concepts and to make forecasts, they are simplifications and imperfect. It is important to understand the imperfections of models to understand expected shortcomings. Shortcomings can lead to misapplication of a model and errors in forecasts. That does not mean that we do not understand what is occurring. It also does not mean that we cannot use the model to forecast. The shortcomings just mean that there are minor considerations not included that can have major implications if the forecaster is not aware of the shortcomings.

This chapter discusses some of the major planetary circulations and cycles including the Earth's general circulation and the water cycle. These processes link all the Earth spheres: atmosphere, biosphere, cryosphere, geosphere, and hydrosphere. The conceptual models discussed in this chapter use the physical laws and observed patterns to simplify complex natural processes. It provides the basis for our ability to forecast the weather and climate.

Earth's General Circulation Conceptual Models

For several hundred years, human exploration and trade made us aware of the **prevailing wind** and temperature pattern around the world. The prevailing winds are the usual or average direction of the wind over some geographical area. Mariners in the 16th century were aware of the tropical **trade winds, midlatitude westerlies**, and the locations of the subtropical deserts. Pattern recognitions such as these are a good start to formulating a conceptual model.

By the second century B.C., we knew that warm air rises and cold air sinks (Archimedes Principle). By the 17th century, we knew the Earth rotates and revolves around the sun with the rotation axis pointed toward the North Star. Galileo Galilei used observational evidence to prove this last discovery originally conceived by Nicolaus Copernicus. Galileo is considered the father of the scientific method for using observations to prove the Copernicus heliocentric model. Isaac Newton also proved the laws of motion and gravity in this century. From these laws we know that air is forced from areas of high pressure to low pressure.

Using known weather patterns and these physical laws, Lord Hadley was able to build one of the first conceptual models of the **Earth's general circulation of the atmosphere**. In fact, the motion of the atmosphere is much more complex than captured in these early conceptual models. However, by considering a few important principles, Lord Hadley attempted to describe the main patterns of the general circulation.

This process of taking some simple principles and envisioning the effects on a system leads to the creation of a conceptual model. Conceptual models are not mathematical models. In the next couple of chapters, mathematical models such as weather and climate models are discussed. Mathematical models are based on these early conceptual models.

Single-Cell Circulation Model

Initial attempts at conceptually modelling the Earth's general circulation envisioned a simplified Earth-like planet. The sun heats this planet more at the equator than the poles. However, the similarities stop there. To simplify this planet, the conceptual planet is not rotating and completely water-covered. Applying the scientific principles known at the beginning of the 18th century, Lord Hadley attempted to build a conceptual model of the Earth's general circulation. This model can be compared to the known patterns of the Earth's climate system.

In this simplified model, because the Earth is warmest at the equator, we would expect air here to expand outward and rise upward. Likewise, because the Earth is coldest at the poles, we would expect air here to contract inward and sink downward. The expanding air at the equator would cause less air to weigh on the ground reducing the surface pressure. In contrast, contracting air at the poles would cause more air to weigh on the ground increasing the surface pressure. Therefore, we would expect high surface pressure at the poles and low surface pressure at the equator. The difference in pressure would force surface air from the poles to the equator. With no planetary rotation, there is no Coriolis force to deflect this movement.

In addition, because the air at the poles contracts and sinks, a disproportional amount of weight is near the surface. Therefore, the relatively high surface pressure at the poles would become a relatively low pressure near the top of the atmosphere. Similarly, because the air at the equator expands and rises, a disproportional amount of weight is at the top of the atmosphere. Therefore, the relatively low surface pressure near the equator would become a relatively high pressure near the top of the atmosphere. The upper atmosphere pressure gradient would force air from high pressure at the equator to the low pressure at the poles and complete the convection cell.

Such a planet would have a circulation like the planet in Figure 8.1. A single vertical circulation cell would exist in the northern and the southern hemispheres. The vertical circulation cell is called the Hadley cell and this conceptual model is called the single-cell circulation model. For this planet, air would generally rise at the equator and sink at the poles. At the surface, this planet would have a northerly surface flow (from north-to-south) in the northern hemisphere and a southerly surface flow in the southern hemisphere.

In comparison to Earth, the only features that this model replicates is the rising air at the equator and sinking air at the poles. This conceptual model is insufficient to capture the easterly trade winds or the midlatitude westerly wind patterns of the Earth's observed general circulation. When we include one more feature of the Earth, we can explain these patterns. That feature is the Earth's rotation.

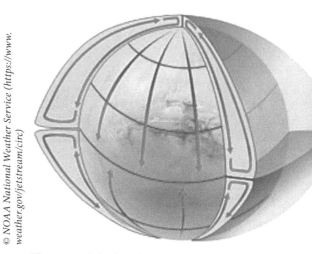

© NOAA National Weather Service (https://www.weather.gov/jetstream/circ)

Figure 8.1 Single-cell circulation model on a non-rotating water-covered planet is shown. Surface winds (red arrows) and vertical north-to-south wind circulation (red and blue arrows) are provided.

Three-Cell Circulation Model

If we consider the previous conceptual simplified planet but add the Earth's rotation to this planet then some major changes occur. As the air at the equator rises and hits the top of this planet's troposphere, the air spreads poleward. As this air moves poleward, it experiences an increasing Coriolis force that turns the air to the right in the northern hemisphere, which is toward the east. This continues until about 30° latitude where the air cools by radiation emission and sinks to the surface. Therefore, the Hadley cell does not extend past 30° latitude on this planet (Figure 8.2).

When the descending air in the Hadley cell hits the surface, air spreads both poleward and equatorward. A decreasing Coriolis force deflects the air that moves equatorward to the right (left in the southern hemisphere). The deflected surface air creates the northeasterly (southeasterly in the southern hemisphere) trade winds in the tropics. The air in the two hemispheres converge at the equator producing the Inter-Tropical Convergence Zone (ITCZ). An increasing Coriolis force deflects the air that moves poleward to the right (left in the southern hemisphere). A stronger deflection of surface air creates the stronger westerly winds in the midlatitudes.

Like the single cell circulation model, air over the poles is still the coldest air on this planet and that air descends at the poles. When the air hits the surface, it spreads out and moves equatorward. This air is deflected to the right (left in the southern hemisphere) creating the strong polar easterlies in the Arctic and Antarctic. The Arctic air gradually moves equatorward to converge with the surface midlatitude winds moving from the tropics. The resulting surface temperature gradient between the two air masses creates the polar front. Air ascends at the polar front spreading at the top of the atmosphere and completing two more vertical circulation cells; the polar cell (60° – 90° latitude) and the Ferrel cell (30° – 60° latitude). With the Hadley cell, that makes three vertical circulation cells in each hemisphere.

GLOBAL ATMOSPHERIC CIRCULATION

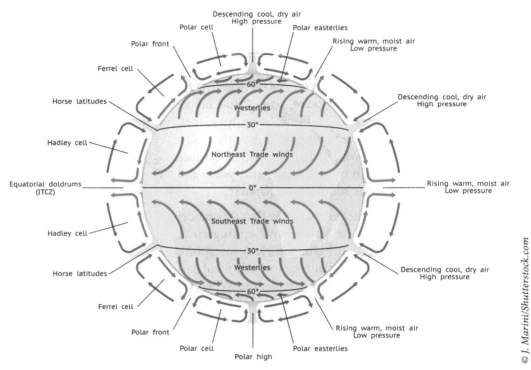

Figure 8.2 Three-cell circulation model on a rotating water-covered planet is shown. Surface winds (arrows on globe) and vertical wind circulation (arrows surrounding globe) are provided along with predominant surface pressure at the equator, 30° latitude, 60° latitude, and poles.

This **three-cell circulation model** explains a number of patterns that we see on Earth. The easterly trade winds, midlatitude westerlies, and polar easterlies are all observed in the lower tropospheric winds on Earth. The ITCZ, bands of rising air and cloudiness at the ITCZ and the polar front and sinking dry air at the poles and subtropics are all observed vertical circulations. The diverging air above the ITCZ and the polar front creates belts of surface low pressure at these latitudes. Similarly, the converging air at the subtropics and poles creates belts of high pressure at these latitudes. All of this is found on Earth when observing annual means.

If you envision this conceptual planet to have a tilted rotation axis, then you get seasons. On Earth, the rotation axis is tilted by 23.5° so the ITCZ would not always be at the equator. The ITCZ follows the latitude of direct radiation. The ITCZ would be near 23.5° N (Tropic of Cancer) during the northern hemisphere summer solstice. It would then shift southward thereafter reaching 23.5° S (Tropic of Capricorn) at the northern hemisphere winter solstice. All the other belts and circulation cells would shift accordingly.

Beyond the Three-Cell Circulation Model

The three-cell circulation model is relatively simple and explains much, but not all, of the Earth's general circulation. For example, Earth has continents that create heating differences from the ocean-covered conceptual planet. In the winter hemisphere, the continents are colder than the ocean and in the summer hemisphere, the continents are warmer than the ocean. This causes the pressure pattern seen in Figure 8.3. In January,

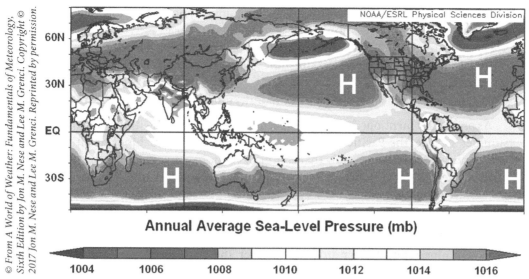

Figure 8.3 Annual average sea-level pressure (color shading) highlighting the subtropical semipermanent high-pressure centers.

when the continents are colder in the northern hemisphere, the belts of high pressure move toward them because cold air is denser. In July, when the continents are warmer in the northern hemisphere, the belts of low pressure (and the ITCZ) moves toward them. This creates alternating high (in the cold season) and low (in the warm season) pressure over the continents and semipermanent highs over the ocean. The term semiperma-nent means that the high-pressure centers may not always be in the same region on a day-to-day basis. However, averaging the pressure over a month, these high-pressure centers will show up in their expected locations (Figure 8.3).

The semipermanent highs and their associated circulation greatly affects coastal weather. The Pacific High dominates the weather on the U.S. west coast. In the summer, the Pacific High is centered at the latitude of Northern California (Figure 8.4). The flow around high pressure at the surface is spiraling out of the center. Therefore, the wind along the west coast is onshore north of the latitude of high pressure and offshore south

Figure 8.4 Semipermanent high locations during summer affecting North America coastal weather is shown with expected air circulation (blue arrows).

of it. Onshore flow means maritime air, and its humidity, is moving toward land bringing with it clouds and precipitation. That is why cities like Seattle, WA and Vancouver, BC are often rainy. Offshore flow means continental air, and its lack of humidity, is moving over coastal cities bringing with it sunshine and dry conditions. That is why cities like Los Angeles, CA are sunny all summer long. In fact, the average rainfall for Los Angeles is less than a total of half an inch for the three-month summer period of June, July, and August.

As previously mentioned, these semipermanent highs move with the seasons. After the summer solstice, the Pacific High moves south eventually reaching the latitude of Baja California and the offshore flow that southern California experiences all summer gradually becomes onshore (Figure 8.5). The majority of the annual rainfall in Los Angeles falls in the three winter months of December, January, and February. At latitudes similar to the location of the Pacific High, the winds blow parallel to the coast from the north. This has an effect on the coastal ocean temperatures, which is discussed later.

The semipermanent **Bermuda High** over the Atlantic Ocean greatly affects the weather in the eastern U.S. The Bermuda high does not move north or south much over the seasons. However, it does move closer to Europe in the winter so its influence on eastern U.S. is weaker in winter (Figure 8.5). Because the Bermuda high always causes air to flow onshore on the U.S. Gulf and East coasts, the eastern third of the U.S. is often humid. In the summer, hot humid conditions prevail as maritime tropical air masses are often over this area. In the winter, these air masses are less frequent and do not reach as far inland, but where it does, the warm humid air mass moving over the cold land produces fog.

Another major shortcoming of the three-cell circulation model is that the baroclinic instability and cyclone formation that dominates the midlatitudes are not included in the model. We saw these effects in the previous chapter and in the rotating fluid tank. Whenever rotation occurs with a temperature gradient, baroclinic instability will occur and cyclones will form. The midlatitudes are characterized by a strong temperature gradient

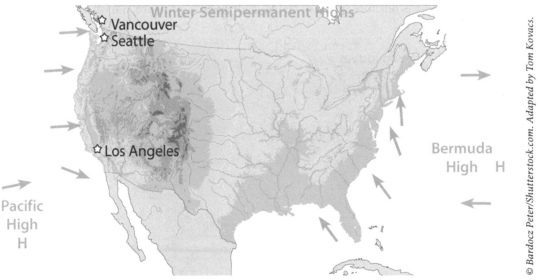

Figure 8.5 Semipermanent high locations during winter affecting North America coastal weather is shown with expected air circulation (blue arrows). The Pacific high moves south and the Bermuda High moves east from its summer position causing some of its influence to weaken (thinner blue arrows).

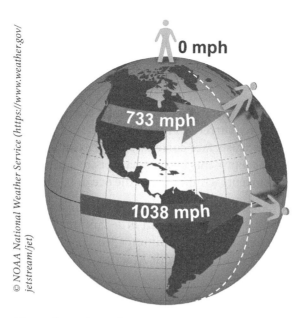

Figure 8.6 The Earth's surface has the greatest rotational velocity at the equator (1038 mph) and zero mph at the poles. When air moves poleward, it attains a
larger angular velocity because the distance to the rotation axis decreases and its
velocity is higher in accordance with the Law of Conservation of Angular Momentum.
Air moving poleward attains a faster eastward (i.e. westerly) velocity. Of course,
friction slows this wind down so winds greater than 300 mph are not found in the
subtropical jet stream.

often concentrated in the polar front. The upper airflow is also wavy, often with large
amplitude north-south planetary or Rossby waves. Jet streams also bracket this area to the
north with the polar jet and to the south with the subtropical jet.

The subtropical jet stream exists at the junction of the Hadley and Ferrel cells while the
polar jet stream exists at the junction of the Ferrel and Polar cells. The polar jet stream
exists because of the temperature gradient along the polar front. The temperature gradient creates a pressure gradient that, in balance with the Coriolis force, forces air from
west-to-east (westerly). The subtropical jet stream exists because of the Law of Conversation of Angular Momentum. The angular velocity of the Earth's surface at higher latitudes is slower and drops to zero at the poles (Figure 8.6). According to the law, the air
moving poleward would keep its angular momentum (product of **angular velocity** of
the air and radius of its rotation). Air that moves poleward moves faster toward the east
(i.e. westerly) relative to the Earth's surface. Friction does slow the winds; otherwise, the
subtropical jet would be much faster than it is.

On Earth, the static stability of the stratosphere prevents this air from penetrating the
stratosphere. Therefore, air spreads poleward at the top of the troposphere and the Hadley,
Ferrel, and Polar cells all exist within the troposphere. The layer above the troposphere
have different processes that affect its circulation. Some of these processes is covered in
Chapter 12 as they pertain to long-range forecasting (i.e. forecasts for more than a week).

Ocean Circulation Conceptual Models

The ocean is of major importance to weather and climate forecasting. It covers over 70%
of the Earth's surface and the ocean circulation transports a lot of energy from the tropics to the poles. Oceans are also important regulators of greenhouse gases. The ocean's

impact depends on its two different circulations. The ocean has a surface circulation and a thermohaline deep ocean circulation forced by different mechanisms.

Surface Currents

The world's surface ocean currents are shown in Figure 8.7. The atmospheric general circulation directs the surface currents. Prevailing winds are the main force that accelerates the surface water. However, surface currents are not exactly the same as the atmospheric general circulation. The continents become barriers to surface currents creating numerous localized surface currents within each of the ocean basins.

The prevailing winds direct the Antarctic Circumpolar Current, equatorial current, and North Atlantic and Pacific drift. With little land mass in the Southern Ocean, the surface water circles the world mostly unimpeded creating the eastward flowing Antarctic circumpolar surface current. South America, Africa, and Australia deflects some of this current to produce the Peru/Humboldt, Benguela, and West Australia currents, respectively. All these are cold currents because they are moving from an area of the world that is colder to an area of the world that is relatively warmer. This mechanism is how the ocean redistributes some of the Earth's energy imbalanced by the differential heating by the sun.

The continents of Africa and Asia impede the westward flowing equatorial current. Usually, when continents impede the surface current, the water branches both north and south. In this case, both branches are warm currents of water because the source of water

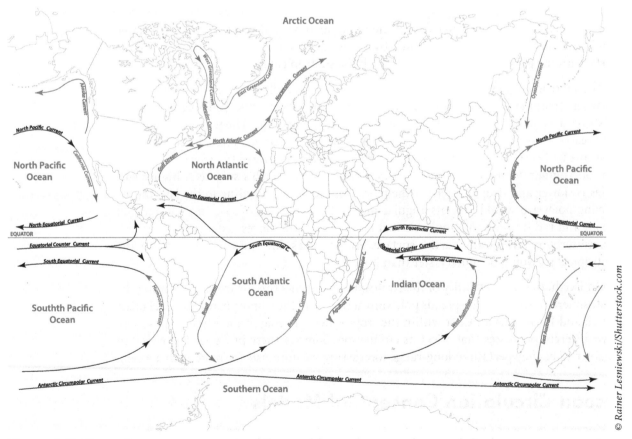

Figure 8.7 The surface ocean currents of the world are shown and named. Red arrows represents warm currents and blue arrows represents cold currents.

is located in the warmest part of the ocean. In the Atlantic Ocean, the northern branch becomes the Gulf Stream and moves into the Caribbean Sea and then the Gulf of Mexico. Eventually, this current enters the Atlantic Ocean through the Straits of Florida and hugs the U.S. coastline before making its way toward Europe. Europe would be much colder if it were not for this warm current of water. In the Pacific Ocean, the northern branch of the equatorial current becomes the Kuroshio Current and moves along the eastern side of Asia. Both the Gulf Stream and Kuroshio Current help energize many of the tropical cyclones in the northern hemisphere.

The Gulf Stream branches apart at the European continent. The southern branch becomes the Canary Current and is cold while the northern branch becomes the North Atlantic drift and warms Scandinavia. The North Pacific Drift branches at the North American Continent. The southern branch becomes the California current and is cold while the northern branch warms Alaska.

The surface ocean water is a well-mixed layer of water usually 100 m deep or so. The exact depth depends on season, latitude, and turbulent mixing of water due to wind and waves. The thermocline is a layer of rapid cooling with depth that separates the surface water above and the deep ocean below.

The force of the moving water at the top of the ocean surface layer forces the movement of water lower down in this surface layer. The top of the surface layer and each successive layer below is in balance with the Coriolis force. However, each successively lower layer is deflected to the right in the Northern Hemisphere. This Coriolis deflection causes the top of the surface layer to move at about a 45° angle to the right of the prevailing wind. Each successively deeper layer is deflected further to the right (Figure 8.8). The change in direction of the water as you go deeper into the surface layer is called the Ekman spiral. Because of the Ekman spiral, the average transport of water in the surface layer tends to be to the right of the prevailing wind.

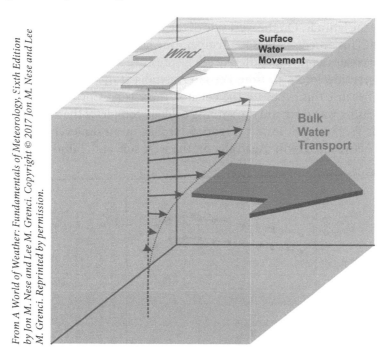

Figure 8.8 Diagram of the changing direction of the ocean current (blue arrows) as you go down within the surface layer of the ocean forced by the prevailing wind (yellow arrow).

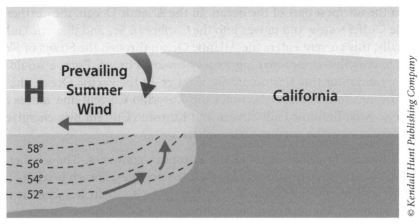

Figure 8.9 In the summer, prevailing winds (purple arrow) around the Pacific High parallels the coast around San Francisco. Ekman transport of surface water occurs to the right (toward the west in this case) of the prevailing wind motion causing colder water to upwell (blue arrows).

Ekman transport of surface water has an important weather and climate impact. Where winds parallel the California coast around the Pacific High, Ekman transport of surface water occurs away from the coast (Figure 8.9). Of course, water levels do not drop much on the west coast because water from lower down rises to the top in a process known as upwelling. This upwelling water is colder and nutrient rich, which leads to a vibrant marine life and cold surface waters. This effect is greatest in summer when the Pacific high is about at the latitude of San Francisco making summers in San Francisco not much warmer than winters (Figure 8.10).

A similar effect occurs along the coast of Peru, making water temperatures here relatively cold for the latitude. On the west side of the Pacific Ocean, the water temperature is much warmer. This difference in water temperature between the east and west sides of the Pacific Ocean creates a pressure difference. The pressure difference, with low pressure on the warmer west side, forces air from Peru to Australia at the surface and accelerates the trade winds. Because this occurs at the equator, there is no Coriolis force deflection. In addition, the rising warm air and the sinking cold air completes the atmospheric circulation called the Walker circulation (Figure 8.11). The mean sea level pressure difference is monitored between Darwin, Australia on the west side and Tahiti on the east side. It

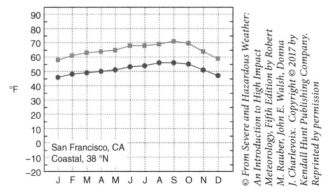

Figure 8.10 Average daily high (red) and low (blue) temperatures for San Francisco for each month of the year.

December - February Normal Conditions

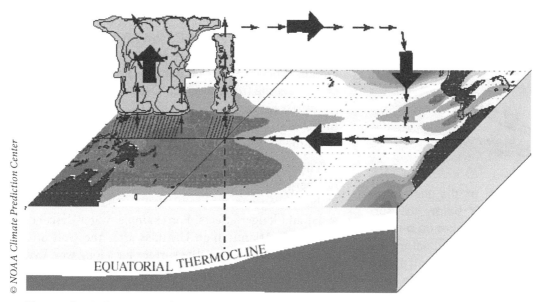

© NOAA Climate Prediction Center

Figure 8.11 Diagram of the Walker Circulation (black arrows), which are forced by warmer surface ocean water (yellow/orange shaded contours) on the west side of the equatorial Pacific Ocean and cooler surface ocean water (blue shaded contours) on the east side of the equatorial Pacific Ocean.

oscillates over a period of around three years and is known as the Southern Oscillation. A southern oscillation index is computed based on the mean sea level pressure differences between Darwin and Tahiti. The Walker circulation causes water to pile up on the west side of the Pacific Ocean creating higher pressure in the ocean water below the top of the surface layer. This high pressure in the ocean forces water eastward and creates the Equatorial countercurrent.

When the Southern Oscillation Index is in its negative phase (above normal pressure at Darwin) for a long period of time, the trade winds decrease and can reverse direction. With less force on the equatorial current, the higher water pressure causes a wave of warm water to move toward Peru. The wave of warm water stops the upwelling and warms the surface water temperatures in the eastern equatorial Pacific Ocean. This warming of the surface water temperatures on the east side of the Pacific Ocean is known as El Nino. In contrast, when the Southern Oscillation Index is in its positive phase for a long period, it causes a strong Walker circulation. Abnormally cold surface water on the east side of the Pacific Ocean known as La Nina forms. Both El Nino and La Nina have dramatic effects on weather and climate. These effects are not felt only along the coasts of Australia and South America, but worldwide because of its effects on the atmosphere's general circulation. A number of major internal climate oscillations like El Nino and La Nina affect the weather worldwide. These oscillations are monitored for seasonal forecasts, which are discussed later in this chapter and in Chapter 12.

Thermohaline Circulation

The deeper ocean circulation known as the thermohaline circulation is not directed by winds, but by temperature (thermos-) and salt content or salinity (halide). In reality, density differences direct this circulation because colder and more saline water is

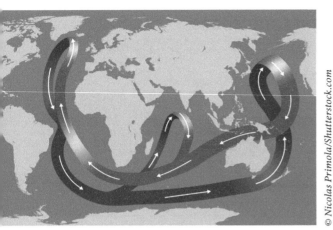

© Nicolas Primola/Shutterstock.com

Figure 8.12 Diagram of the thermohaline circulation, which is below the surface (100 m) water and makes up a large majority of the ocean. Water enters the deep ocean circulation in the North Atlantic shown by the descending red to blue arrows and Antarctica. It comes back to the surface in the Indian and Pacific Oceans shown by the ascending blue to red arrows.

denser than warmer and less saline water. Deep ocean bottom water largely originates at high latitudes in the North Atlantic and the Antarctic (Figure 8.12). The Antarctic is the source of the densest water in the ocean. Water temperatures, often below 0° C, will lift the North Atlantic sourced water to the surface in the Southern and Indian Oceans. The deep ocean water does not freeze because the salt lowers the freezing point. Deep water also upwells to the surface in the North Pacific Ocean. Water surfacing in the North Pacific Ocean is some of the oldest water, spending hundreds of years in the deep ocean.

The thermohaline circulation transfers a large amount of energy, gases, and dissolved substances around the globe. Changes in the circulation can have dramatic seasonal and longer effects. For example, water descends in the North Atlantic high latitudes after the Gulf Stream carries this water along the surface for a long way. Evaporation at the surface causes the water to become saltier and denser until it descends in the high latitudes of the North Atlantic. However, because of melting glaciers in Greenland and sea ice in the Artic, fresh water is mixing with this salty water making it less dense. This additional fresh water slows the thermohaline circulation. Natural changes to the climate may have led to a slowing of this circulation during the Younger-Dryas period (12900 – 11700 BC). The circulation may be slowing again although not due to natural changes this time. Continued slowing of the Gulf Stream would cool the climate of Europe. It would also lead to a buildup of water in the Northern Hemisphere Atlantic Ocean exacerbating sea level rise in coastal areas. Observations show that this is currently happening with sea level rise on the U.S. east coast exceeding the global sea level rise by as much as a factor of four[1].

Major Atmospheric Cycles and Teleconnections

Seasonal to decadal climate system cycles occurring in small areas of the Earth can have major global impacts on atmospheric conditions because of **teleconnections**. Teleconnections are environmental effects separated on planetary scales connected to a long-term change. Sometimes the effect can be on the opposite side of the Earth. Longer-term impacts on the order of seasons help forecasters provide seasonal forecasts.

El Nino, La Nina, and the related Southern Oscillation affect the longwave pattern and the jet stream. El Nino and La Nina change the equator-to-pole temperature gradient. El Nino warms the equatorial Pacific and increases the temperature gradient between the equator and poles. This strengthens the jet stream, particularly the subtropical jet. Figure 8.13 illustrates the strengthening of the subtropical jet caused by El Nino. This stronger west-to-east flow in the southern U.S. states causes wetter and cooler conditions in this part of the U.S. mostly during winter and spring. Without the meander of the jet streams and lack of troughs and ridges, the midlatitude cyclones that normally bring precipitation to the northern U.S. and Canada are missing. Lack of midlatitude cyclones causes drier winters in these areas. Lack of snow warms this region too because

[1] Sallenger Jr., A.; K. Doran; and P. Howd (2012) Hotspot of accelerated sea-level rise on the Atlantic coast of North America. *Nature Climate Change*, **2**, 884-888.

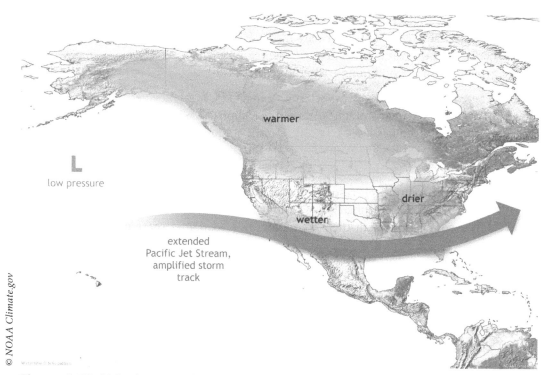

Figure 8.13 U.S. climate effects from El Nino

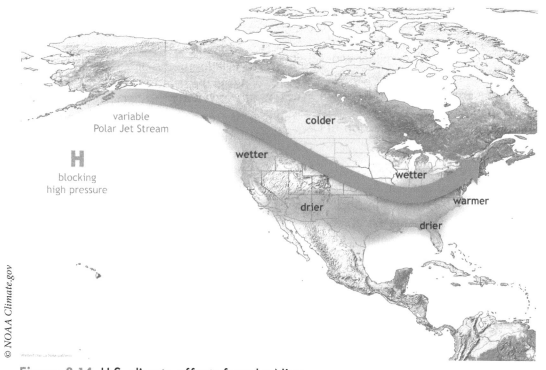

Figure 8.14 U.S. climate effects from La Nina.

the absence of snow cover scatters less sunlight into space allowing the ground to absorb more energy. In the summer, El Nino's main effect is on tropical cyclones. This affect is discussed in Chapter 12.

Figure 8.14 shows how La Nina conditions causes the subtropical jet to disappear and the polar jet stream to meander and become wavier. Wavier troughs and ridges produce a colder winter in the trough in eastern Alaska, much of western Canada, and the northern U.S. Wetter winter conditions occur in the Pacific Northwest with a stronger onshore flow and in the Great Lakes and northeast regions, which are downstream of the trough. Warmer and drier conditions are found to the south.

These patterns do not always set up as expected nor do they necessarily persist for the entire winter. As meteorologists learn more about El Nino/La Nina and the Southern Oscillation, it becomes clear that the specific regions of warming or cooling locations within the tropical Pacific Ocean creates different patterns of temperature and precipitation anomalies.

Other known atmosphere-ocean oscillations such as the Arctic Oscillation (AO), North Atlantic Oscillation (NAO), and Pacific Decadal Oscillation (PDO) also cause teleconnections with their own effects that can alter these patterns. The AO and

Digging Deeper

Internal Climate Oscillations

The Arctic Oscillation (AO) surface pressures are measured more closely to the Arctic than the North Atlantic Oscillation (NAO). Otherwise, the two oscillations are similar. When pressures are higher in the tropics, the AO and NAO are in their positive phase. During the positive phase of the NAO and AO, polar jet stream winds are strong. These winds keep the cold air bottled up in the Arctic and contributes to milder winters in the U.S. During the negative phase of the NAO and AO, jet stream winds are weak and wavier. Just like during La Nina, the wavier jet stream winds lead to a greater production of midlatitude cyclones.

The AO and polar vortex weakening are related. The polar vortex is a ring of winds in the polar stratosphere extending down into the upper troposphere that develop due to the extremely cold air that forms during the polar night (remember the polar night is months long). During the negative phase of the AO, polar vortex winds are weak, and the stability of the polar vortex is low. On top of this, a wavier jet stream leads to the shedding of long-lived vortices from the poles to the midlatitudes. These vortices contain extremely cold air and lead to polar vortex outbreaks in North America and Asia. More detail is provided in the "Digging Deeper Box" in Chapter 12.

The Pacific Decadal Oscillation (PDO) is a change from normal Pacific Ocean sea surface temperatures between the North American coast near Alaska and the north central Pacific Ocean. The PDO is a much longer lasting oscillation than the other oscillations, thus the 'decadal' in the name suggesting the phases last for decades. Its affects are somewhat similar to El Nino/La Nina, but even more complex and less well known.

The Quasi-Biennial Oscillation (QBO) is a 28-29-month oscillation of the direction of the equatorial winds in the stratosphere from easterly to westerly. Like the AO, the QBO has an effect on the polar vortex and is discussed in more detail in the "Digging Deeper Box" in Chapter 12. The Madden-Julian Oscillation (MJO) is an eastward propagating wave of enhanced and suppressed convective activity on a 20-80-day cycle that helps guide outlooks of precipitation. The MJO affects the activity of convection in the tropics and midlatitudes. When identified, the MJO's normal behavior is to move from west to east across the tropics and circles the globe in about 30-60 days. The MJO is particularly important for U.S. and Canada west coast precipitation events in their wet winter season.

Like the southern oscillation, the AO, NAO, and PDO have positive and negative phases depending on the sign of the differences in pressures that determine the state of these oscillations. The QBO has easterly and westerly phases. Teleconnections are based on the sign or direction of these phases.

NAO are a measure of the difference in surface pressure between the tropical regions and the Arctic that directly affects the polar jet stream. One major effect of the AO is in its relationship to polar vortex outbreaks (see the "Digging Deeper Box"). The Pacific Decadal Oscillation (PDO) is similar in effects to El Nino but lasts for a much longer time.

These oscillations do not just cause regional effects but can affect global warming. Besides the teleconnections, El Nino causes an increase and La Nina causes a decrease in global annual mean temperatures. In a similar manner, the PDO can change the global annual mean temperatures. The other oscillations can alter jet stream and weather patterns. None of the oscillations causes the global climate to change over the long term but must be considered when observing global and regional climates. However, the oscillations themselves and their teleconnections can change and may be part of climate change. The impact of these teleconnections on forecasting are covered in Chapter 12.

Water Cycle

The water cycle represents the flow of water in all its phases from the atmosphere to the global oceans and back. However, it is much more detailed than that (Figure 8.15). Water cycles through all of the Earth's spheres. Besides the atmosphere and hydrosphere, which includes the fresh and salty water systems, water cycles through the biosphere, cryosphere, and geosphere. Changes to land and water use have become so profound that these changes affects the weather and climate by altering the flux (flow or transport) of water to the atmosphere.

Figure 8.15 The water cycle is shown. Labeled yellow arrows highlight fluxes or transport of water by various processes and phase changes.

The water cycle has no starting point and can take an infinite number of pathways. In fact, over time, you may be drinking water breathed by Julius Caesar and that passed through dinosaurs. Unfortunately, you have an even better chance of drinking water that you pollute because you obtain your water and do most of your polluting locally. A good place to start to describe the cycle would be the ocean because it is the largest reservoir of water.

Oceans contain about 97% of the Earth's water. Ocean water is a salty buildup of minerals accumulating over millions of years. Ocean water can evaporate and increase the humidity of the atmosphere. The evaporation is not salty because the salt remains behind. The water can recondense into the liquid form or deposit into the solid form to produce various clouds. Maritime air masses eventually bring this water over land. A transfer of water to the land occurs during precipitation. More water evaporates from the ocean than precipitates onto it for this reason. The water that precipitates is the main source of our fresh water, which all organisms, including humans, need to survive.

About 90% of the remaining water on Earth is frozen (glaciers, permafrost, etc.) or in groundwater. Most water for human use comes from groundwater, but only a few percent of it is useable. Lakes, soil, wetlands, reservoirs, rivers, streams, organisms, and the atmosphere contain the remaining water for human use. Despite the extensive amount of water on Earth very little is useable to humans. In fact, we are nearing our limit of available water[2].

Nearly all this water comes from liquid or solid precipitation. Precipitation can be stored in any of the land reservoirs. Snow and glaciers also melt as they flow to lower, warmer latitudes or through seasonal warming. Liquid precipitation and meltwater can infiltrate, or enter, the ground to become part of the soil moisture or groundwater. If the soil is too moist or the precipitation rate too high the water can runoff on the ground. Excessive runoff causes flooding, as does the flow of groundwater and runoff into streams, rivers, and lakes, which are depressions in the ground into which water eventually drains. Much of the water in these water reservoirs on land eventually flows back to the ocean. This flow into the ocean mostly balances the water lost by the ocean through excess evaporation.

Human changes also dramatically affect local water budgets and can have an effect on flood and drought forecasting, weather and climate. Building development often changes pervious ground to impervious ground. Impervious ground means that water cannot infiltrate the ground. If the reduced infiltration is not accounted, flooding can result. Large-scale development can change humidity transport from ground to atmosphere also known as moisture flux. The changing moisture flux can affect heating, cloudiness, and precipitation patterns. A major example of this is the urban heat island effect where temperatures in urban areas can exceed outlying areas at night by several degrees Celsius. A recent impact that can cause a much more abrupt change to our climate system is the Amazon wildfires of 2019. Loss of trees can affect the flux of water from ground to atmosphere so much that the climate can change to the point that the Amazon forests would completely disappear.

---

[2] Abbott, B.; K. Bishop; K. Zarnetske, J. Minaudo; C. Chapin III; F. Stuart; S. Krause; D. Hannah; L. Conner; D. Ellison; S. Godsey; S. Plont; J. Marçais; T. Kolbe; A. Huebner; R. Frei; T. Hampton; S. Gu; M. Buhman; S. Sayedi; and G. Pinay (2019): Human domination of the global water cycle absent from depiction and perceptions. *Nature Geoscience*. **12**. 1. 10.1038/s41561-019-0374-y.

Summary

Patterns have been found in the complex atmospheric motions that we see in satellite imagery. Prevailing wind patterns such as the polar easterlies, midlatitude westerlies, and tropical trade winds have also been known by mariners and farmers for centuries and determines how weather moves. Considering a conceptual simplified water-covered planet that does not rotate and is heated at the equator is a first step in understanding the Earth's general circulation. This conceptualization leads to a single vertical circulation cell model that does not resemble the Earth's circulation much. Nonetheless, this conceptual model lays the framework to consider a rotating planet that leads to the three-cell circulation model. The Hadley, Ferrel, and Polar vertical circulation cells and the Coriolis deflection creates a pattern of pressure and winds that are observed in seasonal averages of the Earth. Once the tilt of the rotation axis and continents are considered, the seasons and semipermanent highs help explain coastal weather and climates.

The ocean circulation also has weather and climate affects. The ocean has a surface and deep thermohaline circulation that are set in motion by different processes. The surface ocean circulation is forced by the Earth's general circulation. However, it is modified by continents that represent impassable boundaries for ocean water. The deep ocean circulation is forced by density differences caused by temperature and salt content. Water enters the deep ocean where it is densest in the North Atlantic and Antarctica and returns to the surface in the Indian and north Pacific Oceans. This circulation transports energy throughout the world with climate effects if it is interrupted.

Surface currents within the surface ocean layer transfer momentum to lower levels with increasing Coriolis deflection to the right in the northern hemisphere and is called the Ekman spiral. The result is an Ekman transport of water at right angles to the winds that transports water away from west coasts of continents causing upwelling of cold air. In the tropical Pacific Ocean, the upwelling off the coast of Peru is interrupted by a pressure oscillation known as the Southern Oscillation that can alternately strengthen and weaken the equatorial trade winds and surface ocean currents. This leads to a warming or cooling of water off the coast known as El Nino/La Nina. El Nino/La Nina and other internal climate oscillations leads to teleconnections that affect world weather.

Water not only cycles around the ocean, but because of phase changes and winds can cycle through all of Earth's spheres including the atmosphere, biosphere, cryosphere, and geosphere. The water cycles through these spheres in a complex path that creates fresh water that all living organisms use from saltwater. Flooding occurs when water into a watershed cannot enter the ground or flow out of the watershed quickly enough.

Key Terms

Prevailing Wind

Midlatitude Westerlies

Trade Winds

Earth's General Circulation of the Atmosphere

Hadley Cell

Single-Cell Circulation Model

Inter-Tropical Convergence Zone (ITCZ)

Polar Easterlies

Polar Cell

Ferrel Cell

Three-Cell Circulation Model

Semipermanent Highs

Pacific High

Onshore

Offshore

Bermuda High

Angular Velocity

Surface Ocean Currents

Gulf Stream

California Current

Thermocline

Ekman Spiral

Ekman Transport

Upwelling

Walker Circulation

Southern Oscillation

El Nino

La Nina

Internal Climate Oscillations

Thermohaline Circulation

Salinity

Water Cycle

Flux

Groundwater

Infiltrate

Runoff

Flooding

Impervious Ground

Teleconnections

Arctic Oscillation (AO)

North Atlantic Oscillation (NAO)

Pacific Decadal Oscillation (PDO)

Questions and Problems

1. If you took a plane from New York, NY to Rome, Italy, would you expect a head wind or tail wind based on the Earth's general circulation? What about a flight from Hawaii to the Philippines? Explain why.

2. What is a major difference in assumptions and results of the single-cell and three-cell circulation models? Which is more similar to actual global winds?

3. The Sahara, Mojave, Gobi, Atacama, and Kalahari deserts are all found near 30° north and south latitude. Based on what you know about the three-cell circulation models and cloud and precipitation formation, why are most of the world's hot deserts found at this latitude?

4. Where do the jet streams form relative to the three circulation cells and why do they form here? (Note: make sure you contrast the formation of the polar and subtropical jet streams)

5. Given that the Bermuda High typically provides the steering current for hurricanes in the Atlantic Ocean, would you predict more landfalling hurricanes when the Bermuda High was closer or further from North America and why?

6. Why does southern California receive almost no rain in the summer months?

7. Why is it so rainy year-round in Seattle, WA and Vancouver, BC?

8. What is the difference in the way the surface and deep ocean circulations form (i.e. what forces them to circulate)?

9. Why is the water temperature off the west coast of the U.S. often more than 10 °F colder than off the east coast?

10. Use the prevailing winds and the surface ocean currents to explain why England is warmer than Maine even though England is further north.

11. What causes the water temperature off the coast of California to be cold in summer?

12. What is the characteristics of the surface water in the North Atlantic Ocean that causes it to be a major source of deep ocean water? What would change if fresh (salt-free) glacial melt were to increase from Greenland?

13. Where does most of our drinking water come from and how does polluting our land ultimately enter our drinking water?

14. How can a rapid spring thaw lead to flooding? Name two ways.

15. What happens to the ocean water temperature along the South American coast during El Nino?

16. What is the relationship between El Nino and the Southern Oscillation?

17. What is the relationship between the Walker Circulation and the Southern Oscillation?

18. How does El Nino affect the subtropical jet stream?

19. What would you forecast for your area in an El Nino winter?

20. What would you forecast for your area in a La Nina winter?

Other Resources

https://www.emich.edu/geography-geology/weather for links to useful weather data to go along with this textbook and updates to any broken links in the textbook.

https://www.metoffice.gov.uk/weather/learn-about/weather/atmosphere/global-circulation-patterns provides animations of the Earth's General Circulation

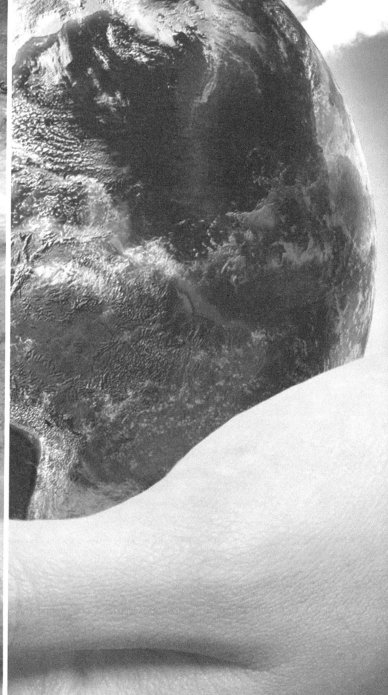

Unit 3

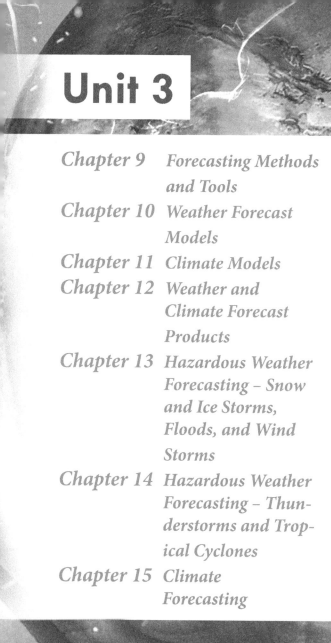

Weather and Climate Forecasting

Chapter 9

Forecasting Methods and Tools

Introduction

This chapter begins the highest level of the scientific method: **forecasting**. Scientific forecasting requires careful observation, data gathering, and the use of all the scientific laws, theories, and principles to make a forecast of what will happen in the future. Experience also helps separate a great from an average forecaster, but scientific data and principles are at the foundation of all weather and climate forecasts. For the beginning forecasters and non-scientists, one scientific practice that is important to remember is to use observations and principles to come up with conclusions. Oftentimes, people will rely on what they hear from others or what they remember from the past. Non-meteorologists probably will not make many weather forecasts. However, the practice of using observations and principles is what helps you make a sound and persuasive argument. This skill helps in any field and in our everyday lives.

Each year, taxpayers pay approximately $5.1 billion for the weather forecasting services of the National Weather Service. Yet, they derive over $30 billion of value from those forecasts.[1] Weather forecasting is a proven valuable application of the scientific method. A scientist would question the derived value based on this text alone. However, the source is documented from a peer-reviewed scientific journal. That is an example of a sound and persuasive argument based on data about the value of the National Weather Service and weather forecasting.

Forecasting Methods

This chapter will focus on weather forecasting. The book discusses climate forecasting later. The focus here will be on forecasting methods and tools that forecasters use to put together their forecast. Weather forecasting has its roots in folklore. Beginning with folklore will help demonstrate the difference between scientific forecasting and non-scientific forecasting. Some folklore sayings are based on observations, testable, and therefore scientific. Some may not work well, but modern forecasts are not perfect either.

Scientific laws, theories, and principles should be repeatable. However, applying them to weather forecasts may not be perfect because of the complexity of the system forecasted. For example, you know that a tree will fall if you cut it due to the law of gravity. However, which way it falls depends on a number of other factors that are difficult to predict. Including all the important factors may still not create a perfect forecast. However, including as many factors as possible to create the best possible forecast is part of the science of weather forecasting.

---

[1] Lazo, J. K., R. E. Morss, and J. Demuth, 2009: 300 billion served: Sources, perceptions, uses, and values of weather forecasts. Bull. Amer. Meteor. Soc., 90, 785–798.

The invention of weather instruments such as Galileo Galilei's thermoscope in 1593 and Evangelista Torricelli's mercury barometer in 1643 allowed observations of various weather parameters. These observations were regularly recorded in the 18th century. However, it was not until the invention of the telegraph in 1837 by Samuel Morse that a network of observations could be established. Once scientists moved past folklore, an international effort to gather data began in the late 19th century. Several countries created weather services in the 1860s and 1870s. Ultimately, the international community established the first International Meteorological Organization in 1880 to organize these efforts. Armed with this data, forecasters were able to pick out patterns, which led to the earliest instrument-based weather forecasting methods. However, the complexity of the atmosphere hampered these efforts. Each weather event is different and forecasting by weather patterns had limited accuracy and future range.

Not until a mathematical technique, applied by Lewis F. Richardson, to calculate the weather was operational, that accuracy began to improve rapidly. Using a large set of weather observations made available for World War I in 1910, he made the first mathematical **weather model** forecast. However, this technique did not become plausible until computers became powerful enough in the 1950s. Mathematical weather forecasting now forms the basis for all modern weather forecasts.

Folklore Forecasting

A groundhog in the U.S. and a badger in Germany make some of the most well-known folklore forecasts. In the U.S., the most famous groundhog is Punxsutawney Phil who on February 2 of each year emerges from hibernation to prognosticate the arrival of spring. The folklore is that if the groundhog emerges and sees its shadow, because the sky is clear, we will receive six more weeks of winter. If it does not see its shadow, then spring is near. Groundhog Day has its roots in the Pagan and Christian celebration of Candlemas where the folklore is that we should expect a prolonged winter if it is clear on this day. It is unclear where this prediction applies since different areas may experience an early spring or long winter within the same year. In fact, in Punxsutawney, PA, the prediction does not show any forecasting skill.

In the case of Groundhog Day, the folklore has no basis in observation or principle and therefore no basis in science. The correlation between the clearness of the sky on a single day does not determine the weather for the next 6 weeks. There are, however, some folklore that are based on observations and therefore based on science. In fact, we now know the principles behind these folklore sayings.

One popular mariner folklore saying is, "Red sky at night, sailors delight; red sky in morning sailors take warning." Observations by mariners is that the time of day of the redness of the sky portend the weather, is the basis for this saying. Although this saying does not always apply, it does have some predictive skill and is based on scientific principles. Mariners' general experience is the source of this saying, which by itself is not scientific. Planning and carrying out an investigation is a scientific practice needed to determine if this folklore is valid. Mariners would need to set up an experiment to determine the number of times the redness of the sky determined some objective measure of the type of weather produced. However, the folklore is measurable and therefore an experiment can be developed to test this hypothesis.

If someone developed such an experiment, it would probably show that the saying is true more often than not. The principle behind the folklore is that a red sky at night can happen if the horizon is clear in the west where the sun sets. The sun's filtered rays would shine scattered red sunset light on clouds further east. Remember that air molecules selectively scatter the short visible wavelengths (cf. Chapter 4). The filtered transmitted light that scatters off clouds further east makes the sky red. Any clouds in the sky are to the east and moving away and clear skies are moving in toward the observer in the midlatitudes. Therefore, any storm clouds would be leaving the area and you can "take delight" if you are a sailor. If the sky were red in the morning when the sun is in the eastern sky, then the red filtered sunlight would illuminate clouds further west (Figure 9.1). These clouds would be moving toward the observer. Of course, this folklore only holds true in the midlatitudes where the prevailing winds are from the west.

© Maria Onoper/Shutterstock.com

Figure 9.1 Sunrise over the sea shown reddening dust and clouds further west.

There are a number of other valid scientific folklore sayings such as, "If a ring forms around the moon, 'Twill rain or snow soon". This saying is also based on observation and scientific principles. The ring is the halo formed in cirrostratus clouds, which form ahead of warm fronts. Nonetheless, people want more detail in their forecasts like temperature, winds, precipitation amounts, etc. For those details, weather forecasting needs to employ more observations.

Persistence and Climatological Methods

Two simple forecasting methods do not require much knowledge of weather principles but does require observations. The simplest is the persistence method. It works by forecasting the same weather in the future as is currently experienced. For example, if today's high and low temperatures are 20 °C (68 °F) and 10 °C (50 °F), respectively, then you would predict the same high and low temperatures tomorrow. This method works fairly well in the tropics and in the middle of a large air mass. However, it does not work well in areas and times of changeable weather.

The climatological forecast is similarly simple but requires more data. In this case, the climatological means for an area are used as a basis for a weather forecast. For example, if tomorrow your forecast area has a mean high of 25 °C (77 °F) and a mean low 15 °C (59 °F), then that is what you would forecast for tomorrow. This method works well when the weather is unvarying and is correct within about 3.3 °C (6 °F) most of the time. Nonetheless, most people want a more precise forecast, especially for days that will be far different from normal. They also want precipitation, wind, and sky cover, which varies much more.

These two techniques may seem so simple that they cannot possibly have any use, but they are used as a reference to determine forecast skill. Forecasts have skill if they can routinely beat a climatological forecast. Skill must be verified for all time ranges of a forecast. Skill, in this case, means that the users of these forecasts are receiving value out of them. The National Weather Service forecasters are providing more accurate forecasts than simply using climatology to make a forecast beyond seven days. In fact, seven-day forecasts were as accurate in 2018 as three-day forecasts were 30 years earlier (Figure 9.2).

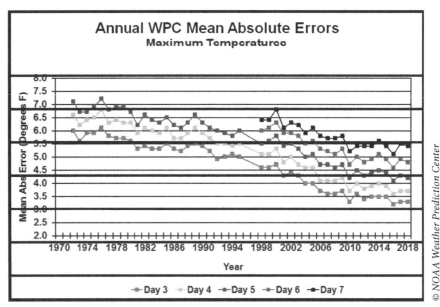

Figure 9.2 Forecast error for daily maximum temperatures in °F shown for 3-7 day forecasts from 1972-2018.

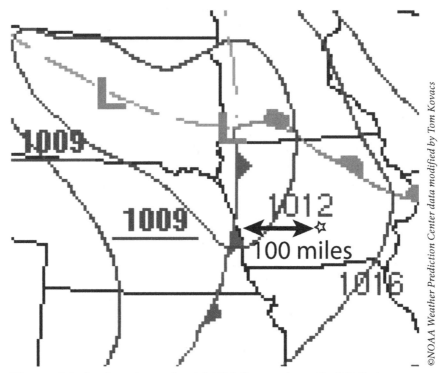

Figure 9.3 Surface fronts for 15 UTC September 12, 2019 showing a cold front that is 100 miles from Des Moines, IA (star) and moving in its direction.

Steady State (or Trend) and Analog Forecast Methods

A **trend forecast** is based on the assumption that weather systems will not develop or change movement speed. This assumption is called the **steady-state** assumption and sometimes this forecasting method is called the steady-state method. For example, if a front were moving at a constant speed, a surface weather map can be used to make a forecast based on the movement of air masses. For example, in Figure 9.3, Des Moines,

IA is located 160 km (100 miles), east of a cold front that is moving toward Des Moines at 40 km/hr (25 miles/hr). A steady-state forecast would conclude that the weather would become colder in Des Moines in about 160 km divided by 40 km/hr or 4 hours. In fact, the weather found 40 km/hr × 24 hr = 960 km (600 miles) behind the cold front will likely be Des Moines' weather 24 hours from now.

Trend forecasts are still used in operational weather forecasts in the very short term (<6 hours). Beyond six hours, weather systems develop to the point that the trend forecast loses skill. Once international weather networks regularly provided surface and upper air data, weather forecasters used various types of analog methods to forecast the weather. The analog method uses the forecasters' experience of spotting patterns they have seen before. For example, forecasters noticed that, in winter, stations south of the track of a midlatitude cyclone received mostly liquid precipitation while stations north of it received mostly frozen precipitation.

One often-used analog method is known as forecasting by weather types. Forecasting, by weather types, used a large number of cases to distill the atmosphere into several types. A forecaster then recognizes a general pattern of pressure and fronts and assign the atmosphere a type. The type would guide the forecaster to make a forecast for the next five days. Of course, the atmosphere is much more complex than a small number of types. Forecasts had limited skill beyond a few days into the future with this method.

Despite their shortcomings, the analog method is still used today. For example, forecasters have a number of competing computer products available to them to guide their forecasts. These products may not all agree, and it is up to the forecaster to determine when to favor a certain product. In addition, forecasters must know how to adjust a forecast based upon how these products handled past situations. Longer-term forecasts called outlooks still use analog seasons to guide seasonal forecasts. Chapter 12 discusses these outlooks.

Weather Forecasting Models

In the early twentieth century, weather forecasters noted that other sciences were able to predict things like the motions of planets to great precision. These sciences had data of initial conditions (e.g., locations, velocities, etc.) and applied the physical laws to calculate their changes. Up to this point, weather forecasters were simply looking at trends and recognizing patterns. They were aware of the same physical laws, but they had not attempted to use initial conditions and the laws to calculate the change in the weather.

Lewis F. Richardson, a mathematician, made the first attempt to calculate changes in initial weather parameters using physical laws (e.g. Law of Conservation of Energy and Mass, Laws of Thermodynamics, Newton's Laws of motion, etc.). He calculated the change in the surface pressure for a couple of points over Europe on May 20, 1910. A large amount of upper-air data was available on that day in Europe, which along with the surface data gave him the initial condition data he needed. He also developed a technique to use the equations from the physical laws to predict a future state of the atmosphere. He performed the calculations by hand, which took over six weeks! Nevertheless, besides also being grossly inaccurate, the calculation laid the groundwork for one of the most important tools used in weather forecasting: the weather forecasting model.

It was not until computers became powerful enough to do these calculations faster that research on weather models matured. Operational weather models began in the 1950s and replaced forecasting by weather types as the primary forecasting guidance in the 1960s. Global Climate Models began in the 1960s. The first regional (non-global) weather

Using Mathematics and Computational Thinking

Mathematics is central to a deep understanding of how science is practiced. Mathematics allows a numeric representation of weather parameters, symbolic representation of weather processes, and calculations of future change. Computational tools allow for a much finer pattern recognition than any human can perform. For example, averaging can pull out a signal from noise. That signal can be an upward trend such as shown in Chapter 2 for global mean temperatures. It can also be a repeating pattern or relationship such as the relationship of wind speed and pressure gradient established in Chapter 5. Mathematical representation of waves or cycles can be used to pull out a repeating pattern in long-term climate data (cf. Chapter 15). Mathematics also serves as a communication tool to scientists. It can precisely express patterns, uncertainties, magnitudes, and probabilities that can be used to make decisions and identify new concepts. For this reason, mathematics is often considered the language of science.

The next two chapters will show how mathematics and computational tools are used to simulate the atmosphere to make mathematical forecasts. Computers allow more computations in one second than every human being on Earth can make in several days. This speed combined with computational tools to convert physical laws to equations allow computers to consider weather processes over several days better than any human. However, mathematical weather forecast models are not perfect and it is important to be aware of computational weaknesses. Nonetheless, the development of weather models elevated weather forecasting from pattern recognition to intentionally including physical laws and using them to compute change. Today, weather models are the primary forecasting tool allowing us to forecast the weather with skill out to more than seven days. Mathematics also allows us to calculate forecasting skill that counters the prevailing opinion that meteorologists are always wrong.

models developed in the 1970s. Further development in weather models continued to increase forecast accuracy. Forecast temperatures three days into the future, began showing skill in the 1970s and seven days into the future began showing skill in the 1st decade of the 2000s (Figure 9.2).

Weather model output does not directly relate to the surface conditions. The increased complexity of the Earth's surface and the turbulence associated with the planetary boundary layer made extrapolating model data to the surface difficult. Statistical methods began transferring the output of weather models to specific stations the 1970s. Called Model Output Statistics (MOS), these used the past performance of models and the actual surface conditions to make a statistical forecast from the model output.

The next chapter provides detail on the weather forecast model method. It is there that it will become clear that several approaches are available to model the highly complex atmosphere. In the 1990s, meteorologists realized that they could run multiple different models to analyze the spread of model forecasts. This technique is known as ensemble forecasting. Ensemble forecast techniques also include running a single model with slightly different inputs to test uncertainties within the model. Ensemble forecasting gives the meteorologist a way to quantify how well a model or ensemble of models can handle an atmospheric situation. Because forecasters use weather models as guidance, forecasters now had an idea of how much to trust the model guidance.

Weather models have become the main forecast guidance because they can take into account much more than an individual forecaster. Forecasters still add skill by using the analog forecast method. For example, they are aware of the situations and weaknesses that cause individual weather models to fail. Furthermore, current operational weather models have trouble forecasting events that are strongly dependent on small-scale (<10 km) factors. Many severe weather events fall into this category. Chapters 13 and 14 discuss the special case of severe weather forecasting. Still, many tools besides weather models help the forecaster in these situations. The special applications of these tools are discussed next.

Forecasting Tools

Weather models are not the only forecasting tool employed by modern weather forecasters. Radar, satellite, weather stations, and weather balloons are important sources of data for modern weather forecasts. Currently, this data serves as the initial weather conditions to run weather models. They also support weather analysis for making short-term forecasts that impact decisions made by the public for comfort and safety. Each of these tools have applications for severe weather, air quality, and even climate change. The rest of this chapter discusses how forecasters currently use these tools in ways not related to weather models.

These tools provide weather data in real-time. Features in time and space are resolved well below what weather models can support. For this reason, critical severe weather warnings are based on these tools. Nonetheless, forecasters may not be able to contend with the volume of data in the short time necessary in life-saving situations. Luckily, synthesizing this data and alerting forecasters of potentially life-threatening situations utilizes computer software. Furthermore, much of this information is more technical than most of the public is accustomed to receiving. Therefore, a discussion of technology used to present this information in a timely and digestible manner is also discussed.

Radar

Conventional Doppler radar, which began widespread use in the 1980s replacing non-Doppler radars, can run in two modes providing reflectivity and wind velocity. A maximum radius of 290 km (180 miles) is available for each of these parameters. Multiple Doppler radars in reflectivity mode provide a much larger image of precipitating weather systems in the U.S. (Figure 9.4). Doppler radars in velocity mode can scan at different elevations. Where radars overlap, it is possible to get the horizontal and vertical velocities. Despite the limited data parameters, much can be determined from radar alone and in combination with other data.

Radar shows the location of precipitation and, by looping images together, the direction the precipitation is traveling. Figure 9.4 shows that an individual thunderstorm cell moved 100 km to the east-northeast in 80 minutes, which is 75 km/hr (47 miles/hr). Individual high-reflectivity cells are typically individual cumulonimbus clouds. From this loop, one could also determine whether individual cells are strengthening or weakening. In the case of the cell highlighted in Figure 9.4 the reflectivity weakened over that time (comparison image not shown). The dozens of radars in this figure show that these individual cells are part of a line of thunderstorms that extends across Michigan and Indiana. Looping the image shows that the line itself was moving east at 40 km/hr (25 miles/hr) and the individual cells were moving northeast along the line. The line was part of a cold

Figure 9.4 US radar composite of dozens of radar images in reflectivity mode for 1308 UTC September 13, 2019. The black arrow (100 km in length) is the distance traveled by the thunderstorm cell (orange blob at the end of the arrow) in 80 minutes).

front extending from a low-pressure center in Canada. Knowing these speeds help forecasters know the timing and location of the worst weather impacts.

It is not possible to know precipitation type with radar alone. Radar on the Internet or television often shows precipitation type. However, that information comes from combining radar, weather station, weather balloon, and satellite data. Computer programming software that TV stations or weather apps possess or purchase from vendors produce much of those data enhanced products. The National Weather Service uses a software package called **AWIPS (Advanced Weather Interactive Processing System)** discussed later.

Precipitation rate can be determined from radar data. You can obtain one hour and storm total rates at www.weather.gov by clicking on radar and clicking inside the national map. Precipitation rate comes largely from reflectivity. However, special computer algorithms determine the type of precipitation and clouds to estimate the rainfall rate and rainfall accumulation from the reflectivity. The special algorithms take into account that snow does not have as large of a reflectivity as rain and melting snow has a much larger reflectivity than rain. Figure 9.5 shows the precipitation amount produced for the one-hour period starting at the time of Figure 9.4 along with the button to click

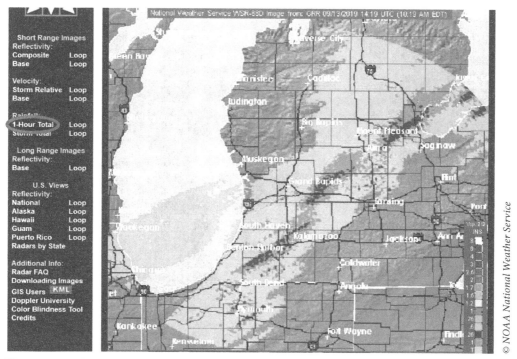

Figure 9.5 Shown is the Grand Rapids radar estimated 1-hour total precipitation for the 1-hour period after the radar image in Figure 9.4. To get this image, press the button circled in red.

to get this data. Using the legend in the lower right, the thunderstorm cell highlighted in Figure 9.4, east of Grand Rapids, produced a quarter inch per hour (moderate intensity) precipitation rates.

During severe weather, patterns on Doppler radar can determine the type of severe weather produced. First, reflectivity values > 65 dBZ (purple on most radar images) are likely to contain hail because no other precipitation creates this much reflectivity. Increasingly, depolarizing Doppler radars, which can also pick out hail with more precision, are being used. Dual polarization Doppler radar receives information on other parameters such as the differential amount of reflectivity from perpendicularly polarized pulses. Because non-spherical objects reflect electromagnetic waves differently in perpendicular direction and hail are non-spherical, distinguishing hail from spherical raindrops is easy with this radar.

A radar bow echo indicates strong straight-line winds (Figure 9.6) in a line of thunderstorms. The shape of bow echoes resembles a hunter's bow and occur where the thunderstorms' outflow has been constrained in some way. The center of the bow is where the highest winds are located, because this is where the thunderstorm cells are moving ahead at a much faster rate than the rest of the line.

Doppler radar cannot resolve tornadoes themselves, but patterns can point to the potential for a tornado. In reflectivity mode, the mesocyclone of a strongly rotating cumulonimbus cloud known as a supercell produces a hook echo on the radar image (Figure 9.7). The heaviest precipitation wraps counterclockwise around the rotating updraft producing the characteristic hook. The updraft itself is usually devoid of precipitation so the inside of the hook is called a bounded weak echo region. It is within this hook that a tornado would be located, if present.

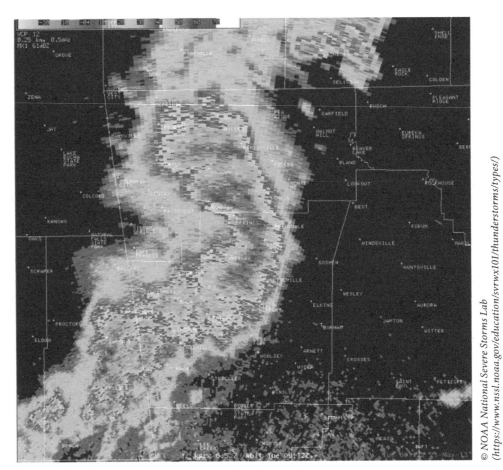

Figure 9.6 Doppler radar image of a bow echo.

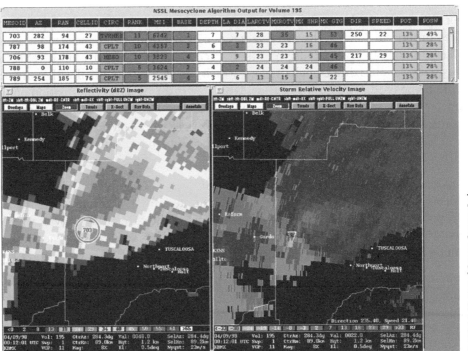

Figure 9.7 Doppler radar image of a hook echo in the circle in reflectivity mode (left) and a tornado vortex signature (TVS) in velocity mode (right) is shown.

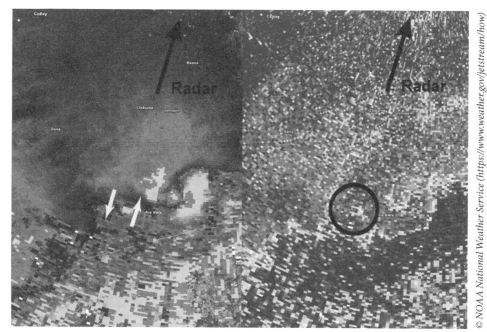

© NOAA National Weather Service (https://www.weather.gov/jetstream/how)

Figure 9.8 Doppler radar is shown in velocity mode (left) and depolarization mode (right) during an active tornado. The radar is located off the image in the direction of the black arrows. On the left, red is outbound and green is inbound wind with the yellow arrows showing a tornado vortex signature (TVS). On the right blue indicates non-spherical objects and red indicates spherical objects. The circled blue dot is collocated with the TVS and shows debris lofted by a tornado.

A couplet of winds in opposite directions known as a tornado vortex signature (TVS) appears in thunderstorms with strong rotations (Figure 9.7 right and Figure 9.8 left). The TVS is a much stronger indication of a funnel cloud though not necessarily a tornado, which is a funnel cloud that makes contact with the ground. A debris ball causes the end of the hook to become more circular is an even stronger indication that a tornado is on the ground. Debris lofted around the tornado causes the debris ball. Dual polarization radar provides additional evidence that a tornado is on the ground because debris is non-spherical (Figure 9.8 right).

Satellite

The first satellite images for weather forecasting started in the 1960s. NOAA and NASA polar- and geostationary-orbiting satellites have instruments that provide weather data for forecasting. The geostationary orbiting satellites are the satellites that most of the public and weather forecasters experience directly. Beginning in the 1970s, the first in the Geostationary Orbiting Environmental Satellites (GOES) began observing. It observed with a 0.9 km resolution in the visible and 9 km resolution in the infrared every 20 minutes. The most recent GOES satellites observe with a 0.5 km resolution in the visible and 2 km resolution. The polar orbiting satellites have instruments that provide data used in weather models and for analysis in air quality, climate, hydrological, and space weather forecasting.

Among the polar orbiting satellites, managed or co-managed by NOAA are JASON-3, Suomi-NPP, NOAA-20, and Cosmic-2. JASON-3 primarily measures sea-level height, but also identifies warm pools of water in the ocean for tropical cyclone intensity and

Jason-3

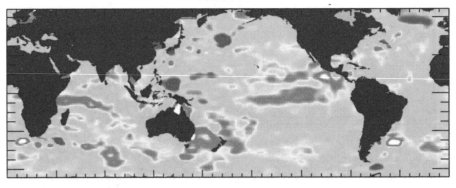

Jason-2

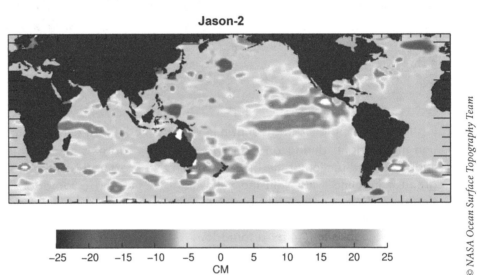

© NASA Ocean Surface Topography Team

Figure 9.9 JASON-2 and JASON-3 sea surface height anomalies (cm) are shown averaged over February 12-22, 2016. Higher height anomalies (red) indicate warmer than average water and lower height anomalies (purple) indicate colder than average sea surface temperatures. El Nino is evident as the red blob in the eastern equatorial Pacific Ocean, west of the Americas.

El Nino/La Nina forecasting. Because warmer water expands, height anomalies in the eastern equatorial Pacific are useful to monitor El Nino/La Nina (Figure 9.9). Suomi-NPP and NOAA-20 have instruments that observe sea-surface temperature, temperature and humidity profiles, and ozone measurements (Figure 9.10). COSMIC-2 are a constellation of satellites that provide data for weather models, climate monitoring, and space weather.

NASA manages the Global Precipitation Measurement (GPM) satellite, which provides global observations of snow and rain. The GPM core observatory consists mainly of the GPM Microwave imager and the Dual frequency Polarization Radar (DPR). It serves as a global radar in space. The combination of the two instruments along with data from other satellites that makes up GPM allows precipitation typing and intensity. Figure 9.11 shows one of the strengths of this satellite: the ability to observe precipitation over the ocean where surface radars often miss.

The geostationary satellites, GOES 16 (GOES East) and GOES 17 (GOES West), provide 16 imaged wavelength bands in the visible and infrared part of the EM spectrum. They also provide a lightning mapper and an instrument that monitors space weather. Images and loops from all bands can be found at https://www.star.nesdis.noaa.gov/goes/ and

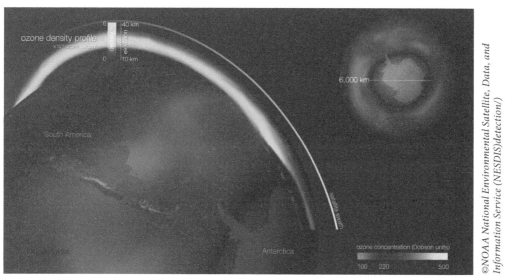

Figure 9.10 Ozone density profile from Suomi-NPP satellite (green-scale) and total vertical ozone concentration (anomalously low in red) from numerous other satellites.

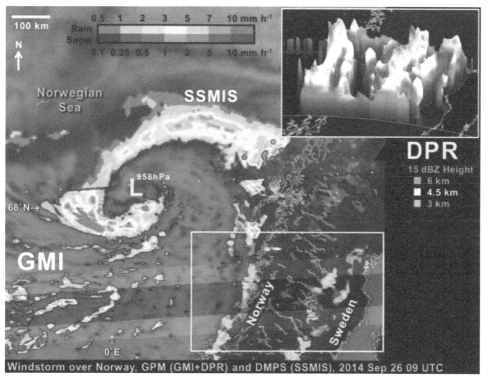

Figure 9.11 NASA GPM core observatory image (GPM microwave Imager (GMI) and Dual frequency polarization radar (DPR)) of a midlatitude cyclone with a mixture of precipitation approaching the coast of Norway on 09 UTC September 26, 2009.

https://rammb-slider.cira.colostate.edu. The satellites are also capable of obtaining 30 second (compared to five minutes) higher resolution (mesoscale) image loops for requested weather of interest.

The 16 imaged wavelength bands are sensitive to specific atmospheric constituents helpful to weather forecasting. For example, the GeoColor product uses the first three

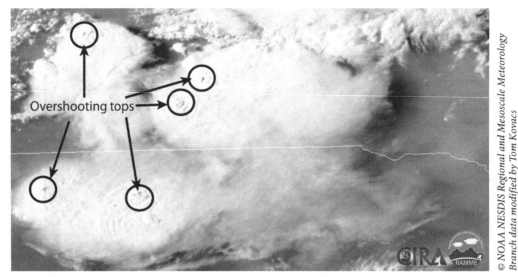

© NOAA NESDIS Regional and Mesoscale Meteorology
Branch data modified by Tom Kovacs

Figure 9.12 GOES East image on 2347 UTC August 26, 2017 is shown with thunderstorm overshooting tops circled on the border of South Dakota and Nebraska (white line).

bands to show what you see from space during daytime. At night, the GeoColor product uses band 7 for lower liquid water clouds shaded blue and band 13 for high ice clouds given a grayscale (not shown). A static night-lights background image from another satellite accompanies the night image. GeoColor product loops provides a forecaster information about cloud cover and movement, particularly for lower clouds. Lower clouds have more water and appear brighter in the visible. In addition, because thunderstorms typically form in the late afternoon when the sun angle is low, strong thunderstorms will produce **overshooting tops** that cast a shadow on the anvil cloud below (Figure 9.12). These overshooting tops help identify thunderstorms that may be severe.

The water vapor wavelength bands (bands 8-10) are helpful in identifying cyclones (low-pressure systems) and anticyclones (high-pressure systems). These bands are sensitive to atmospheric water vapor in the upper (band 8), middle (band 9), and lower (band 10) troposphere. It can identify the dry conveyor belt in midlatitude cyclones and dry air in the tropics surrounding a tropical system (which would weaken it). Band 10 is useful to identify the source of water vapor from low-level moisture jets in midlatitude cyclones. Figure 9.13 (top) shows a developing midlatitude cyclone with strong water vapor transport (blue) during development. Twelve hours later Figure 9.13 (bottom) shows the water vapor source is cutoff by an increasingly strong dry conveyor belt (brown).

Weather Maps

There are a number of weather maps important to forecasting. Probably the most important is the surface map because it provides the conditions where we live, on the Earth's surface. The high- and low-pressure systems and fronts are some of the most important features on a surface map for forecasting. These features show the location of air mass boundaries, the direction they are moving, and whether to expect rainy and changeable weather (i.e. low pressure) or dry and fair weather (i.e. high pressure). With the station models, you also have the surface observations: temperature, humidity, sky cover, winds, and any significant weather such as rain, snow, storms, etc.

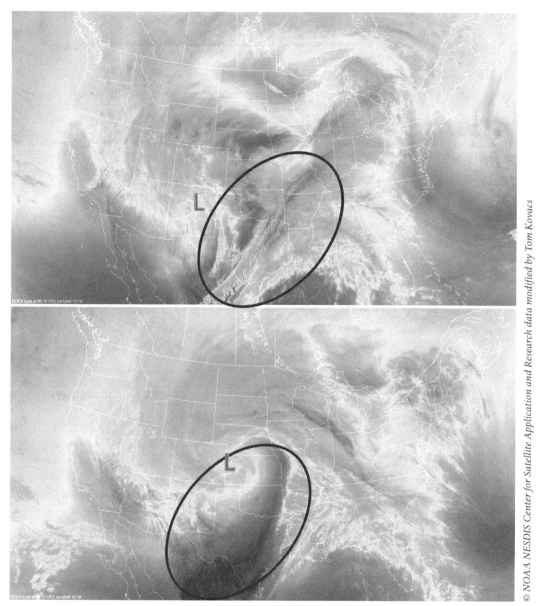

Figure 9.13 GOES lower tropospheric water vapor image (band 10) on 445 UTC March 13, 2019 (top) and 1645 UTC March 13, 2019 is shown with surface low-pressure center indicated. Darker blue shading represents increasingly high water vapor content while darker brown shading represents increasingly low water vapor content.

Briefly, the standard upper air maps have the following features important to forecasting (see Figure 9.14 as a reference):

1000 mb map –The main purpose of the 1000 mb map is to calculate the difference between the height of the 500 mb map and the 1000 mb map. This difference gives the 1000-500 mb thickness parameter. These thicknesses are an excellent indicator of the temperature of an air mass. Small thickness means a cold air mass and large thickness means a warm air mass. A sharp gradient in thickness values are good for identifying surface fronts. The 5400 m thickness line is also a good reference thickness for identifying the rain/snow line in winter.

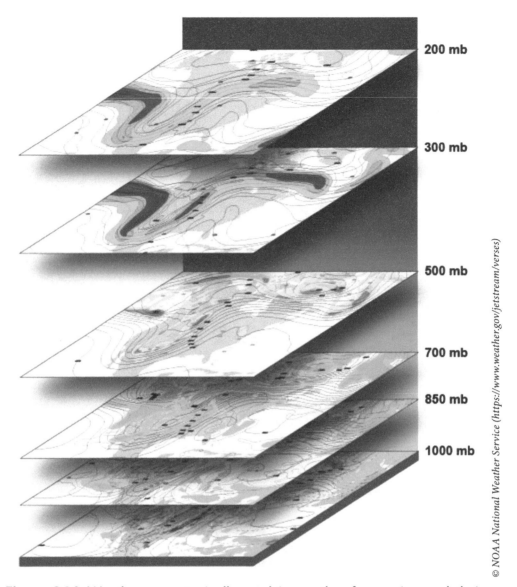

200 mb

300 mb

500 mb

700 mb

850 mb

1000 mb

Figure 9.14 Weather maps typically used in weather forecasting and their relative locations in the vertical are illustrated.

850 mb map – 850 mb is about 1400 m above sea level and is typically the first level above the planetary boundary layer. This layer is the lowest layer where most of the temperature changes from day to night no longer occur. Low clouds form and precipitation falls from clouds at this level. A quick reference for whether these clouds will produce rain or snow is the temperature at this pressure-level.

700 mb map –700 mb is the top of the lower troposphere and the low clouds. Humidity is important at this layer. High humidity extending from the surface can mean that a surface system has ample moisture available to produce heavy rain. For forecasting thunderstorms and severe weather, dryness here can mean that water in a developing cumulonimbus cloud will partially evaporate when it reaches this level. The evaporation cools the air and makes the rising air more buoyant. Chapter 14 discusses how cooling the air well above the Earth's surface can help thunderstorms to grow. Shortwaves are also best observed at this level. Shortwaves provide energy to strengthen longwave troughs.

500 mb map –Because 500 mb is half of the surface pressure, this level is the center of mass of the atmosphere. Winds at this level, which blow parallel to the height contours, move large weather systems such as air masses, fronts, tropical cyclones, and low- or high-pressure systems. Therefore, looking at the height contours at this level gives you a map of how large weather systems move.

200 and 300 mb map –Winds, troughs, ridges, jet streams, and jet streaks are most important at these levels. The horizontal location relative to troughs and ridges greatly influences the development of surface low- and high-pressure systems. Areas of upper-air divergence are found downstream of troughs. Low-pressure centers form and develop under upper-air divergence. Jet streaks have a pattern of upper air convergence and divergence. Divergence is found in the right entrance and left exit regions of the jet streak. The 300 mb map is better for identifying the polar jet whereas the 200 mb map is better for identifying the higher subtropical jet.

300 and 500 mb hemispheric map – Hemispheric maps are helpful for longer term forecasting and forecasting along the west coast. The 500 mb shows if there are any blocking patterns that may cause the long wave pattern to stall creating persistence in the type of weather (e.g. warmer or dryer than normal) experienced in a region. The number of longwave wavelengths around the world guides longer wave forecasts such as was shown in Chapter 7 (cf. Figure 7.12). The 300 mb hemispheric map helps to see the jet stream winds over the Pacific to help in forecasting coastal weather.

Skew-T Diagrams

Skew-T diagrams of weather balloon data contain a wealth of information representative of a region. With the vertical profile of temperature, dewpoint temperature, and winds a forecaster is given valuable information in relation to cloud height, maximum and minimum temperatures, precipitation type, stability, wind shear, air quality, and severe storm potential. This unit will discuss many, but not all of these applications. Weather balloons are released twice a day (0 Z and 12 Z), but special releases are made for areas of interest. Weather models can also calculate future Skew T diagrams (https://mag.ncep.noaa.gov/).

Computing the lifting condensation level (LCL) from Skew-T diagrams was discussed in Chapter 5. This value provides the height of low-level cloud bases for air rising from the surface. In order for air to rise to this height a front, topographical barrier, or an area of surface convergence would have to force it to this height. In addition, on summer afternoons, the sun is often strong enough to give the surface air enough buoyancy that it makes it to the LCL to produce cumulus clouds. Air then rises moist adiabatically in the cumulus cloud.

Following a dry adiabat from the 850 mb, air temperature in a morning sounding down to the surface is a good forecast of the surface high temperature (Figure 9.15). Daytime heating, on clear days, typically warms the layer between 850 mb and the surface to be dry adiabatic.

The type of precipitation largely depends on the temperature profile. As discussed in Chapter 6, rain forms in all above-freezing clouds and in below-freezing clouds that have no ice crystals. Expect ice crystals to be present where the air is nearly saturated and the coldest temperatures in the cloud are below –10 °C (14 °F). However, supercooled water drops are also likely until the temperature is below –20 °C (–4 °F). To forecast precipitation type, any level with saturated air and the temperatures below this level must be considered.

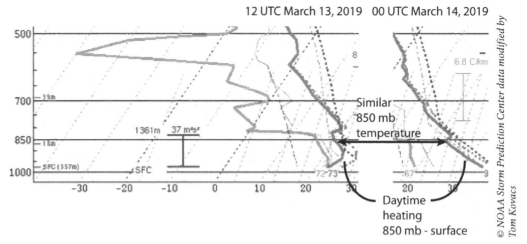

© NOAA Storm Prediction Center data modified by Tom Kovacs

Figure 9.15 Skew-T diagram for Oklahoma City, OK with observed dewpoint temperature (green) and air temperature (red) shown for 12 UTC March 13, 2019 (left) and at 00 UTC March 14, 2019 (right). Heating on clear days raises the temperature from 850 mb to the surface causing the environmental lapse rate to be dry adiabatic (i.e. parallel to the dry adiabats – yellow lines).

The vertical temperature profile helps identify stability, which is useful in air quality and severe weather forecasting. For air quality forecasting, the stability of the atmosphere determines how much clean air is available to mix with polluted air. When polluted air is injected into a stable layer, very little mixing occurs, and the concentration of the pollutants can become large and cause health problems. If you ever experienced a firework display at night during stable conditions the smoke appears to not move or dissipate. Unstable layers allow polluted and clean air to mix. However, the amount of clean air this pollution can mix with depends on stable layers above and below the unstable layer. For example, during the evening the air in the lowest 100 m becomes very stable on clear nights with little wind. In order to rise above the nighttime stable layer, which is often about 100 m in height, industrial stacks are tall to mix its polluted emissions above this stable layer.

A number of severe thunderstorm indices are calculated from morning soundings to alert forecasters of locations that are likely to experience severe weather. Two of the most used indices are the lifted index and the Showalter index. They are similar in that both are a measure of the difference between the actual temperature at 500 mb and the temperature of an air parcel that rose from the surface to 500 mb. The difference between the indices is in how the surface temperature is calculated. The **lifted index** uses the actual surface temperature whereas the **Showalter index** uses the dry adiabat that runs through the 850 mb temperature (cf. Figure 9.15). Therefore, the Showalter index uses a forecasted surface high temperature for a clear day while the lifted index uses the actual surface temperature. In practice, the Storm Prediction Lab will compute the lifted Index for the current and calculated maximum surface temperature along with other important starting points (Figure 9.16 in table). They also plot an air parcel that starts at the modeled high temperature from the surface to the top of the troposphere (Figure 9.17 dotted maroon line). Higher negative indices (i.e. the higher the parcel temperature at 500 mb is than the actual temperature at that level) indicate a better chance of cumulonimbus clouds and thunderstorms.

The height the cumulonimbus cloud reach and the velocity that air rises in the cumulonimbus cloud depends on the **Convective Available Potential Energy (CAPE)**.

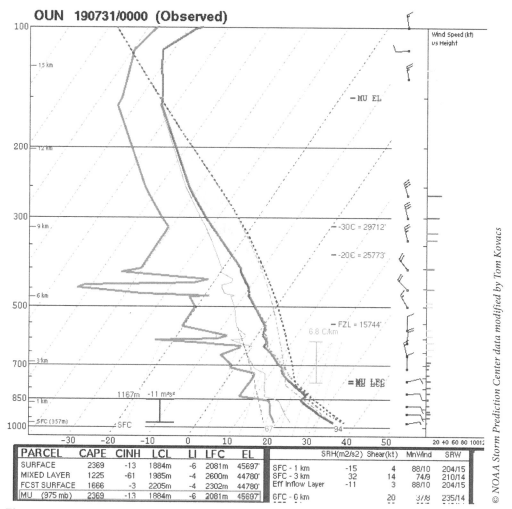

PARCEL	CAPE	CINH	LCL	LI	LFC	EL		SRH(m2/s2)	Shear(kt)	MnWind	SRW
SURFACE	2369	-13	1884m	-6	2081m	45697'	SFC - 1 km	-15	4	88/10	204/15
MIXED LAYER	1225	-61	1985m	-4	2600m	44780'	SFC - 3 km	32	14	74/9	210/14
FCST SURFACE	1666	-3	2205m	-4	2302m	44780'	Eff Inflow Layer	-11	3	88/10	204/15
MU (975 mb)	2369	-13	1884m	-6	2081m	45697'	SFC - 6 km		20	3/8	235/14

Figure 9.16 Skew-T diagram for Oklahoma City at 00 UTC March 14, 2019 (same as right side of Figure 9.15) is shown. Dewpoint temperature (green) and air temperature (red) are plotted along with the calculated most unstable parcel (maroon dotted line). The blue shading represents the area that the moist unstable parcel is buoyant or above the observed temperature. The blue shaded area represents CAPE and its value is calculated in the table (orange box) under CAPE (units are J/kg).

CAPE is a cumulative measure of the amount rising air is warmer than the environment throughout the troposphere. It is essentially a measure of the buoyant area created on a Skew-T diagram (Figure 9.16 blue shading). The width of this area is the difference in the temperature of the rising air and the environmental air. The depth of this area is the difference in height between the top and bottom of this buoyant layer. Air rises faster with higher CAPE.

Vertical wind shear can also be calculated on the Skew-T diagram. Vertical wind shear is the difference between the wind speeds at two different levels. The most used wind shear values are calculated between the surface and 1, 3, and 6 km (Figure 9.16 in table). Wind shear is the difference between the winds at 1, 3, and 6 km from the winds at the surface. As will be discussed in Chapter 14, thunderstorms become severe when the wind shear between the surface and 6 km is large. Wind shear between the surface and 1 km and the surface and 3 km is more important for tornadic thunderstorms.

Wet Bulb Temperature and Precipitation Type

The figures in Chapter 6 show the different temperature profiles for snow, sleet, and freezing rain. However, precipitation falling from clouds into dry air can melt, sublimate, or evaporate partially or completely. All these phase changes require energy to be absorbed from the air, lowering the temperature below the cloud (Figure 9.17). Sublimation and evaporation also add to the amount of water vapor in the air, which raises the dewpoint temperature (melting does not). The lowered temperature and raised dewpoint causes the temperature below the cloud to approach the wet-bulb temperature (see Chapter 1). Therefore, when forecasting precipitation type it is important to consider the wet-bulb temperature below the cloud. With enough sublimation, melting and evaporation the air temperature can decrease to the wet-bulb temperature once precipitation begins to fall. This can lead to an initial rainfall turning into a snowstorm.

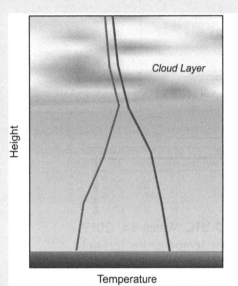 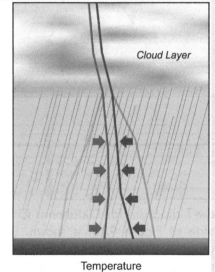

© From A World of Weather: Fundamentals of Meteorology, Sixth Edition by Jon M. Nese and Lee M. Grenci. Copyright © 2017 Jon M. Nese and Lee M. Grenci. Reprinted by permission.

Figure 9.17 Illustration of the effect of precipitation on the temperature (red) and dewpoint temperature (green) profile. The two temperatures approach the wet bulb temperature after precipitation begins.

AWIPS

The National Weather Service (NWS) and other forecasters also need ways to analyze the data, generate products, and get their products out to their customers. When you go to a weather app, watch a weather broadcast, or receive a weather warning you are the forecasters' customer. You are paying for this information usually through taxes in the case of NWS forecasts or through advertisements or subscriptions through apps or cable TV. The main products that forecasters provide is discussed in Chapter 12.

For NWS forecasters the primary analysis and communication software is called the Advanced Weather Interactive Processing System (AWIPS). AWIPS processes data from many sources. It then allows the forecaster to display these products in ways helpful to the forecaster (Figure 9.18). For example, it may be helpful to not only see the current

Figure 9.18 AWIPS terminal shown at the Louisville National Weather Service.

surface map, but also the surface map over the next few hours from computer models. Furthermore, forecasters cannot constantly monitor radar and other data for hail and tornado signatures. However, the system can notify the forecaster when Doppler radar has spotted a tornado vortex signature and provide the direction of movement. Then, forecasters can produce warning boxes for communication to the public. The system also allows forecasters to communicate these boxes directly to warning centers and customers around the U.S.

Broadcasting the Weather

Broadcasting weather information to the public is a multi-billion-dollar industry. Weather information is one of the few scientific products communicated to the public daily. Weather apps must capture the attention of the user and be interesting along with informational. Each weather app spends a lot of money on creating graphics to attract people to use their app much like any other app available.

Weather broadcasts must do the same with a weatherperson that the public trusts and can provide information they can understand. Increasingly, this person is expected to not only broadcast a forecast on television, but also engage with the public on websites and social media. During severe weather, this same person must interrupt television broadcasts to communicate situation and safety information. Weatherpersons risk the ire of the public, but this information may be the only way some people can receive life-saving information. A person that has credentials and can communicate this information in an easily understandable and occasionally entertaining way usually earns trust. TV stations have almost entirely gone to employing meteorologists for this job. The American Meteorological Society (AMS)

© Korey Miracle

Figure 9.19 Kylee Miller, Certified Broadcast Meteorologist presenting the weather. The top picture features the chrome key, also called the green screen. The bottom photo is what the viewer sees on TV. Here you can see her pointing to a specific location with a temperature. The box at the bottom with her name and seal is used at times during the newscast when she is on live TV.

created a certification called the Certified Broadcast Meteorologist (CBM) seal that communicates the credentials of the weatherperson. Only a certified meteorologist with a full college meteorology degree can obtain the AMS seal.

The on-air weatherperson presents a large number of scientific graphics and must explain and point out features of importance. These graphics are displayed with the help of the **Chroma key compositing technique** (aka green screen). The weatherperson appears to stand in front of all the maps they are displaying. In actuality, the weatherperson is standing in front of a green screen (also sometimes a blue screen), which is edited out and replaced with weather maps (Figure 9.19). This is where the weatherperson can see weather images using the monitors (one on either side of green screen) and the front camera. In Figure 9.19 you can see the monitors allow the on-air weather person to see the weather graphics and herself, showing her what the viewing audience sees.

Summary

Forecasting is the result of the scientific method that rests on data and observations and all the experimental work using this data to establish laws, theories, and principles. Folklore forecasting provides examples of the first forecasting, some based on scientific evidence and some not. Scientific weather forecast methods include persistence, climatological, steady state or trend, analog, and weather model forecasting.

The persistence method assumes tomorrow will be similar to today. The climatological method assumes tomorrow will be similar to the average for that date. Both are simplistic but based on data. These methods are accessible to anybody to practice and are used to establish a baseline for determining skill of a professional forecast. The steady state or trend method assumes that large-scale weather features, such as air masses, will move at constant speed and not develop. Forecasters then calculate how far upstream to look for weather conditions on surface weather maps that will move into the forecast area. Forecasters still employ this method on short-term (< 6 hour) forecasts as a baseline. Analog methods use previous forecaster experience to forecast the future based on similarities to past weather situations. Forecasting by weather types is a more formal way of doing this using a large database of scenarios and typing them into a smaller number of forecast results. Weather forecast models were developed to use scientific laws, theories, and principles to calculate future weather changes.

Weather models have limitations particularly in small space and time scales. Other forecasting tools are still used for very localized and short-range forecasts. Radars can alert the public to approaching precipitation and forecasters to severe weather. Satellites can show the public when skies will clear or become overcast and forecasters when El Nino is developing, or weather systems are strengthening. Weather maps provide a wealth of information in cross-sections from the surface to the jet stream level. Each mandatory level (i.e. 1000 mb, 850 mb, 700 mb, 500 mb, 300 mb, and 200 mb) provides data of importance to that level within large-scale weather systems. At one location, Skew-T diagrams provide data at all these levels and are especially used for air quality and severe weather forecasting.

All of this data can be overwhelming and not particularly useful in their raw formats. For this reason, software packages have been developed to provide weather data for specific purposes. Some websites and apps combine radar, weather balloon, and weather model data to provide precipitation intensity and precipitation type in a simple graphical format. Forecasters use software packages to combine multiple data products or to alert them to hazardous weather. Broadcasters use software packages to present complex scientific data to an audience with a large range of scientific background in a short amount of time.

Key Terms

Forecasting

Weather Model

Persistence Method

Climatological Forecast

Forecast Skill

Trend Forecast

Steady State

Analog Method

Forecasting by Weather Types

Model Output Statistics (MOS)

Ensemble Forecasting

AWIPS (Advanced Weather Interactive Processing System)

Dual Polarization Doppler Radar

Radar Bow Echo

Supercell

Hook Echo

Bounded Weak Echo Region

Tornado Vortex Signature (TVS)

Debris Ball

Overshooting Tops

500-1000 mb Thickness

Lifted Index

Showalter Index

Convective Available Potential Energy (CAPE)

Vertical Wind Shear

Chroma key compositing technique

Questions and Problems

1. What is the return on investment (search the internet to calculate) of the government's weather forecasting enterprise based on the numbers provided in this text?

2. How is the mariner's saying, "Red sky at night, sailors delight; red sky in morning sailors take warning" more scientific than the Groundhog Day declaration?

3. For your location, if today's high is 57 F, what would be the correct persistence and climatological forecast for tomorrow? Note: for consistency, take tomorrow as the homework due date.

4. What does a weather forecaster need to do to show that their forecasts have skill?

5. Find a surface map (perhaps 2 maps to get the rate of movement) from one of the links in this textbook at a time that a front is about to move through your location within the next 24 and 48 hours. Use the steady state method to predict the weather 24 and 48 hours after the date and time on the map. Circle the observations on the surface map that you are using to base your forecast.

6. What is the mean absolute error for three-day forecasts of high temperatures in 2018? How much of an improvement is that compared to 1972? What are the most important improvements in forecasters' tools that likely led to this improvement?

7. If you want to know if it is going to rain in the next hour as you prepare to walk across a large college campus, what forecasting tool is best and how would you use it?

8. What is the best evidence of a tornado from looking at radar?

9. What evidence on radar or satellite are there that hail is being produced by a thunderstorm?

10. If you want to know what time cloud cover will dissipate this afternoon, so you can decide when to go to the beach to tan, what forecasting tool is best and how would you use it?

11. If your parents in your home city are under a tornado warning, what forecasting tool can you use to determine if the tornado is heading toward their house? Describe exactly how you would use this tool and what features you are looking for.

12. Provide a one sentence summary of each mandatory level (i.e. 1000, 850, 700, 500, 300, and 250 mb) including one important weather parameter from each map and how it is applied to weather forecasting.

13. Describe how you can use a morning (12 UTC) Skew-T diagram to forecast the surface high temperature in the afternoon on a sunny day.

14. Obtain a Skew-T diagram from a location where the surface temperature is below 50 °F and point to features that you would look at to determine the precipitation type if it were to precipitate that day. Based on this analysis, forecast the precipitation type.

15. Forecasters utilize large amount of data that is continuously being produced. All this data is difficult for weather broadcasters to present to a public without a meteorology degree. What kinds of technologies are used to help digest all this data for forecasters and broadcasters?

16. What weather product would a meteorologist examine to observe the hook echo?

17. If our broadcaster in Figure 9.19 chose to wear a green blouse, what would the viewing audience see on their television and why?

18. Describe several things that a weather broadcaster must do besides standing in front of a television camera and give a public forecast.

Other Resources

https://www.emich.edu/geography-geology/weather for links to useful weather data to go along with this textbook and updates to any broken links in the textbook.

Chapter 10

Weather Forecast Models

Introduction

Weather forecast models have revolutionized weather forecasting. They helped make forecasts of maximum and minimum temperatures, rain probabilities, sky cover and winds highly accurate over a seven-day forecast period. Because of the complexity of the method and the importance of this tool to forecasting, weather forecast models have their own chapter. This chapter will describe the operation of weather forecast models. Chapter 11 describes climate models.

Making of a Weather Forecast Model

In many ways, operating the weather forecast model (hereafter weather model) is a perfect example of the scientific method in action. Weather data, the foundation of the scientific method, is also the foundation of weather modeling. Weather models use the laws of physics to calculate the future weather much like the scientific method uses the laws of physics to make forecasts. In this section, each step of modeling the weather is described separately.

Step 1: Gathering Data

Weather data is extensive and new data sources become available all the time. Different weather models have different data ingested. For example, a regional weather model for North America does not need data from Asia, but a global model does. To get an idea of the vastness of data used in these weather models, this section discusses the data ingested into the Global Forecast System (GFS) model in 2019. The GFS is a global weather model run by the U.S. National Weather Service (NWS).

Computer programs download data from several platforms and various computer servers. The NWS provides both surface data from weather stations and upper-air data through weather balloons. This data has been discussed in previous chapters. Augmenting the surface-based datasets are buoys, commercial ships, lighthouses, offshore platforms, and tide gauges. Augmenting upper-air datasets are commercial aircraft, Doppler radar, SODAR, and wind profilers. A number of satellite-based instruments provide global vertical sounding data including the geostationary network from the NOAA NESDIS (GOES East and West), European EUMETSAT (Meteosat), Japanese (GMS), and India (INSAT). In addition, polar orbiting satellites from NASA (MODIS and GPM), NOAA NESDIS (Suomi NPP, NOAA 20, COSMIC 2, and JASON), U.S. Air Force (GPS network), and European EUMETSAT (METOP) provide data.

Once all this data is downloaded, weather models **assimilate** the data, which means that data is prepared for use in the weather models. For the GFS model, the Global Data Assimilation System (GDAS) operated by the National Center for Environmental Prediction (NCEP) assimilates all the data.

Step 2: Assimilating Data

The second step of operating a weather model is to assimilate all the available data. Models **interpolate** data to a static grid of points on which the future weather is calculated. Future weather is not calculated at the locations the data are observed because there would be too many non-uniformly distributed data points. Each location would not have data from all the data sources either. Therefore, a grid is created to perform the assimilation and calculations. The speed of the computers, amount of data, and the number of calculations largely determines the spacing between grid points. A weather model forecast must be completed well in advance of the forecast period otherwise; it is not of much value. Therefore, **grid point spacing** has limits.

Figure 10.1 shows a fictitious computer model grid to illustrate a realistic distribution of grid points in relation to a map of weather stations. Grid points are uniformly spaced, but are not necessarily collocated with the actual observations. If in Figure 10.1, the grid points are spaced every 10 km then each represents a 10 km × 10 km area and covers a **model domain** of 60 km × 60 km. The grid spacing and domain for this model requires a total of 6 × 6 = 36 grid points.

Dividing the model domain by the area the grid points represents determines the number of grid points that require calculations. As discussed in the previous chapter, the first attempt at a 24-hour forecast for pressure at a single location took a person two years to complete. In order to be relevant the calculation for a 24-hour forecast must take considerably less than 24 hours.

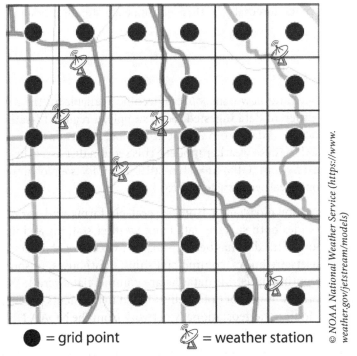

© NOAA National Weather Service (https://www.weather.gov/jetstream/models)

● = grid point   📡 = weather station

Figure 10.1 Demonstration of a distribution of grid points and weather stations projected on a map of a region.

In regards to what features you are trying to include in your simulation, the most important consideration is model resolution. For example, when you are taking a portrait of somebody with your camera the created image contains a number of pixels, which are very much like grid points. Your camera has millions of pixels, each one focused on a small part of the image. If your portrait image has 1000 pixels in the horizontal and 1000 pixels in the vertical then the portrait image is composed of 1000 × 1000 = 1,000,000 pixels or 1 megapixels. The nose, eyes, and ears may have thousands of pixels focused on them providing a lot of detail for each of them. If you were to take the picture twice the distance away, the person's face would appear twice as small in the picture. There may now only be hundreds of pixels each on the nose, eyes, and ears and you would see much less detail. If you took the picture a hundred times the distance away, only a few pixels each would be on the nose, eyes, and ears. You may not be able to see them at all. As a rule, you need approximately five pixels in each direction in order to resolve a feature like a nose, or eyes, or ears.

Figure 10.2 illustrates a somewhat analogous effect of grid spacing and resolution. The two pictures of the same scene, but the picture on the right is about five times higher resolution. Because the picture on the right has about five times better resolution, it has about 5 times the number of pixels for each feature. The picture on the left allows you to see that this is an intersection with lane markings and possibly trees on the two corners with a path to a lower area in the bottom right. The picture on the right allows you to see the arrows in the lanes, branches in the trees, and stairs to the lower area in the bottom right.

© Data retrieved from DC Data Catalog (http://data. dc.gov/) modified by Tom Kovacs

Figure 10.2 Two pictures of the same scene with different resolutions are shown. The left image has a resolution about 5 times more coarse than the right.

Now, this is not exactly the same in weather modeling, which deals with equations and not smoothed images, but it shows the importance of resolution. A general rule of thumb is that you need approximately five grid points in each direction in order to resolve an atmospheric feature. If you want to simulate a 10 km by 10 km thunderstorm, you need to have five grid points in each direction to cover the 10 km × 10 km area. That means that the spacing between grid points would need to be 10 km × 10 km divided by 5 or 2 km × 2 km. Therefore, to resolve and simulate a thunderstorm you need a grid point spacing of 2 km. This grid spacing is less than current operational weather models, which cannot resolve individual thunderstorms. Even smaller atmospheric features like precipitation and clouds are not resolved. We will see shortly how computer models handle these seemingly important shortcomings.

The model domain itself is also an important consideration for weather modeling. If you wish to simulate a thunderstorm, 25 grid points spaced 2 km apart is enough to resolve the thunderstorm, but it may not be all you need to model it. The weather at a location depends on what is happening above and upstream of that location. If you are making a one-day forecast, the weather that will affect your location may be 500 km

(310 miles) upstream of your location. If your model domain does not contain these locations the model will unlikely be able to calculate the weather correctly. The 2 km grid spacing must be distributed over a much larger domain.

Unfortunately, it is not possible to have microscopic grid spacing and global domains because of the number of calculations needed. The size of the model domain and the spacing of the grid points are two factors in determining the number of model calculations. Each grid point requires a number of calculations. The various calculations needed in a weather model are discussed in the next step. However, let us use a nice round number of ten calculations to illustrate the large number of calculations that a model would need to compute.

For example, we can see how quickly the number of calculations in a model grows for a model domain that covers the entire U.S. The U.S. is approximately 4400 km (2750 miles) in the east-west direction and 2400 km (1500 miles) in the north-south direction. With a 10 km grid spacing, the model would need 4400/10 × 2400/10 = 440 × 240 = 105,600 grid points. Because we also need to have grid points in many levels from the Earth's surface to the upper stratosphere, the model would need to repeat this grid many times for each of the levels. For 50 model levels, the model would have 105,600 × 50 = 5,280,000 grid points. The model also needs to do a number of calculations at each grid point. If the model were to do 10 calculations at each grid point, it would have to make 5,280,000 × 10 = 52,800,000 calculations.

The model domain for the GFS model is global. For a global model domain in our above example, the total number of calculations would be over 8 billion. This number of calculations is for only one model time step. Typically, models calculate about five minutes forward in time requiring a repeat of this calculation 288 times for each modeled day in the future. For a one-day forecast, that is a trillion calculations. Actual weather models have more than ten calculations to perform in each model's step. The NWS computer is fast, but computers have limitations, which limits the spacing of the grid points (Figure 10.3).

Prior to making the calculations to forecast the weather, the observed data must be interpolated to the grid points. Various interpolation schemes exist. For example, you can simply interpolate the closest observation to the grid point. However, you may find that you can get a more accurate representation if you took an average of several data points surrounding the grid point. Even more accurately, you can take an average of all the data points surrounding the grid point, but weight the observations by the distance they are away from the grid point (Figure 10.4). Operational weather models employ more complicated interpolation schemes. However, these examples give you an idea of how various

Figure 10.3 Supercomputer used by the NWS shown that can perform 8400 trillion operations per second.

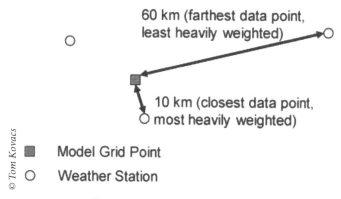

■ Model Grid Point

○ Weather Station

Figure 10.4 Illustration of interpolating weather station data to a model grid point using a weighted average.

models can employ different interpolation schemes to interpolate data to the model grid points. In conclusion, once all the data is gathered the second step in operating a weather model is to interpolate all the data to all the grid points.

Step 3: Calculating the Changes in the Weather Parameters

The equations based on the physical laws discussed in Chapters 4-8 allow models to calculate the change in time of each of the weather parameters. For example, Newton's Laws govern air motion or the winds. The following equation expresses the change in winds from Newton's Laws:

$$\frac{\Delta v}{\Delta t} = PGF + CF + Friction$$

where v is the wind velocity, t is time, PGF is the pressure gradient force, CF is the Coriolis force, and Friction is the frictional force. This is Newton's Law for a unit mass of air (i.e. 1 kg). The right-hand side is the sum of all the forces on air, which was discussed in Chapter 5.

Most mathematical equations experienced before college are written in the following form:

$$y = f(x)$$

That is y is a function of some other variable, x. For example, the following equation expresses the well-known linear line equation,

$$y = mx + b$$

where m is the slope of a linear line and b is the y-intercept. Knowing the slope and the y-intercept allows you to calculate y for every x because y is a function of x only. Some may have experienced nonlinear equations where y is a function of x raised to some power. The weather model equations are all nonlinear functions solvable with complex math beyond the level of this textbook.

In fact, the weather model equations are even more complicated than that. The equation for the change in temperature comes from the First Law of Thermodynamics. It is repeated here from Chapter 4,

$$\frac{\Delta U}{\Delta t} = q - w$$

where U is the change in internal energy, q is heating, and w is work. If there is no phase changes then the change in internal energy, U, is just the change in temperature, T. The equation can be written as

$$\frac{\Delta T}{\Delta t} = q - w$$

By substituting the different heating mechanisms and work processes discussed in Chapter 4,

$$\frac{\Delta T}{\Delta t} = radiation + convection + radiation - adiabatic\ expansion$$

Remember that convection is related to the movement of air, which is in the equation for Newton's Law. Therefore, weather models are a system of coupled equations because they depend on each other. The set of equations to simulate weather are a set of coupled nonlinear equations. Do not worry if you have no clue how to solve or calculate these equations because nobody has solved them. They actually lead to a branch of mathematics known as chaos. Chaos causes the uncertainties in weather models to grow with time leading to a theoretical limit of applicable forecast range of around two weeks.

Students know that not being able to solve the equations means that you cannot come up with the correct answer. Unfortunately, we have not come up with a correct answer for how all the weather parameters change. Fortunately, the father of numerical weather prediction, Lewis Richardson came up with a way to approximate the equations. The equations can be written as a sum of better and better approximations. Technically, if you produced an equation infinitely long using Richardson's approximation you would come up with the exact answer. Therefore, another difference between different computer models is how the equations are approximated.

Digging Deeper

Limits on Spatial and Temporal Model Resolution

The time step of computer models has limits other than computer processing speed. The time is limited by the grid-point spacing due to a mathematical condition called the Courant-Friedrichs-Lewy (CFL) condition. The CFL condition is that the grid-point-spacing, Δx, divided by the time step, Δt, must be less that the velocity of travel of anything that has a significant impact on the weather parameters. For example, if a thunderstorm were to travel from one grid point to the next in less than the time step of the model, the thunderstorm would essentially skip grid points. It would be at one grid point and appear two grid points away without traveling through the intervening grid point.

Physically, this sounds like teleportation and is not physically real. Mathematically, this leads to instability in the calculations causing model parameters to be wrong at best and crash the computer running the model at worst.

Therefore, if you are already at the CFL threshold and you reduce the grid-point-spacing, you must proportionally reduce the time step. Not abiding by this condition can cause the calculations to become unrealistic. Lewis Richardson's first attempt at mathematical weather forecasting was inaccurate because he violated the CFL condition of which he was unaware.

Calculations of the approximate equations must be done for small steps forward in time to make for a better approximation. When a model produces a 24-hour forecast, it does not just calculate the change in each parameter over the 24-hour period in one step. It does so in a large number of smaller steps. Storms can form and dissipate in that 24-hour period and these changes need to be captured by the model. The computer processing speed limits the time step, like the grid-point spacing.

Unfortunately, calculating the approximations to the physical laws are not the only calculations that weather models must make. As mentioned in the previous step, current weather models cannot resolve thunderstorms, clouds, or precipitation. Weather models would not have much benefit if they cannot predict precipitation! Nor can they resolve the smaller scale effects these have on heating or the smaller scale effects that the Earth's surface can have on them. These phenomena are called subgrid scale phenomena.

Luckily, there are two ways to handle subgrid scale phenomenon. First, models can nest other models within the larger model using the parameters of the model. Second, models can simply handle the subgrid scale phenomenon in a simpler way using the modeled parameters. Either way, they are using the parameters that the model calculates and so this technique is called parameterization.

A good example of parameterization is the convective parameterization. Convection produces rising air and often leads to thunderstorms if the air is unstable and there is enough humidity. Humidity and the vertical temperature profile (needed to calculate static stability) are weather model parameters. Researchers observe the relationship of weather model parameters to cloud size, precipitation, strength of updrafts and downdrafts, etc. These clouds affect the precipitation type and rate, distribution of temperature, humidity, energy, and winds inside and outside of the cloud (Figure 10.5). All of these are also parameters in the weather models. Therefore, the model parameters are used to determine if a cloud forms and the effects this cloud has on the model parameters without modeling the process itself.

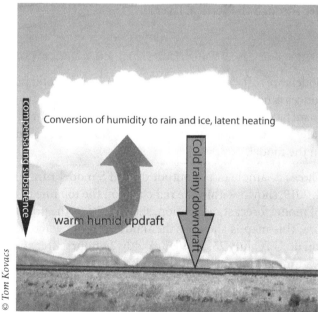

Figure 10.5 Convection clouds affects the redistribution of energy, temperature, humidity, winds, and all phases of water. These are all weather model parameters, but the processes that cause the redistributions are not.

Cause and Effect

All of science works under the assumption that there are a few natural and physical laws that underlie all causes and their effects. All effects in the world have an underlying scientific cause. For example, noises at night could be attributed to the supernatural, which is often invoked when the causes are not clear. To be a scientific explanation, that cause must be traced back to the natural and physical laws. Supernatural causes by definition are not traceable to natural laws. Any tentative scientific explanation or hypothesis that some cause leads to an effect requires a chain of interactions that connect the cause and effect. Oftentimes, novice scientists confuse the cause and the effect. A cause-and-effect relationship does not necessarily mean that the effect will lead to the same cause.

For example, although we learn that unstable air causes rising air, clouds, and precipitation it is not true that precipitation causes unstable air.

Parameterization is an application of cause-and-effect. Although we know that unstable air leads to precipitation, the chain of processes from cause to effect occurs at a scale that is not resolvable by current weather models. However, because unstable air often leads to precipitation, a model of how much precipitation is produced by a certain level of unstable air can be created. The amount will depend on other model parameters such as humidity, temperature, wind shear, vertical wind velocity, and other values that can be calculated from model parameters.

Parameterization is used during each time step. In addition, the parameterization can keep track of subgrid scale parameters such as water in all phases and the fraction of sky covered in clouds. These parameters may also be used as input into other parameterizations such as nested radiative transfer models. Radiative transfer models need to know the distribution of clouds and water in all phases to know how shortwave and longwave radiation transfer through the vertical layers.

Step 4: Weather Model Post-Processing and Broadcasting

Computer models are software that are "run" like any computer program. Each weather model run produces a number of output data products called **prognostication maps (progs)** such as surface and upper air maps, Skew-T diagrams, radar images, etc. These maps are generally produced hourly or every three hours, but could be produced at each time step within the model.

Figure 10.6 shows a sample of the output of a GFS model run. The model run time is 00 UTC July 24, 2019, shown within the red circle on the top line of text. The data is valid after 24 hours of model forecast calculation, shown within the green circle on the top line of text. Therefore, this map is showing the model forecast calculation for these parameters expected on 00 UTC July 25, 2019 or exactly 24 hours after the model was run. The map is actually a forecast for a time in the future of when the model was run, shown in the blue circle on the top line of text.

The equivalent mean sea level pressure (EMSL) are the black contours, three-hour precipitation amount is the green shading, and 850 mb temperatures are the colored contours. These are all model-calculated values after 24 hours. The data and units of measurement are described in the bottom line of text. The map shows that high pressure will dominate the eastern half of the U.S. (as shown by the light blue H over Illinois). Multiple low-pressure centers are affecting the western half of the U.S. and Mexico (red 'L's on the

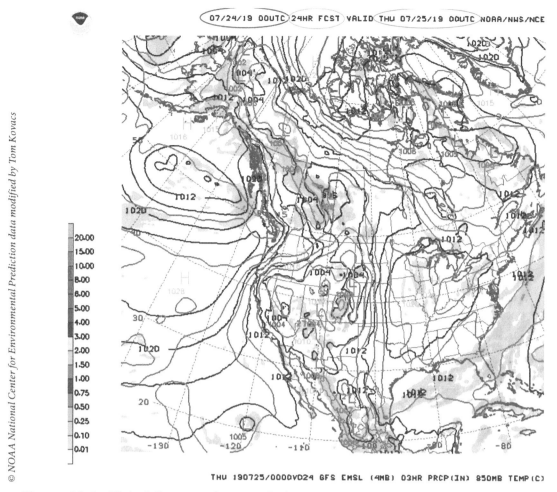

© NOAA National Center for Environmental Prediction data modified by Tom Kovacs

07/24/19 00UTC 24HR FCST VALID THU 07/25/19 00UTC NOAA/NWS/NCE

THU 190725/0000V024 GFS EMSL (4MB) 03HR PRCP(IN) 850MB TEMP(C)

Figure 10.6 Global Forecast System (GFS) model output for a model run on 00 UTC July 24, 2019 and valid 24 hr later on 00 UTC July 25, 2019. Included is 3 hr precipitation (color shading), sea-level pressure (black lines), and 850 mb temperature (red lines). The red circle at the top is the time of the model run, the green circle is how many hours into the future this map represents, and the blue circle is the time in the future the map is valid.

map) causing precipitation (green shading). The 850 mb temperatures, have the important 0 °C contour colored purple (see far northern Canada). All isotherms hotter than 0 °C are colored red and all isotherms colder than 0 °C are colored blue to identify above- and below-freezing temperatures. Spotting the purple isotherm helps identify areas that should expect frozen precipitation (blue contour side of the purple line) and areas that should expect rain (red contour side of the purple line).

Users of weather models like to know the model forecast for specific surface locations instead of trying to analyze all the maps. However, mentioned in the previous chapter, weather models do not do a good job of forecasting the surface weather conditions at specific stations. After the model has run, it generates Model Output Statistics (MOS) to interpolate the model output data statistically to surface locations. These statistics are based on the statistical relationship between past computer model output and the weather parameters at surface locations.

For example, Figure 10.7 shows MOS statistics for Orlando, FL for the GFS model run at the same time (00 UTC July 24, 2019) as the map in Figure 10.6. The top row shows that GFS model data are statistically interpolated for Orlando International Airport. The

Weather Forecast Models **223**

```
ORLANDO INTL
 KMCO   GFS MOS GUIDANCE    7/24/2019   0600 UTC
 DT /JULY 24         /JULY 25              /JULY 26              /
 HR   12 15 18 21 00 03 06 09 12 15 18 21 00 03 06 09 12 15 18 00 06
 X/N         89       73             89          73          91
 TMP  77 85 85 80 77 76 74 74 76 85 86 80 77 75 74 74 76 84 87 80 76
 DPT  75 75 74 74 74 73 73 73 74 73 72 73 73 72 72 72 73 73 72 72 73
 CLD  BK BK OV OV OV OV BK SC BK BK OV OV OV OV OV OV BK BK BK OV BK
 WDR  19 23 25 27 28 25 20 20 18 21 23 27 06 09 15 17 17 21 22 26 20
 WSP  06 10 11 09 06 04 02 02 03 07 08 06 07 09 05 04 03 07 08 05 03
 P06      50    70    25    11    27    69    37    18    30 55 33
 P12      83          29          76          46          62
 Q06       2     4     0     0     0     5     1     0     0  3  1
 Q12       5           0           5           1           3
 T06    51/ 2 86/ 4 18/ 5  2/ 0 31/ 1 74/ 9 24/ 1  6/ 0 29/ 1 27/ 1
 T12       86/10       31/ 3       74/10       29/ 1 79/ 8
 CIG   8  8  7  6  7  8  8  8  8  8  7  6  5  5  8  8  7  7  6  8  8
 VIS   7  7  7  7  7  7  7  7  7  7  7  5  6  7  7  7  7  7  7  7  7
 OBV   N  N  N  N  N  N  N  N  N  N  N HZ  N  N  N  N  N  N  N  N  N
```

Figure 10.7 MOS statistics from the GFS model run on July 24, 2019 at 06 UTC for Orlando, FL.

second row shows the four-letter code for the station (KMCO). It also shows that this is GFS MOS Guidance and the date and time of the model run. The third row is the date (DT) and the fourth row is the hour that each column of data is valid. The rest of the rows are the MOS forecasted weather parameters for this station.

The X/N row provides the max/min temperature for each day. Sometimes this line is written N/X if the minimum temperature comes first on the row. In Figure 10.7, the first value on this row, 89 °F, is the forecasted maximum temperature between 12 UTC and 00 UTC for July 24. The maximum is always for the period between 7 am and 7 pm local standard time, which in this case is 12 UTC to 00 UTC because Orlando is in the Eastern Time zone. The value is written under the end of this day, 00 UTC, which starts July 25. Because the maximum temperature for July 24 appears under July 25, this often leads to confusion. However, this maximum is for the previous 12 hours so it is the maximum temperature for July 24. The second value on the row, 73 °F, is the forecasted minimum temperature between 00 UTC and 12 UTC for the early morning hours of July 25. Again, this can be confusing because the TV and online weather forecast will usually say on July 24 that tonight's low will be 73°F. In reality, that low is usually reached in the early morning hours of the following day and the MOS statistics reflects this.

The next two rows are the forecast air temperature (TMP) and dewpoint temperature (DPT) in °F for the time and date given for each column under the 'DT' and 'HR' rows. The value under the July 24 (DT) at 12 UTC (HR) column shows a forecasted air temperature (TMP) of 77 °F and a dewpoint temperature (DPT) of 75 °F. Continuing across the row are the air temperatures and dewpoint temperatures forecasted every three hours. Notice that the highest forecasted temperature on the TMP row within July 24 is 85 °F. However, the forecasted maximum temperature on the X/N row is 89 °F. The maximum temperature probably occurs within the three-hour gap in the provided temperature data.

The next row, 'CLD' is the coded cloud cover. The code is as follows (definitions in Chapter 1): clear (CL), few clouds (FW), scattered clouds (SC), broken (BK), and overcast (OV). The next row is the wind direction (WDR) and wind speed (WSP). The wind direction is given in tens of degrees as described in Chapter 1. Therefore, the first value for 12 UTC on July 24 is 190° or winds from slightly west of south. The wind speed is six knots.

The following six rows are related to precipitation probabilities and amounts somewhere in a 48 km (30 mile) box centered on the station. The 'P06' and 'P12' rows are the probabilities in percent that at least 0.01" of liquid equivalent precipitation will be observed in the preceding 6- and 12-hour period, respectively. The 'Q06' and 'Q12' rows are categories for the liquid-equivalent precipitation amounts for the preceding 6 and 12 hours, respectively. The categories are defined as follows: 0 = no precipitation expected; 1 = 0.01 – 0.09 inches; 2 = 0.10 – 0.24 inches; 3 = 0.25 – 0.49 inches; 4 = 0.50 – 0.99 inches; 5 = 1.00 – 1.99 inches; and 6 = > 2.00 inches. The 'T06' and 'T12' rows are the probability of thunderstorms and severe thunderstorms for the preceding 6- and 12-hour periods, respectively. The thunderstorm probability is to the left of the '/' and the severe thunderstorm probability is to the right. Sometimes, in cold weather locations other precipitation categories will be available. See https://www.nws.noaa.gov/mdl/synop/tpb/mdltpb05-03.pdf for more information on all these rows.

The last operational part of this step is to convert the weather model output to a data format that other users can obtain and use. Some smaller-scale computer models use the GFS model output as input to their models. Some of these smaller-scale models will be the focus of the different computer models discussed in the next section of this chapter. Because this is public government data, all raw model data is available to everybody. The NWS also provides all the maps and other graphical output formats at http://mag.ncep.noaa.gov.

Examples of Weather Models

By now, the reason for the existence of many different weather models should be clear. A different group of scientists with different forecast interests develops each weather model. Some are more interested in daily weather, some in tropical cyclones, and some in the development of individual clouds or storms. In addition, different locations of interest require different model domains. By reducing the domain size, it is possible to reduce the grid point spacing since the grid covers a smaller area. The tradeoff is that the model does not know anything about outside the model domain, which creates problems with how to handle the boundaries. This boundary condition problem also reduces the number of days that a computer model can reliably forecast into the future. For example, the global GFS model can calculate what is happening around the world so that there is never any air that will affect any station that the model has not already calculated. The North American Model (NAM), however, has a model domain that extends through North America, and the adjacent oceans (Figure 10.8). The model is no longer reliable once the air in Asia affects the weather in California. Partially for this reason, the NAM model only forecasts for 84 hours (3.5 days). Whereas the High Resolution Rapid Refresh (HRRR) Model has an even smaller domain that only covers the U.S. and only forecasts for 18 hours (Figure 10.8).

The GFS, NAM, and Rapid Refresh models are all operational models run by the National Center for Environmental Prediction (NCEP) of the NWS. However, other scientific organizations run other models. Europe run the European Center for Medium

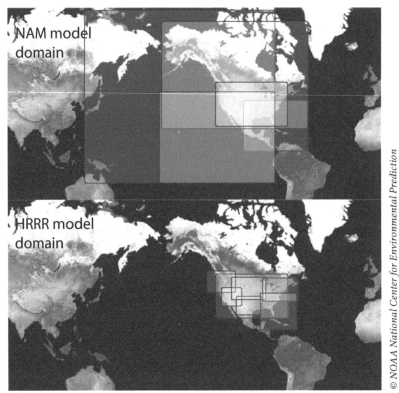

Figure 10.8 NAM (top) and HRRR (bottom) model domains are approximated by the total area covered by the sum of all the red outlined data output boxes.

© NOAA National Center for Environmental Prediction

Range Weather Forecasts (ECMWF) model, Canada runs the Global Environmental Multiscale (GEM) Model, United Kingdom (UK) has the UK Met Office (UKMO) model. There are also specialized computer models for climate, air quality, and hurricanes and numerous research models for nearly every weather phenomenon of interest. In this section, the 2019 operational weather forecast models from NCEP are discussed.

Global Forecast System Model (GFS, GEFS)

The global model that NCEP operates is the Global Forecasting System (GFS) model. The grid spacing of the GFS is currently 28 km (18 miles) in the horizontal and has 64 vertical levels that extend from the ground to the top of the stratosphere. Vertical levels are rarely evenly spaced for any model (Figure 10.9). Because of the amount of complexity near the surface compared to higher levels, the levels are closest together near the surface. The stratosphere rarely has a large number of levels because of its extreme stability and therefore lack of vertical motion. The stratosphere would not change much over short time periods and have little effect on shorter range forecasts. However, the stratosphere does affect longer range forecasts and a global model that produces longer range forecasts must consider these. That is why the GFS is considered a medium to long-range forecasting model because of its large horizontal (global) and vertical (to the top of the stratosphere) domain.

The parameterizations for the GFS are often simpler compared to shorter range regional forecast models. This textbook will only compare the radiative transfer and convective parameterizations. The GFS uses the Rapid Radiative Transfer Model (RRTM) to handle both shortwave and longwave radiation. This model separates the shortwave

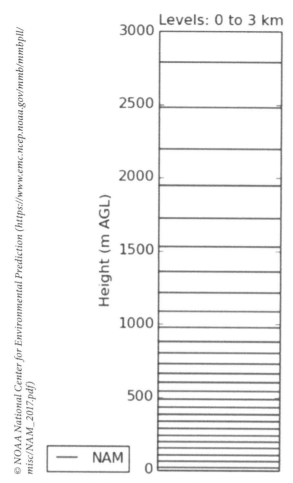

Figure 10.9 Vertical model grid levels for the North American Model (NAM) from 0-3 km are shown. The levels continue to spread further apart above 3 km.

and longwave radiation into a number of wavelength bands and then calculates how each band transfers through the atmosphere. The calculation is based on parameters from the model and other parameterization schemes. It also uses a mass flux convection parameterization known by the scientists that proposed it, Arakawa-Schubert.[1] This scheme treats the updraft and downdraft of air and their effects on heating and precipitation for the entire grid-point. It also uses model parameters to determine the fraction of clouds within that grid point. It does not treat individual clouds.

The GFS model is run four times a day (00, 06, 12, an 18 UTC) and publicly accessible maps can be obtained at http://mag.ncep.noaa.gov under 'model guidance'. Each of the four model runs in a 24-hour period are selectable. Map output is provided for different selectable regions. Output includes several precipitation amounts and accumulations, a simulated radar, and surface and upper-air maps. Users can also select 'forecast soundings' instead of 'model guidance' to select calculated soundings. For each model run, all maps are provided every hour for 5 days and less often out to 16 days. All soundings are provided every 3 hours for 5 days.

---

[1] Arakawa, A and W. H. Schubert (1974) Interaction of a cumulus cloud ensemble with the large-scale environment, Part I, *J. Atmos. Sci.* 31, 674–701.

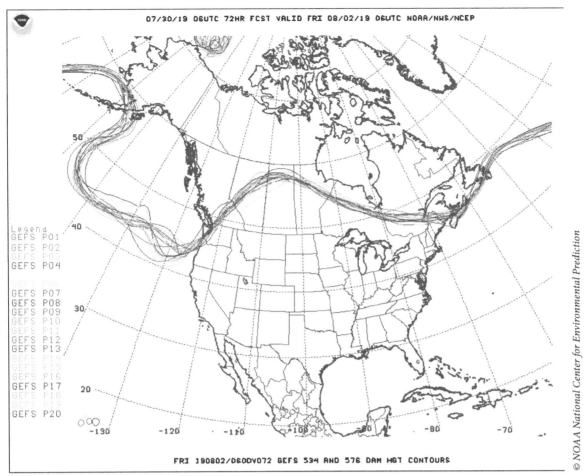

Legend
GEFS P01
GEFS P02
GEFS P03
GEFS P04

GEFS P06
GEFS P07
GEFS P08
GEFS P09
GEFS P10
GEFS P11
GEFS P12
GEFS P13
GEFS P14
GEFS P15
GEFS P16
GEFS P17
GEFS P18
GEFS P19
GEFS P20

FRI 190802/060DV072 GEFS 534 AND 576 DAM HGT CONTOURS

© NOAA National Center for Environmental Prediction

Figure 10.10 GEFS spaghetti plot for the 72-hour forecast of the 5340 m (north of Alaska) and 5760 m (south of Alaska) contours of the 500 mb level valid for 06 UTC August 2, 2019 for the 20 perturbed model runs on 06 UTC July 30, 2019.

Ensemble forecasts for the GFS are also available from the Global Ensemble Forecasting System (GEFS). Observations are perturbed to produce 20 different inputs that are run separately. The ensembles are provided as means and standard deviations or as **spaghetti plots** for individual parameters every 6 hours for 7-and-a-half days and every 12 hours for 16 days. Figure 10.10 shows a spaghetti plot for the 72-hour forecast of the 5340 m and 5760 m contours on the 500 mb level. These values are valid for August 2, 2019 at 06 UTC for the ensemble model run on July 30, 2019 06 UTC. Spaghetti plots provide an idea of model uncertainties of locations and intensities of atmospheric features. Areas for which contours for the 20 individual runs are relatively close together shows high confidence in the model forecast results. Where the contours for the individual runs are widely spaced shows low confidence in the model forecast results.

North American Model (NAM, NAM HIRES, SREF)

NCEP operates a regional model for North America called the North American Model (NAM). The model domain includes North America and a good portion of the Atlantic and Pacific Oceans (Figure 10.8). The NAM has a grid spacing of 12 km (7.5 miles) in the horizontal and has 60 vertical levels that extend from the ground to the middle of the stratosphere. It also has a NAM HIRES version that has a grid spacing of 3 km (2 mile) for smaller model domains. The grid spacing of these models are smaller than the GFS model, but do not extend as high in the stratosphere because the NAM is a shorter-range forecasting model. Because it is not a global model, the boundaries of the model domain are initialized and updated throughout the model run. The way the NAM model does this is by using a 6-hour-old GFS model to define the features on the model boundaries throughout the model run.

The parameterizations for the NAM are slightly different from the GFS model. It also uses the Rapid Radiative Transfer Model (RRTM) to handle longwave and shortwave radiation. However, it uses the Betts-Miller-Janjic convective adjustment scheme.[2] In this scheme, the temperature and humidity profiles are adjusted to some reference profiles based on observational studies of tropical convection. The adjustment to model parameters takes into account the effects of shallow (stratiform) and deep convection (cumuliform) separately. The HIRES version does not have a cumulus parameterization. The model has a high enough resolution to resolve convection.

The NAM model is run four times a day (00, 06, 12, an 18 UTC) and publicly accessible maps can be obtained at http://mag.ncep.noaa.gov under model guidance. Each model run in a 24-hour period is selectable. Map output is provided for different selectable regions. Output parameters and soundings for the 12 km NAM are similar to the GFS model. The 3 km NAM HIRES output parameters include more severe weather parameters and parameters related to visibility. For the 12 km NAM, all maps and soundings are provided every hour for 84 hours (3.5 days). For the 3 km NAM HIRES, all maps are provided every hour for 60 hours (2.5 days). Similar to the GFS model, short-range ensemble forecast (SREF) products are also provided.

Rapid Refresh Model (RAP, HRRR)

NCEP also runs a smaller regional model for the continental US called the Rapid Refresh Model (RAP). The model domain includes the U.S., Canada, and Alaska and small parts of the Pacific and Atlantic Ocean, which is smaller than the NAM's model domain (Figure 10.8). The RAP has a grid spacing of 13 km (8 miles) in the horizontal and has 50 vertical levels that extend from the ground to the middle of the stratosphere. It also has a Hi-Resolution Rapid Refresh 'HRRR' version that has a grid spacing of 3 km (2 mile) for smaller model domains. The spacing is similar to the NAM model with fewer vertical levels. The boundaries are updated like the NAM and the parameterizations are similar. The big difference is that the model is run every hour with updated or 'refreshed' input data.

The RAP and HRRR models are run every hour and publicly accessible maps can be obtained at http://mag.ncep.noaa.gov under model guidance. Each model run in a 24-hour period is selectable. Map output is provided for different selectable regions for the HRRR. Output parameters for the HRRR are similar to the NAM HIRES model, whereas the RAP model has much fewer output maps. For the RAP, all maps are provided every hour for 39 hours for the 03, 09, 15, and 21 UTC model runs otherwise maps are provided every hour for 21 hours. For the HRRR, all maps are provided every hour for 36 hours for the 00, 06, 12, and 18 UTC model runs; otherwise, maps are provided every hour for 18 hours. No model soundings are provided.

Many other weather model products are produced by NCEP and available at the same website. These products include multi-model ensemble forecasts, other high-resolution models, fire weather models, sea ice models, ocean wave models, and coastal water level

---

[2] Janjic, Z. I., 1994: The step-mountain Eta coordinate model: Further developments of the convection, viscous sublayer, and turbulence closure schemes. *Mon. Wea. Rev.,* **122**, 927–945

models. Numerous other research models that have other applications including hurricanes, air quality, hydrological (flood and drought), cloud, turbulence, tornadoes, etc. exist. Many of these are not operational or are produced by non-governmental organizations. Often operational models apply knowledge gained by these research models. Weather models have certain characteristics discussed in the next section that limit how far into the future they can simulate.

Model Limitations and Weaknesses

Weather models suffer from a number of weaknesses that may have been apparent in the previous sections. First, input data is sparse in some locations, but satellite data is increasingly covering traditional areas that lack data including the polar-regions, oceans, and mountains.

Second, the equations are not solved exactly, and the calculations will always be approximations. Related to this, some phenomena occur below the resolution of the models and parameterizations are required. Convective parameterizations were one of those featured. However, increasingly these parameterizations are not needed because operational models' grid spacing is approaching the scale to resolve convection. Many issues arise with these convection-allowing models, primarily because smaller-scale processes such as turbulence becomes more important[3]. It is unlikely that a model will be able to forecast where specific thunderstorms and tornadoes will occur. However, probabilities of these important phenomena may become model forecast products of the future.

Finally, the ultimate limitation is that the equations from the physical laws that govern the predictability of the atmosphere are nonlinear, coupled, and sensitive to the initial conditions. This statement is roughly the definition of a chaotic system as first postulated by Edward Lorentz. A small difference in the initial input to computer models will eventually lead to wildly different results. The uncertainties in this nonlinear system will grow and overwhelm the actual signal.

A popular example scenario of chaos relates to whether the flapping of a butterfly's wings can cause a tornado several days later. That means that if the observations input into weather models have some uncertainties (no instrument can measure perfectly) and the data is not interpolated perfectly to the model grid then model simulations will eventually lead to chaos. We are already near the expected limits of predictability for weather models (i.e. 10-16 days). Chaos theory provides an estimate of the limits of predictability based on the dynamics of the system. Climate models, which are probabilistic and not deterministic, do not have the same sensitivity as weather models and can forecast much further into the future. Nonetheless, climate models also have some limits due to chaos theory.

Summary

Weather models are an excellent example of the scientific method in action. The first step in making a weather model is gathering all the weather data for your model. For global models, which provide longer-range forecasts, data comes from surface weather stations, weather balloons, buoys, commercial ships, lighthouses, offshore platforms, tide gauges, commercial aircraft, Doppler radar, SODAR, wind profilers, and satellites. The second step is assimilating the data into the model. Data sources are not evenly distributed across the world making assimilation difficult. Weather models create a uniformly spaced

---

[3] Yano, J.-I., and Coauthors, 2018: Scientific challenges of convective-scale numerical weather prediction. Bull. Amer. Meteor. Soc., 99, 699–710, https://doi.org/10.1175/BAMS-D-17-0125.1.

horizontal grid and interpolate available data to these grid points. That means that not all grid points receive the same amount of data and data may be spatially and temporally distributed unevenly. Interpolation schemes are created to handle estimates of weather parameters on each grid point from these disparate sources.

Once the initial data is included on the model grid for the entire model domain, the model is run. Running the model involves calculating the changes in all the model parameters. These calculations are based on the physical laws written as mathematical functions. Because of the complexity of the atmosphere, the mathematical equations are approximations. The approximations limit the accuracy and forecast range of these models. The equations must also be calculated in a time step that is a small fraction of the total forecast period because many weather processes and phenomena occur in periods much less than the forecast period. Some processes occur on a scale too small for weather models. These subgrid processes are parameterized, which means they use model parameters and empirical relationships to estimate the final effect on model parameters. Parameterization avoids simulating the subgrid processes.

Once the model run is complete, data are plotted on prognostic maps, usually hourly, for the period of the model run. These progs provide the time the model was run, the forecast range, the time the prog is valid, and the parameters plotted with their units of measure. For specific surface stations, a statistical interpolation is done to provide three-hour resolved forecasts, known as model output statistics (MOS).

The NWS runs several operational weather models, each with a specific purpose. The Global Forecast System (GFS) model has a global domain and simulates higher in the stratosphere, but has a more coarsely resolved grid and simpler model physics. The GFS is used for longer range forecasting. The North American Model (NAM) has a regional domain and does not simulate as high in the stratosphere, but has a finer resolved grid and more complex model physics. The NAM is used for shorter range forecasting. The rapid refresh model (RAP) is similar to the NAM model, but with a smaller domain. It is run more often so it is more rapidly updated with newly available data. RAP models are used for same day forecasting. All these models can also be run in ensemble modes, which provides an average and spread of several weather parameters. Ensemble models give the forecaster an idea of where model forecasts are less uncertain.

Key Terms

Assimilate	Model Levels	Parameterization
Interpolate	Model Time Step	Prognostic Maps (progs)
Grid Points	Coupled Equations	Boundary Condition Problem
Grid Point Spacing	Chaos	
Model Domain	Subgrid Scale	Spectral Models
Model Resolution	Nest	Spaghetti Plots

Questions and Problems

1. If you were to play a really long game of scavenger hunt where you can drive all over the U.S., list six weather observation platforms, with a sketch of what they look like, that you would see on the Earth's surface (land or coast) that might be providing data for weather models.

2. Draw a 50 km × 50 km grid of model grid points with a grid spacing needed to resolve a 10 km × 10 km thunderstorm. Outline the grid points where the thunderstorm could be within your grid.

3. What is meant by the time step of a weather model? What is the typical time step in a weather model?

4. According to a general rule, how large would a cloud need to be for a weather model with a horizontal grid spacing of 10 km to resolve **fully**?

5. Why would model resolution of cities like New York City, NY and Aspen, CO be more of a problem than a city like Des Moines, IA.? (Hint: Look at the location of these cities)

6. If you wanted to determine how well a weather model forecasted temperature three days into the future at your location, what time (in your local time zone) would you go outside to measure the temperature for a model run January 1 1200 UTC?

7. How many computations would a weather model need to make a 24 hour forecast if it had a time step of 1 hour, a grid spacing of 10 km and a domain of 100 km × 100 km (Note: assume 1 equation and 1 vertical level)?

8. Find the most recent 00 UTC GFS model run 24-hour forecast for the "850_temp_mslp_precip" parameter. Provide the image URL and include a copy of the map in your answer. What time and date is this map valid?

9. What does parameterization mean? Give an example of a process that is parameterized and two model parameters that may be needed to parameterize the process.

10. Go to http://www.nws.noaa.gov/mdl/synop/products.php and select "GFS" under "text guidance". Provide the high and low temperature for the 24-hour period for the closest station on the day your homework is due. Also, supply the MOS table you used.

11. Would a thunderstorm (10 km diameter) need to be modeled or parameterized by the GFS and NAM? Why?

12. What is a weather model ensemble? What additional information would an ensemble forecast of an upper air trough give that a single model forecast would not?

13. Which weather model would you select in the morning to help determine how much snow you will receive during that day? Describe why you chose that model.

14. Which weather model would you use to look at forecast weather maps for: a) today, b) tomorrow, and c) 1 week from now?

15. Provide a weather model map that includes all of the U.S. showing the polar jet stream 7 days from when the model was run. Circle the highest wind speeds and provide their value.

16. Provide a weather model map that includes all of North America that shows precipitation amounts where you can also determine the type of precipitation forming

in low clouds 2 days from when the model was run. Circle an area of precipitation that is likely rain and another area that is likely snow and explain what you see on this map to determine precipitation type.

17. With the existence of weather models, why are weather forecasters still necessary?

18. Other than weather courses, what college courses do you think are necessary to pursue a career in developing weather models?

19. If computer resources were unlimited, would weather model forecasts be perfect? Provide at least one reason for your answer.

Other Resources

https://www.emich.edu/geography-geology/weather for links to useful weather data to go along with this textbook and updates to any broken links in the textbook.

https://sites.google.com/a/ucar.edu/model-encyclo-determ provides a more thorough description of the models mentioned in this textbook and a few others not mentioned.

http://climatemodels.uchicago.edu/ includes several radiation, climate, hurricane, and carbon cycle models with simple user inputs to play with.

Chapter 11

Climate Models

Introduction

Skeptics often say something to the effect of, "How can climate scientists forecast what will happen in 100 years when they cannot even get the weather forecast correct for tomorrow?". Although we have seen that weather models are actually quite accurate one day into the future, the skepticism is understandably misguided. They do not understand that climate models do not forecast the high and low temperature 36,500 days (100 years) in the future for a specific location like weather models do for tomorrow.

Climate models are probabilistic not deterministic. That is, they forecast means and other statistics, not specific weather on specific dates. Weather forecasts are part probabilistic and part deterministic. High and low temperatures for example are deterministic; "Tomorrow's high will be 50 °F", is deterministic. Chance of precipitation is probabilistic; "Tomorrow we have a 50% chance of rain", is probabilistic. However, there is an understanding, probably more by the forecaster, that the high temperature forecast is actually probabilistic. Some days those probabilities are lower like with an approaching front. For the probabilistic precipitation forecast, it can never be completely correct. Tomorrow can never half rain; it rained, or it did not. Nevertheless, the number of times it rains when a forecast is 50% is remarkably close to 50% of the time.

Climate models currently resolve midlatitude cyclones but forecasting when a cyclone affects a specific area a year into the future is not realistic. However, forecasting the number of midlatitude cyclones and a mean amount of precipitation in that future year is realistic. This forecast depends more on the distribution of energy and humidity averaged over a year, which is far easier than forecasting the distribution of energy and humidity on a specific day. The forecast of means dramatically reduces uncertainties, which allows a forecast much farther into the future. It is akin to the analogy used in Chapter 2. It is difficult to predict a single coin toss, but easy to get close to the number of 'heads' or 'tails' in 100 flips. That ability allows confidence in climate models to simulate future climate because it forecast the averages.

This chapter focuses on how climate models forecast future climates. It will compare climate and weather models and describe how they are tested. Current climate models are three-dimensional models that couple the atmosphere, hydrosphere, cryosphere, geosphere, and biosphere. However, to focus on the climate models' ability to predict energy balance, the chapter starts with a zero-dimensional radiation balance model discussed in Chapter 4. The chapter then moves to one-dimensional models. These models highlight energy distribution and their relation to the horizontal and vertical movement of air and energy. With this background, General Circulation Models (GCMs), which considers the transport of mass and energy by the Earth's general circulations discussed in Chapter 8 are described. Climate models are also GCMs, but they are also referred to as Global Climate Models (also GCMs). I hope that it will be clear how the focus on energy changes and probabilistic forecasts allow climate modeling to make predictions of climate change for decades.

Zero-Dimensional Climate Model

Zero-dimensional climate models mean that they do not vary in any spatial or temporal dimension. Zero-dimensional climate models produce one globally annual mean temperature based on an energy budget. The digging deeper box in Chapter 4 derived the simplest zero-dimensional climate model. In the case of the Earth with no atmosphere, the absorbed incoming solar radiation, $(1-\alpha)S_0$, equals the outgoing infrared radiation for an Earth with no atmosphere, $4\sigma T^4$, as follows:

$$(1 - \alpha)S_0 = 4\sigma T^4.$$

The albedo, α, is the fraction of solar energy, S_0, reflected by the Earth so $(1-\alpha)$ is the fraction of solar energy absorbed by the Earth. The right-hand side is the amount of energy emitted by the Earth, σT^4. It is multiplied by a factor of 4 due to the ratio of areas of the Earth emission (Earth surface area) versus solar absorption (Earth cross-section area). This leads to a radiative equilibrium temperature of 255 K.

This zero-dimensional climate model allows one to determine the effects of the Earth's global mean temperature based on the Earth's albedo and solar input. The values used are approximately realistic for the Earth at the top of the atmosphere. The resulting temperature is the effective emission temperature of the Earth. Raising this temperature to the fourth power and multiplying by σ would give the emission energy of Earth, 240 W/m^2. This emission energy is observable by satellite when observing just the Earth's infrared emission.

The solution is steady state so the system is assumed to be in equilibrium. New values of solar constant or albedo can be used to simulate a changing solar output or an ice age. The problem with assuming steady state is that different parts of the real climate system change at different time scales. In addition, some climate feedbacks in the climate system can dramatically increase the changes. A familiar example of a feedback is the loud sound produced when sound from a musical instrument is sent to an amplifier, a speaker and an amplifier over-and over again (Figure 11.1). The resulting loud sound is caused by this feedback. To incorporate these and other real effects, higher dimensional climate models must be used. Examples of climate feedback is discussed with higher dimensional climate models in the next few sections.

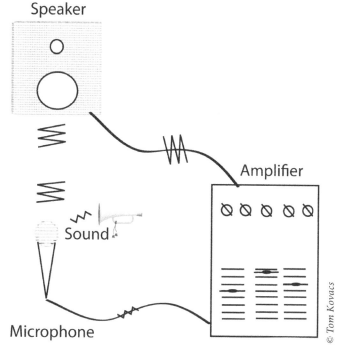

Feedback Loop

Speaker

Amplifier

Sound

Microphone

© Tom Kovacs

Figure 11.1 When a sound enters a microphone that is too near a speaker, a feedback loop creates a much louder noise. The sound enters a microphone, where the sound signal is amplified and then sent to a speaker. If the amplified sound enters the microphone, it will be reamplified creating a feedback loop.

One-Dimensional Climate Models

One-dimensional climate models are not necessarily older than Global Climate Models (GCMs). The simplification of one-dimensional models over the three-dimensional GCMs suggests that they were created at a time of less computer power. However, they were developed around the same time. One-dimensional climate models are still used because of their simplicity. New parameterizations and other tests are often performed on one-dimensional models to understand their effects before incorporation into GCMs. This section uses that simplicity to demonstrate how climate models work before moving to the more complicated GCMs.

Energy Balance Climate Models

Energy balance climate models are one-dimensional climate models where the variation occurs in latitude (north-south direction). They are similar to zero-dimensional models in that the amount of energy added depends on the difference between the radiation in and out of the climate system. However, these one-dimensional models encompass latitudinal variation in energy, which means that the amount of energy present at a given latitude is not constant across the globe. Things such as albedo can vary latitudinally (for instance, low albedos over the ocean and high albedos over ice caps and deserts), which have strong impacts on energy balance that can be incorporated into these climate models.

These models can give one simple equilibrium answer or change over time. Therefore, we can simulate how things like ice ages occur or what will happen with global warming. Unlike weather models, these climate models do not provide a weather forecast at any one location 40 years from now. However, based on energy balance you can calculate how much the mean temperature will change in 40 years. If the model includes reservoirs of energy such as glaciers and it parameterizes processes like glacial melting rates, it can also calculate sea level rise.

In the energy balance model, energy into the climate system is not just balanced by energy emitted back into space. It is also possible to lose energy latitudinally. Therefore, a term that represents the flux of energy latitudinally, F_i, is included. So, our one-dimension model becomes

$$\left(1-\alpha_i\right)S_i = E_i^\uparrow - F_i.$$

In each case, the i subscript is for the latitude. The term $E_i^\uparrow$ is the emission of energy lost to space, which in the zero-dimensional model was equal to $4\sigma T^4$. If you have latitudes from 0° N to 90° N in 10° intervals, then you have ten of the above equations for each latitude. For the first equation, all the subscripts are i=1 to represent the equator (0°), the second equation has all the subscripts i=2 to represent 10° N, and so on. The F_i represents the flux of energy from one latitude to another (Figure 11.2). The simplest way to represent

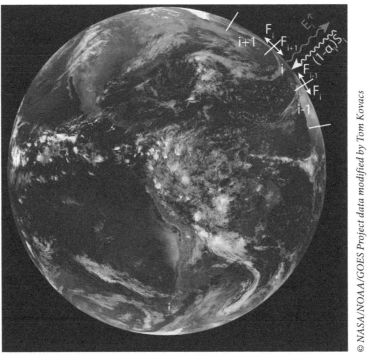

Figure 11.2 Energy transfer represented in an energy balance model is shown for latitude *i*. Fluxes are represented out of (*F_i*) and into (*F_{i-1}* and *F_{i+1}*) latitude *i*. Earth radiation (red curvy arrow) to space (*E_i^↑*) and solar radiation (yellow curvy arrow) absorbed at Earth ((1-α)S_i) are also shown.

this is to make F_i dependent on temperature difference so that more energy is lost from warmer to colder latitudes. Midlatitude cyclones are the physical mechanism that transports warm air ahead of low pressure and cold air behind. Wavy jet streams and the ocean currents also serve this purpose on the real Earth.

These models are very sensitive to small changes in albedo causing ice-free or ice age states with small albedo changes. One potential reason for the sensitivity is that these models simulate real positive feedbacks. The ice-albedo feedback is a positive feedback where a warmer surface temperature causes a loss in ice causing a lower albedo. The lower albedo causes more energy absorption causing a warmer surface temperature and the process then repeats.

Another problem with this model is it assumes that either the lapse rate remains constant or all the heating occurs at the surface. No vertical energy flux exists. In addition, the model allows changes that only depend on surface temperature or surface albedo. Clouds are important to the energy balance but are weakly dependent on surface temperature. Clouds are more dependent on temperature and humidity profiles, which are not included in these models. Some of these necessary vertical processes can be included in the other one-dimensional model: the radiative-convective climate model.

Radiative-Convective Climate Models

Radiative-convective climate models are one-dimensional climate models where the variation occurs in the vertical. These models simulate the energy input into the atmosphere at different altitudes. Unlike energy balance models, there is no energy flux in the horizontal. However, these models could include an energy flux in the vertical, which would be a real physical simulation of convection.

Digging Deeper

Creating a One-Dimension Climate Model

Figure 11.3 shows a simple form of a radiation model. A single layer atmosphere has both solar and Earth radiation transferring through it to the ground and to space. We can simplify the model by assuming that the effective Earth emission temperature is the same as given in the zero-dimension model, 255 K. This tells us how much energy is exiting the atmosphere. The model assumes that the atmosphere does not absorb solar radiation (close to reality). It also assumes that the atmosphere absorbs all the infrared emission from the Earth's surface (close to reality). This simulation is essentially an atmosphere filled with greenhouse gases and no ozone layer.

Greenhouse gases are those that absorb more infrared than solar wavelengths. The small amount of solar absorption that occurs in the real atmosphere is mostly by ozone, which causes the stratosphere to warm. Therefore, the absence of the atmosphere absorbing solar radiation by ozone means this model will not produce a stratosphere. However, it is possible to add other layers and one of those could be a layer that absorbs solar radiation. Just like the real atmosphere, the absorption of solar radiation would produce a stratosphere-like temperature layer that increases with height.

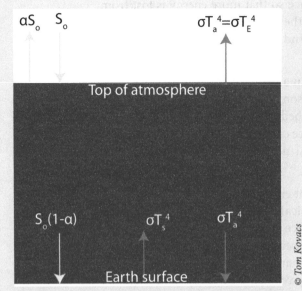

Figure 11.3 A one-layer radiation model shown with the one layer (blue shading) representing the atmosphere. Yellow arrows are solar radiation fluxes and red arrows are Earth radiation (infrared) fluxes. S_o is the solar radiation constant, α is the albedo of the Earth and atmosphere, σT_s^4 is the Earth surface emission, σT_a^4 is the Earth atmosphere emission, and σT_E^4 is the effective Earth emission at the top of the atmosphere from the zero dimensional model.

The yellow arrows in Figure 11.3 are the solar radiation fluxes. The Earth surface and atmosphere reflects about 30% of solar radiation (α) and absorbs all the rest of the energy ($1 - \alpha$). The reflected solar radiation is what you would observe when looking at the dayside of the Earth from space. The absorbed radiation is balanced by the effective emission of the Earth and atmosphere (σT_E^4). This value is calculated in the zero-dimensional climate model and is shown as the red arrow pointing up at the top of the atmosphere. In this model, the only emission reaching the top of the atmosphere is from the single-layer atmosphere. Therefore, we set the top of atmosphere emission to equal the effective emission of the Earth. To calculate the surface temperature, we calculate the energy balance in the atmosphere. The atmosphere is losing energy that it emits toward the ground

and out to space. It is gaining energy absorbed from the emission of the Earth's surface. At equilibrium, the energy gained would equal to the energy lost as follows

$$\sigma T_s^4 = 2\sigma T_a^4.$$

Because $\sigma T_a^4 = \sigma T_E^4$, substituting gives

$$\sigma T_s^4 = 2\left(\sigma T_E^4\right).$$

From the zero-degree model $T_E = 255$ K. Solving for the surface temperature gives

$$T_s = \sqrt[4]{2T_E^4} = \sqrt[4]{2(255K)^4} = 303K.$$

Because the atmosphere loses energy at the top and bottom and the ground only loses energy at the top, the atmosphere must be colder. In addition, because all the emission into space comes from the atmosphere, its temperature must equal the effective Earth emission calculated with the zero-dimensional climate model. This model allows us then to calculate the temperature of the Earth's surface to achieve radiative balance in the atmosphere.

The problem with the purely radiative model is the comparison of the lapse rate created in this model with the real Earth's atmosphere. Most of the greenhouse gas absorption and emission in the Earth's atmosphere comes from the lowest 3 km of the atmosphere. This near-surface layer is the location of the highest concentration of water vapor. That would mean that the effective temperature at 3 km would be 255 K. From Chapter 1, the atmospheric lapse rate, Γ_a, from 0 to 3 km is calculated as the following,

$$\Gamma_a = -\frac{\Delta T}{\Delta z} = -\frac{T_2 - T_1}{z_2 - z_1} = -\frac{255K - 303K}{3km - 0km}$$

$$= 16\frac{K}{km} = 16\frac{°C}{km}$$

This lapse rate is absolutely unstable (i.e. greater than the dry adiabatic lapse rate of 10 °C/km), which would result in rapid convection. Not including convection in this model creates unrealistic lapse rates. Therefore, the convection part of this model would need to include a term that allows for an extra energy flux upward. In the simplest radiative-convective models, the model parameterizes a threshold lapse rate using convective adjustment. Convective adjustment means that once reaching a critical lapse rate, convection redistributes energy in the vertical. Physically, cumulonimbus clouds (thunderstorms) play this role in the real atmosphere.

Including a layered atmosphere allows study of the effects of the solar and Earth emission on convection. Varying greenhouse gases, solar input, or Earth surface changes tests their effects on stability, cloud cover, and the global mean surface temperature. Like the energy balance models, radiative convective models give one simple equilibrium answer or change over time. Time dependent models calculate a change over time using an iterative method where changes occur causing fluxes of energy, which produces more changes, etc. This is different from the zero-dimensional model, which provided an input and produced a single answer. Most mathematics in elementary and secondary school is similar to this latter functional form.

Varying the amount of greenhouse gases or other model parameters allows consideration of other real feedbacks. The water vapor-temperature feedback occurs where a warmer surface temperature causes more evaporation, increasing the water vapor concentration. The increased water vapor increases the greenhouse effect, which increases the surface temperature completing the positive feedback loop (Figure 11.4).

A similar feedback process occurs with carbon dioxide and methane. The dissolution of carbon dioxide out of water decreases with warmer surface ocean temperatures. Subsequently, a warmer ocean surface would cause more carbon dioxide to remain in the atmosphere, increasing the greenhouse effect. The increased greenhouse effect causes warmer surface ocean temperatures, which completes the positive feedback loop. The melting of permafrost in the Arctic release methane, a potent greenhouse gas. Therefore,

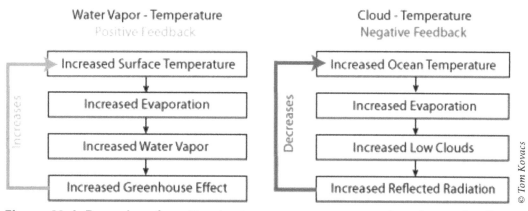

Figure 11.4 Examples of positive (water vapor - temperature) and negative (low cloud - temperature) feedback loops

melting the permafrost would lead to an increase in the greenhouse effect and more melting of the permafrost. There are many more of these positive feedbacks, which amplifies change. Some feedbacks are negative feedbacks, which restrains change. For example, an increase in ocean surface temperature increases surface evaporation causing more low clouds. Low clouds reflect solar radiation back out to space, which lowers the ocean surface temperature (Figure 11.4). Realize that the terms positive and negative do not mean good and bad. They refer to the amplification of the initial change where positive increases and negative decreases the initial change.

The lack of flux in the horizontal is unrealistic in radiative-convective models. Similarly, not distributing the energy in the vertical is unrealistic in energy balance models. Therefore, you need to do both, which is what Global Climate Models (GCMs) simulate. The strength of these one-dimensional models is in their simplicity, which allows scientists to test cause-and-effect. Because one-dimensional models are not as computer intensive as GCMs, they also allow scientists to test more complex processes or parameterizations. They can then compare the one-dimensional models with single columns in GCMs to see if the results are significantly different.

Global Climate Models (GCMs)

Global Climate Models (GCMs) are essentially a combination of energy balance models and radiative convective models. However, GCMs allow the full interaction between vertical and horizontal mass and energy fluxes. This important difference allows internal climate components to change in response to the changes in the heating due to increased greenhouse gases. The interaction of the climate components internal to the climate system leads to internal climate variability. Even in the radiation-convection models, the convection did not fully respond to all the internal components such as convergence. With the full three-dimensional interaction, parameterizations that were needed because of a lack of dimensionality are no longer needed. However, GCMs still include parameterizations to handle subgrid processes (See Chapter 10 for a description) or because of limitations of computer resources. In GCMs, the atmosphere and hydrosphere can fully interact. Even within the atmosphere, physical processes such as winds, pressure, phase changes, and precipitation are free to interact with the heating (Figure 11.5).

Details of the transport in the horizontal and vertical have increased throughout the years such that weather and climate models have become similar. The main differences between the two are the resolution, parameterizations, required initialization time, and output. As of 2014, climate models have a horizontal grid space less than 100 km (61 miles), more than 30 vertical levels, and a time step less than 30 minutes (Figure 11.5). These resolutions are almost a factor of 10 coarser than weather models of the time. Parameterizations must account for the fact that more processes are subgrid scale in climate models. In addition, climate models must be initialized to reach an equilibrium state so that the statistics match present conditions.

The use of climate model output also differs from weather models. Weather models are more frequently using ensemble model runs (see Chapter 10). However, climate models must be run in an ensemble mode to produce probabilistic predictions. Initial conditions are varied about the mean in order to produce climate simulations with a mean and variation around the mean. The real observed present climate includes these random variations from year-to-year. The real observed, annual mean global surface temperature has always varied about some short-term mean.

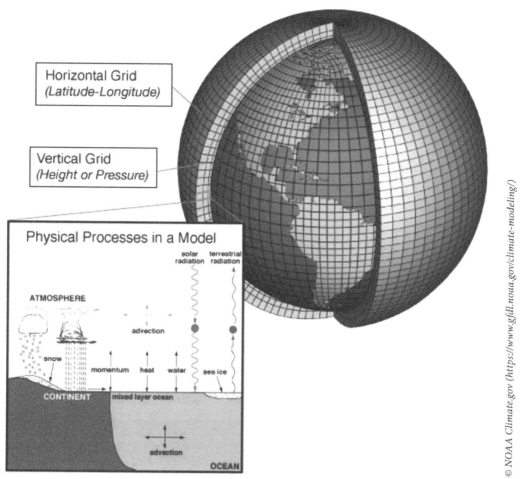

Figure 11.5 Diagram showing the grid spacing of the global atmospheric model and the various ways that other climate components (e.g. snow, sea ice, and ocean) are coupled to the atmospheric model.

© NOAA Climate.gov (https://www.gfdl.noaa.gov/climate-modeling/)

GCMs are run as an ensemble with varying initial conditions or with multiple GCMs. Ensemble runs provide a number of benefits. First, by varying the initial conditions within a GCM, they provide a test of sensitivity of the models. Second, they provide a mean and range of possible climate states in the future. This range provides an estimate of the range of possible levels of global warming or sea level rise, for example. Finally, running an ensemble of multiple climate models with different physics provides an estimate of uncertainty of the models' representation of physical processes (i.e. the parameterizations). Testing GCMs is discussed in more detail at the end of the chapter.

Another big difference between GCMs and weather models is that running a model beyond a couple of weeks requires systems other than the atmosphere to also change. The atmosphere is the most dynamic of the climate systems and responds to changes on faster time scales. For example, when forecasting changes in the atmosphere in the U.S. (i.e. weather) for two weeks, local changes in winds are important while loss of sea ice is not. However, when forecasting climate decades or centuries into the future, local wind changes are not important, but loss of sea ice is.

The World in Global Climate Models

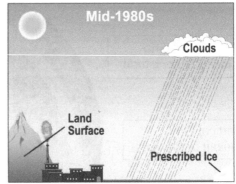
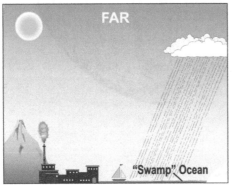
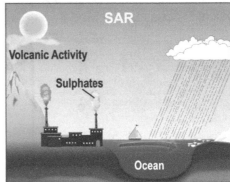
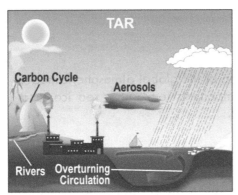
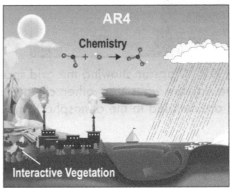

Figure 11.6 Illustration of the evolution of the Earth systems considered in global climate models is shown. Included are the state of climate models in the mid-1970s, mid-1980s, and four International Panel on Climate Change (IPCC) assessment reports: First Assessment Report (FAR, 1990), Second Assessment Report (SAR, 1995), Third Assessment Report (TAR, 2001), and Fourth Assessment Report (AR4, 2007).

Because things like land use, sea surface and deep ocean temperature, atmospheric composition, and permafrost melting are important, atmosphere models must be coupled with other **Earth system models** (Figure 11.6). Increasingly, atmospheric GCMs (AGCMs) are coupled with land, cryosphere, ocean, atmospheric chemistry, and other biosphere models in order to allow those systems to change and not be parameterized (Figure 11.6). Recently, Earth System Models (ESMs) have been developed that include all those systems as modules with a coupler that allows the systems that run on different spatial scales to fully interact. Because of the computer resources such models require, tradeoffs are made in the simplification in parameterizations.

Systems and System Models

A system is a group of related objects or components that form a whole. Systems are often considered completely isolated, but external systems may exchange forces, matter, and energy. The key here is that the system can be studied or modeled in isolation. Part of any experimental design of the system is to ensure that the system is physically isolated, and any external conditions are controlled. For example, when studying the effect of a carbon dioxide increase on a specific plant, it is important to isolate the plant's environmental air from the air external to this system. The components of a system are interdependent, and the functioning of the system can be very different from the functioning of the individual components.

Climate models are an attempt to model the climate system. In this case, the climate system are all the components, forces, feedbacks, and boundaries of the Earth's climate. Originally, the climate system was modeled as just the atmospheric system with all other systems providing some type of external effect or forcing (Figure 11.6). The sun, land, ocean, cryosphere, and biosphere were all external systems that provided an increasingly complex external forcing to the atmosphere. Even the atmospheric chemistry was originally considered an external forcing with the greenhouse gases prescribed as an external forcing. Modern Earth system models operate as a series of isolated systems that externally force one another.

Earth System Models of Intermediate Complexity (EMICs) have also been developed that tradeoff forecasting range or resolution to allow for the more sophisticated parameterizations. Chapter 15 will discuss climate models that go even farther and include non-physical processes such as technological, social, political, and economic changes. These **Integrated Assessment Models (IAMs)** allow a calculation of climate change in the future based on these social changes.

The rest of this section will describe an operational GCM. This GCM is the operational model run by NOAA's National Center for Environmental Prediction and used by NOAA's Climate Prediction Center (CPC) for intraseasonal and seasonal forecasts about one year into the future. It is also run for longer periods both to understand past climate changes and to predict future climate.

Climate Forecast System v.2 Climate Model (CFSv2)

Modern GCMs are similar in structure to weather models and many of the details of data assimilation, grids, and the meaning of parameterization is described in Chapter 10. This section will focus on the differences of a GCM.

The first step in making a forecasting model is gathering data. If you learn anything from this book, hopefully, it is that all science requires observations and data at its foundation. The data needs for GCMs are much more extensive than weather models. Whereas weather models use weather data gathered over less than a six-hour period, climate models typically use at least 30 years of data. Because models are predicting probabilities and other statistical measures, they must be initialized so that the statistics match the beginning of the period that they are forecasting. Therefore, before a GCM can be considered ready to forecast the future climate, it must be able to replicate the statistics of the past climate.

For the Climate Forecast System v.2 (CFSv2), the initial calibration data comes from a reanalysis of observational data from the period 1979-2009. Reanalysis is a method of observations and an Earth System model (e.g. weather, ocean, etc.) that simulates one or more aspects of the Earth system to generate a synthesized estimate of gridded climate data. The components, process, and the data are referred to as the Climate Forecast System Reanalysis (CFSR).[1] The process for producing the reanalyzed weather data is a combination of observed data assimilation and weather model. Essentially, a six-hour weather model forecast from a previous analyzed time serves as the beginning data grid for the new time. Then, new observational data within a six-hour period is assimilated in a similar way as described in Chapter 10. Then, the process repeats for the next six-hour field.

The recently observed data is the same data described in previous chapters in this book. Older observed data comes from some of the same data sources, but some weather stations and satellites are no longer functioning. This assimilation and running the model from a period long ago to ensure a statistical match to the current observations only needed to be completed once, which is good because it took 2 years! An ongoing assimilation process is much more operational (much shorter assimilation time) and uses recent data.

The weather model forecast used for producing the reanalyzed atmospheric data comes from the GFS model. The model runs at an equivalent grid spacing of around 38 km and 64 vertical levels. Unlike weather models, GCMs do not just consist of atmospheric models, but also model other parts of the climate system. In the case of CFSv2 model and CFSR data reanalysis, data are also reanalyzed and produced for the ocean, land, and sea ice.

A similar process produces the ocean and sea-ice reanalysis data. The data for ocean and sea ice comes from the Global Ocean Data Assimilation System (GODAS) and the ocean model is the Modular Ocean Model v.4 (MOMv4) with a coupled sea ice model. The ocean model works similar to an atmospheric model except sea salt distribution is also modeled (Figure 11.7). Sea ice (Figure 11.8) is modeled anywhere ice can form on

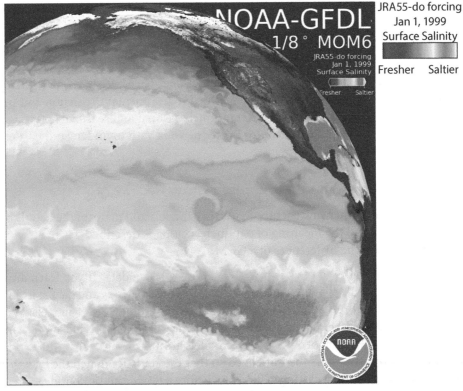

Figure 11.7 Modular Ocean Model v.6 sea salt concentration from Global Ocean Data Assimilation System (GODAS) data.

[1] Saha, S., and Coauthors, 2010: The NCEP Climate Forecast System Reanalysis. *Bull. Amer. Meteor. Soc.*, **91**, 1015–1057.

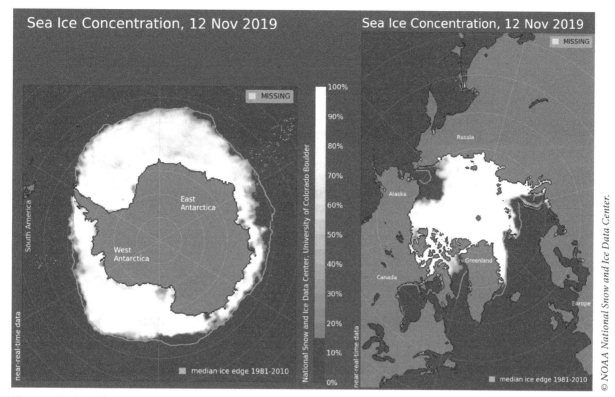

Figure 11.8 Observed sea ice concentration as a percentage of ocean surface on November 12, 2019 compared to 1981-2010 median value from Global Ocean Data Assimilation System (GODAS, orange outline). Data are shown around the South Pole (left) and North Pole (right).

water including the Great Lakes in winter. Typically, the model simulates three layers: one snow and two ice layers of varying thickness. Formation of melt ponds in summer are also considered because of their effect on surface albedo.

The data for the land and soil comes from the Global Land Data Assimilation System (GLDAS) and the land model is the Noah Land model (Figure 11.9). Land height, vegetative cover, snow cover, soil temperature, and soil moisture are some of the things modeled in a land model. GCMs already fully couple the water cycle but are just starting to couple the carbon and nitrogen cycles from the land to the atmosphere and oceans. However, the operational CFSv2 currently uses a prescribed carbon dioxide concentration.

All the modules interface with each other when running the operational CFSv2 model. For example, ocean surface temperature, sea ice melt, sea salt, and snowmelt within the ocean model depend on atmospheric temperature and solar radiation from the atmosphere model. Likewise, albedo in the atmosphere model depends on sea ice from the ocean model and snow and vegetative cover from the land model.

CFSv2 operational model output is hourly and on an approximate 56 km (35 miles) grid. A tight schedule of forecasts allows ensembles to be produced, which are then available for the once per month long-range outlook forecasts described in Chapter 12. Data is available publicly for the reanalysis data from the CFSR and the operational CFSv2. The data is available at the National Center for Environmental Information (NCEI, www.ncei. noaa.gov). Application of CFSv2 and other GCMs for century long model forecasts are discussed in Chapter 15.

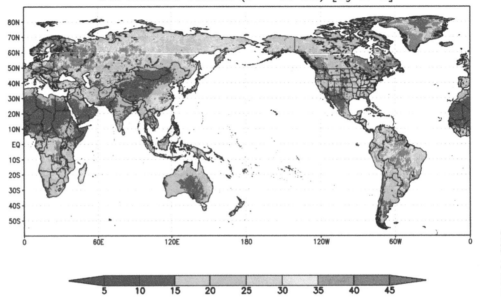

Figure 11.9 Noah Land Model v.2.1 soil moisture content (kg/m² in upper 0 – 10 cm layer) from Global Ocean Data Assimilation System (GODAS) data.

Other GCMs

Several other Global Climate Models (GCMs) are developed and maintained by several different universities and science centers around the world. In the International Panel on Climate Change (IPCC) assessment report 5 (AR5) there were 65 coupled GCMs assessed. Australia, China, Canada, U.S., Russia, Japan, and several European countries manage their own models. Some countries developed multiple climate models. In the U.S., the National Center for Atmospheric Research (Community Earth Science Model), Geophysical Fluid Dynamics Laboratory (CM 2, CM 3, ESM2M, ESM 2G), NASA Goddard Institute for Space Studies (E2-R), and NCEP (CFSv2) all maintain climate models. These models have different methods for handling air movement, different parameterizations, and different data input. Furthermore, the other Earth systems such as the ocean, sea ice, and land use different modular models. Some of the models are beginning to couple carbon, nitrogen, and other biological cycles instead of prescribing them. This is important in studying and representing the feedbacks of permafrost melting and carbon uptake in oceans. It is also useful in understanding biological climate effects such as plant growth, animal migration, habitat health, etc.

Regional Climate Models

With the certain climate changes facing us, many communities are interested to know more specifics about how changes will affect them. No longer is it sufficient to calculate a global mean temperature change or global sea level rise. Climate risk lies in the local impacts on storm water systems, food production, fisheries, and water availability. Municipalities around the world want to know how to become more resilient to these changes and how they will need to adapt. These are tough decisions that affect livelihoods, cost billions of dollars, and affect future policy.

A typical large city like Kansas City, MO is about 50 km (31 miles) across. Even a median sized state like Iowa is about 400 km (250 miles) across. With a grid spacing of 56 km (36 miles) for the CFSv2 climate model, states are just starting to be resolved.

Large cities can be completely contained within one grid point. If that grid point contains a large lake and a large city, like Chicago, IL or Detroit, MI, the temperatures from the GCMs can be a mixture of land and water surface. These cities would not have the information needed to make actionable decisions from GCMs.

One method for determining local effects is by statistically downscaling climate models to local scales. Downscaling is a process used to produce high-resolution data from low-resolution data. The process involves finding statistical relationships between large-scale variables from climate models and observed local scale variables. For example, statistical relationships exist between GCM temperatures around coastal cities, like Chicago, IL, and local city temperatures. In this way, downscaling hopes to produce the city's temperature change from climate model variables. Often this is as simple as determining the change in climate from some control run added to the mean, maximum, and minimum of a local variable. A disadvantage of this technique is that it does not capture any changes in variability. For example, the range between the minimum and maximum temperatures may change, but downscaling may not represent this.

A second method for determining local effects is by dynamically downscaling climate models to local scales. This technique uses the GCM as the boundary condition for a regional scale climate model. Chapter 10 showed how a global scale weather model (e.g. GFS model) is used as the boundary condition for regional weather models (e.g. NAM model). These models provide much skill in areas where regional scale features dominate the local climate variables such as the coastal cities.

Global Climate Model Testing

Model performance can only be tested with past or present climates. It would take too long to make a future climate forecast and wait to compare to observations decades from now. Climate models are continually improved and those decades ago are already obsolete. We can look back at historical climate model forecasts though.

For the late 19th and much of the 20th century, climate models calculated the change in global mean temperature based on a doubling of the carbon dioxide concentration. In 1896, Svante Arrhenius used a zero-dimensional climate model to calculate that doubling carbon dioxide would lead to a 5 °C global temperature change.[2] In a 1967, landmark paper by Syukuro Manabe and Richard Wetherald,[3] the estimate was lowered to 2 °C. That is remarkably consistent to observations from the past 100 years where carbon dioxide has increased by 50% and global temperatures have increased by 1 °C, both half of the 1967 estimate.

In 1990, the International Panel on Climate Change (IPCC) began issuing assessment reports based on climate model results.[4] Carbon dioxide increases were now being estimated based on estimates of future emissions. They concluded that the globe would warm 1 °C above 1990 values by 2025. As of 2018, the globe has warmed by 0.6 °C from 1990. At the current rate of warming, that forecast will also be close.

Models can be compared with other models through ensemble forecasting and sensitivity testing. Although this provides an idea of the precision of climate models, it fails

[2] Arrhenius, Svante (1897). "On the Influence of Carbonic Acid in the Air Upon the Temperature of the Ground". *Publications of the Astronomical Society of the Pacific*. **9** (54): 14-24.

[3] Manabe, S. and R. Wetherald, 1967: "Thermal Equilibrium of the Atmosphere with a Given Distribution of Relative Humidity". *Journal of the Atmospheric Sciences*, **24**(3), 241-259.

[4] Houghton, J.T., G.J. Jenkins, and J.J. Ephraums. Climate Change: The IPCC Scientific Assessment: Report Prepared for IPCC by Working Group 1. Cambridge: Cambridge University Press, 1990.

Recent Climate Model Intercomparison Results (CMIP5)

Recent CMIP intercomparisons have performed well in matching observed global mean temperatures. Figure 11.10 shows the results of CMIP5 for 36 GCMs and 12 EMICs from the 2013 IPCC Fifth Assessment Report. Model output was compared to three different global mean temperature datasets (black lines) from over 140 years. The mean of the GCM results plotted as a temperature anomaly (thick red line) shows many of the trends and fluctuations as the observed temperatures. Even the global cooling that occurs after the five major volcanic eruptions highlighted with green dashes is simulated well.

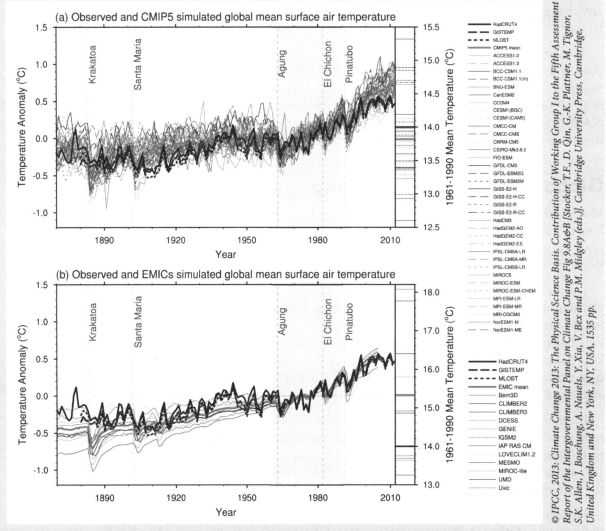

Figure 11.10 Simulation of global mean surface air temperature for all a) Coupled Model Intercomparison Project 5 (CMIP5) GCMs and b) Earth System Model of Intermediate Complexity (EMICs) assessed in IPCC AR5. Individual model line colors are in the legend. Observed mean temperatures (black) and the mean temperature of all CMIP5 GCMs and EMICs (red) are provided. Credit IPCC AR5.

When multiple models are compared with the same input data then the differing model dynamics and physics can be tested. Figure 11.11 shows how individual GCMs output correlates with observations of surface temperature, outgoing longwave radiation, precipitation, and shortwave cloud radiative effect. From CMIP3 (2003-2005) to CMIP5 (2010-2014) correlations improved and are now nearly perfectly correlated for global mean surface air temperatures and outgoing longwave radiation. Precipitation and cloud radiative effect improved by a larger amount and are high, but still have room for improvement.

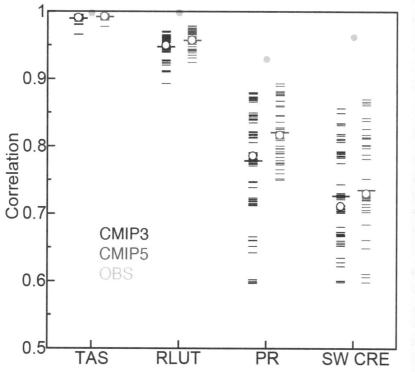

© IPCC, 2013: Climate Change 2013: The Physical Science Basis. Contribution of Working Group I to the Fifth Assessment Report of the Intergovernmental Panel on Climate Change Fig. 9.6 [Stocker, T.F., D. Qin, G.-K. Plattner, M. Tignor, S.K. Allen, J. Boschung, A. Nauels, Y. Xia, V. Bex and P.M. Midgley (eds.)]. Cambridge University Press, Cambridge, United Kingdom and New York, NY, USA, 1535 pp.

Figure 11.11 Comparison of correlation for Coupled Model Intercomparison Project 3 (CMIP3) (2003-2005) and CMIP 5 (2010-2014) GCM simulations of surface air temperature (TAS), outgoing longwave radiation (RLUT), Precipitation (PR) and shortwave cloud radiative effect (SW CRE) compared to observations. Two observation data sets were considered and the correlation of the two datasets are given by the green dot. Credit IPCC AR5.

to provide its accuracy. Nonetheless, the combination of replicating past climates and sensitivity testing provides strong evidence that GCMs are providing an accurate range of potential future climates. Reducing that range is important in determining large-scale future impacts. Reducing the resolution and increasing the climate system's interactions increases the potential for capturing important feedback processes and the accuracy of GCM forecasts. This latter goal also increases the ability to determine local impacts, which is where the climate risks become clear and is more actionable for policy makers.

The World Climate Research Programme (WCRP) coordinates and facilitates climate research. One of their activities is the **Coupled Model Intercomparison Project (CMIP)**. CMIP prescribes a number of inputs and experiments for international modeling programs to simulate and provide their data. Experiments are set up to determine how models perform in simulating past climate for which verification data exists.

Creating the input changes in the variables that cause climate change such as greenhouse gases is an uncertainty. Greenhouse gases depends on population growth, technology advance, economic development, policies, and a host of other societal changes. The process for determining these changes are discussed in Chapter 15.

An important goal of the CMIP program is to allow model output from the various international models be accessible in a standardized format for the international community to analyze. The International Panel on Climate Change (IPCC) produces assessment reports that assesses CMIP data to determine future climate change and their impacts. The U.S. Global Change Research Program produces a National Climate Assessment that also uses this data.

Summary

Climate models differ from weather models in one very important way. Climate models are run as probabilistic and not deterministic. They forecast means and variances over a long period instead of forecasting a specific value of a weather parameter on a specific day. They are run in ensemble mode to produce these probabilities. This difference allows climate models to forecast over much longer ranges of time than weather models.

The simplest climate model is a zero-dimensional climate model in which only one value is produced. These models balance the amount of energy entering and leaving the Earth's climate system to calculate a radiative equilibrium temperature. One-dimensional climate models vary over one dimension. For energy balance climate models, the dimension of variation is latitude and a flux of energy to adjacent latitudes is allowed if temperatures vary. For radiative-convective climate models, the dimension of variation is vertical and a flux of energy to adjacent vertical levels is allowed if lapse rates become large. Full three-dimensional Global Climate Models (GCMs) are essentially a combination of these two models where fluxes can occur horizontally and vertically.

NOAA's National Center for Environmental Prediction (NCEP) runs an operational GCM known as the Climate Forecast System v.2. (CFSv2). Data assimilation is different for this model in that it uses 30 years of data to initialize the model before its forecasts are used. Initially this process took two years but is now updated with more recent data on an ongoing operational schedule that is much more time sensitive. The Climate Prediction Center uses this model for intraseasonal and seasonal forecasts.

CFSv2 along with a number of other national and international climate models creates longer period forecasts. These models have varying resolutions, data sources, and parametrizations like weather models. Unlike weather models, these models require an interface with other Earth system models in order to fully couple with the other Earth spheres. Ocean models, sea ice and glacial models, land models, biological models, and chemical models are examples of the modules required to interface with weather models in GCMs. These models are assessed by several assessment organizations such as the International Panel on Climate Change and the U.S. Global Change Research Program. The Coupled Model Intercomparison Project (CMIP) organizes intercomparisons.

Key Terms

Probabilistic

Deterministic

Climate Models

Zero-dimensional Climate Models

Climate Feedbacks

One-Dimensional Climate Models

Energy Balance Climate Models

Positive Feedbacks

Radiative-Convective Climate Models

Negative Feedbacks

Global Climate Models (GCMs)

Internal Climate Variability

Earth System Models

Earth System Models of Intermediate Complexity (EMICs)

Integrated Assessment Models (IAMs)

International Panel on Climate Change (IPCC)

Statistically Downscaling

Regional Scale Climate Model

Coupled Model Intercomparison Project (CMIP)

Questions and Problems

1. Explain the difference between a deterministic and a probabilistic forecast and give an actual weather or climate forecast example of each from an online source.

2. What is the dimension in one-dimensional climate models? How, then, is there a zero-dimensional model?

3. What is the purpose of having a one-dimensional model? Why not just have full GCMs?

4. Why is the ratio of the Earth emission to the solar absorption have a geometrical factor of 4 in the zero-dimensional climate model?

5. In the energy balance model, describe how the alpha term would change from the equator in Africa to the South Pole. Use the following indexing: α_1=0° latitude or the equator, α_2=10° S latitude, …, α_{10}=90° S latitude or the South Pole. You should have 10 values for the alpha term. What latitudes would change most if all the glacial ice melted?

6. Which one-dimensional model would be best to test the following and why: a) global warming effects on cloud cover, b) global warming effects on glacial melting

7. Draw a flow chart, like Figure 11.4, of the positive feedback that is produced when a microphone is placed near a speaker. Note: Sound from a microphone goes through an amplifier before getting to the speaker.

8. Describe (not just list) two major differences between global climate models (GCMs) and weather models.

9. Based on Figure 11.6, provide a timeline with at least five times showing the progression of processes added to GCMs. Also, include a future addition that has yet to be included based on this text.

10. Why is it necessary to use 30 years of data to initialize a climate model when weather models only need about six hours of data?

11. How is ocean water and sea ice assimilated into GCMs?

12. Why is it important to include ocean water and sea ice in a GCM used to forecast future global temperatures?

13. Why are regional climate models necessary and who uses them?

14. Why are regional climate models considered superior to statistical downscaling? In your answer, focus more on what statistical downscaling is and why it may be perilous to use.

15. Based on CMIP testing, what are climate models good at simulating and what do they have some difficulties in simulating?

Other Resources

https://www.emich.edu/geography-geology/weather for links to useful weather data to go along with this textbook and updates to any broken links in the textbook.

http://climatemodels.uchicago.edu/ includes several radiation, climate, hurricane, and carbon cycle models with simple user inputs to play with.

Chapter 12

Weather and Climate Forecast Products

Introduction

Most people do not realize that professional weather forecasters are providing products. A 2-day forecast is very different from a 3-month outlook, for example. The public are not the only customers of weather forecasts. Retail businesses, energy traders, farmers, pilots, utilities, and others all need weather forecast products. Schools need 6-hour forecasts to determine whether schools will close, and pilots need them to file a flight plan. Utilities need forecasts of varying length to determine the energy capacity they need on hand. Energy traders need 3-month outlooks to set prices for trade and farmers need them to decide on when and what to plant. Many want the 7-day forecast to know if they need to bring an umbrella tomorrow or to alter their weekend plans.

All of these uses dictate the forecast composition and the forecast period or forecast range for weather products. The period or range of the forecast is how many hours, days, or seasons into the future weather conditions are forecast. Composition includes cloud cover, precipitation, temperatures, winds, severe weather and more. Of course, modern scientific forecasts have limitations. Forecasting whether it will rain for a wedding two months into the future is not possible. However, forecasting that it will be a wetter than normal season is possible. In this chapter, the focus will be on the wide array of weather and climate forecast products and the data and tools used to produce them.

Nowcasts

The typical weather forecasts received on Internet, television, or radio are actually composed of three different products. Information given for the next 6 hours is different from information given 5 days into the future. Information within the next 6 hours includes things like snow accumulations, storm start and end times, and severe thunderstorm location and movement. This product is known as the nowcast.

To produce nowcasts, long-range weather models like the GFS (see Chapter 10) are not much help. In fact, weather models are not as significant for nowcasts as radar, satellite, Skew T diagrams, and surface- and upper-air maps. Finding surface boundaries on satellite or trending radar data are more precise real (not simulated) data. Forecasting where in a metropolitan area flooding rain or severe storms will occur is below the resolving capabilities of weather models. Related information such as river heights, road conditions, eyewitness reports, safety precautions, etc. may be included in these nowcasts to give specific local information. Severe and hazardous weather forecasts employ some forecasting methods that are not based on weather models. These forecasts are also nowcasts but are discussed separately in the next couple of chapters.

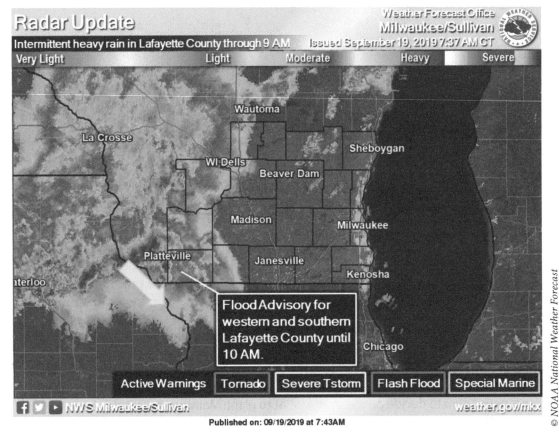

Figure 12.1 Example of a nowcast for Lafayette County Wisconsin issued 12:37 UTC (7:37 AM CDT) September 19, 2019. A text description and safety precautions for flooding were included with this graphical forecast.

The trend method is particularly important in the nowcast. For example, Figure 12.1 shows how radar is used to observe the trend of heavy rain approaching a county in southwest Wisconsin. The nowcast informed residents that heavy rain should be expected for the next hour-and-a-half leading to a flooding advisory. Flood stage information for local rivers showed that hydrologic information was also considered in the nowcast. In addition, the flood advisory provided safety information. Although safety information is not part of the forecast, it is an example of the ancillary products provided in nowcasts.

Short-Range Forecasts

The **short-range forecast** spans the period of 6 hours (0.5 days) to 60 hours (2.5 days). The short-range forecast does not forecast the specifics, extreme weather, or ancillaries that the nowcasts provide. For example, Figure 12.2 provides a National Weather Service (NWS) 7-day forecast, which includes the short-range and mid-range forecast. The forecast for the current day does not mention flooding or the period of heavy rain to within the half hour that the nowcast provides. In fact, the forecast precipitation amount mentions half-three quarters of an inch generally in the broader countywide forecast area. Whereas the flood advisory mention 1-3 inches of precipitation in specific parts of counties. The variability in precipitation intensity shown in Figure 12.1 is difficult to forecast and communicate until the precipitation is present and nearby. This difference in precipitation amount highlights the difficulty in forecasting extreme precipitation amounts beyond a few hours.

Detailed Forecast

Short-range forecast

Today	Showers and thunderstorms, mainly before 1pm. Some of the storms could produce heavy rainfall. High near 79. South wind around 5 mph. Chance of precipitation is 100%. New rainfall amounts between a half and three quarters of an inch possible.
Tonight	A 30 percent chance of showers and thunderstorms, mainly after 1am. Patchy fog after 4am. Otherwise, mostly cloudy, with a low around 64. South wind around 5 mph becoming calm.
Friday	A 30 percent chance of showers and thunderstorms, mainly after 1pm. Patchy fog before 9am. Otherwise, partly sunny, with a high near 83. Calm wind becoming south around 5 mph in the afternoon.
Friday Night	Partly cloudy, with a low around 67. Southeast wind around 5 mph.
Saturday	A 50 percent chance of showers and thunderstorms. Mostly cloudy, with a high near 77. South wind 5 to 15 mph, with gusts as high as 30 mph.
Saturday Night	Showers and thunderstorms likely, mainly before 1am. Mostly cloudy, with a low around 65. South wind 5 to 10 mph. Chance of precipitation is 60%. New rainfall amounts between a quarter and half of an inch possible.

Mid-range forecast

Sunday	A 40 percent chance of showers and thunderstorms. Mostly cloudy, with a high near 74. West wind around 5 mph.
Sunday Night	A 20 percent chance of showers and thunderstorms. Partly cloudy, with a low around 56. West wind around 5 mph becoming calm.
Monday	Sunny, with a high near 73.
Monday Night	Mostly clear, with a low around 55.
Tuesday	A 20 percent chance of showers and thunderstorms. Partly sunny, with a high near 73.
Tuesday Night	A 30 percent chance of showers and thunderstorms. Mostly cloudy, with a low around 58.
Wednesday	A 20 percent chance of showers and thunderstorms. Mostly sunny, with a high near 73.

Figure 12.2 Example of a short- and mid-range forecast provided for southwest Lafayette County Wisconsin (same area as highlighted in Figure 12.1) on the morning of Thursday September 19, 2019.

The short-range forecast will typically include precipitation accumulations, wind speed and directions, and exact probabilities of precipitation. In the sample forecast, wind speed and direction are included in the first day of the mid-range forecast and precipitation probabilities throughout the 7 days. These details are up to the local NWS office and reflects the forecaster's judgement of the ability to forecast these details beyond the short-range.

Short-range forecasts are driven more by weather models particularly the high resolution (e.g. RAP, HRRR) and regional models (e.g. NAM). MOS and ensemble forecasting (see Chapter 10) becomes important for this forecasting period. Ensemble model forecasts provide a level of confidence to weather models by looking at the spread or standard deviation of the ensemble. In addition, forecasters still utilize trend forecasting.

The forecaster's experience of how weather models handle various situations (analog method) is also invaluable and can improve the forecast skill. The forecaster's experience is particularly valuable when the spread of ensemble forecast is large. The forecaster will have to select the models to trust most for the given situation. In addition, forecasters know that weather models do not forecast thunderstorms or areas of extreme rainfall well. Forecasters know these processes are sub-grid and modify the guidance from weather models accordingly.

Mid-Range Forecasts

Mid-range forecasts cover the range of 2.5 days to 10 days. Some forecasters will combine methods for long-range forecast outlooks, climatology, and weather models to provide a 16-day and 30-day forecast. However, these forecasts stretch the abilities of weather models and have not been shown to have any skill.

Mid-range forecasts typically provide sky cover (i.e. sunny, cloudy, etc.), high and low temperatures, and a mention of a chance of precipitation though not always an exact percentage (Figure 12.2). MOS statistics and the trend method becomes unreliable farther out in the forecast period. This restricts the amount of information that forecasters can provide.

Weather models almost entirely guide these forecasts. However, a good forecaster will be able to use their experience to know which weather models to favor. Global weather models (e.g. GFS) are necessary as you move beyond 2.5 days. Chances increase that the air affecting local weather will come from outside a regional weather model domain. The weather model domain of importance may not be just horizontal. The stratosphere can become an increasingly important consideration when forecasting this far in the future (see the "Digging Deeper" box).

Digging Deeper

Stratosphere Effects on Surface Weather

The stratosphere, the bottom of which is around 10 km or near the 250 mb level, is a very stable part of the atmosphere. Changes here are slow to affect the weather in the troposphere. However, over the long term, processes in the stratosphere can have profound effects on the weather at the surface.

Polar vortex outbreaks are one example of dramatic weather events that have roots in the stratosphere. These outbreaks may be predictable a couple weeks in advance due to observing the warming in the Arctic stratosphere.[1] During sudden stratosphere warming events, the arctic stratosphere can warm by 50 K (90 °F) in a week (Figure 12.3). This warming weakens the polar vortex and leads to the shedding of smaller polar vortices (upper-level lows) that can move equatorward (high potential vorticity in Figure 12.3). These polar vortices then move overpopulated areas of Asia, Europe, and North America and cause record-breaking cold Arctic air outbreaks.

The polar vortex is a fall and winter phenomenon arising from the effects of the polar night,

which also lowers ozone in the stratosphere (green areas under ozone in Figure 12.3). Sudden stratospheric warming events are normal and occur every year in the spring, however, a weakening of the polar jet stream can help an earlier breakup and polar vortex outbreak. A negative Artic Oscillation (AO) index can lead to a weakening of the polar vortex and polar vortex intrusions into lower latitudes. Furthermore, the easterly phase of the Quasi Biennial Oscillation (QBO) is associated with more events of sudden stratospheric warming, a weaker Atlantic Ocean jet stream, and colder winters in eastern U.S. and northern Europe. The westerly phase has the opposite effect.

In addition, long-term tropical precipitation cycles can be dependent on the equivalent of atmospheric tides in the stratosphere caused by heating of the stratospheric ozone layer.[2] Much like the ocean tides that are forced by the gravitational pull of the sun and moon on the oceans, the solar heating causes pressure changes in the stratosphere. These pressure changes, which follows the sun's path, affects convection at the surface.

[1] Kretschmer, M.; D. Coumou; L. Agel; M. Barlow; E. Tziperman; and J. Cohen, (2018) More-persistent weak stratospheric polar vortex states linked to cold extremes. *Bull. Amer. Meteor. Soc.*, **99**, 49–60, https://doi.org/10.1175/BAMS-D-16-0259.1

[2] Sakazaki, T; K. Hamilton; C. Zhang; and Y. Wang (2017) Is there a stratospheric pacemaker controlling the daily cycle of tropical rainfall? Geophys Res Lett 44:1998–2006. https://doi.org/10.1002/2017GL072549

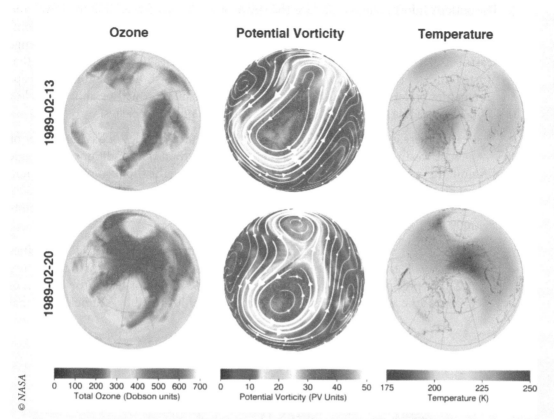

| Ozone | Potential Vorticity | Temperature |

1989-02-13

1989-02-20

© NASA

0 100 200 300 400 500 600 700
Total Ozone (Dobson units)

0   10   20   30   40   50
Potential Vorticity (PV Units)

175   200   225   250
Temperature (K)

Figure 12.3 Measurements in the stratosphere around the 50 hPa (50 mb) level on two days during a stratospheric warming event between February 13, 1989 (top row) and February 20, 1989 (bottom row). First column are total column ozone (Dobson units), second column are potential vorticity, which is a measure of vorticity, and third column is temperature. The North Pole is near the center of all circles and warmed nearly 50 K (90 °F) over this period.

Ensemble forecasting becomes much more important in the mid-range forecast because the uncertainties in weather models become large. Locations where spaghetti plots have small spread give forecasters' confidence. Alternatively, areas with substantial spread suggest to the forecaster that variable weather is coming, but uncertainty is high. Forecaster experience also becomes important because spaghetti plots of different weather models can highlight where some models are known to get Earth system physics wrong. This knowledge allows forecasters to know which weather models are more likely to get the situation correct.

Long-Range Outlooks

The Climate Prediction Center (CPC) produces long-range forecast outlooks that cover the period starting from 6 to 90 days. The products include 6-10-day, 8-14-day, 3-4 weeks, 1-month, 3-month, drought, U.S. hazards, and global tropical hazards. All these forecasts can be found at www.cpc.ncep.noaa.gov. They are all called outlooks because they typically provide only probabilities of above-, below-, or near-normal conditions, except drought. Because the forecasts are a comparison to recent 30-year means, they are considered climate forecasts. Outlooks do not provide specific maximum and minimum temperatures nor conditions on specific days.

The outlook information is valid for the entire outlook period even if both above- and below-average daily conditions can be expected within that period. The 6-10-day outlook overlaps the mid-range weather forecast. This overlap is partially because mid-range forecasts have moved beyond 5 days. However, some industries like the information that a climate outlook provides in comparison to a weather forecast. For example, landscaping companies prefer to know if temperatures and precipitation will be above or below normal. They are less interested to know the conditions on specific days.

The reason there is skill in these outlooks is that the probabilities of having above- or below-average weather over a period is easier to forecast than the conditions on a single day. A similar example given previously would be forecasting the flip of a coin. You would be correct about 50% of the flips if you forecasted the result. However, forecasting a 50% occurrence of heads for a large number of throws will be within a few percentage points nearly 100% of the time.

All NWS outlooks use the same format for presenting probabilities. Probabilities are color-shaded if the probability of being above- or below-normal for temperature (Figure 12.4) or precipitation (Figure 12.5) exceeds 33%. The color bar at the bottom of the image shows the assigned colors for where the probabilities of above- or below-normal

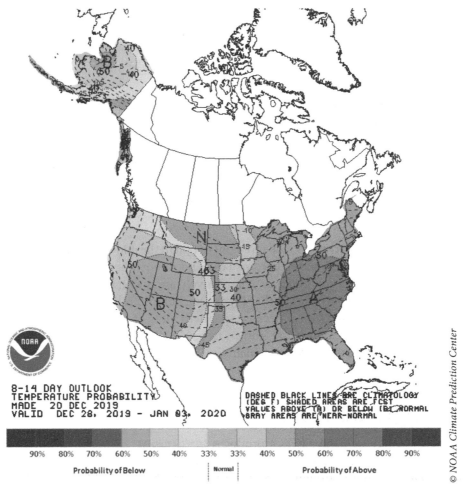

© NOAA Climate Prediction Center

Figure 12.4 8-14 day temperature outlook issued on December 20, 2019 and valid for December 28 – January 3, 2020 is shown. Color shading is defined at the bottom and represents the probability of the period averaging above or below at least 20 of the same one week periods in the prior three decades (in this case 1981-2010).

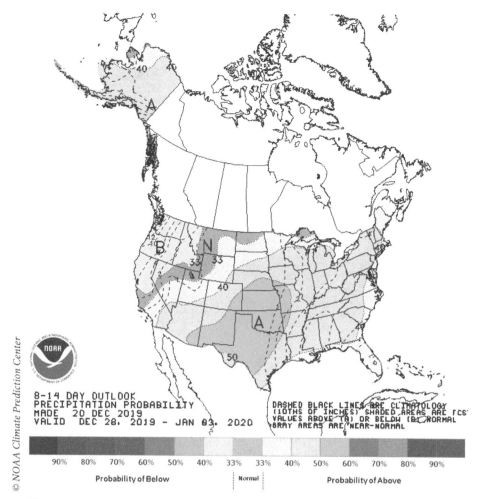

8-14 DAY OUTLOOK
PRECIPITATION PROBABILITY
MADE   20 DEC 2019
VALID   DEC 28, 2019 - JAN 03, 2020

DASHED BLACK LINES ARE CLIMATOLOGY
(10THS OF INCHES) SHADED AREAS ARE FCS
VALUES ABOVE (A) OR BELOW (B) NORMAL
GRAY AREAS ARE NEAR-NORMAL

90% 80% 70% 60% 50% 40% 33% 33% 40% 50% 60% 70% 80% 90%

Probability of Below   Normal   Probability of Above

Figure 12.5 8-14 day temperature outlook issued on December 20, 2019 valid for December 28 – January 3, 2020 is shown. Color shading is defined at the bottom and represents the probability of the period averaging above or below at least 20 of the same one week periods in the prior three decades (in this case 1981-2010).

conditions exist. The reason that 33% is the lower threshold is because all comparisons to normal are for the three-decade period ending on the most recently completed decade. Therefore, for 2020, the normal is defined as the three-decade period 1981-2010. For example, if the temperature is expected to be warmer than the warmest 20 years for this one-week period in this 30-year reference period then it has a 33% chance of being above-normal.

6-10 Day Outlook

NWS 6-10-day outlooks rely on weather model ensembles to estimate temperature and precipitation and are updated daily. The main consideration is where locations lie within the modeled 500 mb height contour trough/ridge pattern. The models used in this case are the global weather models such as the GFS and GEFS. The ensemble data provides both a mean and standard deviation of all the models or model runs that make up the ensemble (Figure 12.6). These statistics provide the strength of the troughs and ridges (given by the trough/ridge pattern of the mean wind) and the probability of the pattern occurring (given by the spread). Analogous years are selected from a database of previous 500 mb height contours that most nearly match the current pattern to aide in determining

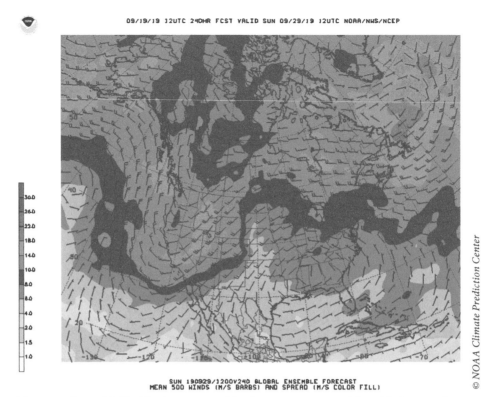

SUN 190929/1200V240 GLOBAL ENSEMBLE FORECAST
MEAN 500 WINDS (M/S BARBS) AND SPREAD (M/S COLOR FILL)

© *NOAA Climate Prediction Center*

Figure 12.6 GEFS 10-day ensemble forecast run on 12 UTC September 19, 2019 valid 12 UTC September 29, 2019 showing the mean (wind barbs) and spread (color fill) of the 500 mb winds.

the likelihood of being above- or below-normal. The forecaster provides additional skill by knowing which models to weight in creating the average guidance pattern. Not shown in this figure is the forecast for days 6-9, which showed the troughs and ridges gradually forming and amplifying over the U.S. Because weather model output is still somewhat accurate over this forecast period, the individual days are also considered in the forecast.

Whether locations lie in a trough or ridge determines whether that area will be colder or warmer than average. Remember in Chapter 7, troughs form when the layer beneath the trough axis is cold. Therefore, where troughs are located, the air is typically colder than average. The opposite is true for upper-air ridges, which are produced by warmer layers of air. The probabilities of being above- or below-average is based on a combination of the ensemble spread and the strength of the troughs and ridges. Figure 12.6 shows a strong trough building in the west and ridge building in the east side of the U.S. (see wind barbs in Figure 12.6). A relatively small spread (blue contours in Figure 12.6) exists in the 10-day ensemble forecast. This pattern suggests a high confidence of warmer than normal temperatures in the east and central U.S. and colder than normal conditions in the west. Figure 12.7 shows the official NOAA Climate Prediction Center 6-10-day temperature forecast for the period that corresponds to the period in Figure 12.6.

For precipitation, the same trough/ridge pattern informs storm track likelihoods. Areas downstream of the mean 500 mb trough axis are typically locations of upper-air divergence, rising air, and precipitation. Areas downstream of the mean 500 mb ridge axis are typically locations of upper-air convergence, sinking air, and no precipitation. Likely locations of surface fronts and maritime flow patterns at the surface are also locations of a higher probability of precipitation. Figure 12.6 suggests that the Rockies will be wetter than normal because they lie east of the trough axis in the 10-day ensemble mean.

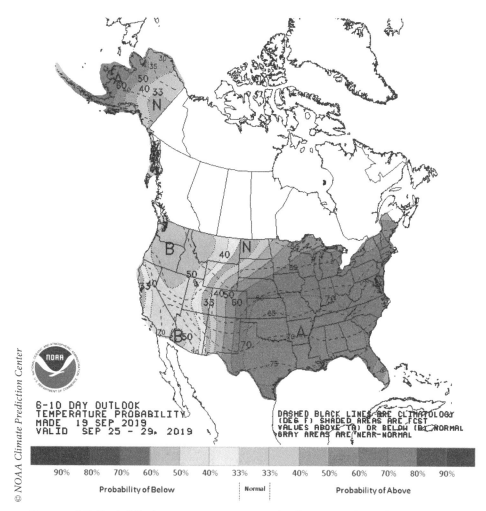

Figure 12.7 6-10 day temperature outlook created on September 19, 2019 valid for September 25-29, 2019.

States from Texas north have maritime flow and are likely to be wetter than normal. The east coast lies east of the ridge axis and are likely to be dryer than average. Figure 12.8 shows the official NOAA Climate Prediction Center 6-10-day temperature forecast for the period that corresponds to the period in Figure 12.6. Notice that the highest above average probability in the continental U.S. is downstream of the mean trough where the modeled winds are greatest.

8-14 Day Outlooks

These outlooks are released daily like the 6-10-day outlooks. They also consider much the same tools as the 6-10-day outlooks because the global models (GFS, Canadian model, ECMWF model, Ukmet model, etc.) all produce model calculations to at least 14 days. For the 6-10-day outlook, only the main outlook considerations were described. However, as forecasting periods become longer, other longer time-scale influences are considered. Surface features, such as snow cover, soil moisture, sea surface temperatures, etc., can have a major influence on weather patterns. For example, an anomalously warm blob (actual name) of water has been persistent in the northern Pacific Ocean in the Gulf of Alaska for much of the fall of 2019 (Figure 12.9). Because of predicted westerly winds,

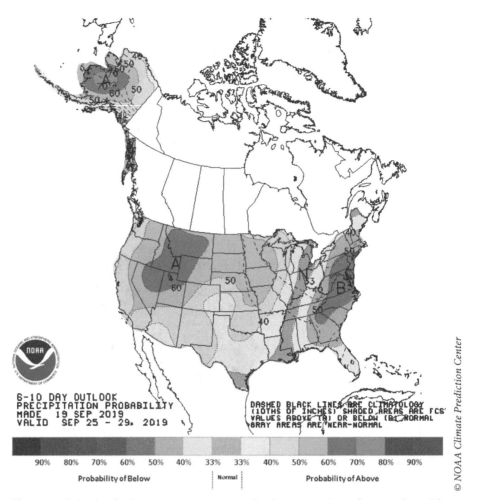

Figure 12.8 6-10 day precipitation outlook created on September 19, 2019 valid for September 25-29, 2019.

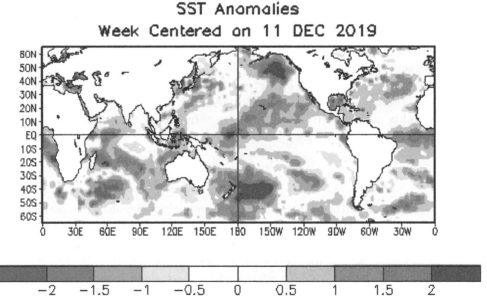

Figure 12.9 Sea Surface Temperature (SST) anomalies averaged for the week centered on December 11, 2019 are shown. Temperature anomalies are given in the scale at the bottom.

the official 8-14-day temperature outlook by the CPC (Figure 12.4) for the southern pan-handle of Alaska is a high probability of above average temperatures even though the rest of Alaska's temperature outlook was for below normal temperatures.

Knowledge of the ridge/trough pattern is often modified with knowledge of surface land conditions too. A deep snowpack greatly reduces surface temperature because of latent heating, solar scattering, and infrared emission. Reduced temperatures are likely with a thick snowpack even with an expected ridge. In addition, once a drought is estab-lished in summer, precipitation often evaporates before reaching the surface due to the dry surface air. The effects of a drought can last an entire season.

3-4 Week, One-Month, and Three-Month Outlooks

The 3-4-week outlook covers the two weeks after the 8-14-day outlook. The 3-4-week outlooks are released every Friday and the 1- and 3-month outlooks are released on the third Thursday of each month. The monthly and 3-month outlooks are valid for the fol-lowing calendar month or 3 months. Although, 3-month outlooks are also provided for three-month periods for the entire year. Because of the date of release of the 1-month and 3-month outlooks, the 1-month outlook approximately covers the 30-day period after the 8-14-day outlook. The 3-month outlook is approximately a full season. Oftentimes, 3-month outlooks are presented to the public as an outlook of what a specific season's temperatures or precipitation will be compared to average. For example, an outlook of a cold and snowy winter comes from the seasonal outlook.

Weather prediction models have no skill past two weeks as chaos takes over and the uncertainties grow too large. These outlooks use climate models instead of weather pre-diction models. The National Center for Environmental Prediction (NCEP) runs the Climate Forecast System v.2 (CFSv2) model, which is an ensemble model, run with 40 dif-ferent perturbations to the initial observations. The CPC uses this model and models run at ECMWF and Japan. They also use the North American multi-model ensemble, which is an ensemble of 6-8 models from the U.S. and Canada. Using multiple models pro-vides a better estimate of forecast uncertainty. Climate models were discussed in detail in Chapter 11, but a point of emphasis is important to mention here. Climate models predict means and other statistics, not specific weather on specific dates. For example, a climate model may forecast the mean number of tropical cyclones in an ocean basin over time.

For these outlook periods, there are some longer time scale influences that are known to have an effect on long-range means. Some of these were discussed already such as soil moisture, sea surface temperature, and snow cover. Tropical cyclones during the hurri-cane season are difficult to forecast weeks and months into the future and can dramati-cally affect long-range outlooks. Tropical cyclones transport a lot of moisture and energy and can affect the movement of longwaves.

The CPC uses two different statistical models. Statistical models are not based on physical laws like weather and climate models, but on past statistics. One of the statistical models is the Constructed Analog (CA). The CA uses a combination of past seasons to construct an atmospheric and oceanic state that is similar to the current state. Because we know the results of those past years, we can make a statistical guess as to what will hap-pen in the future. A second statistical model is the Canonical Correlation Analysis (CCA), which attempts to correlate the recent behavior of the Pacific Ocean and its effects on U.S. temperatures and precipitation. Both of these statistical models provide guidance and it is up to the forecaster's experience in how to apply them to the outlooks.

Furthermore, outlooks must consider the current state of important internal climate cycles and the planetary-scale oscillations and their teleconnections discussed in Chapter 8. The greatest effects of the El Nino Southern Oscillation (ENSO), Arctic Oscillation (AO), North Atlantic Oscillation (NAO), and the Pacific Decadal Oscillations (PDO) are in winter in the northern hemisphere, but these sometimes extend into the spring. In the summer and fall, the major jet streams are weaker, and the polar jet stream moves into far north Canada, so the teleconnections are less influential. The exception is the effect on the subtropical jet stream and tropical cyclones.

NOAA's Tropical Prediction Center puts out a seasonal forecast for tropical cyclones multiple times prior to and throughout the northern hemisphere tropical season (June-December). These forecasts are based on sea surface temperatures, location and strength of semipermanent highs, and teleconnections. For example, during El Nino conditions, the stronger upper-troposphere winds, which tends to produce strong wind shear, reduces tropical cyclone production over the Atlantic Ocean. Because the western Pacific cools in an El Nino, the subtropical jet stream here weakens. Consequently, the reverse pattern of weaker upper-troposphere winds increases tropical cyclone production over the Pacific Ocean. During La Nina conditions, weaker wind shear over the Atlantic Ocean favors tropical cyclone production while stronger wind shear in the Pacific reduces tropical cyclone production.

Figure 12.10 provides the three-month forecast for the October, November, and December 2019 period. Above-average temperatures are forecasted for the entire forecast area. Forecasters considered El Nino/La Nina (considerations provided in available

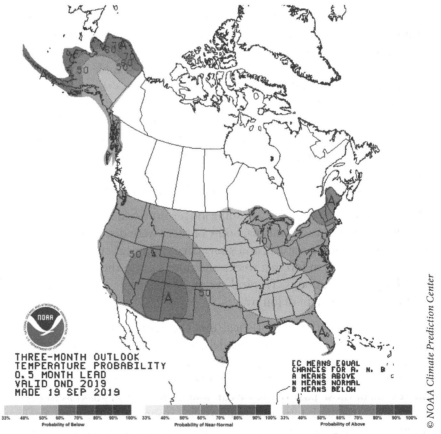

Figure 12.10 Three-month temperature outlook for the months of October, November, and December 2019 are shown. Percentage of exceeding the mean temperature for the same months in the 1980-2010 period are color-coded with the legend shown at the bottom.

forecast discussions), which for this period was forecast to be absent. Other internal climate oscillations had been weak at this time. Very high percentages (>70%) of exceeding temperature averages were expected in Alaska because of the forecast of the high sea surface temperatures surrounding Alaska (Figure 12.9). The outlook has high confidence here because the warm temperatures are also captured in the dynamical and statistical models. In the rest of the continental U.S., dynamical and statistical models agreed with above-average temperatures, but the percentages were less in the northern states. The lower confidence was because of the uncertainty of the effects that an active period of tropical cyclones at the beginning of the forecast period would have on the longwave pattern. Furthermore, the AO has trended negative to this point suggesting that cold air is more likely to move south into these areas making for variable temperatures throughout the period.

Figure 12.11 provides the same outlook period, but for precipitation. In this case, the probabilities are not as high as the temperatures because there is not the same decadal increase in precipitation from global warming. High probability of above-average precipitation exists in Alaska because the expected warmth should delay the onset of sea ice surrounding the state, which increases humidity transport into the state. Humidity transport from the expected increased activity of tropical cyclones in the Pacific and Atlantic Ocean also leads to expected above-average precipitation in the green shaded areas. The below-average precipitation in the northwest is attributed to the climate and statistical model guidance.

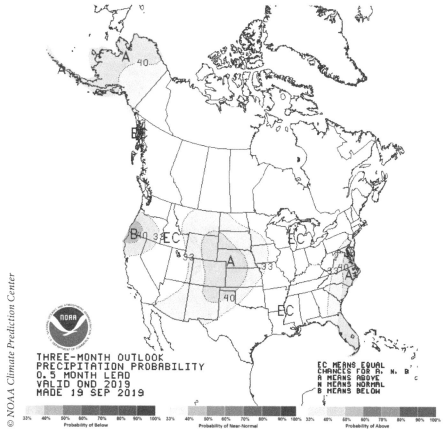

Figure 12.11 Three-month precipitation outlook for the months of October, November, and December 2019 are shown. Percentage of exceeding the mean precipitation for the same months in the 1980-2010 period are color-coded with the legend shown at the bottom.

Hazardous Weather Outlooks

The Storm Prediction Center (https://www.spc.noaa.gov/) issues an 8-day **convective outlook** and **fire outlook** with forecasts of thunderstorm, severe weather, and fire threats. For the day 1-3 convective outlooks, the probability of a thunderstorms or severe thunderstorms occurring in a 40 km (25 mile) area are given (Figure 12.12). The 4-8-day outlooks outline areas where severe thunderstorms are at least 30% likely. The **convective outlook risk categories** for the day 1-3 convective outlooks are as follows:

Thunderstorm—10% probability of severe or non-severe thunderstorms for each area.

Marginal—isolated severe thunderstorms (5% chance) of short duration and/or coverage

Slight—Scattered severe thunderstorms (15% chance) of short duration and/or coverage with some isolated intense storms

Enhanced—More widespread severe weather (30% chance) of longer duration and/or coverage and more intense storms

Moderate—Widespread severe thunderstorms (45% chance) that are long-lived and intense.

High—Severe thunderstorms are likely (60% chance) with a strong likelihood of significant severe weather (i.e. very large hail or particularly violent tornadoes).

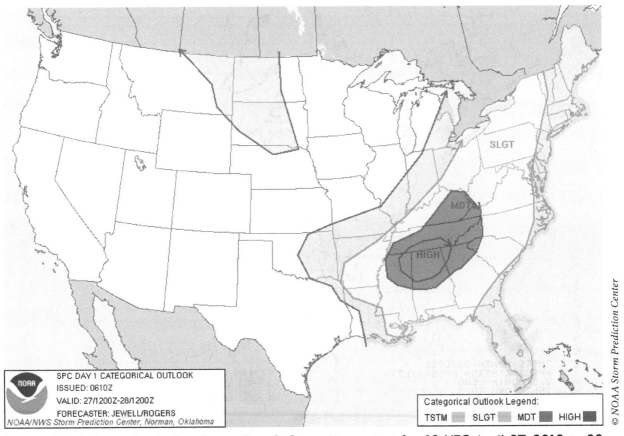

Figure 12.12 Storm Prediction Center Day 1 Convective output for 12 UTC April 27, 2019 to 02 UTC April 27, 2019 issued at 06 UTC April 27, 2019. Later this day 292 tornadoes were reported.

Fire hazard forecasts utilize a combination of temperature, relative humidity, and thunderstorm forecasts. High temperature and low relative humidity particularly over a long time provide the fuel for wildfires. Lightning from thunderstorms provides the spark. When dry wood is available, the likelihood of wildfires from human influence is higher. Specific thresholds are given for elevated, critical, or extremely critical.

The Weather Prediction Center (https://www.wpc.ncep.noaa.gov/threats/threats.php) issues a 3-7-day **weather hazards forecast**. Hazards include flooding; heavy ice, rain, or snow; severe storms; excessive heat; high winds; much above/below normal temperatures; significant water waves; wildfires; and drought. Although some of these hazards overlap with those predicted by the Storm Prediction Center, this outlook provides all the possible weather hazards in one location. The Climate Prediction Center (https://www.cpc.ncep.noaa.gov/products/predictions/threats/threats.php) also issues an 8-14-day weather hazards forecast. However, the risks are confined to precipitation, temperature, and wind hazards.

Watches and Warnings

The NWS is solely responsible for the issuance of official watches and warnings in the U.S. (Figure 12.13). Over 40 different official watches and warnings exist. Only those related to the severe weather discussed in the next two chapters are described in this section. Some watches and warnings differ depending on location. For example, wind chill advisories are issued for southern Florida when wind chills are expected to be below 2 °C (35 °F), whereas, the threshold for Minneapolis, MN is –32 °C (–25 °F). On the other hand, heat advisories are issued for heat indices (combination of effects of temperature and dewpoint) greater than 38 °C (100 °F) for Minneapolis, MN, whereas, the threshold for Houston, TX is 43 °C (110 °F). All other watches and warnings are standardized for all locations.

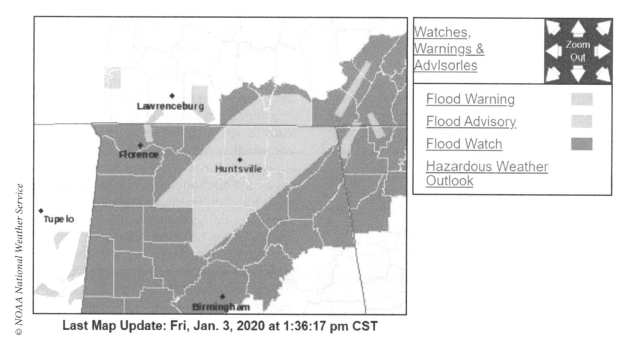

© NOAA National Weather Service

Last Map Update: Fri, Jan. 3, 2020 at 1:36:17 pm CST

Figure 12.13 The National Weather Service issues watches by county or portion of a county and warnings with smaller polygons within counties as shown by these flood watches and warnings from the Huntsville, AL NWS office on January 3, 2020.

Obtaining, Evaluating, and Communicating Information

Reading, writing, and understanding scientific literature is extremely important to the scientist and to becoming a scientifically literate citizen. For a novice scientist, scientific writing is difficult for three reasons. First, scientific writing has a set of jargon that makes writing easy. However, those unaware or first learning this jargon may find it difficult to understand. Much of this jargon may not be found in standard dictionaries making it even more difficult. Second, scientific text is often information dense and individual words contain very precise meaning. Reading scientific texts require more concentration than popular literature such as novels and newspapers. Scientific texts cannot be read like a novel and doing so will often lead to a lack of comprehension. Finally, scientific writing is often multimodal. Scientific texts often contain words, equations, tables, diagrams, graphs, illustrations, etc. For this reason, graphical novels like comic books are more akin to scientific writing than novels. Contrary to what seems to be popular opinion, comic books are actually sophisticated reading materials.

Writing and speaking in science is as fundamental as learning to draw for an artist. The central role of communication in science is often surprising to aspiring scientists. Scientists are stereotypically introverts who find communication in written or spoken form more difficult. Assuaging this difficulty is the specific form of much of scientific writing.

Scientific writing starts with an introduction that includes background knowledge, thesis statement, objectives, and layout of the paper. The hypothesis and analysis performed is included in a thesis statement. The thesis statement often begins with the words, "The purpose of this paper ..." or "This paper will ..." and appears near the end of the Introduction. The reason that it appears at the end of the introduction is that the reader may need the background information to understand it and some of the paper's jargon. The methodology is the second section and includes materials used, data sources, dates (if relevant), statistics used, models, rejection of data with reasons, and a summary of procedures. Results are the next section and includes data in the form of figures, images, graphs, tables along with a description of the important features in the data relevant to the objectives. Finally, a discussion of the results is included especially in relation to the thesis statement in the introduction. These discussions are interpretations of the results, comparisons to other studies, relationships to relevant scientific theories or the thesis statement. The formulaic way of writing provides a good model for understanding how a scientist expects to communicate.

Unfortunately, communication to the public cannot follow this form, which makes it difficult for scientists to communicate more generally. The weather broadcaster (TV, radio, or newspaper) must communicate the weather in short and simplified broadcasts or articles for quick consumption of information. Communication of public safety information must convey precise descriptions of the dangers and important safety information. Usually the focus of weather broadcasts is on results. However, the lack of background and methodology leads to scientifically literate citizens to question whether the information they are receiving is valid, considers all important factors, or has a valid methodology. A perfect example of this is the complex concept of global warming. Questions always arise about whether natural changes have been considered or how such changes differ from past changes. The absence of methodology often leads to these questions. The problem is that including such information requires too much time for most of the public to tolerate.

The NWS issues the following winter, flood, wind, and foggy weather watches and warnings for the U.S.:

Frost advisory: issued when maximum temperature is forecasted to be 0° C (32 °F) to 3 °C (36 °F) on clear and calm nights.

Freeze watch/warning: issued when minimum temperature is forecasted to be below freezing, 0 °C (32 °F). Watches are for conditions within 24-36 hours and warnings are issued for within 24 hours. All frost and freeze advisories are issued during the growing season only. The growing season varies by location, but usually begins with the last frost and ends at the first freeze.

Winter weather advisory: Issued when any amount of freezing rain or 2-4 inches of snow/sleet/freezing rain is forecasted.

Winter storm watch/warning: issued when ¼"of freezing rain, 5" of snow/sleet accumulation in 12 hours, and/or 7" of snow/sleet accumulation in a 24-hour period is forecasted. Watches are issued within 48 hours and warnings are issued within 24 hours.

Ice storm warning: issued when ¼" of freezing rain is forecasted.

Blizzard warning: issued when snow and/or blowing snow is forecasted to reduce visibility to ¼ mile or less for 3 hours or longer with sustained winds of 30 knots (35 mph) or greater.

Flood/flash flood watch/warning: issued when flooding or flash flooding is possible for a watch or imminent for a warning. Flash floods are rapid rises of water usually occurring within 6 hours of the start of heavy rain or due to dam breaks. Ocean, lake, and rivers can also reach flood stage resulting in coastal, lake, and river flood warnings.

Wind advisory: issued when sustained winds of 25-35 knots (31-39 mph) for an hour or more or wind gusts of 40-50 knots (46-57 mph) are forecasted.

High wind watch/warning: issued when sustained winds greater than 35 knots (40 mph) or wind gusts greater than 50 knots (58 mph) are forecasted. Watches are issued if conditions are possible and warnings are issued if conditions are occurring or imminent.

Dense fog advisory: issued when fog is forecasted to reduce visibilities to ¼ mile or less for at least 2 hours.

The forecasting of most of these severe weather events are covered in Chapter 13. Chapter 14 will cover thunderstorm and tropical severe weather events. NWS issues the following thunderstorm and tropical cyclone watches and warnings for the U.S.:

Severe thunderstorm watch/warning: issued when winds of 50 knots (58 mph) or greater, and/or hail 1" in diameter, and/or tornadoes are forecasted. Watches are issued if severe thunderstorms are possible. Warnings are issued when severe thunderstorms are occurring.

Tornado watch/warning: issued when tornadoes are forecasted. Watches are issued if tornadoes are possible, warning are issued when tornadoes are occurring.

Tropical storm watch/warning: issued when tropical storm conditions (i.e. winds 35-65 knots or 39-73 mph) are forecasted. The storm producing these conditions could be a hurricane, but hurricane conditions are not forecasted in the advised area. Watches are issued when tropical storm conditions are forecasted within 48 hours and watches are issued when conditions are forecasted within 24 hours.

Hurricane watch/warning: same as tropical storm watch/warning except hurricane conditions (i.e. winds 65 knots (74 mph) or greater) are forecasted.

Summary

Weather forecasters produce a number of products for public consumption. The most public of these products are the seven- or ten-day forecasts seen on weather broadcasts. These are actually three different products. The shortest-term product is the nowcast, which is the weather forecast for the next 6 hours. It includes things like snow accumulations, storm start and end times, and severe thunderstorm location and movement. Forecasters employ the steady state method for nowcasts. The short-range forecast is for the period 6 hours to 2.5 days. It typically includes precipitation accumulations, wind speed and directions, and exact probabilities of precipitation. Regional and higher resolution weather models provide most of the forecast guidance for this period. The Mid-range forecast is for the period 2.5 to 10 days. It typically provides sky cover (i.e. sunny, cloudy, etc.), high and low temperatures, and a mention of a chance of precipitation. Global weather models and ensemble modeling provides most of the guidance for this period.

Long-range outlooks are climate forecasts in that they only provide probabilistic forecasts relative to average. The outlooks include the 6-10-day, 8-14-day, 3-4-week, monthly, and three-month forecasts. Information provided is a probability of temperature or precipitation above or below average compared to a recent past 30-year average. The 6-10-and-8-14-day outlook primarily use weather models and ensemble models for guidance. However, they will also use snow cover, soil moisture, and sea surface temperatures upstream of a location to guide these forecasts. The other products use dynamical and statistical climate models, known teleconnections, and internal climate oscillations.

The Storm Prediction Center (SPC), Weather Prediction Center (WPC), and Climate Prediction Center (CPC) also have hazardous weather outlooks. The SPC provides an 8-day convection (i.e. thunderstorm) and fire outlook. The WPC provides a 3-7-day weather hazards forecast. Hazards include flooding; heavy ice, rain, or snow; severe storms; excessive heat; high winds; much above/below normal temperatures; significant water waves; wildfires; and drought. The CPC provides an 8-14-day weather hazards forecast with less specific precipitation, temperature, and wind hazards. Many of these hazards have specific thresholds for watches and warnings to be issued to the public.

Key Terms

Forecast Composition

Forecast Range

Nowcast

Short-Range Forecast

Mid-Range Forecast

Long-Range Forecast Outlooks

Convective Outlook

Fire Outlook

Convective Outlook Risk Categories

Weather Hazards Forecast

Questions and Problems

1. Find and provide a nowcast like in Figure 12.1. Discuss the important information the nowcast is conveying and the data used to put together the nowcast forecast.

2. Find a short- and mid-range forecast like in Figure 12.2 for your area and point out information that is conveyed in the short-range forecast that is not conveyed in the mid-range forecast. Based on your knowledge of weather forecasting describe why it would be difficult to convey the information not in the mid-range forecast.

3. Contrast the data used in a short-range forecast from one used in an 8-14-day outlook.

4. Describe a couple of different forecast products and the importance each one may be to you.

5. Provide the forecast range and composition for two forecast products that are not adjacent (i.e. nowcasts and short-range forecasts are adjacent in time).

6. Find and provide an 8-14-day outlook map for your area and describe what information it conveys to you for your area.

7. Find and provide a 3-4-week outlook map for your area. Look at the forecast discussion and describe some of the things mentioned in this textbook that was considered for an area that has a high probability of above or below average temperature or precipitation.

8. For a 3-month outlook issued on February 16 for the spring months of March, April, and May, what will the forecast tell you about the weather to be expected on April 15?

9. How are weather models used differently in short-range forecasts from long-range outlooks?

10. When do outlooks go from relying on weather models to climate models and why is this?

11. Why does a thick snowpack often lead to an extended period of cold temperatures?

12. How would an El Nino year affect tropical cyclones in the Atlantic Ocean and why?

13. What is the National Weather Service criteria for an ice storm?

14. Why are wind-chill warnings and advisories influenced by geographic location?

15. If a winter storm warning is upgraded to a blizzard warning in your area, what additional features of the expected winter storm are the National Weather Service now likely predicting?

16. What is the difference between severe thunderstorm and tornado watches from severe thunderstorm and tornado warnings?

Other Resources

https://www.emich.edu/geography-geology/weather for links to useful weather data to go along with this textbook and updates to any broken links in the textbook.

Chapter 13

Hazardous Weather Forecasting – Snow and Ice Storms, Floods, and Wind Storms

Introduction

This chapter discusses the special forecasting considerations for hazardous weather that occurs during snow, ice storms, non-tropical floods, and windstorms. Hazardous cold weather includes snowstorms and blizzards, lake-effect snow, and ice storms. Tropical cyclones also produce flooding, and along with thunderstorms, can produce damaging high winds, but they are covered in the next chapter.

Weather models will provide measured amounts of heavy rain, snow and ice, and high winds. However, weather models have limitations covered in Chapter 10 that limits the predictability of more hazardous weather. Weather models do not have the resolution to simulate the processes and small-scale variability that leads to most cases of hazardous weather. Hazardous weather forecasting requires more densely packed data because the special forecasting considerations require observing smaller-scale features.

Up until now, this textbook discussed processes that are classified as synoptic scale (e.g. fronts, midlatitude cyclones, etc.) and microscale (precipitation formation, radiative transfer, etc.), but analyzing hazardous weather requires a middle scale. Forecasters call this middle scale, mesoscale. The Storm Prediction Center's Mesoanalysis website (https://www.spc.noaa.gov/exper/mesoanalysis/) provides the needed denser data analysis that is used in these next two chapters. Forecasting these mesoscale features also restricts us to a shorter time-scale, which is often the case in dealing with smaller spatial scales. The focus in these chapters is predominantly on nowcasting and some short-range forecasting. Make sure to visit the mesoanalysis website when referenced throughout the chapter.

Snowstorms and Blizzards

From late fall to early spring, the combination of a more southerly-positioned jet stream, and a larger surface temperature gradient lead to stronger midlatitude cyclones. The cold weather also leads to frozen precipitation from these cyclones producing snowstorms and blizzards. Chapter 7 highlighted preferred areas of cyclogenesis and these areas cause different types of snowstorms that affect different areas of North America. This section will move west-to-east and start with a discussion of western U.S. snowstorms.

Scale, Proportion, and Quantity

In weather and climate, like all sciences, important processes vary over a large range of time, space, and energy. Oftentimes, things that happen over short time periods such as the time it takes for air to rise, expand, and adiabatically cool does not need to be considered in the time that it takes the air to rise. The expansion is essentially instantaneous and the cooling happens no matter how fast air rises in most weather applications. The time scale of these processes are far different and can be considered as two separate processes. Scale or the relative size or extent, is an important scientific concept for distilling the most important components of a scientific process. On a spatial scale, the whirls in the smoke coming out of a chimney does not appreciably influence the flow of air in a city.

Related to scale are the concepts of proportion and quantity. Proportion can simply be a fraction or parts of a whole. Water makes up 1 in 100 molecules of air while carbon dioxide makes up 400 in 1,000,000 molecules, which is also 400 parts per million (ppm). Quantity is the total amount and can be expressed as a fraction, but it is not parts of a whole like proportions. For example, velocity is related to distance traveled and time. The quantity expresses the magni tude of the velocity or speed. However, unless you know the units of scale you would not be communicating speed even if you divide the two numbers. Those numbers must have a scale and appreciating the magnitude of the units of scale helps to appreciate quantity.

Up until now, this textbook has focused on fronts, pressure centers, air masses, etc. Meteorologists categorize these features as synoptic scale, which have a scale of several hundred kilometers (hundreds of miles) or more and weather models do an excellent job of simulating this scale. Meteorologists categorize features that are several hundred kilometers (few hundred miles) down to a few kilometers (about a mile) as mesoscale. Regional weather models simulate only half this scale and high-resolution models (NAM HIRES and HRRR) are just starting to get into the low end of this scale. Microscale features are those less than about 1 km (0.6 miles) and include turbulent processes, precipitation formation processes, etc. The separation into these scales help meteorologists consider processes that are important on one scale without worrying about processes on the smaller scales that may have little impact.

Gulf of Alaska Low – Coastal and Mountain Snowstorms

The Gulf of Alaska is a preferred area of cyclogenesis because of the strong temperature gradient between the cold land and the ocean water. The warm current of water offshore moves north from the North Pacific drift. These Gulf of Alaska lows have a large temperature gradient, ample humidity from the Pacific Ocean, and the rapid rise in elevation forcing rising air as the maritime air comes ashore. Midlatitude cyclones often form here, but the upper-air divergence is what determines the reduction in surface low pressure. Stronger surface winds result from the lowering of the surface pressure, which leads to a stronger pressure gradient, faster circulation around the low-pressure center and stronger surface winds. With a lack of surface friction from the smooth ocean, the winds can be quite strong as they come onshore.

Besides the central surface pressure and upper-air divergence, the amount of precipitation largely depends on access to humidity. Warmer sea surface temperatures and a thicker layer of humidity produce higher precipitation rates. Typically, the sea surface temperatures in the northern hemisphere are warmer farther south. Occasionally, an atmospheric river will set up to provide ample humidity for these systems. In the western half of the U.S., these rivers typically form when the jet stream splits in the central Pacific with a portion of the jet stream moving south to tap into warmer sea surface temperatures (Figure 13.1). The generated waviness of the jet stream allows the southern branch of the jet to collocate with the cyclogenesis and upper-air support of the northern branch.

Heavy precipitation, warm air, and rapid elevation changes produce melting snowpack and mudslides along the Coastal, Sierra, Cascade, and Rocky Mountains. Figure 13.2 shows the varying topography of the coastal mountains of California within the first 75 km (45 miles) from the ocean. Elevations quickly rise to over 5000 feet and farther northeast to over 8000 feet. Slopes are steep enough to produce mudslides especially in areas that have recently experienced wildfires. Local forecasters must be aware of steeply sloped land that wildfires have stripped of vegetation. Coastal storms often leads to mudslides on this land.

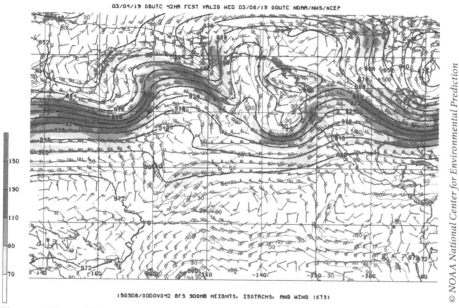

Figure 13.1 300 mb map for 00 UTC March 6, 2019 showing a split polar jet stream with a northern branch (blue) eventually creating an area of upper-air divergence downstream of a deep trough and on the left exit region of a 110-130 knot jet streak. The southern branch produces an atmospheric river (green arrow) from the equatorial Pacific to the west coast of North America.

Figure 13.2 View of the Los Angeles, CA coastline shown.

The rapid elevation changes and condition of the land over small distances are not captured well in weather models. Furthermore, data are sparse in mountainous areas and radar has difficulty penetrating the rugged terrain. Despite these limitations, local forecasters must forecast numerous mountain storm effects that are below the resolution of weather models.

In mountainous areas, the temperature decreases as elevation increases. Oftentimes, even if you know how much liquid will fall from the sky, the rapid changes in elevation and temperature causes the rain/snow line to vary horizontally and vertically and both must be forecasted. Precipitation type can change rapidly over small distances, so snow accumulations are often given by elevation. The snow ratio, ratio of snow accumulation to liquid water content (see Chapter 6), varies over large ranges. Mountain snows often have very high snow ratios because of the cold dry air at elevation. A small amount of liquid can produce a large accumulation of powdery snow. Snowstorms often produce two or three feet of snow on the windward side of mountains and mountain passes in the western U.S.

Forecasters also need to carefully consider the precise wind direction and the orientation of the mountain passes and peaks for local enhancements of rising air and precipitation rates. Wind speeds can also vary over small distances as air becomes constrained, causing it to accelerate in mountain passes. Local forecasting offices generally have experience with these smaller scale considerations and use the analog forecasting method on top of weather model guidance. For all these reasons, mountain snowstorms (and mountain weather in general) are some of the most difficult weather to predict. Many people think their weather is changeable, but the most dramatic changes in weather occur in the mountains.

Alberta Clipper

Cyclogenesis often occurs downstream of the Canadian Rockies in Alberta, Canada producing a cyclone often referred to as the Alberta Clipper (cf Figure 7.3). Upper-air support can make these cyclones intense, but they lack the temperature gradient and humidity source of many other areas of cyclogenesis. Some of the more intense Clipper systems will tap into Gulf of Mexico moisture, but setting up a low-level jet of humidity from the Gulf to Canada is rare. The Clipper systems themselves are typically not large enough to reach this far south. As the system moves further south, the potential to tap into Gulf moisture must be monitored by watching surface to 700 mb winds and dewpoints. However, precipitation from these systems are usually more dependent on the speed of motion of the system. Clippers, more often than most cyclones, produce mostly snow and affect southern Canada and the north central plains and Great Lakes areas. Because of the lack of humidity, accumulations are usually limited to several inches.

Colorado Low

Similar to the Alberta Clipper, the Colorado Low forms downstream of mountains, in this case the Colorado Rockies. Also, like the Alberta Clipper, Colorado Lows do not have the strong temperature gradient, but being further south means maritime tropical air is not as far away. A case study of a bomb cyclone that formed in south central Colorado on March 12, 2019 illustrates the important ingredients necessary for a strong midlatitude cyclone.

Starting at 00 UTC March 13, 2019, the ingredients that led to its rapid development were taking shape. The surface pressure at the center of the low at this time was 995 hPa

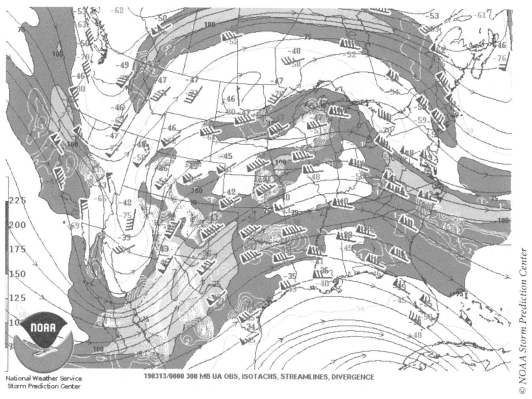

National Weather Service
Storm Prediction Center

190313/0000 300 MB UA OBS, ISOTACHS, STREAMLINES, DIVERGENCE

© NOAA Storm Prediction Center

Figure 13.3 300 mb map on 00 UTC March 13, 2019 showing the strong jet streak winds (shaded light blue) in excess of 125 knots (144 mph) over a preferred area of cyclogenesis in southern Colorado and New Mexico.

(995 mb). Figure 13.3 shows the 300 mb map at 00 UTC March 13, 2019. Two features are important to notice here. First, there is a deep trough producing strong upper-air divergence over central Colorado and New Mexico. This area is collocated with the preferred area of midlatitude cyclogenesis east of the Colorado Rockies. Second, this area is on the left exit region of a jet streak with winds in excess of 125 knots (144 mph). This is a strong jet streak by most standards.

More clues exist at 500 mb in Figure 13.4. At the same time as the previous figure, a strong trough exists at 500 mb, but there is a shortwave going through the trough. The shortwave will deepen the trough and the trough axis will become negatively tilted. In Chapter 7, a negatively tilted trough is defined as one that is sloped from northwest to southeast. Figure 13.5 shows how the pressure trough went from positively tilted at this time to negatively tilted 12 hours later producing extreme upper-air divergence.

Conditions in this cyclone also illustrates the environment for the promotion of a snowstorm to a blizzard. Figure 13.6 shows the cyclone low at 12 UTC March 13, 2019 in the middle of this rapid decrease in central pressure. At this time, the central pressure had dropped 19 hPa (19 mb) in 12 hours to a central pressure of 976 hPa (976 mb) and dropped an additional 8 hPa (8 mb) in the next 6 hours to a central pressure of 968 hPa (968 mb). That is the equivalent central pressure to a category 2 hurricane. The large pressure gradient and cold temperatures in western Nebraska and eastern Colorado produced snow, reduced visibilities to less than a ¼ mile, and sustained winds in excess of 35 mph. These are the threshold conditions for a blizzard.

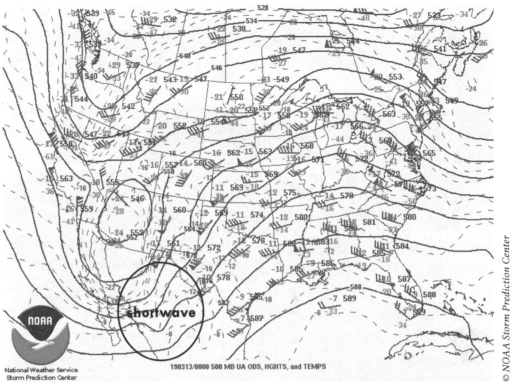

Figure 13.4 500 mb map on 12 UTC March 13, 2019 is showing a shortwave trough moving through a longwave trough. The shortwave trough can be seen in Mexico where the height contours are shaped like a small trough.

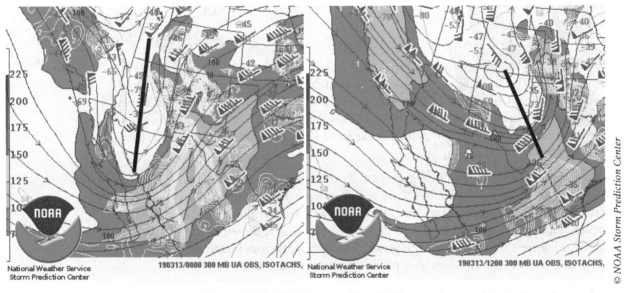

Figure 13.5 300 mb maps on 00 and 12 UTC March 13, 2019 are shown. Black line shows the positively tilted trough (left) becomes a negatively tilted trough (right) in less than 12 hours.

This midlatitude cyclone produced blizzard conditions in northern Colorado, Nebraska and South Dakota in an area to the northeast of the surface low located in southern Colorado (Figure 13.6). This quadrant (northeast) of the midlatitude cyclone is often where the heaviest accumulations occur. The warm conveyor belt rises over the well-formed occluded front (purple front) producing a TROWAL. The surface winds from the Gulf of

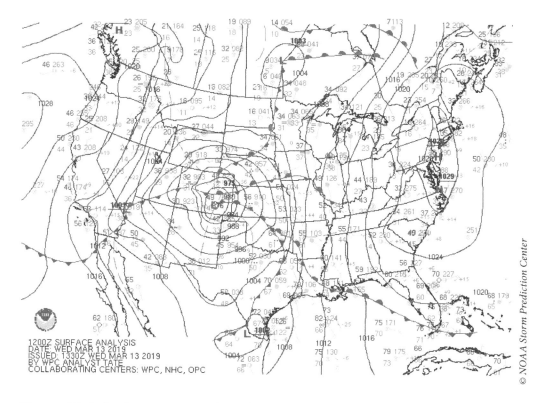

map imagery with the copyright text on the right edge:
© NOAA Storm Prediction Center

Figure 13.6 Surface map on 12 UTC March 13, 2019 showing a Colorado low in the middle of its rapid development with a central pressure of 975 hPa (975 mb).

Mexico parallel this front representing a well-developed low-level jet of maritime tropical air. Dewpoints observed at the coastal Gulf States are approaching 70 °F, which is quite high especially for early March. Therefore, this cyclone had a significant source of humidity transported north to an area where snow formed. Colorado lows like these rarely produce the accumulations of west coast mountain snows, but strong snowstorms like these approach accumulations of 2 feet particularly if the cyclone moves slowly.

Gulf of Mexico and Hatteras Lows and the Nor'easter

Along the Gulf of Mexico coast and the Atlantic seaboard, conditions are favorable in all the ways of the Gulf of Alaska Lows, but with warmer temperatures and higher humidity. In fact, the warm Gulf Stream produces some of the largest temperature gradients just off the east coast near Cape Hatteras in winter. Figure 13.7 shows that the 20 °C (68 °F) isotherm exists immediately off the coast of Cape Hatteras. When a low-pressure center brings air cold enough for snow into Virginia and North Carolina the temperatures can differ by 20 °C or 36 °F over a distance less than 100 km (60 miles). That is a distance drivable in less than an hour.

A major difference between Gulf of Mexico Lows and Hatteras Lows is the position of the upper-air trough and surface cold air. Both Lows form when a cold air mass reaches the coast, but which coast it reaches largely depends on the upper-air trough. When the upper air trough is further west and south polar and arctic fronts will extend to the Gulf of Mexico and with upper-air divergence in place a low will form there. A strong wavy subtropical jet also increases the likelihood of the formation of a Gulf Low. In fact, El Nino years, which causes a stronger subtropical jet, leads to more Gulf Lows.

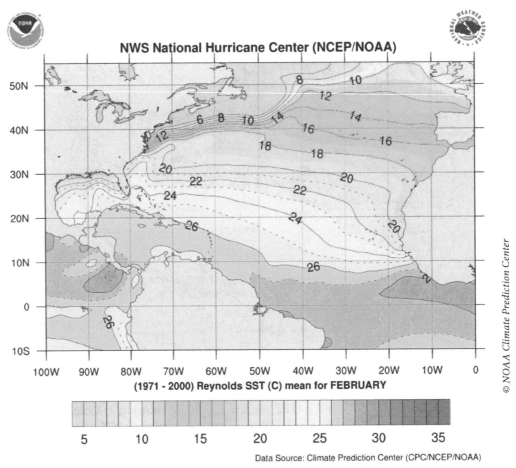

Figure 13.7 1971-2000 Mean sea surface temperature for the month of February.

Hatteras Lows are more likely when the upper air trough is further east and the cold front of a Colorado Low or Alberta Clipper approaches the Atlantic coastline. The combination of the upper-air divergence east of the trough and the large temperature gradient between the cold air mass and the warm Gulf Stream often produces midlatitude cyclones of the coast of Cape Hatteras.

Such extreme temperature gradients provide a large amount of potential energy for these coastal storms called **Nor'easters**. The name Nor'easter comes from the strongest onshore winds from the storm being from the northeast, which benefit from the lack of friction over the water. The longer these storms stay close to the coastline, the more humidity they transport onshore. Therefore, the speed and direction these storms move are critically important in order to get the correct combination of temperature gradient, humidity flux, and proximity to the coastline to maximize snowfall accumulations. Remember that the largest accumulations are found to the north and east of the surface low, which for an east coast storm would be mostly offshore if not for the southwest-to-northeast shaped coastline. Therefore, the largest accumulations in Nor'easters occur in slow moving Nor'easters that remain offshore, but close to the coastline. Of course, the temperature profile needs to be cold enough to produce snow so forecasting this is also key to precipitation forecasts.

One example of how this can mess up a forecast happened with a March 17, 2017 Nor'easter. The storm dumped nearly 3 feet of snow in some places approaching

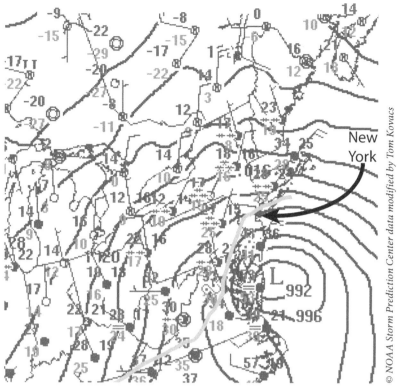

Figure 13.8 Surface map at 12 UTC March 14, 2017 during a major Nor'easter is shown. The green line represents the approximate location of the rain/snow line with New York City barely on the rain side.

accumulations only found in west coast mountain snowstorms. New York City had a forecast for a foot of snow, but ended up with four inches. Although to most this sounds like a big miss, the forecasters had missed the rain/snow line by only a few miles (Figure 13.8).

Although coastal storms brings ashore a lot of warm humid air, it is the prediction of the surface cold air that can make or break a forecast. As long as surface cold air is in place prior to the storm forming and entering the area, it will often remain cold because of cold-air damming. With strong northeasterly winds on the north side of a midlatitude cyclone, the Appalachian Mountains dams the heavy surface cold air and the warm humid air rises up and over this air. Otherwise, a strong flow of cold polar air from the north would need to be in place.

Lake-Effect Snowstorms

Lake-effect snowstorms are special cases of snowstorms that occur downstream of a large body of water. They can also be called ocean-effect snowstorms. The Great Lakes produce the most lake-effect snow. Sometimes the effect occurs during a regular snowstorm adding to the accumulations near a lake. In this case, locally they would be called lake-enhanced snowstorms. Some of the strongest lake-effect snowstorms can rival and even surpass west coast mountain snows with 4-foot snow accumulations not unheard of. The big difference is that these large accumulations are typically only found in a very small geographic zone. In fact, areas a few miles away from 4-foot snow accumulations can experience no accumulation.

Dendritic Growth Zone

Snowfall amount also depends on how the snowflakes grow. Chapter 6 showed how snow crystals could grow into different habits depending upon the temperature and amount of moisture in the cloudy environment. Accumulating snow grows faster as dendrites. Dendrites form in temperatures between –17 °C (1 °F) and –12 °C (10 °F). The vertical area between these temperatures is called the dendritic growth zone. Characteristics such as the physical depth of this layer and the relative humidity within this depth help determine the location of the heaviest snowfall. Weather models parameterize this process and use it to calculate accumulation rates.

The storm prediction mesoanalysis (https://www.spc.noaa.gov/exper/mesoanalysis/) cal-

culates the depth of this layer, which can be plotted along with the relative humidity. Upon selecting a region, maps for these parameters are found under the winter weather tab. Figure 13.9 provides a sample map for a winter storm that occurred on January 1, 2020. The figure shows the depth of the dendritic zone and the relative humidity. Circled is the area that has a combination of the largest dendritic zone depth collocated with high relative humidity. It is here, all other considerations equal, that you would expect the largest snow accumulations. Of course, other factors such as the temperature profile, snow accumulation to liquid water ratio, horizontal humidity flux, and speed of the storm movement also play a role in snow accumulations.

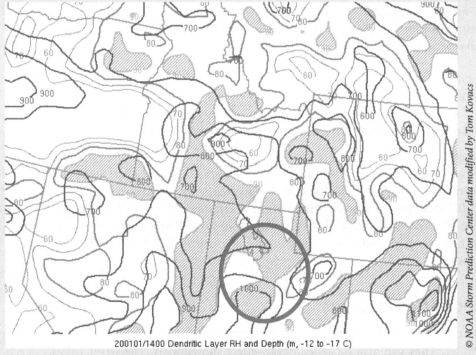

200101/1400 Dendritic Layer RH and Depth (m, -12 to -17 C)

© NOAA Storm Prediction Center data modified by Tom Kovacs

Figure 13.9 Diagram of dendritic layer relative humidity (green shading is RH > 80%) and depth (m, blue lines) on 14 UTC January 1, 2020. The red circle is where over a foot of snow was expected and is also where the dendritic layer depth and relative humidity are highest.

Lake-effect snowstorms occur when a continental polar (cP) air mass blows over a lake that is significantly warmer than the air (Figure 13.10). As cP air moves over a warm lake, the bottom of the air mass gains warmth and humidity. Because the air mass is warming from below this increases the temperature lapse rate and makes the air mass more unstable. When the air mass makes it to the other side of the warm lake it moves onto a surface with increased friction and possibly some elevation change. The increased friction slows the winds down and causes convergence and with the elevation change forces rising air. The rising air occurs in an unstable air mass and produces rows of cumulonimbus clouds that align with the wind direction producing lines of cumulonimbus clouds that can be seen in radar and visible satellite imagery (Figure 13.11).

Cumulonimbus clouds with snowfall is rare because it is difficult to get unstable air masses with the weak sun of winter. They often form in lake-effect snowstorms when there is a particularly large difference between the temperature of the lake surface and the temperature of the surface air moving over the lake. Elevated thunderstorms also occasionally occur in other snowstorms when unstable maritime tropical air moves over cold air. They produce heavy snowfall, lightning, and thunder and are popularly called thundersnows.

There are three main things important to consider when forecasting lake-effect snowstorms: fetch, surface convergence, and the difference between air and lake temperature. Fetch is the distance that cP air travels over the warm lake water. The

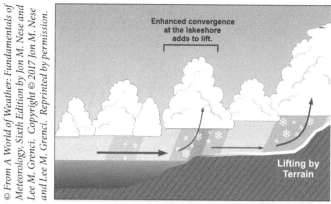

Figure 13.10 Illustration of the process for lake-effect snow production is shown. The blue arrow is cold continental polar air moving over an unfrozen relatively warm body of water. Convergence and frontal lifting as the air comes onshore lifts unstable air upward to form cumulonimbus clouds.

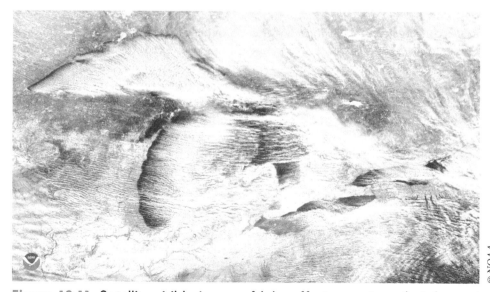

Figure 13.11 Satellite visible image of lake effect snowstorm that dumped 1.5 m (5 feet) of snow in Erie, PA December 24-27, 2017.

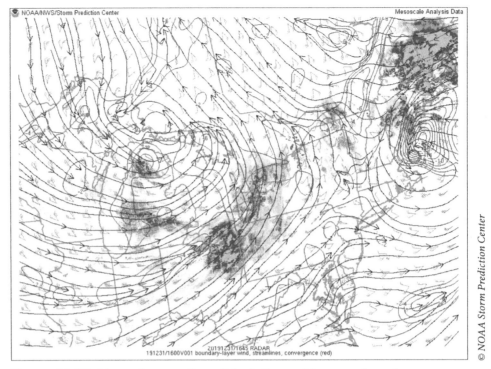

Figure 13.12 Map of streamlines (black lines with arrows), surface convergence (red contours), and radar reflectivity on 16 UTC December 31, 2019.

cities of Buffalo and Syracuse, NY and Marquette, MI are notorious for large lake-effect snowstorms. These cities all average more than 2.4 m (94 inches) of snow each year. The reason these cities have so much snow is because they are located at the end of a long fetch of water. Marquette, MI lies south of the longest fetch across Lake Superior. Buffalo and Syracuse, NY lies to the east of the longest fetch of Lakes Erie and Ontario, respectively.

Surface convergence and rising elevations provide a mechanism for causing air to rise. Going to the mesoanalysis link at the beginning of the chapter and choosing winter weather provides lake effect snow maps. One will give a map of surface convergence and streamlines for the Great Lakes (Figure 13.12). Remember from Chapter 3 that convergence is the negative of divergence. Larger negative values mean stronger surface convergence, which forces stronger rising air. The streamlines, which shows the path surface air will take, provide an idea of the fetch. Higher elevations force this air up producing the largest accumulations. In Figure 13.12, the highest reflectivities are found where streamlines are moving from the lakes (mostly Lake Michigan) to land with the highest values of convergence.

Once air is forced to rise then unstable air will determine how rapidly the air will rise. Faster rising air will lead to heavier snowfall rates and the possibility of thundersnows. For lake-effect snow, the difference between surface and 850 mb temperatures is the important parameter. Typically, 9 °C (16 °F) difference is the threshold to produce a conditionally unstable atmosphere and lake-effect snow. Following the mesoanalysis link at the beginning of the chapter and choosing a different lake effect snow winter weather map will give a map of relative humidity and surface – 850 mb temperature difference (Figure 13.13). Larger values for these two parameters leads to larger snow accumulations. Similar to Figure 13.12 the highest radar reflectivities are found downstream of the largest temperature differences.

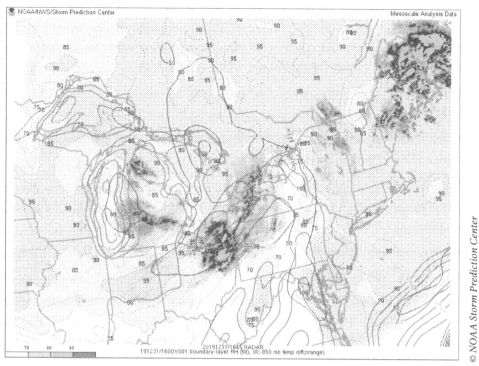

Figure 13.13 Map of planetary boundary layer relative humidity (green shading) and surface-850 mb temperature difference (orange contours) on 16 UTC December 31, 2019.

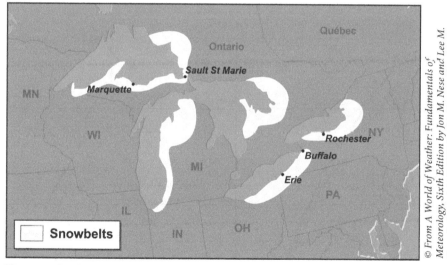

Figure 13.14 Lake effect snowbelts are shown in white. Areas south and east of these belts will also receive lake-effect snow, but it is less likely and often with smaller accumulations.

Figure 13.14 shows the typical lake-effect snow belts. Lake-effect snow typically falls to the south and east of lakes. The reason that lake effect snow does not often fall to the north of lakes is that would require a southerly wind, which is rarely cold enough to produce lake-effect snow. Areas to the west of lakes occasionally gets lake-effect snow, but winds do not typically blow against the prevailing westerly winds.

The lake-effect snow season typically lasts from November to February. Once the lakes freeze over the ice typically cools much faster than the water and the air rarely gets much colder than the ice. Evaporation is also shut down and sublimation of the ice does not produce nearly as much water vapor as a liquid surface. Lake Erie typically freezes over first because it is a much shallower lake. Ice cover maps are a consideration when forecasting for lake-effect snow and can be found at https://www.glerl.noaa.gov/data/ice/#currentConditions.

Ice Storms

Ice storms occur with freezing rain. Oftentimes a mixture of precipitation can fall from clouds that extend to heights that include above and below freezing temperatures. The skew-T diagram is the best tool for identifying precipitation type. Precipitation forms in clouds and clouds form when the air temperature and dewpoint temperature are nearly equal. Therefore, clouds can be observed on skew-T diagrams where the air temperature and dewpoint temperature are nearly equal.

Figure 13.15 shows two cases of wintry precipitation in Detroit, MI and Alpena, MI that is not rain nor snow. In both cases, a thick cloud layer extends from near the surface to about 600 mb and the surface temperature is below the freezing point. The Skew-T diagram for Detroit is typical of a freezing rain or ice storm event. The surface temperature is –2 °C (29 °F), but at around 925 mb or about 400 m altitude the temperature hits the freezing point. Above-freezing temperatures extend from 925 mb up to nearly 700 mb, which is nearly 2500 m thick. Even at the top of the cloud layer the temperature is above –10 C. Precipitation is likely to form as rain and even if ice forms at the top of the cloud, the 2500 m thick layer of above-freezing temperatures that it would need to fall through would likely melt the ice. Furthermore, the 400 m thick layer of below-freezing temperatures at the surface is likely not thick enough to freeze the drops on the way down.

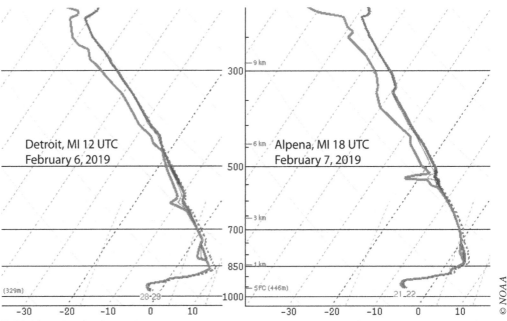

Figure 13.15 Skew T diagrams for Detroit, MI on 12 UTC February 6, 2019 (left) and Alpena, MI on 18 UTC February 7, 2019 (right) are shown. Air temperature (red) and dewpoint temperature (green) are provided. Temperature grid is skewed and parallel to the yellow dashed line. Detroit was reporting freezing rain while Alpena was reporting unknown precipitation.

Figure 13.16 shows a picture of ground conditions just west of Detroit, MI on February 6, 2019 several hours after the Skew-T diagram for Detroit, MI. Ice accumulates on the branches because the precipitation is falling as rain, but the water freezes on contact to the below-freezing surface. Ice accumulation is measured by using a ruler and measuring the ice layer above and below the branch and dividing by two. In this case, the ice is about 0.005 m (0.2 inches) thick or just below the ice storm limit of 0.006 m (0.25 inches). For a large tree with a 10 m radius, r, the amount of ice that sticks to the tree is the product of the cross-section area of the tree and the ice accumulation (e.g. 0.006 m):

$$V = \pi r^2 \times \text{accumulation} = \pi(10 \ m)^2 \times 0.006 m = 1.9 \ m^3.$$

The density of water (ρ) is 1000 kg/m³ so the mass of water that fell on the tree is:

$$mass = \rho V = 1000 \ kg/m^3 \times 1.9 \ m^3 = 1900 \ kg.$$

This mass translates to a weight of about 4200 lbs. of ice. Usually only a fraction of the rain that falls actually freezes to the tree, but even if a quarter of the rain freezes that is over 1000 lbs. of ice. That is why 0.006 m (0.25 inches) of

Figure 13.16 Ice accumulation on a bush near Detroit, MI on February 6, 2019.

freezing rain is the threshold for a damaging ice storm. That weight of ice can easily take down large branches or weak/dead trees. With greater precipitation or wind, ice storms can be quite damaging.

The Skew-T diagram for Alpena (Figure 13.15) is typical of a mixed precipitation event with some freezing rain. The surface temperature is −5 °C (22 °F), and it is not until around 900 mb or about 550 m altitude that the temperature hits the freezing point. Above-freezing temperatures extend from 900 mb up to nearly 750 mb, which is only 1500 m thick. At the top of the cloud layer, the temperature is below −10 C (14 °F). Precipitation is likely to form as rain except at the top of the cloud where it is like to form as snow. The 1500 m thick layer of above-freezing temperatures may not completely melt this snow. Furthermore, the 550 m thick layer of below-freezing temperatures at the ground is likely to freeze some of the drops on the way to the ground. This environment suggests that a combination of snow, freezing rain, and sleet will fall.

The cold side of warm and stationary fronts are prime locations for producing ice storms (Figure 13.17). These fronts tend to have a shallow slope over the cold air allowing for the thin layer of cold air near the surface conducive to freezing rain. Freezing rain falls in a narrow swath on the cold side of the front where the cold layer is still shallow and cold enough not to freeze falling precipitation until it reaches the surface.

Another environment that produces ice storms are cold air damming and cold air trapping events in the Appalachian Mountains. Cold air trapping occurs when a warm front moves into the Appalachian Mountains (Figure 13.18). The terrain traps the denser cold air and the warm air mass is unable to displace the cold air stuck in the valleys. This trapped cold air is usually quite shallow and if the air is below freezing, any liquid precipitation in the area will freeze on the surface. A similar event called cold air damming

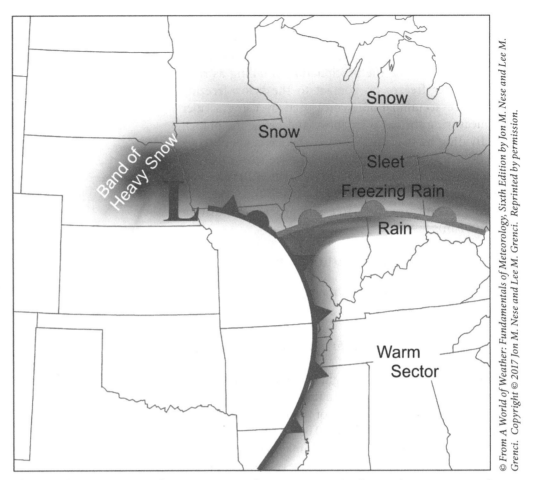

Figure 13.17 Large-scale environment for ice storms is shown. Ice storms tend to occur slightly north of warm fronts where the subfreezing layer beneath the warm front is shallow.

occurs when a midlatitude cyclone is on the coast and warm humid air blows toward the west and the Appalachian Mountains. In this case, the mountains would dam the existing cold air mass with similar effects. The role of cold air damming was also mentioned in the Gulf and Hatteras Low section.

Floods

Hydrological forecasting is related to weather forecasting and the National Weather Service forecasting centers employ hydrologists. Flood and drought forecasting is done by hydrologists and they issue flood and drought statements, watches, and warnings. Forecasting for flooding is complex because flooding does not just depend on weather. Flooding occurs when the amount of liquid water added to a surface is greater than the sum of evaporation and infiltration into the ground. When flooding occurs, water runs off along the surface and fills basements and other low areas when they are in the way of the runoff. To forecast for flooding, hydrologists build **hydrological models** that account for water in snowpack, evaporation, groundwater flow, height and speed of rivers, infiltration, precipitation, soil saturation, temperature, and other important weather variables.

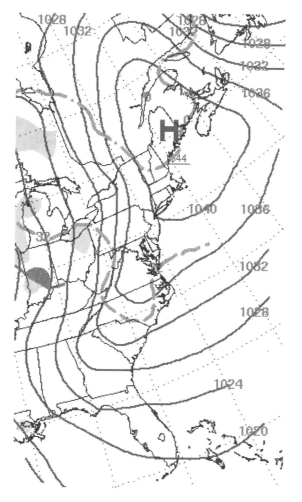

Figure 13.18 Typical cold air damming event is shown. The trough in the isobars extending from the high-pressure center (solid brown) and freezing temperature (dashed blue) is a signal that the Appalachian Mountains trapped cold air in the valleys.

The key weather input into hydrological models is a measure of how much water will be added to a **watershed**. A watershed is an area that falling precipitation will be confined by land elevation to a single outlet. Liquid water can be added into a watershed through melting snow, precipitation, groundwater flow, and rivers. If the amount of water added to a watershed is too much, rivers rise. If the rivers reach flood stage, which is the height from the bottom to the top of the riverbank, the river will overflow its banks and create flooding (Figure 13.19).

Once water precipitates on the ground, infiltration into the ground depends on the **porosity** and **permeability** of the ground. Porosity is the amount of open spaces in otherwise solid material. A sponge, for example, has good porosity because it can hold a large amount of water in its open spaces. However, if the water cannot move through the interconnected open-spaces then infiltration will be slow. Permeability is the ability for water to move through those open spaces. Clay for example has high porosity,

Figure 13.19 River above flood stage causing flooding in homes.

but very low permeability. Ground that has high porosity can hold a large amount of water and if it also has high permeability, it can take in water rapidly. However, water in the ground filling all open spaces eliminates infiltration. A frozen ground also greatly reduces infiltration.

In addition, replacing soil with streets, sidewalks, buildings, and other impermeable materials reduces infiltration. This reduced infiltration is why new neighborhoods build retention ponds to account for the increased runoff. In addition, it is why stormwater systems are built, to redirect runoff to rivers and lakes.

Temperature affects whether the ground, snow, and ice melts and whether frozen rivers will thaw. Taking a core of the snowpack to the ground and melting it determines the amount of liquid water in the snowpack. A foot of fluffy freshly fallen snow has much less liquid water than a foot of old compacted snow. Above-freezing temperatures improve infiltration if the ground thaws, but they also increase liquid water if the snowpack melts. Thawed rivers can lead to broken blocks of ice that can dam a river, known as **ice jams**, and cause flooding (Figure 13.20).

In the warm seasons, when frozen ground and snowpack are not factors, the important weather consideration is the amount of precipitation in a watershed. The intensity, duration, and number of rain events and the size relative to the river watershed are key factors. If a watershed is in a storm track on the longwave pattern, several large rain events in a short period can cause the ground to saturate and then runoff to increase. Equally effective would be a cutoff low that causes a multiday rain event.

An example of a cutoff low event caused over 5 inches of rain to fall in the Tittabawassee River basin on May 18 and 19, 2020. The excessive rain caused major flooding on the river and catastrophic dam failures holding the Wixom and Sanford lakes on the Tittabawassee River upstream of Midland, MI. After the dams broke at approximately 22 z

Figure 13.20 Ice jam causing flooding.

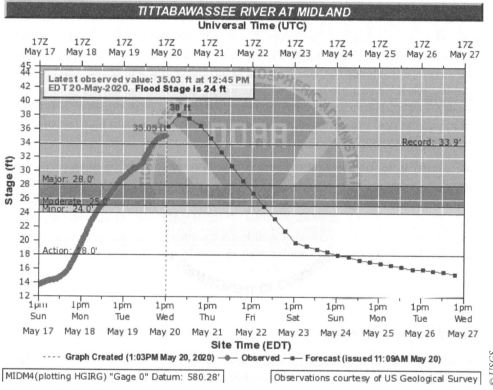

Figure 13.21 River height at the Tittabawassee River near Midland, MI observed at 1645 Z (1245 EDT) May 20, 2020 (observed height in blue). Hydrological forecasting of river heights (purple squares) are also provided and this data can be found at water.weather.gov/ahps. Flood stage is 24 feet and the river crested at 35 feet at the time of this observation.

(1800 EDT) May 19, 2020, all the lake water flowed down the Tittabawassee River causing historic flooding downstream in the city of Midland, MI (Figure 13.21). The river was already at 31 feet (flood stage at 24 feet) when lake water began flooding Midland and increased the river to 11 feet above flood stage in the following 12 hours. In fact, it is possible to get flooding without any precipitation in a watershed if a flooded river upstream brings water into the watershed causing the river to overflow its banks.

Stationary fronts are another large-scale weather feature known to cause flooding rain. Warm humid air can still be forced up and over the cold air at a stationary front. Because the front is stationary, the rain will fall in generally the same area for a long time. Flooding is particularly likely if a low-level jet of maritime air moves toward the stationary front.

Thunderstorms forming on a slow or stationary boundary that sits in an unstable area with good humidity flow are particularly problematic. Thunderstorm precipitation can be much more intense than stratiform precipitation in midlatitude cyclones. Precipitation rates of several inches per hour are achievable in thunderstorms. Because thunderstorms are not resolved in weather models, these are more difficult to forecast. Thunderstorms are not long duration events, but a process known as **training** can cause numerous thunderstorms to form and move over the same area. Training occurs when thunderstorms continually form over the same area like a train of thunderstorms moving past an area.

Tropical cyclones, discussed in the next section, contain exceptionally large amounts of precipitation because of their vast access to warm ocean water and extensive cloud cover. Slow moving tropical and midlatitude cyclones can produce high precipitation amounts if the most intense rain moves slowly over an area causing a long duration intense rain event. This is particularly effective if the cyclones have access to a large amount of humidity. Tropical cyclones maintain access to humidity when over the water whereas midlatitude cyclones maintain access if their warm conveyor belts are connected to a warm body of water. Hurricane Harvey remained over water near Houston, TX through much of a 5-day period from August 25-30, 2017 dumping more than four feet of rain in parts of the Houston vicinity.

Flood severity is defined by a return period based on the probability of an event rising above a specific flood stage or height of the floodwater. For a flood that has a probability of 1% of occurring in a year the return period is expected to be 100 years. A flood of that severity is considered a **100-year flood**. The Midland, MI flooding was estimated to be a 200-year event and Hurricane Harvey a 2000-year event. Insurance companies use this to define flood risks and for the requirement of flood insurance. Nonetheless, climate change is rapidly changing these probabilities so insurance companies and homeowners should be aware.

High Winds Storms

High winds associated with thunderstorms and tropical cyclones will be discussed in the next chapter. When combined with snowfall or blowing snow, blizzard warnings are issued instead, but blizzards have a lower wind threshold because of the danger of reduced visibility is higher. Separate from these storms, high wind warnings are issued for midlatitude cyclones that have sustained winds greater than 35 knots (40 mph) or wind gusts greater than 50 knots (58 mph). Both of these thresholds are considered damaging.

Winds this great occur by two different mechanisms. The first is if the pressure gradient becomes large enough to accelerate winds to these levels. Typically, this occurs with a midlatitude cyclone that has an extremely low pressure. A midlatitude cyclone that has a nearby strong high-pressure center enhances a large pressure gradient and produces strong winds. Surface winds are stronger when the winds are coming onshore from the low friction surface of a lake or ocean. These windstorms are particularly damaging if combined with an ice storm because trees loaded with ice fall more frequently.

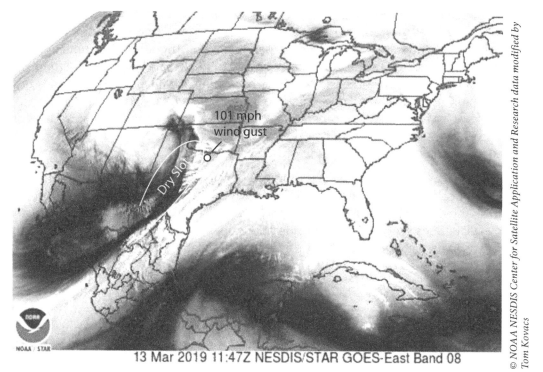

Figure 13.22 GOES-East band 8 upper troposphere water vapor image from 1147 UTC March 13, 2019 showing color-enhanced humidity with humid (green) and dry (yellow) upper troposphere air. A midlatitude dry slot from the sinking dry conveyor belt is highlighted.

The second mechanism occurs in the area where the dry and warm conveyor belt interact. An exceptionally dry dry-slot evaporates convective clouds in the warm conveyor belt causing very strong surface winds to form. The evaporating clouds cause the air to become dense and brings strong upper-level winds to the ground. The descending dry conveyor belt is also forced by upper-air convergence west of midlatitude cyclones. Figure 13.22 shows the location of a 101 mph wind gust reported just northwest of Dallas, TX when the leading edge of a dry slot interacted with the adjacent warm conveyor belt.

Summary

Chapter 13 starts the two chapter hazardous weather chapters. It also starts highlighting the different scales in weather forecasting. Up to now synoptic scale and microscale features were highlighted. Synoptic scale features have a spatial scale of more than hundreds of kilometers or miles and are well simulated in weather models. Microscale features have a spatial scale below 1 km and are parameterized in weather models. In this chapter, we introduced mesoscale features that weather models are increasingly getting better at simulating, but some are still below the resolution of even the high-resolution models.

Snowstorms and blizzards have synoptic scale features that strengthen them such as humidity flux, upper-air divergence, and the development of a TROWAL. However, there are also mesoscale features to consider. Some are on the upper end of mesoscale that weather models handle well such as shortwave interactions with pressure troughs. However, some are on the lower end of the mesoscale that weather models have difficulty resolving. Gulf of Alaska Lows produces mountain snowstorms and the small scale of elevation change leads to rain/snow lines and snow ratios that vary more by elevation. In addition, wind speeds depend on the distribution of mountain passes and peaks, as does rising and sinking motion due to small scale topographic lifting and convergence. Colorado and east coast lows have rain/snow lines and snow ratios that vary rapidly horizontally and can affect snow accumulation forecasts dramatically. East coast lows have small-scale temperature changes (i.e. large temperature gradients) in the sea surface temperature and at the coast and cold-air damming that makes forecasting the rain/snow line difficult.

Lake effect snowstorms change in intensity over small distances because of their dependence on fetch air/water temperature difference, and topography. Longer fetch, cold air moving over warm lake water, and small-scale elevation rises leads to greater snowfall. Besides synoptic scale considerations, ice storms require small vertical scale forecasts to predict precipitation type and ice accumulations. High winds in midlatiude cyclones are sometimes caused by small-scale interactions between the dry and warm conveyor belts.

Key Terms

Synoptic Scale	Nor'easter	Porosity
Microscale	Lake-Effect Snowstorm	Permeability
Mesoscale	Fetch	Ice Jams
Gulf of Alaska Low	Hydrological Forecasting	Training
Alberta Clipper	Hydrological Models	100-year flood
Colorado Low	Watershed	

Questions and Problems

1. Would more snow be expected to fall on the windward or leeward side of a mountain range and why?

2. How does melting level impact where snow falls in mountains?

3. Why are coastal storms usually more intense than Alberta Clippers and Colorado Lows? Give two reasons.

4. What are the central pressures of some of the strong midlatitude cyclones shown in this chapter? How does this compare to the average surface pressure? Also, compare this to a specific hurricane that you find on the Internet.

5. How does cold-air trapping occur in regions such as the Appalachians?

6. In what seasons(s) do East Coast cyclones typically develop? What is special about this season(s) that helps energize these storms?

7. Why do snowfall totals of the northeastern U.S. typically increase as you move inland? How is this related to the possibility of getting a snowfall accumulation forecast incorrect?

8. Why do blizzards associated with Colorado lows have more snow than Alberta Clippers even though Alberta Clippers have colder temperatures?

9. Describe how lake effect snowstorms form describing the importance of the three main ingredients.

10. What time of year is lake-effect snow most likely and why?

11. What effect on future lake-effect snow can people downstream of a frozen lake expect?

12. Why don't small lakes (i.e. not the Great Lakes) produce lake-effect snow?

13. Why is lake-effect snow rare in Toronto, ON despite the fact that it lies on the coast of a Great Lake?

14. From which direction would the wind blow for the heaviest lake effect snow off Lake Michigan and why did you choose that direction?

15. Why would the most damaging ice storms occur when a strong high-pressure center lies north of a midlatitude cyclone? Hint: consider what would happen to the wind and how this would affect damage.

16. What does training mean and how can it lead to flooding rains?

17. If a 100-year flood occurs in your town, can another one occur next year? Explain.

18. Describe three pieces of information in winter that hydrologists must use to forecast for river flooding.

19. What type of front is often associated with flash flooding events and why?

20. What are some things (describe two) you can look for on weather maps or satellite imagery to forecast a high wind event?

Other Resources

https://www.emich.edu/geography-geology/weather for links to useful weather data to go along with this textbook and updates to any broken links in the textbook.

Chapter 14

Hazardous Weather Forecasting— Thunderstorms and Tropical Cyclones

Introduction

This chapter discusses the special forecasting considerations for hazardous weather that occurs during thunderstorms and tropical cyclones. Hazards include lightning, strong surface wind gusts, hail, tornadoes, and flooding. Flooding and high winds were discussed in the last chapter, but there are some features of the flooding and wind specific to tropical cyclones that are discussed here.

Convection is parameterized in weather models, but severe thunderstorms are not parameterized or resolved. Tropical cyclones are usually modeled with global models and regional models specifically for tropical cyclones. High-resolution models (NAM HIRES and HRRR) produce severe thunderstorm parameters such as CAPE (see Chapter 9), wind gusts and a simulated radar. The NAM and GFS also produce simulated Skew-T diagrams. The rapid refresh (RAP) and HRRR produce future mesoanalysis maps.

However, it is the analysis of small features that are subgrid to the models where the forecaster adds skill. Satellites help find small-scale boundaries for thunderstorm initiation and the location and structure of rapidly growing cumulonimbus clouds in thunderstorms and tropical cyclones. Radars help identify severe weather on radar, which supports trained spotters in identifying and characterizing severe thunderstorms once they form. Skew-T diagrams analyze early evidence of environments conducive to rotating thunderstorm updrafts that are precursors to tornadoes. All of these mesoscale analyses is the focus of this chapter.

Ordinary Single-Cell Thunderstorms

Ordinary single-cell thunderstorms are thunderstorms that do not produce damaging hail or wind, but they do produce lightning. They form in conditionally unstable atmospheres where high humidity and some mechanism to force air upward is present. Sometimes that lifting mechanism is convection, caused by the sun heating the ground all morning until air is forced up high enough to produce clouds. Once clouds are produced in a conditionally unstable atmosphere, they will quickly build into cumulonimbus clouds. This scenario is why sometimes you can have a nice sunny day and within an hour have thunderstorms. The updrafts pull humidity from the surface and serves as the inflow of energy into the thunderstorm. Without good inflow, the thunderstorm will die.

Thunderstorms are cumulonimbus clouds that produce lightning. Lightning produces thunder by heating the air to 15000 °C (27000 °F) causing it to rapidly expand, resulting in the sound called thunder. Lightning needs liquid water and snowflakes or graupel

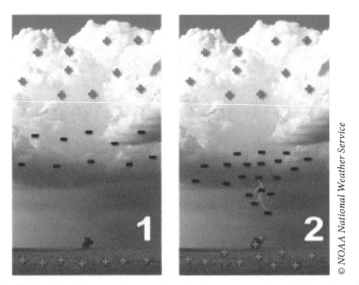

Figure 14.1 Lightning forms when mixed phase cumulonimbus clouds cause a separation of positive (plus signs) and negative (minus signs) charges at different altitudes in the cloud (1). The bottom of the cloud then attracts the opposite sign on the ground (2). Once a large enough voltage to create a current between areas of opposite charge forms will the luminous discharge occur. The discharge can occur in the cloud, between two charged clouds, or from the cloud to the ground. Thunder results from the heated channel of air that lightning travels through at about 15000 °C (27000 °F).

(solid ice) in the same cloud to form with enough separation in distance to separate electric charge (Figure 14.1). These are conditions only cumulonimbus clouds produce. Interestingly, lightning, which is associated with warm season weather, needs snowflakes or graupel to form. It is also possible to get cumulonimbus clouds and lightning in winter if the air is unstable and the clouds grow to at least 1.5 km (5000 feet).

Because lightning travels at the speed of light and thunder travels at the speed of sound, a time gap between when you see the lightning and when you hear the thunder occurs. This gap increases the further you are away from the lightning strike. Because you see the lightning instantaneously, the gap is equal to the time it takes the sound of the thunder to reach your ears. At 343 m/s (767 mph), it takes about five seconds for every mile the lightning strike occurred. Therefore, if the lightning struck 5 miles away, it would take 25 seconds for you to hear the thunder after the lightning strike. The sound of thunder also echoes off buildings, mountains, and clouds to produce the characteristic rumble of thunder.

Cumulonimbus clouds produce precipitation. Precipitation falls and drags air down with it, which produces a downdraft of air (Figure 14.2). To fill the void left in the cloud by the sinking air, air surrounding the cloud is pulled or entrained into the cloud. Because this air is unsaturated, it will partially evaporate the liquid drops in the cloud cooling the air because of latent heating. This cooling offsets the compressional heating of air in the downdraft so that downdrafts are relatively cold when they reach the surface. When the downdraft hits the ground, it spreads out causing a gust front. Gust fronts get their name from the behavior of the winds changing from light to gusty (i.e. variable and strong). This front represents the boundary between the downdraft air outflow from the thunderstorm and the environmental air the thunderstorm resides within. Because it is a mesoscale front, the boundary is often referred to and designated an outflow boundary on weather maps usually with a labeled dashed line.

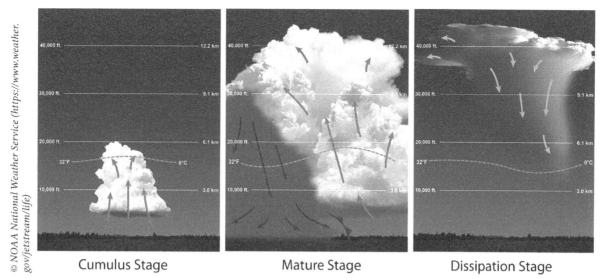

Cumulus Stage   Mature Stage   Dissipation Stage

Figure 14.2 Life cycle of the ordinary thunderstorm shown with updrafts (red), downdrafts (blue), and precipitation (gray).

Severe Thunderstorms

Single-cell thunderstorms can produce lightning, strong winds, heavy rain, and hail, but unless the thunderstorm causes sufficient damage, they are not classified as severe. A severe thunderstorm is a damaging thunderstorm. The National Weather Service (NWS) defines severe thunderstorms as a thunderstorm that produces any one of the following:

1. Hail greater than 1" diameter
2. Wind gusts over 50 knots (58 mph)
3. Tornado

Straight-line winds from thunderstorm downdrafts can generate damaging wind gusts. Sometimes it is not until damage assessment by the NWS that the source of the damage can be determined. Aerial damage assessments can more easily determine if the winds were from a tornado or from straight-line winds. Tornadoes produce damage in a circular fashion with trees falling in multiple directions. Straight-line winds can cause all trees and other structures to fall in a single direction.

Ordinary thunderstorms are structurally different from severe thunderstorms. The structural difference comes about from the presence of vertical wind shear in the environment. Wind shear is a change in wind velocity over a distance. Vertical wind shear refers to change in wind speed and wind direction with increasing altitude. In an ordinary thunderstorm the updraft is nearly vertical and when the downdraft forms it cuts off the updraft and the humidity that the updraft supplies. The importance of vertical wind shear is that it causes the updraft to slant. Figure 14.3 shows a severe thunderstorm developing in an environment with speed shear demonstrated by the increasingly long arrows representing increasing wind speeds at higher altitudes.

When air first enters a cumulonimbus cloud, the cloud drops that are produced are small and do not precipitate. The slant path in a wind-sheared environment produces a shelf cloud at the front of the cumulonimbus cloud, but no precipitation (Figure 14.4). Instead, the updraft continues to the back of the cloud carrying growing raindrops and eventually graupel, hail, and ice crystals. Once the liquid or ice drops are large enough,

Figure 14.3 Illustration of the structure of a severe thunderstorm shown with slanted updraft (orang arrow).

Figure 14.4 Thunderstorm shelf cloud shown hanging over a neighborhood. Although it looks like the cloud is going to crash down on the houses, the shelf cloud represents the inflow of the thunderstorm and the air is actually ascending.

Figure 14.5 A multicell thunderstorm.

they fall to the ground in the back of the cloud. It is here, separate from the updraft that the downdraft forms. That is the key to wind shear: it allows the downdraft to form without killing the updraft and the thunderstorm can continue to develop.

Multi-Cell Thunderstorms

The difference in the type of vertical wind shear, speed or directional, is important in determining the type of severe thunderstorm produced. With significant speed sheer, but little directional shear, the updrafts and downdrafts will still be separated and allow for longer living thunderstorms with more development. The downdrafts and resulting gust fronts cause convergence and updrafts to form new thunderstorms on the southern side of the back of the parent thunderstorm. These **multi-cell thunderstorms** last longer than ordinary thunderstorms and have more time to develop (Figure 14.5). Figure 14.6 shows how the resulting downdrafts eventually cutoff the updraft from the parent thunderstorm but form new thunderstorms on the gust front. Once the new thunderstorm sufficiently develops, much of the inflow of humid air is redirected from the parent thunderstorm, which begins to dissipate.

Multi-cell thunderstorms are rarely severe unless there is sufficient CAPE or the environmental winds are strong. A large CAPE can lead to hail growing to severe limits. The large CAPE can also allow downdraft winds to make it to the ground at a high velocity. If the environmental winds are strong and the multi-cell thunderstorm system

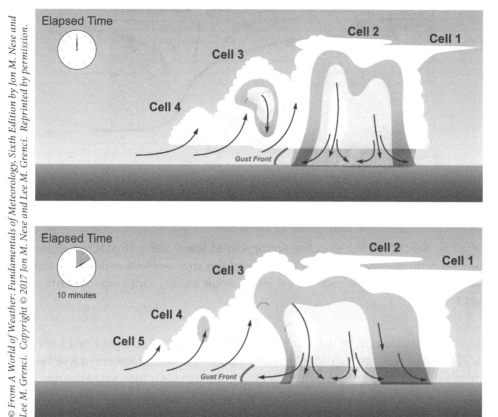

Figure 14.6 Formation of individual thunderstorm cells in a multi-cell thunderstorm showing the evolution of updrafts and downdrafts (black arrows) is shown. a) Cell 3 continues to grow while updrafts feed it humid air, b) Cell 3 downdrafts have now cutoff all updrafts and will begin to die like cells 1 and 2.

is moving rapidly then the resulting downdrafts can cause a gust front to reach severe limits. However, without directional shear tornadoes are unlikely and, if they were to form, are typically weak.

Squall Lines

Sometimes multi-cell thunderstorms can develop into a longer line of thunderstorms called squall lines especially if a large-scale boundary is available such as an outflow boundary from older storms or a front. Again, with sufficient vertical wind shear (speed shear only) these thunderstorms have time to develop with developing thunderstorms often moving ahead of the original boundary. A trailing stratiform region often forms behind the parent thunderstorms (Figure 14.7). The trailing stratiform region develops behind a squall line from ice falling and melting from tall cumulonimbus clouds producing a radar bright brand. The radar bright band is a region of higher reflectivity where ice is melting, which to the radar melting ice looks like a large raindrop. Melting and evaporation in the trailing stratiform region creates a cold pool of air, which is dense and creates surface high pressure. High pressure causes descending air and helps form a rear-inflow jet (Figure 14.7).

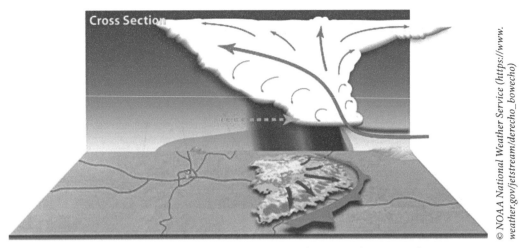

Figure 14.7 Illustration showing the formation of the trailing stratiform region (yellow and orange radar reflectivities behind the stronger red reflectivities of the thunderstorms) and the rear inflow jet (orange arrow) that helps to sustain the gust front.

A **derecho** may form from the rear inflow jet. Derechos are straight-lined high wind events. They differ from gust fronts in that they are longer lasting sustained wind events. Particularly in high-speed shear environments, strong winds are brought to the surface by the rear inflow jet and move outward toward the parent thunderstorms. In this case, new thunderstorms will form on the leading edge of this rapidly moving outflow boundary producing a bow echo on radar (Figure 14.8). Bow echoes are usually indicative of damaging straight-line winds that often reach severe limits.

Squall lines can become severe in high CAPE and high speed-shear environments. The main threat is strong straight-line surface winds, but hail is also possible. Tornadoes are rare although **gustnadoes**, which are tornado-looking vortices that are shallow and surface-based, have been known to form. Gustnadoes form on the leading edge of strong outflow boundaries with strong wind shear. They are not technically tornadoes because they have no connection to the cumulonimbus cloud, but they can be damaging.

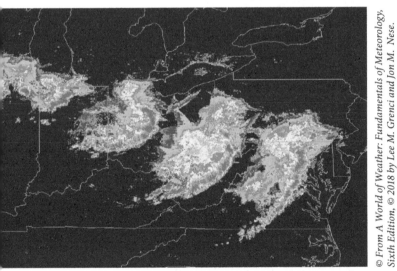

Figure 14.8 Montage of Doppler radar images showing a developing bow echo at five different times. The radar bright band behind the bow echo is the trailing stratiform region.

Supercell Thunderstorms

Supercell thunderstorms produce most tornadoes and nearly all violent tornadoes (Figure 14.9). Supercell thunderstorms have a rotating updraft. Rotating updrafts are produced in environments that include a large amount of directional wind shear. The rotating updraft forms when wind speed shear produces **vortex tubes** as shown in Figure 14.10. If directional shear is also present in the environment, then the surface winds will be

Figure 14.9 Important features of a tornado producing supercell thunderstorm.

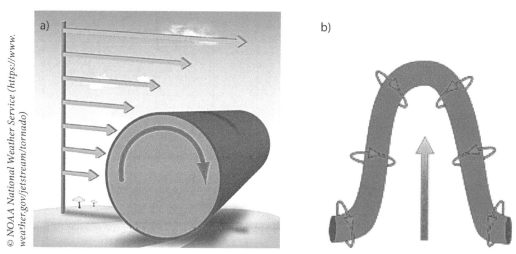

Figure 14.10 Illustration of the production of a vortex tube by speed shear is shown. a) Speed shear causes air to rotate along a horizontal axis creating a vortex tube. b) When surface winds are in a different direction (directional shear) from the upper level winds, this surface air becomes the inflow to a thunderstorm and the vortex tube becomes tilted upward and incorporated within the updraft.

nearly parallel to the axis of the vortex tube. When a thunderstorm forms and these surface winds become the inflow to the thunderstorm, the vortex tube tilts upward and becomes incorporated into the updraft. This incorporation causes the updraft to rotate. The measure of this relationship of speed and directional shear is a complex parameter known as helicity.

Strongly rotating updrafts cause the precipitation to wrap around the updraft. When precipitation wraps around the rear of an updraft, it produces a downdraft in the back of the storm called the rear-flank downdraft near the flanking line (Figure 14.9). The development of a rear-flank downdraft helps constrain the updraft and increases the speed of rotation in the midlevels of the storm. This creates surface low pressure and a lowering

Calculating Helicity

The calculated value of helicity is proportional to the area under a plotted hodograph bounded below by the positive x-axis (Figure 14.11 upper-right). A hodograph is a plot of the wind direction on a 360-degree circle with the distance from the origin proportional to the speed. Each measurement is plotted in order from the surface to the top of the troposphere. The area under this plot is larger if the surface winds are large and from the south and the winds become increasing from the west in the lowest 1-3 km. A large helicity value would mean that the wind shear above the surface and the inflow at the surface are perpendicular. Although the deep (0-6 km) shear better predicts supercell formation, helicity relates more to whether they will be tornadic.

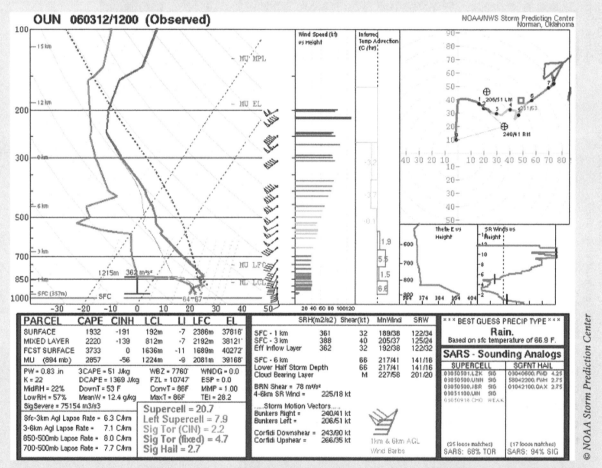

Figure 14.11 Skew t diagram (upper-left) for Oklahoma City, OK on 12 UTC March 12, 2006 is shown. The hodograph (upper-right) is a plot of the wind velocities from the surface upward. Storm Relative Helicity (SRH) is proportional to the area under the plot from the surface to 1 km and the surface to 3 km. Actual SRH values are given in the bottom middle box.

of the cloud surrounding the updraft known as the mesocyclone. The wrapping of precipitation around the mesocyclone produces a hook echo on radar (cf. Figure 9.7). The mesocyclone itself produces the tornado vortex signature in velocity mode (cf. Figure 9.7). On average, 20-30% of mesocyclones produce tornadoes and a tornado warning can be issued when a mesocyclone is observed even if no tornado exists.

Funnel clouds can form within the mesocyclone if surface rotation produced by the rear flank downdraft is sucked and stretched into the mesocyclone.[1] The entrained surface rotation contains humidity from the downdraft, which causes the cloud base to lower producing what is known as a wall cloud because it provides the "wall" from which a funnel cloud would descend to produce a tornado (Figure 14.12). Technically, a funnel cloud is not a tornado until the rotation connects from cloud to ground. Achieving this last step of tornado formation is an active area of research.

© NOAA/NWS, Amanda L. Hill

Figure 14.12 Picture of a tornado shown. The debris that wraps around the funnel gives the tornado its color. In this case, the soil is a light red.

Scientific Practices

Constructing Explanations

The idea of scientific theory was introduced in Chapter 4. Scientists cannot simply formulate theories. Scientists propose hypotheses, which are an attempted explanation of some observation written as a testable question. For example, is it possible that species of animals evolved certain adaptations through genetic diversity driven by a survival of the fittest scenario that favored certain genetic characteristics within the species? That hypothesis would require experimentation to answer, which ultimately led to the theory of evolution. However, a single experimental proof does not make a theory. It simply proves the hypothesis. It is not until multiple experiments by different groups of scientists under different experimental conditions find the same proof that a working theory and ultimately a theory or law is born. Subsequently, scientific observations and theory are used to construct explanations and can further science by developing new hypotheses to be tested.

In constructing an explanation for how tornadoes form, meteorologists have already established that most non-tropical damaging tornadoes form in supercell thunderstorms. Supercell thunderstorms form in environments with large vertical wind shear between 0 and 6 km. This wind shear produces vortex tubes that when sucked up in the updraft causes a rotating updraft. They also know that supercells that form in high helicity surface environments produce strong upper-level rotation because these vortex tubes are more optimally sucked into the updraft by the surface inflow of the storm (i.e. the surface winds and the vortex tubes are more perpendicular). Finally, they know that a rear flank downdraft will constrain the inflow and spin up the rotation in the mid-level of the storm and produce a surface rotation. This constriction leads to a mesocyclone and sucking up the surface rotation produces the wall cloud. How and why the low-level circulation develops in only about 20-30% of mesocyclones is the final piece of the conceptual puzzle. Knowing this will allow meteorologists to explain how a tornado forms. Being able to gather observations of this will help meteorologists forecast which supercells will produce tornadoes. Currently, tornado warnings are issued for many well-developed mesocyclones that do not produce tornadoes. Forming a complete explanation of tornado formation may lead to lowering the false warning rate.

---

[1] Markowski, P. M., and Y. P. Richardson, 2014: What we know and don't know about tornado formation. Physics Today, 67, 26–31.

Tornadoes are categorized on a scale originally created by Ted Fujita and was named the Fujita scale or F-scale. The categorization is assigned after an aerial and ground damage assessment. Recently, the F-scale was overhauled to include more damage signatures in open land and is now the enhanced Fujita scale or EF scale. Both scales spanned from 0-5 with wind speed ranges that were estimated for the F-scale and have been updated for the EF scale based on more field measurements. Full damage determination can be found at https://www.spc.noaa.gov/efscale/ef-scale.html. A sample of damage to single-family houses and apartment buildings is shown in Table 14.1.

Table 14.1 EF scale wind speeds and examples of damage to houses and apartment buildings.

Category	Wind speeds (mph)	Example of damage to houses and apartment complexes
EF 0	65-85	Threshold of visible damage; perhaps loss of shingles
EF 1	86-109	Broken windows, significant loss of roof covering and some roof deck damage; garage doors collapse; collapse of chimney
EF 2	110-137	Much of roof removed; houses may shift off foundation and lose some exterior walls
EF 3	138-167	Most walls collapsed in house except interior rooms; top floor walls collapsed in apartments
EF 4	168-199	All walls collapsed in houses; top two floors collapsed in apartments
EF 5	Over 200	House completely removed from foundation; entire apartment building destroyed

Forecasting Severe Thunderstorms

Forecasting for severe thunderstorms is a complicated endeavor with several important subgrid scale weather model processes. However, consideration of severe weather locations typically starts at the large scale. The first step is to identify areas of surface convergence, upper-air divergence, humidity, instability, and wind shear. These considerations make up the long-range convective outlooks by the Storm Prediction Center (https://www.spc.noaa.gov/products/outlook/).

Areas of surface convergence includes fronts, outflow boundaries, etc. Strengthening fronts are particularly favorable because they are usually associated with some of the other ingredients. Fronts with strong surface winds that converge at the boundaries helps generate rising motion and with sufficient instability can produce cumulonimbus clouds. A special kind of front called the dry front or dryline frequently develops in Texas, Oklahoma, Kansas, and Nebraska (Figure 14.13). This front separates less dense humid Gulf of Mexico air from denser dry desert air from the desert southwest. Even though the desert air is hotter, the density difference due to humidity differences makes this air significantly denser. Humid air is much less dense than dry air. Drylines are known to be a particularly favorable boundary for severe weather because a capping inversion

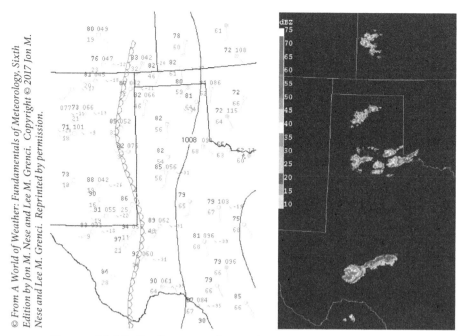

Figure 14.13 Drylines are fronts that separate dry, dense air from moist less dense air and are marked with a line of open semicircles on the side opposite the dry air (left). Half hour after the map on the left, supercell thunderstorms began to appear on radar (right).

(discussed below) keeps the energy in the denser humid air contained longer than other locations. When the cap is broken, updrafts have exceeded 45 m/s (100 mph) and storms grow to 15 km (50,000 feet) in minutes.

In the upper levels of the atmosphere, troughs and jet streaks generate divergence. Areas downstream of the trough axis and within the left exit and right entrance regions of jet streaks are locations of upper-air divergence that will produce rising motion by pulling the air upward. Negatively-tilted troughs (see Chapter 7) are particularly favorable. Anything that helps troughs get stronger like shortwaves or strong surface temperature advection are important large-scale ingredients for severe thunderstorms.

The role of humidity depends on its vertical location. Humidity at the surface helps rising air to saturate and remain buoyant in a conditionally unstable environment. Humidity is necessary to produce clouds, rain, and hail. However, the absence of humidity in the middle layers around the 700 hPa (700 mb) level is more conducive to severe weather. This level is above where rising surface air will already saturate and form clouds. Therefore, cloud drops and raindrops rising into a low humidity environment will cause evaporation. Evaporation cools the air above the humid surface layer, which increases the lapse rate and, therefore, instability. A low-level jet of warm humid air at the surface with dry air at 700 hPa (700 mb) is favorable for increasing CAPE and developing strong updrafts.

Instability is important for creating strong updrafts, but for also inhibiting the release of energy. Large lapse rates in the low to mid-levels (i.e. 850 mb-500 mb) creates large CAPE and strong updrafts. However, in the morning the radiation inversion of the previous evening can lead to a stable layer that inhibits convection (Figure 14.14). When the temperature plot on a Skew-T diagram increases with height, it inhibits convection. If the convective inhibition (CINH) is too high and/or surface heating is too low then cumulonimbus clouds will be unable to form. The atmosphere can have the highest values of CAPE and helicity, but if clouds prevent enough surface heating to break through a cap of CINH, no severe weather will occur. However, if CINH is present but not too large, this is

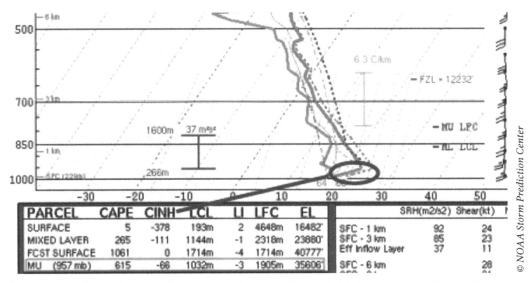

PARCEL	CAPE	CINH	LCL	LI	LFC	EL		SRH(m2/s2)	Shear(kt)
SURFACE	5	-378	193m	2	4648m	16482'	SFC - 1 km	92	24
MIXED LAYER	265	-111	1144m	-1	2318m	23880'	SFC - 3 km	85	23
FCST SURFACE	1061	0	1714m	-4	1714m	40777'	Eff Inflow Layer	37	11
MU (957 mb)	615	-66	1032m	-3	1905m	35806'	SFC - 6 km		28

Figure 14.14 At night, surface air cools more than air higher up creating an inversion (blue oval). The column CINH provides the amount of energy (J/kg) needed to force air from the surface (first row) to a level that it will rise on its own in a layer unstable to the rising air.

an ideal situation for producing severe weather. In this scenario, the energy from the sun heating the surface layer can be stored in the surface layer. If the inversion layer is broken later in the afternoon, the energy stored in the surface layer can be released explosively causing large updrafts. The forecast CINH in Figure 14.14 is 0 J/kg so the daytime heating is expected to break through the capping inversion that afternoon.

Finally, without sufficient wind shear severe weather will not occur. Finding areas where winds are southeasterly at the surface with increasingly westerly winds around the 850 mb layer is favorable. The winds in the 300-500 mb level must be strong and westerly, but strong westerly winds closer to the lower 850 mb level is most favorable.

Forecasting of severe weather occurs in the morning for afternoon severe weather. CAPE values are very low in the morning when computed with surface parcels within a morning inversion. A number of options are available to select the probable expected severe weather parameters for when thunderstorms initiate. Indices discussed in Chapter 9 such as lifted or Showalter indices can provide a rough guide of where to focus for the day. They are computed at heights above the 850 mb level, which is above air affected by nighttime heating. Increasingly negative values are more conducive to the formation of thunderstorms. Wind shear values are also used to assess the probability of those thunderstorms being severe. A number of air parcels are tested on a Skew T diagram other than those rising from the surface. A scan through the lowest 300 mb for the most unstable (MU in Figure 14.14) air parcel and an average parcel in the mixed layer (Mixed layer in Figure 14.14) often provide better estimates of expected CAPE, CINH, and LI. Short-range high-resolution weather models guide forecasters on the development of these conditions throughout the day. The HRRR updates every hour with new data and provides severe weather parameters such as CAPE, helicity, and CINH. Skew-T diagrams are also available from NAM and GFS every three forecast hours.

As thunderstorms near or begin to develop, satellite data is key in observing possible boundaries and the initiation of convection prior to convective cells becoming severe. Radar provides signatures of hail and tornadoes. Rapidly increasing lightning has also been found to be a precursor to severe thunderstorms. Sometimes extra launches of weather balloons in key locations and times will occur.

The next section will discuss more specifically the threshold values that forecasters are looking for on the day of severe weather to determine whether weather watches should be issued.

Surface Wind Gusts

Forecasting wind gusts greater than 50 knots (58 mph) are restricted to straight-line winds in this subsection. These can occur with minimal thresholds of the common severe weather parameters. The helicity threshold is 250 m^2/s^2, CAPE threshold is 1500 J/kg, and the wind shear threshold in the lowest 6 km is 30 knots (35 mph). The wind shear value means that the difference between the winds at the surface and the winds at 6 km is 30 knots (Figure 14.15). CINH values must be more than −500 J/kg (CINH are usually reported as a negative number). If values are closer to −500 J/kg then something must be available to break through the cap such as strong surface heating or a cold front.

Figure 14.15 shows a special weather balloon launch in Birmingham, AL near a time when severe straight-line winds were observed. CAPE values for all tested air parcels and storm relative helicity (SRH) were below threshold values. However, two important

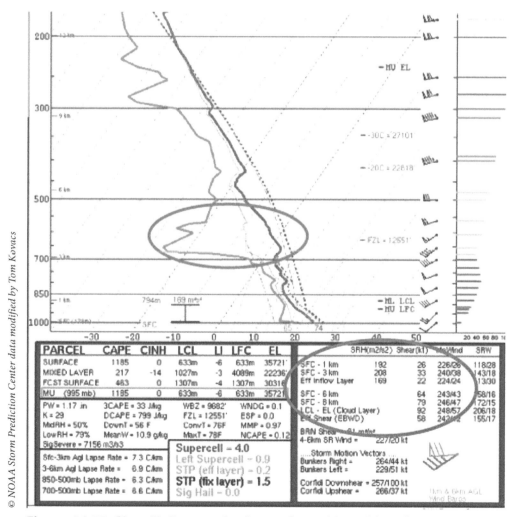

© NOAA Storm Prediction Center data modified by Tom Kovacs

Figure 14.15 Skew T diagram for Birmingham, AL on 18 UTC March 1, 2017 near a time when severe straight-line winds were observed. Helicity and wind shear values were near minimum values (red circle), but a dry layer just above 700 mb (blue circle) likely leads to increasing CAPE values (orange rectangle).

observations suggest that severe straight-line winds were likely. First, surface to 6 km wind shear was extremely high at 64 knots. In addition, the layer between 500 and 700 mb was extremely dry (blue circle). All that was needed were clouds to form and penetrate this layer. The evaporation of raindrops would cool this layer and increase the instability and CAPE values. That would help bring the strong winds in this layer down to the surface. Because CINH was 0 J/kg and the surface layer lapse rates near unsaturated adiabatic lapse rate, this was likely, and a severe thunderstorm watch should have been issued. With SRH values too low, tornadoes were unlikely. In addition, with the low CAPE values and high freezing level (height that air temperature first goes below 0 °C) of 3826 meters (12551 feet), hail greater than one inch diameter was unlikely.

Hail

Hail exists in most thunderstorms, but it must grow large enough to make it to the ground. The vertical distance in above-freezing temperatures that the hail must fall through must be small. Threshold values of the freezing level is about 3500 m in order for that to happen.

Growing hail larger than one-inch diameter requires a strong updraft. The minimum threshold for this size hail is CAPE > 2500 J/kg. However, hail grows best at temperatures between −10 °C and −30 °C. Large updrafts between these temperatures are particularly important and threshold values between these temperatures of CAPE > 1000 J/kg is favorable.

Hail needs time to grow so wind shear must also be at least 30 knots to produce a long-lived thunderstorm. The three parameters discussed here: CAPE between −10 °C and −30 °C, 0-6 km wind shear, and freezing levels can all be found in the SPC mesoanalysis under "multi-parameter fields" (Figure 14.16). Hail > 2" diameter was reported in the area

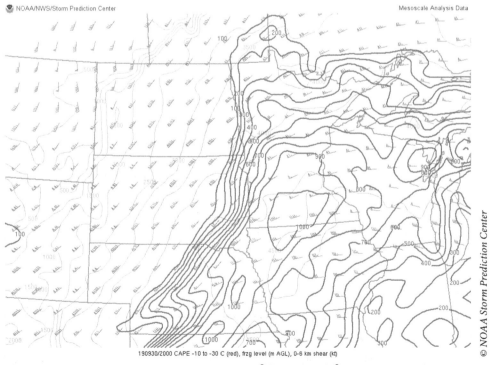

Figure 14.16 Hail parameters: CAPE −10 °C and −30 °C (Red lines), freezing height (blue lines), and 0-6 km wind shear vector (wind barbs) for 20 UTC September 30, 2019.

within the 900 J/kg CAPE contour in eastern and south-central Nebraska on the day of the data in the figure. This occurred despite the CAPE and freezing level (4000 m) being near threshold values for one-inch hail, but the shear vector of 55 knots was quite a bit above the threshold. The wind shear probably allowed thunderstorms to have enough time to grow hail large enough to make it to the ground in the vertical layer that was a bit larger than threshold. This example underlines that these thresholds are simplified guidelines and understanding the process is more important in operational forecasting.

Tornadoes

Although tornadoes can form in non-supercell thunderstorms, the majority of them and nearly all significant tornadoes (EF2 and greater) are produced by supercells. Therefore, the forecast consideration for tornadoes and supercells are nearly the same.

Supercell thunderstorms need the previously mentioned thresholds for severe straight-line winds, but significant helicity is also needed. Threshold values for 0-3 km helicity are typically 250 m^2/s^2 and for 0-1 km helicity are typically 100 m^2/s^2. Although higher 0-6 km wind shear has been known to produce supercells, tornadic producing supercells require the helicity thresholds. It is also not easy to maintain a tornadic circulation over a long vertical distance so a Lifting Condensation Level (LCL) < 2000 m is also favorable.

Significant tornadoes need a higher 0-1 km helicity value, typically greater than 150 m^2/s^2. Significant tornadoes pose significant risk to even well-built houses. All thresholds mentioned for significant tornadoes are included in the significant tornado parameter (STP) found under the composite indices in the SPC mesoanalysis webpage (Figure 14.17). Tornadoes were observed within the STP = 1 contour in southeast Kansas, but not southwest Arkansas. It cannot be stressed enough that looking at a single parameter is not enough to forecast the specifics of severe weather.

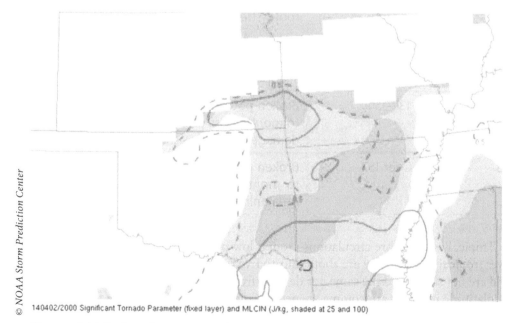

© NOAA Storm Prediction Center

140402/2000 Significant Tornado Parameter (fixed layer) and MLCIN (J/kg, shaded at 25 and 100)

Figure 14.17 Significant tornado parameter (orange lines) and mean layer convective inhibition (blue shading) on 20 UTC April 2, 2014. EF0 tornado reported in southeast Kansas, but no tornado reported in southeast Arkansas.

Tropical Cyclones

Tropical cyclones include tropical depressions, tropical storms, hurricanes, and typhoons. The difference between tropical depressions, tropical storms, and hurricanes are the wind speeds. All have circulation around a central low pressure, but once that circulation reaches 34 knots (39 mph) the tropical depression becomes a tropical storm and a name is assigned. When the circulation reaches 64 knots (74 mph), the tropical storm becomes a hurricane. Hurricanes and typhoons are the same thing; they only differ in where they form. If forming in the North Atlantic or eastern North Pacific they are hurricanes and in the western North Pacific they are typhoons. In the southern hemisphere and Indian Ocean, they are called cyclones.

Like tornadoes, hurricanes have a damage scale. Although unlike tornadoes, the hurricane damage scale is applied while the hurricane still exists. The hurricane scale is called the Saffir-Simpson scale (Table 14.2). The Saffir-Simpson scale is based on sustained wind speed alone and is meant to communicate a typical amount of damage risk based on wind speed and storm surge. Other factors not accounted for in the scale also play a role in damage risk such as movement speed, topography, population, tree density, etc.

Table 14.2 Saffir-Sampson scale wind speeds and examples of damage to houses, trees, and power lines

Category	Wind speeds (mph)	Example of expected damage
1	74-95	Broken power lines, power outages for days, damage to roof covering; Large branches break and some shallow rooted trees topple
2	96-110	Broken power lines, power outages for days to weeks, major damage to roof; many shallow rooted trees topple
3	111-129	Broken power lines, power outages for days to weeks, possible removal of roof; many trees snapped or uprooted
4	130-156	Broken power lines, power outages for weeks to months, loss of roof and some exterior wall damage; most trees snapped or uprooted
5	Over 157	Broken power lines, power outages for weeks to months, many framed houses destroyed; Area uninhabitable for months

© NOAA National Hurricane Center data modified by Tom Kovacs

Tropical cyclones are circulations around low pressure (i.e. a cyclone) that only form over tropical waters. They are about four to five times smaller than midlatitude cyclones and are not structured the same nor develop from the same energy source (Figure 14.18). Midlatitude cyclones are comma shaped because of their fronts while tropical cyclones are more circular. Midlatitude cyclones may be larger than tropical cyclones, but tropical cyclones' wind speeds are significantly larger. Tropical cyclones do not follow the polar front theory nor the conveyor belt model like midlatitude cyclones, which is why they were not covered in Chapter 7.

Figure 14.18 Visible GOES-East image on 1815 UTC October 28, 2018 of the spiral cloud mass of Hurricane Oscar and two comma-shaped midlatitude cyclones with their surface centers marked with an 'L'.

The energy source for tropical cyclones is almost entirely latent heating. Primarily, the condensation and to some extent the deposition of water vapor provides the energy for tropical cyclones. Unlike midlatitude cyclones that use a temperature gradient as potential energy, the tropics have no temperature gradients. Latent heating warms the column of air where cumulonimbus clouds form in the tropics, which causes the air to expand and reduces the pressure at the surface. Once a surface low forms, air circulates counterclockwise in the northern hemisphere, so the Coriolis force is still needed to balance the pressure gradient force. In fact, tropical cyclones rarely form within five degrees latitude of the equator and rarely cross the equator once formed.

To produce enough latent heating, tropical cyclones only form over warm water with a sea surface temperature of at least 26 °C (79 °F). When tropical cyclones move over colder water, they typically weaken. In addition, they cause a lot of upwelling of cold water so that if they become stationary they also tend to weaken. Moving over land almost completely cuts off the water supply. Land also causes increased surface convergence because of the increased friction of the land, which causes the winds to turn more into the now unbalanced pressure gradient. The increased convergence raises the central pressure further weakening the storm. For these reasons, tropical cyclones weaken most rapidly when they move over land.

Like midlatitude cyclones, when surface low-pressure forms the air begins to spiral counterclockwise into the low in the northern hemisphere. This circulation adds mass to the central column of air over the surface. In order to balance this surface convergence, air must diverge at the top of the tropical cyclone. The formation of an upper air high-pressure center diverges air out away from the central column of air over the surface. Unlike midlatitude cyclones, vertical wind shear weakens tropical cyclones because the upper air high-pressure center becomes dislocated from the surface low-pressure center.

The high-pressure center must be immediately on top of the surface low-pressure center in order to remove mass from the center. Sometimes wind shear tears a tropical cyclone apart and the upper-air clockwise circulation is observed on satellite to move away from the surface counterclockwise rotation. When this happens, the tropical cyclone weakens.

The counterclockwise circulation and the forward movement of the tropical cyclone causes air movement, which on the surface is measured as wind. The wind speeds on the right side, relative to the forward movement, of tropical cyclones is larger. The right side of a north moving cyclone would be the east side whereas for a south moving storm would be the left side. Winds constantly blowing the ocean surface on the right side of cyclones leads to a pileup of water. When this pileup approaches land it causes the water level to rise and is called a **storm surge**. The combination of storm surge and the large waves that are typical within tropical cyclones leads to the most damage and risk to life when a tropical cyclone makes landfall. The storm surge is greatest at the coastline and rarely comes more than a mile inland.

The tropical cyclone organizes itself with a surface circulation that does not quite reach the center (Figure 14.19). Like all cumulonimbus clouds, rising air brings humidity to form clouds, but a compensating sinking motion occurs around the cloud. Near the center, the compensating sinking motion clears the air forming the **hurricane eye**. The **hurricane eyewall** contains the tallest cumulonimbus clouds surrounding the eye, which then flows outward at the top in the high-pressure circulation producing a **central dense overcast** over the entire storm. However, sinking motion must occur at numerous radii from the center. Bands of rising and sinking air form with the eyewall as simply one of those sinking bands. Pressure gradients are largest near the eye, which accelerates the winds to their greatest speed in the eyewall. Rising motion is also most intense in the eyewall so that precipitation rates are greatest here. Pressure gradients within the eye are small so not only are tropical cyclone eyes relatively clear, but they are also relatively calm.

Tropical cyclone eyes average between 30 km (20 miles) and 65 km (40 miles) in diameter. Eyes are not evidence of the strength of a tropical cyclone, but evidence of strengthening. Tropical cyclones strengthen most when the eyewall is very tall to maximize heating in the center. It is also important for the outflow to be very strong and

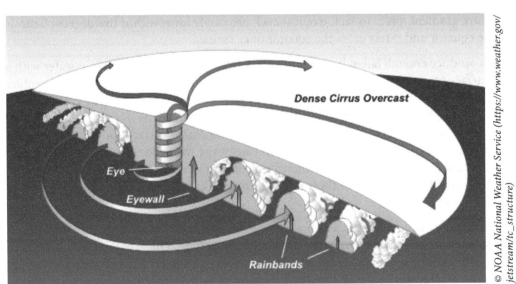

© NOAA National Weather Service (https://www.weather.gov/jetstream/tc_structure)

Figure 14.19 Illustration of the circulation and cloud structure of a mature tropical cyclone is shown. The surface winds spiral inward and upward (green) and upper-air spiral outward and downward (red).

Figure 14.20 Infrared image comparison of Hurricane Dorian on 2215 UTC September 1, 2019 when it was a category 5 hurricane and strengthening (top) and 1624 UTC September 4, 2019 when it was a category 2 hurricane and weakening (bottom). Yellow-orange-red colors show increasingly tall cold clouds.

symmetric to maximize the reduction of the central surface pressure. A perfectly circular and clear eye with very cold cloud tops encircling the eye on infrared satellite imagery is evidence of this structure. The top of Figure 14.20 shows Hurricane Dorian while strengthening with very tall cold cloud tops surrounding a perfectly round clear eye. In contrast, the bottom of Figure 14.20 shows Hurricane Dorian while weakening where the clouds are lower and warmer and not completely encircling the erratic looking cloudy eye.

Forecasting Tropical Cyclones

Data for forecasting tropical cyclones is not as dense as for land-based weather systems. This reduced data availability presents a challenge to forecasting tropical cyclones. Although satellite data is still available, hurricane hunter aircraft often fly into tropical systems to gather data for hurricane weather models. Aircraft gathers flight-level weather parameters, radar, and **dropsonde** data. Dropsondes are similar to weather balloons except they are dropped from the aircraft.

The National Hurricane Center (NHC) hurricane hunter aircraft look for centers of surface low pressure anytime a tropical disturbance is identified. A tropical disturbance is an organized area of cumulonimbus clouds maintained for a long enough period to heat the atmosphere enough to form a surface low-pressure center. Finding this center provides the initial location to weather models and is what initially classifies a tropical depression. Once classified as a tropical depression, the cyclone is given a number.

Between NHC hurricane hunter flights or while the tropical cyclone is far from land, the Dvorak technique is used to estimate sustained wind speeds and central surface pressures. This technique uses visible and infrared satellite imagery to analyze cloud patterns. Tropical cyclones exhibit certain cloud patterns based on their intensity that allows an estimate of these important parameters.

Like traditional land-based weather models, hurricane weather models are initialized with all available data. The equations from the physical laws are computed along with any parameterizations. Hurricane weather models are similar to the models discussed in Chapter 10, with a few differences. Because of some simplifications in the tropical ocean, computer-processing power may be reallocated to improve other facets of modeling such as resolution, model physics, approximations, etc. These models also tend to be run over a shorter forecast period (5-10 days). Global, regional, and ensemble weather models are used as well as statistical models like those used in long-range outlooks.

Typically, the current location, central pressure, maximum sustained winds, movement velocity, **best track forecast** out to 5 days, and a **cone of uncertainty** is communicated to the public (Figure 14.21). The cone of uncertainty is a measure of forecast track error averaged over the past five years. The best track and cone only represent the

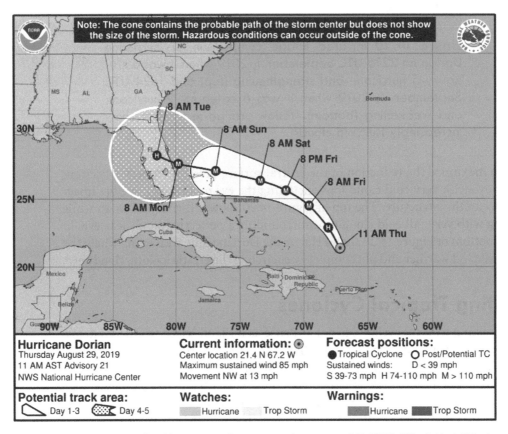

© NOAA National Hurricane Center

Figure 14.21 Warning cone for Hurricane Dorian is shown on 15 UTC (11 AM AST) August 29, 2019. The black line represents the most probable path, the white cone represents the probable track of the center of the storm. The width f the cone represents the 5 year track uncertainty for 1-3 days (solid white) and 4-5 days (stippled areas).

position of the center of the storm and not the wind or damage field. As the tropical cyclone gets closer to land, watches and warnings, precipitation forecasts, wind speed probabilities, and storm surge maps are issued. Storm surge, which is the rise in the mean sea level caused by a tropical cyclone's sustained winds, causes the most fatalities. Local emergency managers will use this data to plan evacuations, mobilize resources, and prepare shelters. Typically, the state and federal government will be involved in emergency planning and communication.

Summary

Most thunderstorms are not severe thunderstorms and determining those that will become severe are important because severe thunderstorms are damaging to life and property. Severe thunderstorms are thunderstorms that produce hail greater than 1 inch, surface wind gusts in excess of 50 knots (58 mph) or tornadoes. Severe thunderstorms can organize in one of three ways: multi-cell thunderstorms, squall lines, or supercell thunderstorms. High-resolution weather models are just starting to forecast these organizations, which are on the low end of the mesoscale. Knowing the organization is important because multicell thunderstorms rarely produce tornadoes while supercell thunderstorms produce most tornadoes and nearly all of the significant tornadoes. Significant tornadoes are those rated on the enhanced Fujita scale of EF2 or greater and cause significant damage to well-built homes.

Skew-T diagrams are the best tool to identify environments where severe thunderstorms will occur. CAPE greater than 1500 J/kg, 0-6 km wind shear greater than 30 knots (35 mph), and helicity values greater than 250 m^2/s^2 are considered minimum thresholds. Other features can modify these values. First, daytime heating makes the air more unstable. Using an air parcel that rises from an average mean layer in the boundary layer on a morning sounding provides a better estimate of afternoon CAPE. Second, convective inhibition (CINH) influences whether energy from the sun will be constrained within this boundary layer to boost CAPE. Finally, a dry layer around 700 mb helps increase instability when clouds form and rise through this layer causing evaporative cooling. For supercell thunderstorms, 0-6 km wind shear must be well-above threshold values and for tornadoes 0-3 km helicity values must also be above threshold. Satellite imagery is useful to identify boundaries where thunderstorms will first develop and radar is useful for finding areas where surface wind gusts, hail, and tornadoes are likely occurring.

Tropical cyclones are areas of low pressure found in the tropics and have energy sources and a spatial structure that is different from midlatitude cyclones. In the absence of temperature gradients, tropical cyclones gain most of their energy from latent heating. They develop in areas where sea surface temperatures are high and cumulonimbus clouds continually form. The latent heating from cumulonimbus cloud formation expands the air and lowers the surface pressure. Satellite imagery is used to monitor the growth of cumulonimbus clouds around the center, which concentrate the heating at the center leading to a stronger tropical cyclone. Wind shear and loss of the source of humidity at the surface due to cooler sea surface temperatures or landfall weakens tropical cyclones.

Key Terms

Ordinary Single-Cell Thunderstorms

Entrained

Gust Front

Outflow Boundary

Severe Thunderstorm

Shelf Cloud

Multi-Cell Thunderstorms

Squall Lines

Trailing Stratiform Region

Radar Bright Band

Rear-Inflow Jet

Derecho

Gustnadoes

Vortex Tubes

Helicity

Mesocyclone

Enhanced Fujita Scale or EF Scale

Dry front or Dryline

Capping Inversion

Convective Inhibition

Significant Tornadoes

Tropical Cyclones

Tropical Depressions

Tropical Storms

Hurricanes

Typhoons

Hurricane Eyewall

Central Dense Overcast

Hurricane Eye

Dropsonde

Best Track Forecast

Cone of Uncertainty

Storm Surge

Questions and Problems

1. If thunder is heard after 15 seconds of a lightning flash, how far away was the lightning? Why does this lag in thunder and lightning exist?

2. A downdraft that falls from 4000 m typically has a temperature of around 0 °C. As it is falling, it compresses and heats at the unsaturated adiabatic lapse rate, which would make the downdraft 40 °C (95 °F) when it reached the surface. Yet, why are downdrafts typically less than 24 °C (75 °F)?

3. Severe thunderstorms need the three environmental ingredients necessary for ordinary thunderstorms plus one other. What are the four necessary ingredients and what types of weather maps or images would you examine for the extra ingredient?

4. What are the three ways that severe thunderstorms organize and what is a distinguishing environmental feature of each?

5. What is a bow echo and how does it usually develop?

6. What indication on radar would alert forecasters to a squall line that is about to or is producing strong straight-line winds?

7. What is the mesocyclone and where is it found in supercell thunderstorms?

8. What feature on radar suggests that a mesocyclone has formed?

9. Draw a vertical cross-section of a tornadic supercell thunderstorm and include the following features: anvil, wall cloud, updraft, downdraft, rain shaft, rain-free base, overshooting top, hail, mammatus clouds, and tornado.

10. How are the EF scale ratings determined for tornadoes?

11. Why are drylines or dry fronts most commonly found in Texas, Oklahoma, and Kansas?

12. Why does air rise over a dryline and what type of air mass is doing the rising?

13. Which variable would forecasters be interested in monitoring in order to forecast the strength of a thunderstorm's updraft?

14. What distinguishes a funnel cloud from a tornado?

15. What causes the initial rotation of a supercell updraft?

16. What is the role of wind shear in the formation of a tornado?

17. Provide three weather parameters and their values that would lead to the forecast of a significant (EF2 or greater) tornado.

18. Provide three weather parameters and their values that would lead to the forecast of large (> 2") hail.

19. Why do hurricanes typically travel east-to-west in the tropics?

20. If a hurricane were moving to the west, which side of the storm would have the strongest winds and highest storm surge when coming ashore?

21. What is storm surge and how does it differ from typical water waves?

22. How is latent heating the primary energy source of hurricanes? How does it lead to lower central surface pressures?

23. What are two mechanisms that lead to a weakening of a hurricane?

24. How can you recognize a weakening hurricane on satellite imagery?

Other Resources

https://www.emich.edu/geography-geology/weather for links to useful weather data to go along with this textbook and updates to any broken links in the textbook.

http://climatemodels.uchicago.edu/ includes several radiation, climate, hurricane, and carbon cycle models with simple user inputs to play with.

Chapter 15

Climate Forecasting

Introduction

Chapter 2 defined climate as the long-term average of weather conditions. Similarly, climate forecasting uses climate models to forecast how the long-term average of weather conditions will change. Chapter 11 showed how this is done for recreating the past climate. Climate modeling requires a thorough knowledge of present and past climates in order to understand the factors that cause climates to change. It also requires a large amount of climate data to ensure that climate models capture all the variance during past climates. The assumption being that future climates contain a similar variance of climate parameters. An important point here, like in previous chapters, is that observations and data form the basis of every climate forecast.

This chapter begins with a list of the main factors that have been shown to cause climates to change. Specifically, the main drivers of climate change cause an imbalance in the energy balance, which leads to changing global mean temperatures. This chapter will focus on changing global temperatures. However, changing global temperatures leads to other climate parameters such as precipitation and winds to change. For this reason, recent global warming and climate change are often used interchangeably although global warming specifically refers to the recent increasing global temperatures.

Many of the factors that affect climate are natural, but some are both natural and human-caused. They all have important time scales to consider when thinking about building and using climate models. For example, the movement of tectonic plates has little impact on the forecasting of climate in the next century because they move so little over that period. However, some of the effects of tectonic plate movement such as volcanoes have a profound effect on climate in the shorter time scales.

Factors That Cause Climate Change

Climates have changed for many reasons over geologic time. Chapter 2 discussed how climate has changed over the past 500 million years and is currently changing. Changes in the distant past were definitely natural because humans were not present more than a couple million years ago. Even the impact of early humans was likely too small to make a significant impact on climate. Humans were certainly present during the ice ages, which were a time of climate change. Humans cut trees and started fires, which could affect climate. The extent of human's effects on climate during these times are an area of active research. However, most scientists regard the Industrial Revolution in the 18th century as the start of when human impacts became significant. During this period, the concentration of greenhouse gases began to increase rapidly, and subsequently global mean temperatures began to increase. In fact, the speed of the change in global temperatures since the Industrial Revolution is very likely faster than at any time in the past half billion years outside of major meteor impacts and volcanic eruptions. One of the questions that interests scientists and the public is whether the recent change in our climate is natural or human-caused. In order to understand that we need to understand all the natural and human causes of climate change.

Scientific Practices

Engaging in Argument From Evidence

Seemingly more and more often the public is exposed to claims that later are 'fact-checked'. In science, a claim can only be offered if it is justified with evidence. Even then, because these claims are published, other scientists can find weaknesses in these claims. However, those weaknesses must be backed with evidence; else, the weakness claims will be justifiably ignored. Argumentation is healthy in science, but only if it is fact- and evidence-based. Argumentation in science takes place in the lab, at conferences, during peer-review, and in journal publications. Likewise, the scientist must make arguments against their own findings. Often, when a scientist finds something new the first thought they have is that their experimentation is flawed. It is dangerous to their career to publish a finding that is not evidence- and fact-based and find later that their experimental setup or interpretation was flawed. Faking the data is a certain career killer that can lead to termination and is likely to be uncovered. Once scientists attack their own findings and assure their interpretation is sound, they publish their results so other scientists can determine if their experimentation or interpretation is flawed. All journal publications are peer-reviewed before publication as a first chance to catch flawed arguments. The publication must make clear the experimental process and the results of those experiments so other scientists can repeat them. Those scientists can then make evidence-based arguments about the validity of the interpretation.

The public must also assess bad science. Unfortunately, most of the public does not have the time or knowledge to make the same assessment. Also, unfortunately, the public often does not assess based on evidence, but on the opinion of those that share their worldview. Opinions are not based on scientific evidence and are not a scientific argument. Typically, the best way to assess science is to go to the source of the scientific claim, which is often a scientific journal. Any scientific concept will be discussed within multiple articles with experimental methods and arguments based on evidence. At the very least, it is best to go with the scientific consensus knowing that the arguments are evidence-based and peer-reviewed.

Climate change is a good example of a scientific argument where much of the public receives their understanding from those people that share their worldview. If the argument is important enough, then a scientifically literate person should be able to access some of the more general scientific journals for the scientific argument. Because of the importance of climate change, a number of scientific bodies provide evidence-based assessments. The International Panel on Climate Change (IPCC, https://www.ipcc.ch) consists of a group of thousands of international climate scientists that provides periodic assessments of global climate change and their impacts. The U.S. National Climate Assessment (https://nca2014.globalchange.gov/) is produced for the U.S. with the help of the various U.S. government climate-related agencies and the U.S. National Academy of Sciences. Both are good evidence-based sources of climate change information written for the science literate (not expert) person.

Natural Causes of Climate Change

This section focuses on time scales to show which natural causes of climate change must be considered as the cause of climate change that we are currently experiencing (i.e. decades-to-centuries). Those causes that change too slowly need not be considered in our current climate change. If the time scale of the changes is not on the order of decades-to-centuries or less, we need not consider them. For example, if you fill a bathtub and climb in for a half hour bath and find that the water level drops in half during that time, you need not consider evaporation as a major factor. Evaporation does cause the water level to drop, but over a half hour, the decrease in water level because of evaporation would be imperceptible. If you wanted to sum the causes to determine how long it would take all the water to disappear, including evaporation would not change the total time enough to bother calculating it.

Plate Tectonics

The theory of plate tectonics states that the crust of the Earth is broken up in different tectonic plates. These plates float on a plastic layer of the upper mantle known as the asthenosphere. Each plate can move somewhat independently of the other tectonic plates on the asthenosphere. Many of the continents and nearby water move on continental plates while oceanic plates move separately. This movement has caused different distributions of continents. All the continents of Earth were connected 250 million years ago in a supercontinent known as Pangaea (Figure 15.1). Over time, this continent broke apart and spread out to their current configuration. What became Antarctica, was near the tropics prior to the periods in the figure and prior to the time of Pangaea. Fossil evidence of tropical plants supports the past tropical location of Antarctica.

Processes, at the plate boundaries, have a large impact on global climate. Mountain building at converging tectonic plates (Figure 15.2) and volcanic processes at subducting (Figure 15.3) and diverging tectonic plates can affect climate on all time scales. As continental plates converge, mountains form such as the Himalayan Mountains when the Indian and Asian continental plates converged (Figure 15.1). Mountains increase chemical weathering, which removes carbon dioxide from the atmosphere and ultimately stores carbon dioxide in limestone rocks in the ocean.

Mountains affect jet streams by making them wavier, which increases the transfer of energy from the equator to the poles. One-dimensional climate models can test the effect of mountains by increasing energy flux across latitudes. Greater energy transfer from the equator to the poles would cause warmer poles and glaciers to retreat to higher latitudes. The receding glaciers activates the ice-albedo positive feedback, which would increase solar absorption and cause global warming.

The arrangement of continents also has a major impact on climate. When Pangaea began to breakup about 250 million years ago, new oceans were created, and the ocean circulation changed. Surface and deep-water ocean circulations redistribute energy just as jet streams do. When Antarctica became isolated around 50 million years ago and the Antarctic circumpolar current formed, energy transfer to Antarctica became restricted possibly causing glaciers to form around 35 million years ago. Carbon dioxide concentrations were lowering at this time, which may have also caused Antarctica to glaciate.

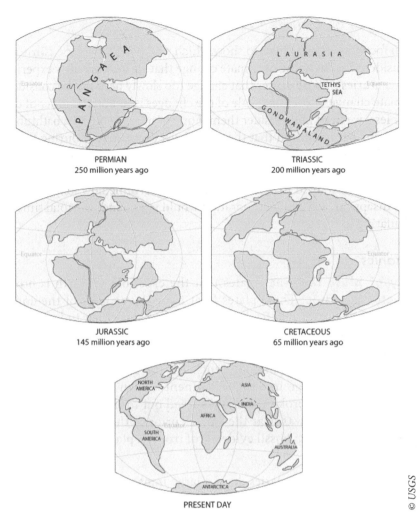

Figure 15.1 Illustration of the breakup of Pangaea starting 250 million years ago to the present day arrangement of continents. Latitude lines 0° (equator), 30°, 60°, and 90° (North and South Poles) are shown.

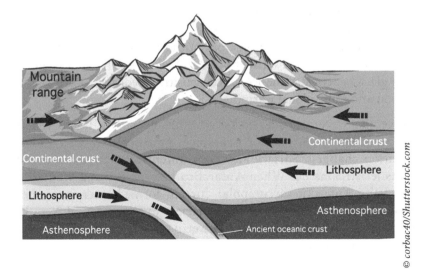

Figure 15.2 Illustration of mountain building at converging continental plates.

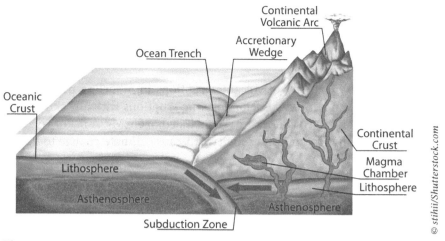

Figure 15.3 Illustration of volcanic activity created by an oceanic plate subducting a continental plate.

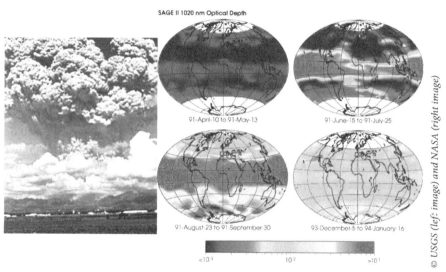

Figure 15.4 Eruption of Mt. Pinatubo on June 12, 1991 is shown on the left. On the right, a proxy for volcanic aerosols (color scale at the bottom) as it spread through the global stratosphere from a month before the eruption (April 10-May 13, 1991) to a couple years later (December 5, 1993-January 16, 1994). Mt. Pinatubo was the last major eruption that dramatically affected the global mean temperature, reducing it by as much as 0.5 °C (1 °F) for a few years after the eruption.

The various effects of plate tectonics and their opposing influences on temperature are complex and still an area of active research. Fortunately, plate tectonics occurs too slowly to affect climate on a decades-centuries time scale and climate forecasting over the next century can safely ignore it. Changes in ocean circulation do have effects on these time scales, but not when caused by plate tectonics. Changes in ocean circulation caused by glacial and sea ice melting do play a role in climate change at the decade-century time scale and will be discussed later. However, there are events caused by plate tectonics that do have effects on climate change at the decade-century time scales and those are volcanic eruptions.

Volcanic eruptions tend to have a short-term cooling effect and long-term warming effect. Volcanic eruptions produce liquid or solid particles that float in air known as **aerosols**. Ash and aerosol forming sulfate from volcanic eruptions pushed into the stable stratosphere can linger for years (Figure 15.4). These aerosols increase the atmospheric albedo and reduce solar radiation absorption at the surface. However, volcanoes also emit greenhouse gases such as water and carbon dioxide. Once the aerosols settle out of the atmosphere in a few years, which occurs faster than carbon dioxide removal, the greenhouse effect dominates to warm the global climate.

GCMs prescribe the effects of volcanic eruptions in modeling past climate changes. However, GCMs cannot forecast major volcanic eruptions with any skill on the decade-century time scale and so volcanoes are not included in GCMs. A major volcanic eruption or a significant change in volcanic activity can cause climate change to be far different from GCM forecasts.

Earth-Sun Orbital Changes

Milutin Milankovitch observed that the Earth's orbital parameters cycle on the order of tens to a hundred thousand years causing global temperature changes and the recent ice ages. The Earth's orbital parameters change because of the gravitational pull of the moon, sun, and other planets. Milankovitch used the calculated changes in these parameters to understand the temperature fluctuations found in the analysis of ice cores over the last million years (cf. Figure 2.3).

Eccentricity of the Earth's orbit The longest period orbital change, on the order of 100,000 years, is the cycle of the eccentricity of the Earth's orbit around the sun. Eccentricity is a measure of the shape of an ellipse, which is essentially a stretched circle or oval (Figure 15.5). A circle is an ellipse with an eccentricity of zero. The Earth's current orbit is actually an ellipse with an eccentricity of 0.017 and decreasing (becoming more circular). The Earth is closest to the sun during northern hemisphere winter (around January 4). This time is also when the Earth is moving fastest. This orbital pattern is why the northern hemisphere winter is around 89 days, whereas the northern hemisphere summer is around 93 days (though it certainly feels like winter is longer!).

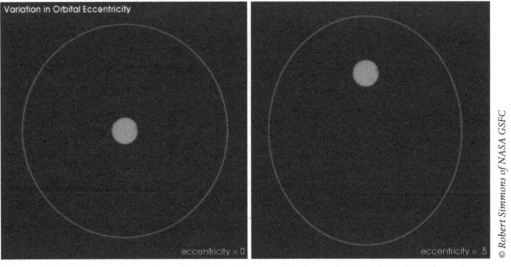

Figure 15.5 Illustration of eccentricity changes in the orbit (red circle) of a planet around the sun (yellow dot)

The effect of eccentricity on global mean temperature is that during their respective summers, the northern hemisphere receives less energy from the sun than the southern hemisphere. The reverse is true for their winters. The summer season is more important when considering glacial advance (ice age). With a colder summer, the latitude at which ice does not melt moves farther equatorward, which is glacial advance. When the eccentricity is smaller, as it is becoming, the northern hemisphere summer will become warmer. However, the eccentricity is closer to its highest value, which should currently favor advanced glaciers in the northern hemisphere and a cooler Earth.

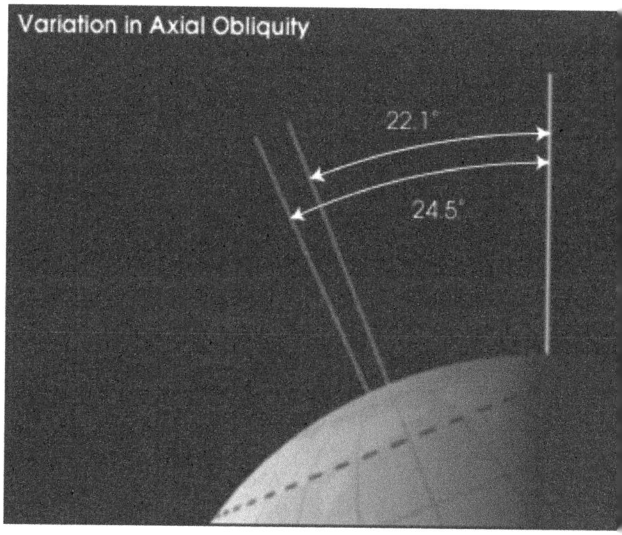

Change in the tilt of the Earth's rotation axis The second longest period orbital change, on the order of 41,000 years, is the change in the tilt of the Earth's rotation axis. The axial tilt is currently at about 23.4° and decreasing. The Earth's axial tilt range is between 22.1° and 24.5° (Figure 15.6). A smaller axial tilt causes summers to be cooler, which would cause glaciers to advance as discussed in the previous paragraph. The Earth is currently midway in its cycle but approaching a tilt that should cause glacial advance and a cooler Earth.

Precession of the Earth's rotation axis The shortest period orbital change, on the order of 23,000 years, is the **precession** of the Earth's rotation axis (Figure 15.7). If you ever played with a spinning top (like a Beyblade) then you may have noticed that when the top slows down, it begins to wobble. The wobble is actually precession. The rotation axis is rotating around the local vertical axis of the spinning top. The Earth has the same precession with its rotation axis. The effect on climate is that 11,500 years from now during northern hemisphere summer, the Earth will be closest to the sun. Therefore, currently the northern hemisphere receives close to its minimum solar energy during summer based on its progression through this precession period. Again, implying that glacial advance should occur, and the Earth should be getting cooler.

The Milankovitch cycles mostly explains the periodic changes in climate that have caused the ice ages. Ice age periodicity is around 100,000 years, which is similar to the eccentricity period. It is also interesting that the three Milankovitch cycles suggest that Earth should be currently entering an ice age. Given the length of the most recent interglacial period, which is similar to past interglacial periods, Earth is due for an ice age. The Milankovitch cycle lengths are at a time scale that are too slow compared to the time scale of warming that the Earth's climate experienced in the past 150 years.

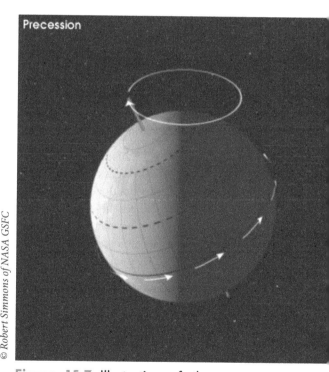

© Robert Simmons of NASA GSFC

Figure 15.6 Illustration of variation in the angle of the Earth's rotation axis (red lines) compared to the orientation of the rotation axis if there were no tilt (white line). This angle is known as axial obliquity.

Figure 15.7 Illustration of the precession of the Earth's axial tilt is shown. The Earth's rotation (white arrows) axis traces out a circle (white circle).

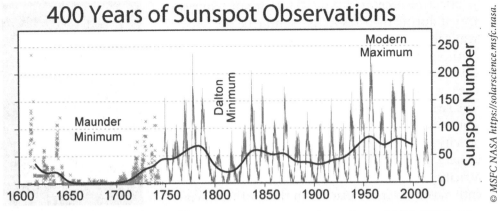

400 Years of Sunspot Observations

Modern Maximum

Dalton Minimum

Maunder Minimum

Sunspot Number

250
200
150
100
50
0

1600 1650 1700 1750 1800 1850 1900 1950 2000

© MSFC NASA https://solarscience.msfc.nasa.gov/SunspotCycle.shtml

Figure 15.8 Graph of monthly mean sunspot numbers from 1610-2015. The Maunder Minimum was a period of relatively few sunspots.

It is also in the wrong direction suggesting an ice age and not global warming. Like plate tectonics, the Milankovitch cycles are a natural cycle that does not act on a time scale that can explain Earth's recent period of warming. Most climate models do not include Milankovitch cycles because the effect is too small over the century time scale that most climate models run.

Solar Output

The sun's solar output changes over a number of different cycles. The most obvious cycle is the **11-year sunspot cycle**. Over this 11-year cycle, the sun goes from active to quiet periods. During active periods, **sunspots** and solar flares increase and the amount of solar radiation reaching the Earth increases. Solar flares affect cell phone service and other electronics so during active sun you would experience more trouble with your cell phones.

A history of sunspot cycles can be retrieved using proxy data for the past several thousand years with direct observations only available for the past 400 years. There have been over a dozen long periods where sunspot maximum was absent. The last such period called the **Maunder minimum**, occurred between 1645 and 1715 (Figure 15.8). This period partially coincided with a period called the Little Ice Age, which was a period of abnormally cold winters for North America and Europe. However, the Little Ice Age began about 50 years before the Maunder minimum.

Recently, the 20th century was one of the most active periods in our record of solar activity. The activity peaked in the middle of the century and then decreased. Although, this activity correlates well with the rise in global mean temperatures in the middle of that century, the drop in activity near the end of the 20th century and the beginning of the 21st century does not. The most recent solar cycle was the weakest in the past couple centuries. Nonetheless, this is a natural cycle on the decades-to-century time scale of current climate change and is included in GCMs.

Ocean Circulation

Ocean circulation changes were mentioned as part of plate tectonics. Tectonics-caused ocean circulation changes have time scales that are too long to be considered relative to our recent climate change. However, the recent melting of Greenland may be reducing the downwelling of water (fresh water is less dense than salt-water) in the North Atlantic. Not only does this have an effect on the deep ocean thermohaline circulation (see Chapter

8), but it may also affect surface currents. For example, the Gulf Stream may be slowing. Europe receives a lot of energy from the Gulf Stream so this change cools Europe. This appears to oppose global warming, which illustrates the complexity of climate change. Over a longer timescale, it reduces the energy transfer from the equator to poles, which may have a number of effects previously discussed (e.g. glacial advance).

In addition, several atmosphere-ocean oscillations have short time scales. Some of these oscillations were mentioned in Chapter 8 such as El Nino Southern Oscillation (ENSO), Arctic Oscillation (AO), and Pacific Decadal Oscillation (PDO). These and other oscillations occur over time scales important to our current climate change. However, the factors that affect these oscillations and their effect on climate remains a source of uncertainty. Nonetheless, the ocean is fairly well observed, at least the surface, and ocean data are included within the data used in GCMs.

Human Causes of Climate Change

Separating natural and human-caused climate change is not easy or straightforward. For example, greenhouse gases and aerosols have both natural and human sources. This section will highlight the human sources of greenhouse gases and aerosols and its relative proportion to natural sources. Humans have also altered the land, which predominantly affects albedo and the water cycle and has other effects on climate.

Greenhouse Gases

Chapter 4 introduced the concept of greenhouse gases. These gases do not work exactly like a greenhouse. Greenhouses have two effects that cause energy to concentrate within them. First, the glass is transparent in the solar wavelengths and opaque at Earth's emission wavelengths (i.e. thermal IR). It is obvious that they are transparent in the solar wavelengths, which is predominantly in the visible part of the electromagnetic (EM) spectrum, because you can see visible light through the glass. If you were only able to see in the thermal IR, the glass would look black because glass absorbs strongly in the thermal IR, which is where the Earth and most things on it emits. Second, the glass provides a barrier to prevent convection from removing energy. Although the latter is probably a larger factor, the former is where the extra energy in the greenhouse comes from. Greenhouse gases work like the former effect.

The main greenhouse gases in the atmosphere are water vapor, carbon dioxide, methane, nitrous oxide, and fluorinated gases. Water vapor has the largest overall greenhouse effect for gases, but clouds, which are not a gas, also have a strong greenhouse effect. However, from a climate change perspective, the importance of a greenhouse gas comes from its emission amount, additional greenhouse effect, and removal time from the atmosphere.

Additional water vapor does not add a substantially greater greenhouse effect because the concentration of water vapor in the atmosphere is already high. Furthermore, additional water vapor tends to condense out of the atmosphere through precipitation rather quickly. Nevertheless, the impact on cloud formation is an important consideration as the climate changes. Increased surface temperature causes more ground water to evaporate into the air. In addition, greenhouse gases are mostly found in the troposphere and tend to warm the surface much more than the upper troposphere. This distribution of heating causes a larger lapse rate, which produces more clouds. Clouds are very complex. Additional clouds do not necessarily add to surface warming if they are low and more reflective. Clouds may radiate strongly in the infrared, but during the daylight, they also reflect solar radiation.

In contrast, carbon dioxide is still at concentrations where additional emissions will have a significant impact on the energy balance. Combustion of fossil fuels and other sources such as cement production and other industrial processes are adding carbon dioxide rapidly (Figure 15.9). In addition, warmer ocean temperatures may release significant concentrations of carbon dioxide stored in the oceans. Carbon dioxide also has a long lifetime in the atmosphere and dissolution in the ocean leads to ocean acidification. For these reasons, the effects of carbon dioxide are the primary greenhouse gas discussed in relation to climate change. The other greenhouse gases are often listed in terms of carbon dioxide equivalent. However, other greenhouse gases have more potential per unit mass to increase global warming. These other greenhouse gases are rated on their potential per unit mass to cause global warming relative to carbon dioxide.[1]

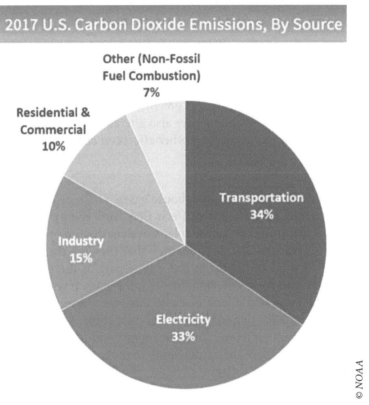

Figure 15.9 Percentage of U.S. carbon dioxide emissions by source in 2017.

Methane has a significant impact on the energy balance, even more so than a similar mass of carbon dioxide. Methane is 25 times more effective at affecting the global energy balance. They are not discussed as much as carbon dioxide because emissions are smaller, and they do not last as long in the atmosphere. Methane also comes from fossil fuels, but it also comes from landfills, permafrost, and just about any place where decaying organic matter is in a low oxygen environment (Figure 15.10). This includes the decaying organic matter (food) within the gut of livestock (i.e. enteric fermentation). The livestock source is often why eating meat indirectly affects climate change. The process of fracking also releases large amounts of methane. Methane is also a component of natural gas.

---

[1] IPCC (2007). Climate Change 2007: The Physical Science Basis. Contribution of Working Group I to the Fourth Assessment Report of the Intergovernmental Panel on Climate Change. [S. Solomon, D. Qin, M. Manning, Z. Chen, M. Marquis, K.B. Averyt, M. Tignor and H.L. Miller (eds.)]. Cambridge University Press. Cambridge, United Kingdom 996 pp.

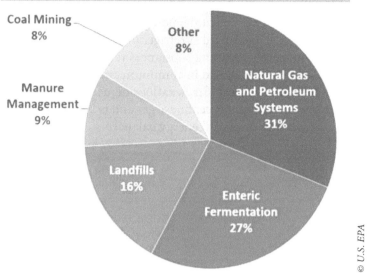

Figure 15.10 Percentage of U.S. methane emissions by source in 2017.

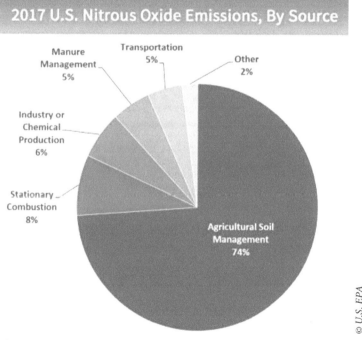

Figure 15.11 Percentage of U.S. nitrous oxide emissions by source in 2017.

Nitrous oxide is emitted in much smaller quantities than carbon dioxide and methane but is 298 times more effective at affecting the global energy balance. They also have a lifetime in the atmosphere that is longer than carbon dioxide. The primary source of human-caused nitrous oxide is agricultural soil management (Figure 15.11). Nitrous oxide is used as fertilizer and is produced in other agricultural soil management processes.

Fluorinated gases are emitted in much smaller quantities than the other greenhouse gases, which is why they are not discussed much. However, most are more than 10,000 times more effective at affecting the global energy balance per unit mass. They also have a potential lifetime in the atmosphere of several thousand years. Unlike the other greenhouse gases, they are all human made. The fluorinated gases are a group of gases that include Chlorofluorocarbons (CFCs), HydroChlorofluorocarbons (HCFCs), and Hydrofluorocarbons (HFCs) that are largely used as refrigerants (e.g. air conditioners, refrigerators) and an alternative to ozone-depleting substances (e.g. Freon) (Figure 15.12). They also include Perfluorocarbons (PFCs) used in aluminum and semiconductor production, water repellents (e.g. Gore-Tex); and sulfur hexafluoride used in electric transmission. Sulfur hexafluoride is the most potent greenhouse gas and is 22,800 times more effective than carbon dioxide at affecting the global energy balance.

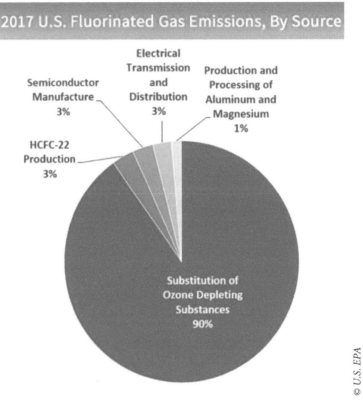

Figure 15.12 Percentage of U.S. Fluorinated gas emissions by source in 2017.

Fossil fuel burning is the majority cause of greenhouse gas increase and global warming. However, agricultural processes, refrigerants, and industrial processes such as cement production also play a significant role. Other than the fluorinated gases, most greenhouse gases have sources that are both natural and human-caused. That dual source leads to the important question about whether the current climate change is natural or human-caused. Chapter 2 discussed how climate models explain much of the observed means and variances in global mean temperature. The left column of Figure 15.13 shows that the observed trend of global mean temperature is replicated only when considering human-caused energy imbalances also known as forcings. The right column of Figure 15.13 also shows that the global distribution of temperature changes can only be explained when including human-caused energy imbalances. The effect on global warming of human-caused energy imbalances are estimated to be well over 50%.[2]

---

[2] IPCC, 2014: Climate Change 2014: *Synthesis Report. Contribution of Working Groups I, II and III to the Fifth Assessment Report of the Intergovernmental Panel on Climate Change* [Core Writing Team, R.K. Pachauri and L.A. Meyer (eds.)]. IPCC, Geneva, Switzerland, 151 pp.

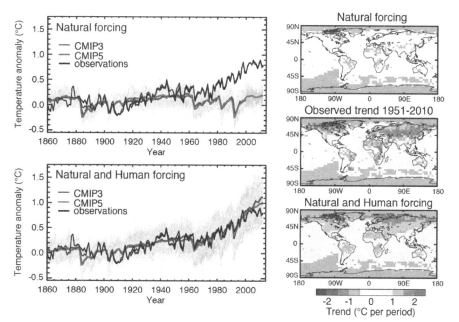

© IPCC, 2013: Climate Change 2013: The Physical Science Basis. Contribution of Working Group I to the Fifth Assessment Report of the Intergovernmental Panel on Climate Change Fig. FAQ 10.1, Fig 1 [Stocker, T.F., D. Qin, G.-K. Plattner, M. Tignor, S.K. Allen, J. Boschung, A. Nauels, Y. Xia, V. Bex and P.M. Midgley (eds.)]. Cambridge University Press, Cambridge, United Kingdom and New York, NY, USA, 1535 pp.

Figure 15.13 Temperature anomaly with an ensemble of climate models from CMIP3 (thin blue) and CMIP5 (thin yellow) and the ensemble means for CMIP3 (thick blue) and CMIP5 (thick red) are shown on the left for natural caused energy imbalances or forcings (top left) and natural and human energy imbalnces or forcings (bottom left) included in GCMs. The three graphs on the right are the global pattern of temperature trends for the period 1951-2010 for natural forcing (top right), observed (middle right), and natural and human forcing (bottom right).

The increased greenhouse gases also have a signature that ties them to fossil fuels. Fossil fuels come from **organic** sources (i.e. carbon sources) that died a long time ago. All life is composed of multiple isotopes of carbon. Isotopes of carbon are carbon of different molecular weights because of additional neutrons in the nucleus. As an organism eats, it constantly replenishes heavier and less stable isotopes of carbon. However, when the organism dies it no longer ingests this heavy isotope of carbon, which is radioactive, and it decays away. Measuring the ratio of the heavy to light isotopes of carbon is how carbon dating works. We can date life based on the amount of the heavier isotope of carbon that it contains. The amount of the heavier isotope of carbon decays by half every 5730 years.

Fossil fuels comes from organisms that died tens of millions of years ago. That means that the amount of the heavier isotope of carbon in fossil fuels is nearly zero. Therefore, if the carbon from fossil fuels is increasing its atmospheric concentration, then the proportion of the heavy isotope of carbon should decrease. The fact that it is provides strong evidence that the increased fossil fuels are from human combustion of fossil fuels.[3] This experiment is just one example of many that ties the burning of fossil fuels to the cause of global warming. As these lines of evidence increase, the cause becomes more definite. Other than volcanic eruptions, natural sources of increased greenhouse gases mostly come from feedback processes caused by global warming. Human causes often start these feedback processes so even most natural sources of greenhouse gases are indirectly human sources.

---

[3] Rubino, M; D. M. Etheridge; C. M. Trudinger; C. E. Allison; M. O. Battle; R. L. Langenfelds; L. P. Steele; M. Curran; M. Bender; J. W. C. White; T. M. Jenk; T. Blunier; R. J. Francey; (2013) A revised 1000 year atmospheric δ13C-CO2 record from Law Dome and South Pole, Antarctica, *J. Geophys. Res. Atmos. 118 (2013): 8482–8499, doi:10.1002/jgrd.50668.*

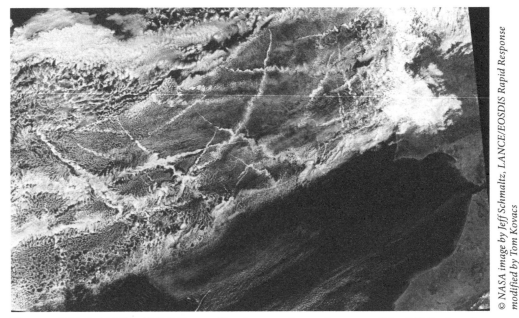

Figure 15.14 NASA MODIS satellite image from January 16, 2018 showing tracks of brighter clouds where ships seeded the clouds with aerosols serving as CCN making more cloud drops and clouds brighter.

Aerosols

Like clouds, the impact of aerosols on the energy balance is complicated. Aerosols directly affect the energy balance by absorbing and scattering solar radiation. A vast majority of aerosols scatter solar radiation, so the direct impact of aerosols is a cooling effect on climate. However, aerosols have an indirect effect on the energy balance in that they serve as condensation nuclei for clouds. Besides affecting the presence of clouds, they can also make clouds more reflective by increasing the reflectivity of them (Figure 15.14).

Land Use

Human development causes changes in the land cover. **Deforestation** and land clearing for agriculture change the energy balance at the surface in a number of ways. Carbon dioxide is used as an energy source, providing most of the mass of all plants. Therefore, removal of plants is essentially like adding carbon dioxide to the atmosphere. Practices such as deforestation and **biomass burning** to clear land are significant losses of carbon sinks and releases the carbon stored in the plants.

Probably the biggest effect of land-use changes is on the water cycle. When we build houses, stores, roads, etc., cement and asphalt replace vegetation. Land once covered by vegetation and replaced with cement and asphalt changes how water infiltrates into the ground and evaporates into the air. Changes in evaporation impacts energy transfer into the atmosphere, which can change the vertical temperature and moisture profile, clouds, and precipitation.

Irrigation and water withdraw have major impacts on lakes, rivers, and streams affecting the water temperature of the bodies of water. That bottled water that people like so much comes from somewhere different from where it is used. In some areas, the water withdraw is so large that rivers cease to flow in areas that they once flowed. During the dry season, the Colorado, Rio Grande, Nile, and Ganges rivers no longer make it to the

Figure 15.15 Rio Grande completely dried in places

sea (Figure 15.15). Large urban developments also lead to the urban heat island effect discussed in Chapter 2.

Global Climate Model (GCM) Forecasts

Global Climate Models (GCMs) were discussed in Chapter 11. This section will discuss how the GCMs are used to make future forecasts. Not every impact that causes climate change needs to be considered if the time scale of the process is too long for the period under consideration. These processes are excluded knowing that some major impacts, like a major volcanic eruption, meteorite impact, or nuclear war, can dramatically change GCM forecasts. Chapter 11 also discussed the data used to model past climates. These data are also used to help forecast future climates by initializing the GCMs. However, data on future solar output, volcanic eruptions, future greenhouse gas and aerosol emissions, and land-use changes must be prescribed. Prescribing this data are discussed in this section. Based on these prescribed processes, the long-term impacts are discussed. Finally, extreme events are the most visible impacts of climate change but attributing these events to climate change is not simple. Nonetheless, a procedure for attributing the effects of climate change on extreme events is discussed.

Modeled Processes

In the section that described the natural causes of climate change, a time scaling argument was made that not all processes that affect climate need to be considered when forecasting over a much shorter period. Plate tectonics and Earth-sun orbital changes do not materially affect the climate over the past or future couple of centuries. These processes affect climate over periods much longer than this, but over a couple of centuries the effects are too small to allocate limited computer resources to include them.

Plate tectonics does cause some short-term impacts that do have major impacts over a much shorter period. Volcanoes are a result of plate tectonics processes and a major volcanic eruption would dramatically affect climate change and could easily overwhelm all the other impacts. Not including plate tectonics in the model means that volcanic eruptions are not a part of the forecast. Not only do we not include these to save computer resources, but also there is little skill in forecasting major volcanic eruptions.

Biogenic processes are just starting to be included in GCMs called Earth System Models (ESMs). Removing a forest would reduce the carbon uptake from the atmosphere. The melting of **permafrost**, which is a subsurface layer of permanently frozen soil in polar regions, would release large amounts of methane. Fully simulating the carbon cycle allows us to understand the effects of these events in future GCM forecasts. For many GCMs, the emission and removal of carbon (i.e. the carbon cycle) are still prescribed.

Prescribed Data

Even for Earth System Models (ESMs) that simulate the carbon cycle, carbon emission from human activities depends on many non-physical processes. The non-physical factors that determine the emission of carbon can be categorized into four different components: population growth, **Gross Domestic Product (GDP) per capita**, **energy intensity of GDP**, and **carbon intensity of energy**. These social and economic determinants are difficult to measure in the future. However, we do know their relative impacts in the past (Figure 15.16).

Population growth is relatively straightforward. More people tend to require more energy, food, and material items that increase greenhouse gases. By multiplying the population growth by the GDP per capita (i.e. the physical stuff you need and want), we can estimate how much more energy, food, and material items the global population uses. Multiplying this by the amount of energy needed to produce these items (i.e. energy intensity of GDP), tells us the additional amount of energy needed for production of our increased needs and wants. Finally, by multiplying this by the amount of carbon

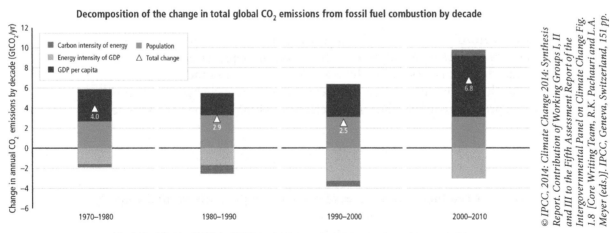

© IPCC, 2014: Climate Change 2014: Synthesis Report. Contribution of Working Groups I, II and III to the Fifth Assessment Report of the Intergovernmental Panel on Climate Change Fig. 1.8 [Core Writing Team, R.K. Pachauri and L.A. Meyer (eds.)]. IPCC, Geneva, Switzerland, 151 pp.

Figure 15.16 The decadal decomposition of fossil fuel consumption change from the 1970-1980 decade to the 2000-2010 decade is shown. The change in annual carbon dioxide emissions are measured in gigatons of carbon dioxide per year. The colors of each of the four factors are included in the legend and the sum of the four factors is given by the white triangle with the value beneath it.

generated by producing this energy (carbon intensity of energy) we know the additional amount of carbon dioxide equivalents emitted.

All of these factors are determined by social, economic, technological, and political factors. Attempts to model these are just beginning. Integrated Assessment Models (IAMs) attempt to couple these non-physical factors with GCMs. The initial attempts produced emission scenarios for the Coupled Model Intercomparison Project v. 3 (CMIP3) and v. 5 (CMIP5) and the third (2001), fourth (2007), and fifth (2013) IPCC Assessment Reports (TAR, AR4, and AR5). Emission scenarios are based on a range of potential futures that included various worldwide population, economic, technological, social, and political "story lines". The IAMs then produce emission scenarios in the 21st century based on these story lines. These emission scenarios serve as a standardized test of various GCMs. In addition, the scenarios provided a range of possible future emission trends to inform international governments on the range of impacts of policy decisions.

Because ESMs were including carbon cycles and atmospheric chemistry, they ended up with varying concentrations of greenhouse gases, which made intercomparisons difficult. For CMIP5 and the fifth (2013) IPCC Assessment Report v. 5 (AR5), emissions that produced a standard set of concentrations of the greenhouse gases by the year 2100 was used to standardize the model intercomparisons. These Representative Concentration Pathways (RCPs) were determined based on a range of predetermined energy imbalance produced in 2100. The range on imbalances selected was from 2.6 W/m² (RCP 2.6) to 8.5 W/m² (RCP 8.5). For comparison, the Earth's emission at the top of the atmosphere (240 W/m²) was calculated in Chapter 11.

These RCPs were the range that published climate experiments were using. This range essentially spanned international mitigation cooperation scenarios (RCP 2.6) to business as usual scenarios (RCP 8.5). Two other intermediate RCPs selected were an imbalance of 4.2 W/m² (RCP 4.2) and 6.0 W/m² (RCP 6.0). The use of RCPs allowed two different experiments. One experiment provided concentration pathways so that all GCMs and ESMs ended up with the same energy imbalance by 2100. The other provided emission pathways so that ESMs could be tested for how they produced different greenhouse gas concentrations and energy imbalances using their carbon cycling and atmospheric chemistry modules.

Long-Term Impacts

The impact of the four RCPs on global annual mean temperature and sea level are shown in Figure 15.17. This figure presents the two climate parameters as an anomaly to the 1986-2005 mean. They essentially represent the expected warming and sea level rise in the 21st century. They also include shading of uncertainty ranges for the RCP 2.6 (blue) and RCP 8.5 (red) scenarios within the graphs and for all four RCP scenarios averaged over 2081-2100. The total global warming in the 21st century for RCP 2.6 is expected to range 0.3 °C (0.5 °F) to 1.7 °C (3.1 °F) and for RCP 8.5 is expected to range 2.6 °C (4.7 °F) to 4.8 °C (8.6 °F). These amounts are on top of the 0.6 C (1.1 °F) of warming already experienced by the end of the 20th century. The rest of this section will highlight the impacts of this range of warming.

Global warming produces many long-term impacts. Most notably, warmer global temperatures melt the world's glaciers, which causes global sea rise. Also presented in Figure 15.17 is the expected global sea level rise for the 21st century, which for RCP 2.6 ranges from 0.26 m (0.85 feet) to 0.55 m (1.80 feet) and for RCP 8.5 ranges from 0.45 m (1.48 feet) to 0.82 m (2.69 feet). For reference, the mean elevation of New York

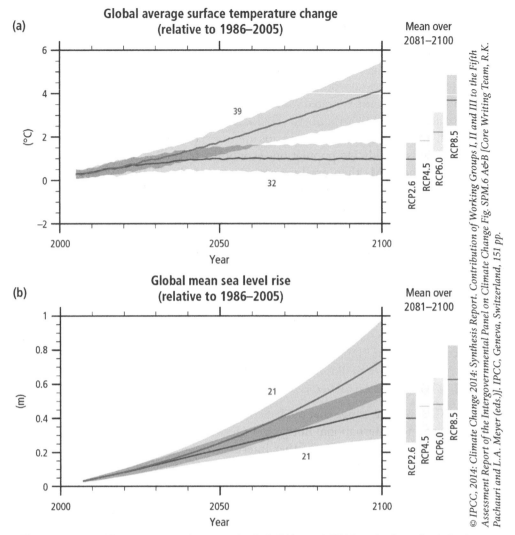

Figure 15.17 The mean and spread of GCM and ESM calculated global mean temperature change (top) and sea level rise (bottom) plotted for RCP 2.6 (blue) and 8.5 (red). The plotted values are an anomaly to the 1986-2005 mean and the number of models that go into the average are labeled above the plotted lines. The mean and spread over the years 2081-2100 are plotted to the right of the graph for all four RCPs.

City is 23 feet, Miami, FL is 6 feet, Venice Italy is 3 feet, and New Orleans. LA is −6 feet. Yes, New Orleans, LA averages 6 feet below sea level and exists due to a series of floodwalls, levees, and pumps. The entire country of the Maldives, and its half million residents, averages 6 feet above sea level. Furthermore, sea level rise near New York City has been twice the global mean because of its location and coastal geometry. These location elevations are also average values with some parts of these cities and countries lower in elevation. In addition, these are elevations relative to mean sea level and does not account for high tide or storm surge.

The speed of the change is also important. Organisms can adapt to a changing climate, but that adaptation is limited by the speed of the change and the accumulation of other stresses to habitats. Past change in climates was slower and allowed organisms to relocate to areas more suitable for life. The current changes are occurring much faster. There is a

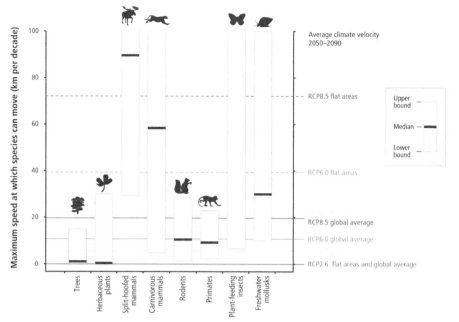

© IPCC, 2014: Climate Change 2014: Synthesis Report. Contribution of Working Groups I, II and III to the Fifth Assessment Report of the Intergovernmental Panel on Climate Change Fig. SPM.5 [Core Writing Team, R.K. Pachauri and L.A. Meyer (eds.)]. IPCC, Geneva, Switzerland, 151 pp.

Figure 15.18 Median speed at which species can move (thick black line, km/decade) compared to the speed at which average temperature isotherms are expected to move (climate velocity) for different Representative Concentration Pathways (RCPs). Climate velocities are faster when there is little elevation change (flat areas). Species that cannot move as fast as the climate velocities are expected to be at risk of extinction.

limit to the speed that organisms can relocate their habitats. Trees and herbaceous plants are the slowest to adapt and anything more than RCP 2.6 is expected to put these organisms at great risk of reduced population or even extinction (Figure 15.18). RCP 2.6 leads to a total warming from the nineteenth century of 1.5 °C to 2 °C, which is often quoted by U.S and international organizations as the point of major irreversible changes. Extinction risk of major ecosystems is one of the reasons for this threshold. Higher emission scenarios put an increasing number of species at risk. Although current extinction rates are more related to pollution, land-use, and invasive species, the combination with climate change can accelerate extinctions.[4]

An effect related to climate change is the acidification of the world's oceans. The increase in atmospheric carbon dioxide concentrations has also led to an increase in dissolved carbon dioxide within the world's oceans. Dissolved carbon dioxide in water leads to the formation of carbonic acid and a lowering of the ocean pH. The pH scale is a measure of the acidity of water ranging from 0 to 14 where seven is neutral, higher values are alkaline, and lower values are acidic (Figure 15.19). Organisms can only survive in an environment with a tight range of pH. The pH scale is not linear with a 0.1 decrease equaling about a 30% increase in acidity.

[4] Settele, J., R. Scholes, R. Betts, S. Bunn, P. Leadley, D. Nepstad, J.T. Overpeck, and M.A. Taboada, 2014: Terrestrial and inland water systems. In: Climate Change 2014: Impacts,Adaptation, and Vulnerability. Part A: Global and Sectoral Aspects. Contribution of Working Group II to the Fifth Assessment Report of the Intergovernmental Panel on Climate Change [Field, C.B., V.R. Barros, D.J. Dokken, K.J. Mach, M.D. Mastrandrea, T.E. Bilir, M. Chatterjee, K.L. Ebi, Y.O. Estrada, R.C. Genova, B. Girma, E.S. Kissel, A.N. Levy, S. MacCracken, P.R. Mastrandrea, and L.L.White (eds.)]. Cambridge University Press, Cambridge, United Kingdom and New York, NY, USA, pp. 271-359.

The pH Scale

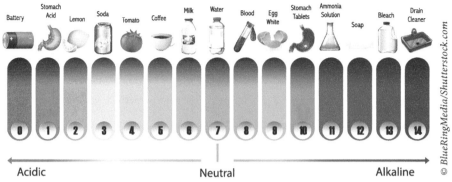

Figure 15.19 The pH scale is illustrated with some common items for each pH value shown above the scale.

During the 20th century the ocean pH has decreased by nearly 0.1 (Figure 15.20). In the 21st century, ocean pH is expected to decrease by another 0.14 for RCP 2.6 scenarios to 0.43 for RCP 8.5 scenarios with the largest decreases found in the Arctic.[5] Lowering pH along with rising water temperatures are a risk to the production of fisheries and causes bleaching of coral reefs. Coral reefs are some of the most biodiverse regions in the world and supports a large number of marine organisms. The bleaching of coral reefs is caused by the loss of algae that lives in a symbiotic relationship with the corals. Eventually bleached coral will die. Biodiversity affects the entire food chain. It also affects drug production. Many drugs that people use and need to stay healthy come from these biodiverse regions.

Attribution to Extreme Events

Chapter 2 defined climate as the long-term average of weather so to change the average, the daily weather conditions must change. However, it is difficult to determine whether climate change causes or worsens any single weather event. Nevertheless, it is possible to determine the likelihood of certain weather events in a world that has not warmed by using GCMs. Through ensemble modeling of a world with no human induced climate energy imbalances, it is possible to measure the **fraction of attributable risk (FAR)**. FAR is calculated as follows,

$$FAR = 1 - \frac{p_0}{p_i}$$

where p_o is the modeled probability of the event in a climate with no human induced energy imbalances and p_i is the modeled probability of the event in a climate with human induced

---

[5] Hoegh-Guldberg, O., R. Cai, E.S. Poloczanska, P.G. Brewer, S. Sundby, K. Hilmi, V.J. Fabry, and S. Jung, 2014: The Ocean. In: Climate Change 2014: Impacts, Adaptation, and Vulnerability. Part B: Regional Aspects. Contribution of Working Group II to the Fifth Assessment Report of the Intergovernmental Panel on Climate Change [Barros, V.R., C.B. Field, D.J. Dokken, M.D. Mastrandrea, K.J. Mach, T.E. Bilir, M. Chatterjee, K.L. Ebi, Y.O. Estrada, R.C. Genova, B. Girma, E.S. Kissel, A.N. Levy, S. MacCracken, P.R. Mastrandrea, and L.L.White (eds.)]. Cambridge University Press, Cambridge, United Kingdom and New York, NY, USA, pp. 1655-1731.

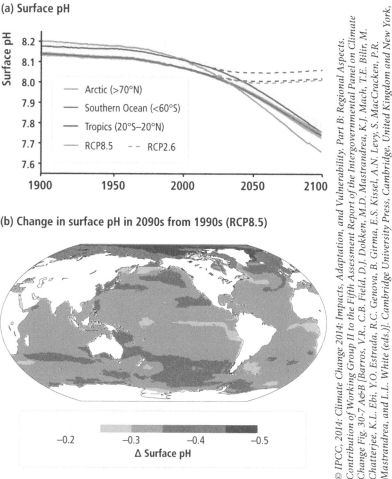

(a) Surface pH

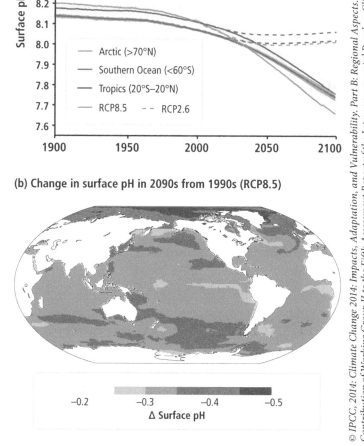

(b) Change in surface pH in 2090s from 1990s (RCP8.5)

−0.2   −0.3   −0.4   −0.5

Δ Surface pH

© IPCC, 2014: Climate Change 2014: Impacts, Adaptation, and Vulnerability. Part B: Regional Aspects. Contribution of Working Group II to the Fifth Assessment Report of the Intergovernmental Panel on Climate Change Fig. 30-7 A&B [Barros, V.R., C.B. Field, D.J. Dokken, M.D. Mastrandrea, K.J. Mach, T.E. Bilir, M. Chatterjee, K.L. Ebi, Y.O. Estrada, R.C. Genova, B. Girma, E.S. Kissel, A.N. Levy, S. MacCracken, P.R. Mastrandrea, and L.L. White (eds.)]. Cambridge University Press, Cambridge, United Kingdom and New York, NY, USA, 688 pp.

Figure 15.20 a) Ocean surface pH values for the Arctic (green), Southern Ocean (blue), and Tropics (red) for RCP 2.6 (dashed) and RCP 8.5 (solid) for the 20th century (observed) and the 21st century (modeled), b) World-wide distribution of the change in surface ocean pH from 1990 to 2090 for the RCP 8.5 scenario.

energy imbalances. For FAR = 1[6], p_o must equal zero, which means that the event is not possible without human induced climate change. For 2016, the exceptionally warm surface water in the north Pacific Ocean known as the "blob" and an Asian heat wave had a FAR = 1 meaning they were not possible without human induced climate change. For 2017, Hurricane Harvey precipitation exceeded an 80,000-year storm, which like a 100-year flood defined in Chapter 13 means that precipitation from Hurricane Harvey is not expected for more than 80,000 years.

Although Hurricane Harvey could have happened in modeled climates with no human induced energy imbalances, it was extremely unlikely. The extreme nature of events like these are increasing and insurance companies are starting to use this increased probability in setting policy rates.[7] Ultimately, this could lower property values and drive people

---

[6] Herring, S. C., N. Christidis, A. Hoell, J. P. Kossin, C. J. Schreck III, and P. A. Stott, Eds., 2018: Explaining Extreme Events of 2016 from a Climate Perspective. Bull. Amer. Meteor. Soc., 99 (1), S1–S157.

[7] Herring, S. C., N. Christidis, A. Hoell, M. P. Hoerling, and P. A. Stott, Eds., 2019: Explaining Extreme Events of 2017 from a Climate Perspective. Bull. Amer. Meteor. Soc., 100 (1), S1–S117, https://doi.org/10.1175/BAMS-ExplainingExtremeEvents2017.1.

away from high-risk areas. Everybody pays higher insurance rates and taxes to support disaster relief for these affected areas. This climate adaptation is an example of the rapidly changing world that climate change can cause for everyone. Climate change is not a rapid calamitous or extinction event, but a slow, yet accelerating adaptation to changing environmental conditions.

Potential Solutions

Although climate change does pose a significant risk to human civilization, humans have combated seemingly overwhelming issues previously. The system of modern plumbing and sewer systems, electricity transmission, wireless communications, the Internet, and the COVID-19 pandemic are all changes made in the past century that approach the solutions necessary to combat climate change. Although, because of the long lifetime of many greenhouse gases, it is likely that even if we stopped emitting greenhouse gases, change will happen. Therefore, climate adaptation and resiliency must be considered. Climate resiliency is making changes to reduce the effects of climate change. An example of climate resiliency is to increase the capacity of storm water systems or reduce the amount of runoff through construction of rain gardens.

In order to mitigate climate change, it is necessary to reduce the factors that lead to the largest increase in greenhouse gases. By far the greatest effect is the burning of fossil fuels. Addressing the four categories of fossil fuel consumption illustrated in Figure 15.16 can reduce the burning of fossil fuels. They are, again, population, gross domestic product (GDP) per capita, energy intensity of GDP, and carbon intensity of energy. This section will address each of these in reverse order.

First, the carbon intensity of energy is the amount of carbon dioxide equivalent created from the energy that we use. The burning of coal, petroleum products, and natural gas are all carbon intensive. We burn these fossil fuels to create electricity, heat homes, and transport people and goods. Solutions that reduce this carbon intensity would help combat global warming. Alternative energy sources such as solar photovoltaics (solar panels), concentrated solar power, wind power, hydroelectric power, geothermal power, hydrogen fuel cells, biofuels, and nuclear power are all examples (Figure 15.21). Some of these have technological issues to overcome while others have other environmental issues to consider. Nonetheless, it is possible to utilize all these options to offset fossil fuel burning with little to no environmental or economic impact. Carbon Capture and Storage (CCS) is another possibility where carbon is captured during fossil fuel burning and stored out of the atmosphere. Examples include using CCS for greenhouses and carbonating soda. CCS currently has issues with large-scale implementation and cost but is a potential future solution.

Second, the energy intensity of GDP is the amount of energy needed to create products. This largely relates to efficiency. Using LED light bulbs instead of incandescent bulbs is an example. Using Energy Star rated appliances and electronics is another example. Residential, commercial, and industrial building can be built or refurbished to be more efficient. Homeowners can simply caulk their houses to reduce energy loss. Cars can run more efficiently or run on batteries (i.e. electric), which are significantly more efficient.

Third, GDP per capita is the number of products that each household consumes. This relates to waste and materialism. The solution here is to simply waste and purchase less. Reduce, reuse, and recycle programs tackle this issue. Composting is also somewhat related in that it prevents organic products, which are largely products required for

(a)

(b)

(c)

© a: Costazzurra/Shutterstock.com; b: esbobeldijk/Shutterstock.com; c: fokke baarssen/Shutterstock.com

Figure 15.21 Alternative energy examples are shown. Starting at left and working clockwise is a geothermal system, solar panels, and a wind energy farm.

survival such as food and clothing, from going to the landfill, which produces methane. It also recycles them because compost helps grow additional crops. Food waste in general is a big problem with nearly half of all grown or raised food products wasted.

The final category is population. Population essentially is a multiplier of all the other categories in the impact on global warming. Population is a multiplier for many issues other than global warming like resource scarcity, access to fresh water, pollution, etc. Population control is generally not a popular solution to mitigate global warming even among environmentalists. However, if the other categories are not controlled, the Earth will eventually control the population, which will eventually bring the energy budget back into balance.

Summary

Climate Change is a natural part of a dynamic Earth and a dynamic atmosphere. It has occurred throughout geologic history. Throughout much of this history, humans played no role in these changes. However, in the past two centuries the effect of human behavior on the Earth's climate has been significant. Determining the amount of that effect and the change we can expect in the future is the focus of long-term century-scale climate forecasting.

A first step in this type of forecasting is to consider all the causes of climate change on this time scale. Being able to exclude natural causes such as plate tectonics and Earth-sun orbital changes makes the climate modelling simpler without sacrificing accuracy. Other natural causes such as solar output and ocean circulation changes cannot be excluded. If major volcanic eruptions occur in the future, GCM results will be affected.

Human causes of climate change such as emission of greenhouse gases and aerosols and changes in land use must also be included in GCMs.

Unfortunately, we know how the human causes of climate change have changed in the past, but we do not know how they will change in the future. These changes must be prescribed based on past behavior and future social, technological, economic, and political changes. Integrated Assessment Models (IAMs) are used to calculate how greenhouse gas and aerosol emissions will change in the future based on these non-physical factors. A range of Representative Concentration Pathways (RCPs) based on these IAMs are used by GCMs to forecast climate change. Based on these expected RCPs, catastrophic changes are expected for all but the lowest RCP, which limits global warming to between 1.5 °C and 2 °C. We are already seeing extreme events that we can now say with confidence would not occur without climate change.

Luckily, potential solutions exist. Reducing greenhouse gas emissions by reducing fossil fuel use is the most impactful. Alternative energy sources that do not emit greenhouse gases and carbon capture and storage are the fastest ways to avoid catastrophic climate change. If we do not reduce climate change, climate adaptation will cost far more than any climate change mitigation solution.

Key Terms

Climate Forecasting

Natural Causes of Climate Change

Theory of Plate Tectonics

Tectonic Plates

Asthenosphere

Pangaea

Converging Tectonic Plates

Subducting Tectonic Plates

Diverging Tectonic Plates

Aerosols

Eccentricity of the Earth's Orbit

Precession

Milankovitch Cycles

11-Year Sunspot Cycles

Sunspots

Maunder Minimum

Human-Caused Climate Change

Fossil Fuels

Lifetime in the Atmosphere

Ocean Acidification

Carbon Dioxide Equivalent

Organic

Deforestation

Biomass Burning

Extreme Events

Permafrost

Gross Domestic Product (GDP) per Capita

Energy Intensity of GDP

Carbon Intensity of Energy

Representative Concentration Pathways (RCPs)

pH Scale

Fraction of Attributable Risk (FAR)

Climate Adaption

Climate Resiliency

Alternative Energy

Carbon Capture and Storage (CCS)

Energy Star

Reduce, Reuse, and Recycle

Questions and Problems

1. How does the moving of the continents affect our climate? Describe two different ways.

2. What factors are thought to have played a role in the cycling between glacial and interglacial periods? Name three and describe how each would lead to advance or retreat of glaciers.

3. Based on Internet research and this textbook, provide a timeline of the latitude location of Antarctica. Include when it began to glaciate, when it broke from Pangea and became isolated, and the geologic periods.

4. What are the values of the Earth-sun orbital parameters that would lead to the best chance for glacial advance in the northern hemisphere?

5. Which of the Earth-sun orbital parameters are we currently more than half-way toward the extreme end that would lead to glaciation?

6. Based on Figure 15.8 and Figure 15.13, what range of years were the solar output (as evidence by the number of sunspots) and the global mean temperature changes correlated and when were they anticorrelated (i.e. one went up while the other went down)?

7. In the movie, "The Day after Tomorrow" (find the synopsis on Wikipedia) current real climate change led to global cooling and a global ice age. What observable changes serve as the basis for this event and what is the real effect it is having on our climate?

8. Which natural causes of climate change can play a significant role in the warming experienced over the last century? Why can't the natural changes that you did not list play a significant role over that time?

9. Three different greenhouse gases fits in these categories: the largest current greenhouse effect, the fastest increasing greenhouse effect, and the largest potential (for the same additional mass) greenhouse effect. What greenhouse gas fits in each category?

10. How do greenhouse gases lead to global warming? What makes them different from nitrogen, for example, which has the highest concentration of gases in our atmosphere, but no greenhouse effect?

11. Why is it difficult to determine the role that clouds, and aerosols play in climate change?

12. One recommendation for removing carbon dioxide from the atmosphere is to pump carbon dioxide into greenhouses and grow plants. How could this remove more carbon dioxide when the plants would take carbon dioxide from the air anyway?

13. What are some of the non-physical processes that have led to an increase in carbon dioxide emission in the decade of 2000-2010?

14. How have GCMs included non-physical (e.g. social, technological, policy) processes?

15. How do scientists determine if an extreme weather event has been affected by climate change?

16. Composting is listed as a potential solution; however, composting produces carbon dioxide. Why is this preferable to throwing food out?

17. According to EnergySage (energysage.com), the average residence uses 10972 kWh of electricity in a year and the average installed solar panel system that would generate this amount of electricity costs $17523 in 2020. In 2019, Massachusetts paid 21.1 cents per kWh. If you paid no additional electricity costs with solar panels, which would be the better deal over 10 years and by how much?

Other Resources

https://www.emich.edu/geography-geology/weather for links to useful weather data to go along with this textbook and updates to any broken links in the textbook.

http://climatemodels.uchicago.edu/ includes several radiation, climate, hurricane, and carbon cycle models with simple user inputs to play with.

Appendix

Appendix A: Units of Measurement and Prefixes

SI Units of Measurement and SI Derived Units of Measurement

Quantity	Name	SI Units	Symbol
length	Meter	m	m
mass	Kilogram	kg	kg
time	Second	s	s
temperature	Kelvin	K	K
Electric Current	Ampere	A	A
Force	Newton	$kg\ m/s^2$	N
Pressure	Pascal	N/m^2	Pa
Energy	Joule	N m	J
Power	Watt	J/s	W
Electrical Potential	Volt	W/A	V

Unit of Measurement Prefixes

Prefix	Multiple	Symbol
Terra	1 trillion = 10^{12}	T
Giga	1 billion = 10^9	G
Mega	1 million = 10^6	M
Kilo	1 thousand = 10^3	k
Hector	1 hundred = 10^2	h
Deca	Ten = 10	da
Deci	1 tenth = 10^{-1}	d
Centi	1 hundredth = 10^{-2}	c
Milli	1 thousandth = 10^{-3}	m
Micro	1 millionth = 10^{-6}	μ
Nano	1 billionth = 10^{-9}	n
Pico	1 trillionth = 10^{-12}	p

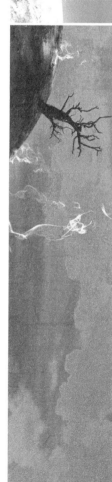

Appendix B: Unit Conversions and Constants

Unit Conversions

Length	Equivalents
1 nautical mile	1.15 mi, 1.85 km, 1850 m
1 mile (mi)	1.61 km, 1609 m, 5280 ft
1 kilometer (km)	1000 m, 3281 ft, 39372 in
1 meter (m)	3.28 ft, 39.37 in, 100 cm
1 foot (ft)	12 in, 30.48 cm, 304.8 mm
1 inch (in)	2.54 cm, 0.254 mm, 0.000254 μm
1 centimeter (cm)	0.39 in, 10 mm, 10000 μm
1 millimeter (mm)	0.039 in, 0.1 cm, 1000 μm
1 micrometer (μm)	0.0001 cm, 0.001 mm, 1000 nanometers (nm)

For Area, square both sides and for Volume, cube both sides (e.g. 1^2 $m^2 = (3.28)^2$ ft^2 or 1 $m^2 = 10.76$ ft^2)

Speed	Equivalents
1 knot	0.51 m/s, 1 nautical mile/hr, 1.15 mi/hr, 1.85 km/hr
1 mile per hour (mi/hr)	0.45 m/s, 0.87 knots, 1.61 km/hr
1 kilometer per hour (km/hr)	0.28 m/s, 0.54 knots, 0.62 mi/hr
1 meter per second (1 m/s)	1.94 knots, 2.24 mi/hr, 3.60 km/hr

Force and Mass	Equivalents
1 Newton (N)	1 kg m/s^2, 0.2248 lb (only on Earth)
1 kilogram (kg)	1000 g, 2.2 lb (only on Earth)
1 gram (g)	0.001 kg, 0.002 lb (only on Earth)

Pressure	Equivalents
Standard Atmosphere	14.7 lbs/in^2, 29.92 in Hg, 1013.25 mb, 1013.25 hPa
1 pound per square inch (lbs/in^2)	2.04 in Hg, 68.93 mb, 68.93 hPa
1 inch of Hg (in Hg)	33.865 mb, 33.865 hPa, 3386.5 Pa
1 millibar (mb)	0.01450 lbs/in^2, 1 hPa, 100 Pa
1 hectoPascal (1 hPa)	0.02953 in Hg, 1 mb, 100 Pa
1 Pascal (1 Pa)	0.01 mb, 1 N/m^2

Energy	Equivalents
1 calorie (cal)	4.186 J
1 joule (J)	0.239 cal, 1 N m

Power	Equivalent
1 watt (W)	1 J/s, 14.34 cal/min
1 calorie per minute (cal/min)	0.07 W

Temperature	Equivalent
Degrees Fahrenheit (°F)	(9/5) °C + 32
Degrees Celsius (°C)	5/9 (°F − 32)
Kelvin (K)	°C +273.15

Constants

Density of dry air at 0 °C and 1000 mb = 1.275 kg/m^3

Density of ice at 0 °C = 917 kg/m^3

Density of liquid water at 0 °C = 997 kg/m^3 (1000 kg/m^3 at 4 °C, which is maximum density)

Earth's surface gravitation acceleration (g) = 9.81 m/s^2

Stefan-Boltzmann Constant (σ) = 5.67 × 10^{-8} W/(m^{2}K^4)

Unsaturated adiabatic lapse rate (Γ_u) = 10 °C/km = 5.5 °F/ft

Viscosity of air = 1.7 × 10^{-5} kg/m·s

Appendix C: Physical Geography and Political Maps of North America

General reference map of the United States

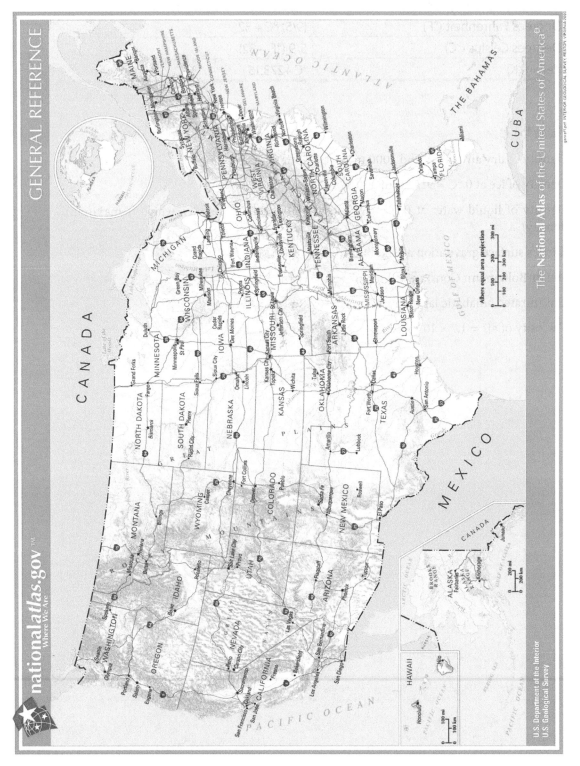

Credit: *National Atlas, U.S. Geological Survey. Public domain.*

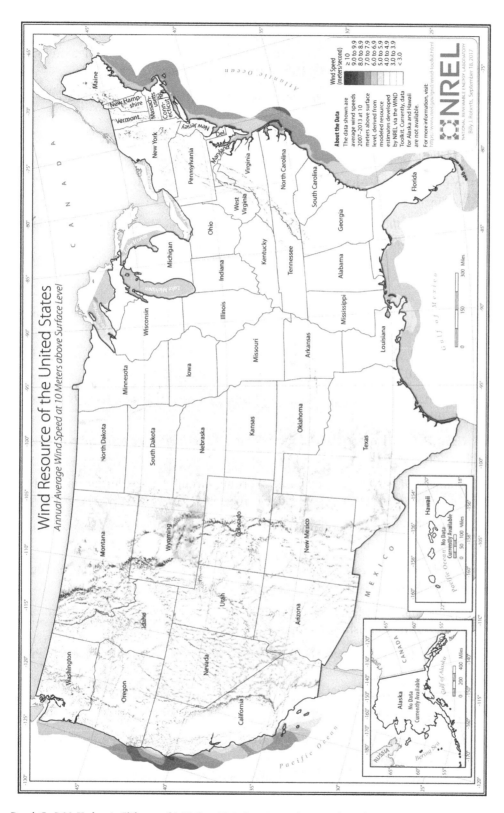

Draxl, C., B.M. Hodge, A. Clifton, and J. McCaa. 2015. Overview and Meteorological Validation of the Wind Integration National Dataset ToolkitPDF (Technical Report, NREL/TP-5000-61740). Publication Date: September 2017. Golden, CO: National Renewable Energy Laboratory. U.S. Department of Energy after National Renewable Energy Laboratory.

Additional Reading Material

Periodicals

Bulletin of the American Meteorological Society. Monthly. The American Meteorological Society, 45 Beacon St., Boston, MA 02108. http://journals.ametsoc.org/

EOS – Transactions of the American Geophysical Union (AGU), Washington D.C. https://eos.org/

Physics Today. Monthly. The American Institute of Physics, 1305 Walt Whitman Rd., Suite 300, Melville, NY 11747. http://www.physicstoday.org

Weather. Monthly. Royal Meteorology Society, James Glaisher House, Grenville Place, Bracknell, Berkshire, England. https://www.rmets.org/weather

Weatherwise. Bimonthly. Taylor & Francis Group, 530 Walnut Street, Suite 850, Philadelphia PA 19106. http://www.weatherwise.org.

Books

Ackerman, Steven, A and John A. Knox. *Meteorology* (3rd ed.) Jones and Bartlett Learning, Sudbury, MA 01776, 2012.

Ahrens, C. Donald. and Robert Henson. *Essentials of Meteorology* (9th ed.) Cengage, Boston, MA, 02210, 2017.

Ahrens, C. Donald. and Robert Henson. *Meteorology Today* (12th ed.) Cengage, Boston, MA, 02210, 2019.

Bohren, Craig F. Clouds in a Glass of Beer: *Simple Experiments in Atmospheric Physics*, Wiley, New York, 1987.

Climate Change 2013, The Physical Basis. Working Group 1 contribution to the Fifth Assessment Report of the IPCC, Cambridge University Press, New York, NY, 2013.

Emanuel, Kerry. Divine Wind – The History and Science of Hurricanes, Oxford University Press, New York, 2005.

Glossary of Meteorology. Todd S. Glickman, Managing ed., American Meteorological Society, Boston, MA, 2000.

Grenci, Lee M. and Jon M. Nese. *A World of Weather: Fundamentals of Meteorology* (6th ed.) Kendall Hunt Publishing Company, 2018.

Hakim G. and J. Patoux. *Weather a Concise Introduction*, Cambridge University Press, 2018.

Markowski P., and Y. Richardson. *Mesoscale Meteorology in Midlatitudes*, Wiley-Blackwell, 2010.

Melieres, Marie-Antoinette and Chloe Marechel. *Climate Change Past, Present, and Future*, Wiley Blackwell, 2015.

McGuffie, Kendal and Ann Henderson-Sellers. *The Climate Modelling Primer* (4th ed.) John Wiley & Sons, Ltd., 2014

Rauber, Robert M., John E. Walsh, Donna J. Charlevoix. *Severe and Hazardous Weather: An Introduction to High Impact Meteorology* (5th ed.), Kendall Hunt Publishing Company, 2017.

Ruddiman, William F. Earth's *Climate: Past and Future* (3rd ed.), Macmillan Learning, 2014.

Wallace, J. M. and P.V. Hobbs. *Atmospheric Science, An Introductory Survey*, Elsevier, Inc., San Diego, CA, 2006.

Washington, W.M. and C.I. Parkinson. *Introduction to Three Dimensional Climate Modeling* (2nd ed.). University Science Books, 2005.

Williams, Jack. The AMS Weather Book: *The Ultimate Guide to America's Weather*, American Meteorology Society, Boston, MA, 2009.

Glossary

100-year flood: A flood that has a probability of 1% of occurring in any year or a return period of 100 years.

11-Year Sunspot Cycles: An 11-year cycle where the sun cycles through an active period of sunspots and increased solar output and a quiet period of relatively few sunspots and reduced solar output.

1-Day Extreme Precipitation: Precipitation events that are above the 90th percentile (i.e. higher than 90% of previous events) of 1-day precipitation amount for each area.

500-1000 mb Thickness: The difference between the height of the 500 mb map and the 1000 mb map at a location. The thickness parameter is proportional to the temperature of the layer and is used to identify fronts and the rain/snow line in winter.

Absolute Humidity: A measure of the abundance of water vapor in the air with its SI unit given as a density, kg/m^3.

Absolutely Stable: Environments where the environmental lapse rate *is less than* both the saturated and unsaturated adiabatic lapse rates.

Absolutely Unstable: Environments where the environmental lapse rate *is greater than* both the saturated and unsaturated adiabatic lapse rates.

Absorption: Conversion of an electromagnetic wave to energy causing the electromagnetic wave to no longer exist and transferring its energy to the absorber.

Acceleration: A vector quantity where the magnitude is the change in velocity of an object with mass and has an SI unit of meters per second squared, m/s^2.

Accretion: Freezing together of two frozen precipitation drops that come in contact often accentuated by a liquid layer forming on the drops.

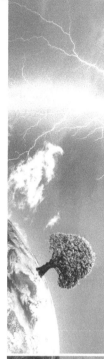

Accurate: The distance between the measurement by an instrument and the true value of the parameter that the instrument is measuring.

Adiabatic: Without heat. A change in temperature that occurs because of work and not because of heating.

Advanced Baseline Imager: Name of the instrument onboard current geostationary weather satellites that record visible and infrared wavelength images of the Earth from space.

Advection: Horizontal convection (see convection).

Aerosols: Liquid or solid particles that float in air.

Air Masses: A mass of air with uniform temperature and humidity (relative to location mean values) between the size of Texas and the size of the entire U.S.

Air Resistance: Drag force that objects experience in air.

Albedo: Percentage of the sun's radiation that is scattered back by a scatterer.

Alberta Clipper: Midlatitude cyclones that originate from Alberta, Canada, a preferred location for cyclogenesis (see cyclogenesis).

Alternative Energy: Energy sources that are alternative to fossil fuel burning and includes renewable energy and nuclear energy.

Altitude: Vertical distance from the Earth's surface.

Altocumulus: Mid-level clouds that look like larger cirrocumulus clouds. From the ground they appear larger than the tip of your finger, but smaller than a fist from an extended arm.

Altostratus: Mid-level clouds that allows the sun through and can predict precipitation because they form ahead of warm fronts.

They differ in appearance to cirrostratus in that there are no haloes; instead the sun appears distorted (not circular).

Analog Method: A scientific weather forecasting method that uses the forecasters' experience of spotting patterns they have seen before to forecast the weather.

Analysis of Variance: A set of statistical techniques used to explain data distributions using sample means and variances. It can be applied to samples of global temperatures at different periods to identify the likely causes of the differences or at least those factors that explain the most variation between the means.

Anemometers: An instrument that measures wind speed.

Angular Velocity: Rotational velocity measured in degrees of rotation per second or revolutions per second.

Anomaly: Difference of a data value from the mean of all the data values.

Archimedes Principle: Scientific principle stating that any object immersed in a fluid is buoyed by a force equal to the weight of the fluid displaced by the object.

Arctic Oscillation: A measure of the difference in surface pressure between the latitude of Iceland and the Arctic that directly affects the jet streams.

Artifacts: A change in the time series of some parameter that is not natural, but caused by flaws in the measurement.

Assimilate: A process of taking data from measurement instruments, preparing the data in the proper form with geographic information, error-checking the data, and interpolating the data to the model grid.

Asthenosphere: Upper layer of the mantle that may deform and convection may cause movement. Tectonic plates float on this layer causing them to move.

Atmospheric River: Low-level jet of humidity akin to a river, but in the atmosphere.

AWIPS (Advanced Weather Interactive Processing System): A software package that combines radar, weather station, weather balloon, and satellite information to produce value-added visual and textual data products.

Baroclinic Instability: An instability formed by winds crossing isotherms. Waves cause air to cross isotherms if a temperature gradient is present. When air crosses isotherms it deepens the waves and causes more air to cross isotherms, which deepens the waves, and so on.

Barometer: An instrument that measures pressure.

Bergeron Process: Cold (ice crystal) growth process of cloud- to rain-drops where the relatively few ice crystals in a cloud grow rapidly at the expense of the far larger number of supercooled drops because the saturation vapor pressure over ice is smaller than over a supercooled liquid drop at the same temperature (see supercooled drops).

Bermuda High: Surface semipermanent high pressure that is centered east and about the latitude of Bermuda throughout most of the year over the Atlantic Ocean. The Bermuda High moves closer to Europe in winter.

Best Track Forecast: A product of NOAA Tropical Prediction Center to the public that is the best forecast of the track of the center of a tropical cyclone.

Biomass Burning: A way to clear land of trees and plants by burning it.

Black Ice: A term that comes about from the fact that freezing rain is often translucent and invisible when freezing on black asphalt roads.

Bomb Cyclone: A special name given for midlatitude cyclones that decrease in surface pressure by 24 hPa (24 mb) in 24 hours.

Boundary Condition Problem: The problem of how to handle what happens at the boundaries of a model domain.

Bounded Weak Echo Region: A pattern on a radar reflectivity image caused by precipitation producing high reflectivity wrapping around (bounding) a rotating updraft. The updraft area is the weak echo region because water drops here are small.

Bow Echo: A pattern on a radar reflectivity image that is shaped like a hunter's bow and occurs in squall lines where the outflow concentrates in a narrow area causing the apex of the bow to rush forward.

Buoyancy Force: Force that is proportional to the density difference between an object and the fluid in which it is submerged as governed by Archimedes Principle (see Archimedes principle).

Calibration: A process of adjusting the scale of an instrument so that its measurement is equal to a calibration standard at several calibration points within the range of the instrument.

California Current: Cold surface ocean current that originates from the southerly directed North Pacific Drift as it branches at the North American Continent.

Capping Inversion: A layer of increasing temperatures with height that inhibits convection and allows the sun's energy to build below. Capping inversions are favorable for severe thunderstorms because the buildup of energy leads to a more explosive growth of thunderstorms rather than spreading the energy over less severe thunderstorms.

Carbon Capture and Storage (CCS): A process of removing carbon from exhaust where carbon is captured during fossil fuel burning and stored out of the atmosphere.

Carbon Dioxide Equivalent: A measure of the potential per mass of a greenhouse gas to cause global warming relative to carbon dioxide.

Carbon Intensity of Energy: The amount of carbon dioxide equivalent created from the energy that we use.

Causation: A cause and effect relationship between two events such that one event clearly causes the other.

Central Dense Overcast: A thick cirrus cover forming from air flowing outward at the top of tropical cyclones in the high-pressure upper-air circulation.

Centrifugal Force: Apparent force caused by an object that is turning because of inertia (see inertia).

Centripetal Force: Balancing force to centrifugal force causing a turning object to maintain its turn and overcome inertia (see inertia).

Chaos: A branch of mathematics that deals with dynamical mathematical systems that appear to be random but are deterministic and highly sensitive to initial conditions (see deterministic).

Chroma key compositing technique: A video editing technique to combine two video images into one. A green screen (or some other color) is used as a background for a second image to be combined with any object in front of the screen.

Cirrocumulus: High altitude cumulus clouds that appear smaller than the tip of your finger when observed from the ground.

Cirrostratus: High altitude clouds composed of ice crystals that refracts sunlight causing halos or sun dogs to form around the sky or moon.

Cirrus: High clouds composed mainly of ice giving them a wispy, feathery shape.

Climate Adaption: Changes in behaviors to survive and thrive because of climate change.

Climate Change: Change in the long-term average of weather parameters. Mostly, the weather parameters include temperature and precipitation, but any weather parameter could be included.

Climate Feedbacks: A process internal to the climate system that can amplify or diminish an external change.

Climate Forecasting: Using climate models to forecast how the long-term average of weather conditions will change.

Climate Models: A scientific mathematical tool using initial conditions and the physical laws to calculate future changes in the average weather conditions. Unlike weather models, they do not forecast conditions on specific days, but provide averages for seasons or years.

Climate Resiliency: The ability to reduce the effects of climate change.

Climate: The long-term average of weather usually requiring at least 30 samples in the average.

Climatological Forecast: A scientific forecasting method that uses the climatological means for an area as a basis to forecast the weather.

Cloud Condensation Nuclei (CCN): Microscopic surfaces such as dust, dirt, sea salt, soot, etc. in the atmosphere for water to condense to form cloud drops.

Cloud Drops: Spherical drops of water that quickly grow in saturated air on cloud condensation nuclei by a factor of 100 to a diameter of approximately 0.01 mm.

Cold Conveyor Belt: The trajectory air takes in a midlatitude cyclone ahead of the warm front at the surface that then spirals into the low as it rises. This makes up the head of the comma shape of the midlatitude cyclone.

Cold Front: A transition zone where a colder air mass is advancing into areas that are currently relatively warm.

Collision-Coalescence: Warm (liquid-only) growth process of cloud- to rain-drops by colliding together and coalescing into a single drop instantly doubling the size of the drop.

Colorado Low: Midlatitude cyclones that originate from Colorado, a preferred location for cyclogenesis (See Cyclogenesis).

Condensation: Phase change from the gas to the liquid state.

Conditionally Unstable: Environments where the environmental lapse rate is less than the unsaturated adiabatic lapse rate, but greater than the saturated adiabatic lapse rate.

Conduction: A transfer of energy when two objects are in contact. It takes place through the movement of the objects' molecules.

Cone of Uncertainty: A measure of forecast track error of the center of a tropical cyclone averaged over the past five years. It is a communication to the public by NOAA Tropical Prediction Center that a tropical cyclone may not follow the best track forecast, but normally can be anywhere within the cone of uncertainty (see best track forecast).

Convection: The transfer of energy by the mass movement of a fluid.

Convective Available Potential Energy (CAPE): A cumulative measure of the amount rising air is warmer than the environment throughout the troposphere. It is essentially a measure of the buoyant area created on a Skew-T diagram when comparing a rising parcel of surface air and the environmental temperature.

Convective Inhibition: When the temperature plot on a Skew-T diagram increases with height, it produces an area of negative Convective Available Potential Energy (CAPE), which inhibits convection (see CAPE).

Convective Outlook Risk Categories: Probability of risk of severe weather and severe weather types for a 40 km (25 mile) area.

Convective Outlook: A weather forecast product provided by NOAA Storm Prediction Center that covers severe weather over the following 8 days.

Converging Tectonic Plates: Area where the Earth's tectonic plates are moving toward one another and colliding. If they are of similar density, mountains form; whereas, if they are of different density, the more dense plate will sink below or subduct the less dense plate.

Conveyor Belt Model: Scientific conceptual model for understanding the structure of a midlatitude cyclone that employs three conveyor belts (warm, cold, and dry) of air currents.

Coriolis Force: An apparent force used to account for the observation that objects in motion above the rotating Earth appear to curve in transit.

Coriolis Parameter: A constant local rotation rate caused by the Earth's rotation, which varies with latitude, but used over a small range of latitudes to help approximate the Coriolis force.

Correlation: A measure of how much the change in two temporally or spatially varying quantities are similar.

Coupled Equations: Equations that depend on the results of each other. Mathematical techniques are employed to handle the coupling of weather model equations.

Coupled Model Intercomparison Project (CMIP): A project to compare and analyze climate models managed by the World Climate Research Programme (WCRP). CMIP prescribes a number of inputs and experiments for international modeling programs to simulate and provide their data.

Cumulonimbus: Cumulus clouds that have extended beyond the lower cloud layer and have begun to produce rain. These clouds often develop an anvil top when the cloud rises to a stable layer, which in unstable environments can be the top of the troposphere.

Cumulus: Low altitude puffy clouds with a flat darker bottom that have a billowy appearance above the base.

Cyclogenesis: The initial formation of a cyclone.

Cyclone: Atmospheric circulation around a center of low pressure.

Daily Mean: Average of a weather parameter sampled over an entire daily cycle (i.e. 24-hour period usually from 00 UTC or midnight local time one day to the next).

Debris Ball: Debris lofted by a tornado causes the end of a hook echo to become more circular (like a ball) and is a strong evidence that a tornado is on the ground (see hook echo).

Deforestation: Permanent removal of forests to make way for agricultural, housing, timber, or other uses.

Dendrites: Type of snow crystal that appear as what most people associate with snowflake shape and are always six-sided. The exact shape of dendrites depends on their own unique trajectory through the cloud. The nearly infinite growth pathways of dendrites give rise to the saying that, "no two snowflakes are ever alike."

Density: A measure of how much matter (i.e. mass) is contained in some volume.

Deposition: Phase change from the gas to the solid state.

Derecho: Sustained straight-line wind events formed from rear inflow jets in a trailing stratiform region (see trailing stratiform region).

Deterministic: A system where the results are determined exactly from causes without any randomness or uncertainty.

Dewpoint Temperature: The temperature air would need to cool down to cause the saturation vapor pressure to drop to the current vapor pressure. At this temperature, water would condense to form dew.

Direct Radiation: Where the sun's rays come in perpendicular to the Earth's surface, causing the amount of solar energy to be maximized over each square meter of the Earth's surface.

Diurnal Cycle: The day-night cycle on a planet due to its rotation.

Divergence: A measure of the spreading out of winds.

Diverging Tectonic Plates: Area where the Earth's tectonic plates are moving apart from one another and magma rises to the surface to form new land or sea floor.

Doppler Effect: The effect to sound that you hear when an object like an automobile is moving past you. Sound travels in waves. An object moving toward you compresses the sound waves so they arrive at your ear with higher frequency. When an object is moving away from you the sound waves spread apart so they arrive at your ear with lower frequency. Radar waves scattering off a moving raindrop exhibits the same effect on the frequency (or the inverse for wavelength) of the scattered waves.

Doppler Radar: Type of radar that is capable of measuring the Doppler effect of a scattered radar pulse to measure wind velocity within a precipitating cloud (see Doppler effect).

Drizzle: Rain drops approximately 0.1 mm (0.01 inch) diameter that must fall from very low clouds to make it to the ground without evaporating.

Dropsonde: Radiometers that are dropped from the aircraft to observe a vertical profile.

Dry Adiabat: Reference line on a Stuve or Skew-T diagram that represents the dry adiabatic lapse rate.

Dry Conveyor Belt: The trajectory air takes within a midlatitude cyclone in the upper atmosphere behind the cold front, which sinks toward the ground as it approaches the surface low. This conveyor belt originates from the jet stream and follows the converging side of a jet streak with sinking cold air behind the cold front.

Dry front or Dryline: A front that separates less dense humid Gulf of Mexico air from denser dry desert air from the desert southwest.

Dual Polarization Doppler Radar: A Doppler radar that transmits two perpendicularly polarized radar beams and analyzes and compares the amount of reflection in the two radar beams.

Earth System Models of Intermediate Complexity (EMICs): Earth System Models where some feature of the Global Climate Models (GCMs) have been simplified (e.g., coarser resolution, limited forecast range) in order to couple other models of the Earth systems.

Earth System Models: Atmospheric Global Climate Models (GCMs) that are coupled with land, cryosphere, ocean, atmospheric chemistry, and other biosphere models.

Earth's General Circulation of the Atmosphere: Scientific conceptual model of the Earth's planetary scale prevailing wind circulation in the horizontal (including trade winds, midlatitude westerlies, and polar easterlies) and vertical (including the Hadley, Ferrel and Polar cells).

Eccentricity of the Earth's Orbit: A measure of the shape of the elliptical orbit of the Earth as it revolves around the sun. A more circular orbit has an eccentricity that approaches zero.

Eddy Viscosity: Friction caused by obstructions to air flow that produce turbulent whirls or eddys that surface heating from the sun can make larger.

Ekman Spiral: The change in direction of the water as you go deeper into the surface ocean layer caused by increasing Coriolis deflection with depth.

Ekman Transport: The average transport of water in the ocean's surface layer caused by the Ekman spiral (see Ekman spiral).

El Nino: The warming of the surface water temperatures on the east side of the Pacific Ocean closely related to the Southern Oscillation (see Southern Oscillation).

Electromagnetic (EM) Wave Spectrum: The entire range of wavelengths of EM waves.

Electromagnetic (EM) Waves: Waves of alternating electric and magnetic fields caused by induction or the production of electric field by magnetic fields and vice-versa.

Elevation: Vertical distance between mean sea level and the Earth's surface.

Emission: the production and release of radiation.

Energy Balance Climate Models: One-dimensional climate models where the variation occurs in latitude (north-south direction). Energy and mass flux along with variations in initial and boundary conditions can vary latitudinally.

Energy Intensity of GDP: The amount of energy needed to create products for a country or municipality.

Energy Star: An Environmental Protection Agency (EPA) and U.S. Department of Energy (DOE) program that labels energy efficient appliances.

Energy: The capacity to do work and has the SI units of the calorie (C) or Joule (J).

Enhanced Fujita Scale or EF Scale: A categorization of tornado intensity on a scale originally created by Ted Fujita. The categorization is assigned after an aerial and ground damage assessment.

Ensemble Forecasting: A forecasting technique to improve model forecasting by running multiple different models or the same model with slightly perturbed initial conditions to analyze the mean and spread of the model forecasts.

Entrained: The act of filling the void left by moving air usually in a cloud by sinking air.

Environmental Lapse Rate: The rate at which the temperature decreases (or lapses) in a vertical column of the atmosphere usually measured by a weather balloon.

Equator: The 0° latitude line.

Evaporation: Phase change from the liquid to the gas state.

Extreme Events: Events that occur well outside the current average distribution of such events, typically defined as above or below 90% of the current historical population of such events.

Extreme Temperatures: Temperatures higher and/or lower than 90% of previous daily means.

Extreme Weather: A weather event that causes a weather parameter greater or lesser than 90% of previous observed data for that parameter.

Ferrel Cell: Planetary-scale vertical circulation cell of the Earth's atmosphere that extends from the rising branch at the 60° latitude to the sinking branch at 30° latitude in the northern and southern hemispheres.

Fetch: The distance that air has to travel over a large body of water before it comes over land again.

Fire Outlook: A weather forecast product provided by NOAA Storm Prediction Center that covers fire threats over the following 8 days.

First Law of Thermodynamics: the mathematical expression of the Law of Conservation of Energy. It states that the change in internal energy of matter, ΔU is the difference between the amount of heating on that matter, q, minus the work that matter does. It is expressed by the formula:

Flooding: Excessive runoff (see runoff).

Fluid: Matter in the gas or liquid phase.

Flux: Flow or transport usually measured in per area of the parameter being transported.

Force: A vector quantity where the magnitude is the amount of acceleration caused on an object with mass and has SI units of Newton, N.

Forecast Composition: The weather parameters and information covered in a forecast. Depending on the forecast and the user this can include cloud cover, precipitation, temperatures, winds, severe weather and/or average seasonal temperatures.

Forecast Range: The number of hours, days, or seasons into the future weather conditions are forecast.

Forecast Skill: An objective measure of the additional accuracy of weather forecasts relative to a forecast based on persistence or climatological data.

Forecasting by Weather Types: A scientific method of forecasting that uses a large number of cases to distill the atmosphere into several types. The forecaster then recognizes a general pattern of pressure and fronts and type the atmosphere. The type would guide the forecaster to make a forecast for the next five days.

Forecasting: A scientific process of careful observation, data gathering, and the use of all the scientific laws, theories, and principles to estimate what will happen in the future.

Fossil Fuels: Anaerobic decomposition of organic matter over a period of millions of years that can be used as an energy source through burning. Coal, oil, and natural gas are examples of fossil fuels.

Fossils: Remains, impressions, or other trace of an organism found in rock, amber, or some other medium that preserves evidence of that organism.

Fraction of Attributable Risk (FAR): A statistical measure of attribution of climate change to an extreme event. FAR ranges from 0 to 1 with FAR = 0 meaning the event is no more likely due to climate change and FAR = 1 meaning the event is not possible without climate change.

Freezing Drizzle: Precipitation that forms in a process similar to freezing rain except by the collision-coalescence process, just like any drizzle. The environment for freezing drizzle that makes it different from drizzle is that the cloud layer is thin and entirely contains supercooled liquid drops.

Freezing Level: The highest height where the temperature remains above freezing. Frozen drops that fall below this height begin to melt.

Freezing Rain: Precipitation that is indistinguishable from rain as it is falling. The distinguishing feature of freezing rain and drizzle is the fact that they freeze <u>after</u> they reach the Earth's surface.

Freezing: Phase change from the liquid to the solid state.

Friction: The sum of a number of forces that oppose motion.

Front: Transition zone between two different air masses. A line with different symbols on surface weather maps symbolizes the type of weather front.

Frontal Lifting: Buoyancy force causing warm air to rise up and over cold air at all fronts because the warm side of a front is less dense.

Geostationary Orbit: An orbit that follows the equator with a height of 35,786 km (22,240 miles). The velocity of the satellite needed to maintain this orbit is equal to the rotational velocity of the Earth (i.e. geosynchronous). This synchrony leads to the satellite always positioned above the same point on Earth.

Geostationary Orbiting Environmental Satellite (GOES): A constellation of geostationary orbiting satellites with onboard weather-observing instruments.

Geostrophic Balance: Name given to air that has the Coriolis and pressure gradient forces in balance horizontally.

Global Climate Models (GCMs): A climate model that allows mass and energy flux in the full spatial three-dimensions. GCMs usually use grid points and vertical levels to calculate the mass and energy fluxes, but can also be spectral, like a weather model.

Global Mean Temperature: Average of a global sample of temperatures around the Earth or other planet. The average is usually the annual mean to average out any seasonal cycle.

Global Warming: Increase in the long-term average of global mean temperatures.

Global Warming: An increase in the global annual mean temperature over a long period usually defined as at least 30 years.

Gradient: A change in a parameter across some distance

Gravity: A force that attracts two masses together. The force leads to a gravitational acceleration, which on the Earth's surface is numerically equal to 9.81 m/s^2.

Green Thunderstorms: Term given to the occasional thunderstorm that turn the sky green. The green color is likely due to a combination of high water content and the angle of the sun in the sky and not due to hail or tornadoes present. Nevertheless, green thunderstorms tend to be strong or severe.

Greenhouse Gases: Constituent atmospheric gases that disproportionately absorbs the Earth's emission, compared to the sun's radiation.

Grid Point Spacing: The uniformly spaced distance between weather model grid points.

Grid Points: Geographically located points used in grid-point weather models that are typically evenly spaced. These points are where all measurement data is interpolated and where all model equations are calculated on and around.

Gross Domestic Product (GDP) per Capita: The amount of products that each household consumes within a country or municipality.

Ground Clutter: Reflection received by radar when the transmitted radar beam propagates anomalously (not follow its expected path). Often at night, the radar beam will bend toward the ground. When this happens objects on the ground will tend to reflect the radar beam back to the receiver.

Groundwater: Water stored in the pores of soil and rock. Less than 1% of water on Earth is groundwater and most water for human use (e.g. drinking water) comes from groundwater, but only a few percent of it is useable.

Gulf of Alaska Low: Midlatitude cyclones that originate from the Gulf of Alaska, a preferred location for cyclogenesis (see cyclogenesis).

Gulf Stream: Warm surface ocean current originating from the northern branch of the equatorial surface ocean current that moves into the Caribbean Sea and then the Gulf of Mexico. Eventually this current enters the Atlantic Ocean through the Straits of Florida and hugs the U.S. coastline before making its way toward Europe.

Gust Front: The leading edge of a downdraft from a thunderstorm as it spreads out along the ground.

Gustnadoes: Tornado-looking vortices that are shallow and surface-based that do not connect to the base of the storm cloud. They are formed by the gust front in a strong wind shear environment.

Hadley Cell: Planetary-scale vertical circulation cell of the Earth's atmosphere that extends from the rising branch at the equator (0° latitude) to the sinking branch at 30° latitude in the northern and southern hemispheres.

Hail: Frozen precipitation that forms by the freezing of raindrops producing layering depending on the speed of the freezing. Large hail is often lumpy due to accretion (see accretion).

Heat Capacity: The amount of energy needed to raise or lower the temperature of 1 g of matter by 1 °C.

Heat Conductivity: The rate at which energy transfers by conduction that mostly depends on the type of substance.

Heat: A measure of the amount of energy transferred, but it can also refer to energy in transfer or the process of transferring energy.

Height: Vertical distance from mean sea level.

Helicity: A measure of the relationship between speed and directional wind shear.

Holocene: The period in Earth's geological history that began the most recent interglacial period. We are currently within the Holocene though a process has begun to formally end the Holocene and determine a new period known as the Anthropocene.

Hook Echo: A pattern on a radar reflectivity image formed by a rotating thunderstorm when the heaviest precipitation wraps counterclockwise around the rotating updraft.

Human-Caused Climate Change: Processes that can lead to climate change that are directly or indirectly affected by humans.

Humidity: The abundance of water vapor in the atmosphere.

Hurricane Eye: Circular area near the center of a tropical cyclone that forms from sinking motion that must compensate the rising air in the eyewall, which clears the air forming the hurricane eye.

Hurricane Eyewall: Circular area near the center of a tropical cyclone that contains the tallest cumulonimbus clouds surrounding the eye.

Hurricanes: Tropical cyclone that have surface winds that equal or exceed 64 knots (74 mph) in the North Atlantic or eastern Pacific Oceans.

Hydrological Forecasting: Forecasting of water and its impact on the Earth's surface such as soil moisture, drought, flood, river flow, snowpack, etc.

Hydrological Models: A mathematical model that considers water in snowpack, evaporation, groundwater flow, height and speed of rivers, infiltration, precipitation, soil saturation, temperature, and other important weather variables to forecast soil moisture, flooding, and drought.

Hydrostatic Balance: Name given to a fluid (usually air in the atmosphere) that has the gravity and pressure gradient forces in balance vertically.

Hypotheses: A question or initial explanation for an observation. The question must be answerable or the explanation confirmable with experimentation and without bias.

Ice Ages: Periods in history where glacial ice existed on Earth.

Ice Cores: a tube of ice drilled out of a glacier. Inside the ice, tiny bubbles preserve the well-mixed atmospheric air when the bubbles formed, which can be sampled.

Ice Jams: Damming of a river or other flowing body of water by chunks of ice formed when the ice cover melts to a point that the ice cover breaks up and flows down river. Water flows around the dam and floods areas outside the river's banks.

Ice Nuclei (IN): Nuclei for water to deposit or freeze to grow ice crystals. The IN needs to look something like an ice crystal (i.e. six sided). Some desert dust, bacteria, pollen, and volcanic ash can act as IN.

Ice Pellets: In the U.S. the same as sleet that forms by the freezing of liquid water. In Canada, ice pellets have the definition that sleet does in the U.S., but sleet is not used in Canada or other commonwealth countries.

Impervious Ground: Ground that water cannot infiltrate or enter into the ground.

Indirect Radiation: Where the sun's rays come in at an increasing angle to perpendicular to the Earth's surface causing the amount of solar energy to be spread over an increasingly larger area of the Earth's surface.

Inertia: Newton's first law is often referred to the Law of Inertia such that an object will stay at rest or at constant velocity unless acted upon by a force.

Infiltrate: In relation to hydrology or geology it means to enter into the ground below the surface.

Infrared (IR) Bands: The radiation band with wavelengths between 0.01 mm (1 μm) and 1 mm.

Integrated Assessment Models (IAMs): Global Climate Models (GCMs) or Earth System Models (ESMs) that include non-physical processes such as technological, social, political, and economic changes.

Interglacial Period: Relatively warmer periods within ice ages where glaciers recede poleward.

Internal Climate Oscillations: Natural oscillations in long-term weather averages that have an effect on short-term climate changes such as El Nino (see El Nino).

Internal Climate Variability: Variability caused by the interaction of the climate components internal to the climate system. In climate models these are usually considered natural changes in the Earth's climate system (i.e. not human-caused, from orbital changes, or from changes of the sun).

Internal Energy: A measure of the potential and kinetic energy within the constituent molecules of matter.

International Panel on Climate Change (IPCC): An intergovernmental Panel of the United Nations made up of climate scientists charged with assessing climate change research and communicating a synthesis of this research to policy makers and the international community. The communication is typically done through a series of assessment reports published about twice per decade.

Interpolate: A process of using representative measurement data to populate weather model gridpoints. Typically, this involves mathematical schemes to average measurement data surrounding model gridpoints because measurement and model gridpoints are rarely collocated.

Inter-Tropical Convergence Zone (ITCZ): Seasonally transient zone where the trade winds in the two hemispheres converge.

Isobars: Map contours of equal values of pressure drawn at uniform pressure intervals (see isopleths for an example).

Isopleths: Map contours of equal values usually drawn at uniform value intervals (e.g. for temperatures 60 °F, 70 °F, and 80 °F are three different isopleths of temperature on many weather maps)

Isotachs: Map contours of equal values of wind speed drawn at uniform wind speed intervals. (see isoplething for an example).

Isotherms: Map contours of equal values of temperature drawn at uniform temperature intervals (see isopleths for an example).

Isotopes of Oxygen: Oxygen atoms of different molecular weights because of additional neutrons in the nucleus.

Jet Streaks: Areas where the jet stream winds are particularly large due to force imbalances (see Jet streams).

Jet Streams: A confined area of the atmosphere near the top of the troposphere (about 1-2 km in the vertical) where winds are the strongest. A polar and subtropical jet stream exists in each of the northern and southern hemispheres and meander in a wave-like pattern around the entire Earth (see Polar jet and Subtropical jet).

Kinetic Energy: The energy of motion and the amount of energy an object uses to move is given by its mass and velocity.

Kohler's Theory: Scientific theory stating that when water condenses onto cloud condensation nuclei they create a solution drop that is no longer pure water. The resulting solution drop dramatically lowers the relative humidity necessary to achieve condensation in the atmosphere.

Köppen Climate Classification System: A system of classification using annually and monthly mean temperature and precipitation data throughout a year to define different climates.

La Nina: The cooling of the surface water temperatures on the east side of the Pacific Ocean closely related to the Southern Oscillation (see southern oscillation).

Lake-Effect Snowstorm: Snowstorms that occur downstream of a large body of water when cold air flows over the relatively warmer water in fall and winter.

Latent Heat: Change in the potential energy of molecules within matter during a phase change.

Latitude: Reference lines used on global maps that run east-west. The 0° latitude line is called the equator with latitude lines increasing in value to 90° latitude at the North Pole and decreasing in value to -90° latitude at the South Pole.

Law of Conservation of Angular Momentum: Scientific law that states that in the absence of forces to reduce spin, such as friction, the product of the radius of spin of a mass around a rotation axis and the angular velocity (e.g. rotations per second) of the mass is constant.

Law of Conservation of Energy: Scientific law that states that energy is neither created nor destroyed.

Laws of Motion: Newton's three laws of motion include the first law that an object will stay at rest or at constant velocity unless acted upon by a force, the second law that quantitatively relates a force to acceleration, and the third law that there are no isolated forces and for every applied force there is an equal and opposite force.

Lee Side: Opposite side of the mountain from where the prevailing winds come from.

Lifetime in the Atmosphere: A measure of the amount of time that a chemical species lasts in the atmosphere before it deposits out on the Earth's surface or reacts to form a new chemical compound.

Lifted Index: An index for alerting forecasters to severe thunderstorms. The index is calculated as the difference between the actual temperature at 500 mb and the temperature of an air parcel that rose from the surface to 500 mb.

Lifting Condensation Level (LCL): On a Stuve or Skew-T diagram, a line parallel to a dry adiabat through the surface temperature and a line parallel to a mixing ratio line through the surface dew-point temperature meet at the height that rising air becomes saturated. Physically, this is the level of the cloud base for low clouds.

Long Waves: Atmospheric waves with wavelengths equal to about the size of the entire length of the U.S. These longwaves do not move with the upper-level winds, the winds move through them.

Longitude: Reference lines used on global maps that run north-south. The 0° longitude line is called the prime meridian with longitude lines increasing in value to 180° longitude going east and decreasing in value to -180° longitude going west. Note that longitude 180° and -180° are the same longitude.

Long-Range Forecast Outlooks: A weather forecast that covers the period starting from 6 to 90 days and provides probabilities of above-, below-, or near-normal conditions.

Madden-Julian Oscillation (MJO): An eastward propagating wave of enhanced and suppressed convective activity on a 20-80-day cycle that helps guide outlooks of precipitation.

Mammatus Clouds: Clouds that form underneath some cumulonimbus anvils and appear to bulge downward. These clouds are the rare cases of clouds that develop downward.

Mandatory Pressure Levels: Upper-air levels that weather balloons are required to record data to produce upper-air weather maps. The mandatory pressure levels in the troposphere are 1000 mb, 925, mb, 850 mb, 700 mb, 500 mb, 400 mb, 300 mb, 250 mb, and 200 mb.

Map Projection: Varying attempts to convert the three-dimensional surface to two-dimensions. All projections cause some form of distortion and the choice of projection depends on the size of the map and area of interest.

Mass: The amount of matter contained in an object or organism with the SI unit of kilograms, kg.

Matter: The physical substance that composes all objects and organisms causing it to occupy space and have mass.

Maunder Minimum: The most recent period between 1645 and 1715 where a sunspot maximum was absent in the normal sunspot 11-year cycle.

Mean Sea Level: Mean elevation of the ocean's surface.

Melting: Phase change from the solid to the liquid state.

Mesocyclone: A surface low-pressure center in a supercell thunderstorm that cause a lowering of the cloud base surrounding the updraft.

Mesoscale: A spatial range that meteorologists define features that are between 1 and 100 km.

Mesosphere: The layer of the Earth's atmosphere above the stratosphere that has a positive temperature lapse rate (temperature decreases with altitude) usually ending around 85 km above the Earth's surface.

Microclimates: Distinction of climate over small areas (typically on the order of 1 km or less in one spatial direction) because of small-scale effects.

Microscale: A spatial range that meteorologists define features that are less than 1 km.

Midlatitude Cyclones: Cyclones that form in the midlatitudes on boundaries of large temperature gradients.

Midlatitude Westerlies: Prevailing westerly (from west-to-east) winds in the midlatitudes (30° to 60°).

Mid-Range Forecast: A weather forecast that covers the range of 2.5 days to 7 days and typically includes sky cover (i.e. sunny, cloudy, etc.), high and low temperatures, and a mention of a chance of precipitation though not always an exact percentage.

Milankovitch Cycles: Cycles on the order of the period of recent, Pleistocene, ice ages in the orbital parameters: eccentricity, tilt of the Earth's rotation axis, and precession that Milutin Milankovitch used to explain the periodic cycles of the ice ages and interglacial periods.

Mixing Ratio: A measure of the abundance of water vapor in the air with its SI unit given as a ratio of the mass of water vapor to the mass of air, g/kg.

Model Domain: The geographical and vertical extent of a weather model. Global models have a global domain, but smaller-scale weather models have domains that are less than global.

Model Levels: A height that a horizontal grid exists for a grid-point weather model or waves are used to represent weather parameters.

Model Output Statistics (MOS): A statistical method to transfer the output of weather models to specific stations based on the past performance of models and the actual surface conditions.

Model Resolution: The spatial size of features that a model can distinguish and simulate. A rule-of-thumb is that models can resolve features if that feature spans five grid points in each spatial direction.

Model Time Step: The change in time that weather models use to calculate the change in model parameters. There are limitations on model time steps that restrict the size of the time step.

Moist Adiabat: Reference line on a Stuve or Skew-T diagram that represents the saturated adiabatic lapse rate.

Molecular Viscosity: Friction caused by the random motions of molecules bumping into one another.

Multi-Cell Thunderstorms: A type of severe thunderstorms where the downdrafts and resulting gust fronts cause convergence and updrafts to form new thunderstorms on the southern side of the back of the parent thunderstorm.

Natural Causes of Climate Change: Processes that can lead to climate change that are not significantly affected by humans.

Near infrared (IR): The shorter IR wavelengths near the visible wavelengths.

Needles: Type of snow crystal that form at the warmest temperatures and look like little needles that would be six-sided columns if seen under a microscope.

Negative Feedbacks: A process internal to a system that diminishes an external change.

Negatively-Tilted Troughs: An upper-air trough that tilts along a line from northwest to southeast, presenting a negative slope on a weather map.

Nest: The act of placing a smaller-scale weather model within the domain of a larger-scale model.

Nimbostratus: Rain producing stratus clouds.

Nocturnal Boundary Layer: The surface layer (typically up to around 100 m altitude) that is affected by the cooling of the ground during the evening hours.

Nor'easter: A midlatitude cyclone that forms off the northeast coast causing strong northeasterly winds. Because of the large temperature gradient along this coast in the winter, these storms are particularly strong.

Nor'easter: A midlatitude cyclone that forms along the Atlantic coast of the U.S. The name comes from the strongest onshore winds from the storm being from the northeast, which benefit from the lack of friction over the water.

North Atlantic Oscillation (NAO): A measure of the difference in surface pressure between the tropical regions (Azores) and the upper midlatitudes (Iceland) that directly impacts the jet streams.

Nowcast: Weather forecast for conditions within the next six hours includes things like snow accumulations, storm start and end times, and severe thunderstorm location and movement.

Occluded Front: A special case where a cold front appears to overtake a warm front, the transition zone between the cold and warm air masses disappears at the surface. The appearance of occluded fronts mark an important stage in the life cycle of a midlatitude cyclone.

Ocean Acidification: The reduction of pH of the ocean caused by the dissolution of chemicals in the ocean that react with water to form an acid.

Offshore: Continental air, and its lack of humidity, that flows toward coastal cities bringing with it sunshine and dry conditions.

Omega Block: A pattern in the atmospheric long-wave pattern where a longwave has a large amplitude ridge downstream causing the longwave pattern upstream to remain constant with unchanging and extreme weather.

One-Dimensional Climate Models: A climate model that varies in the latitudinal (See energy balance models) or vertical direction (see radiative convection models). These models allow mass and energy flux in one direction and the initial and boundary conditions to vary in the same direction.

Onshore: Maritime air, and its humidity, that flows toward land bringing with it clouds and precipitation.

Ordinary Single-Cell Thunderstorms: Thunderstorms that do not produce damaging hail or wind.

Organic: Substances that are usually associated with life. On Earth all life is carbon-based so organic refers to carbon-based.

Outflow Boundary: A boundary between the downdraft air outflow from a thunderstorm and the environmental air the thunderstorm resides within.

Overshooting Tops: Updrafts of strong thunderstorms will overshoot the stable tropopause and produce cloud tops that are higher than the rest of the anvil. In the late afternoon, the overshooting tops cast a shadow on the anvil cloud below seen on visible satellite imagery.

Pacific Decadal Oscillation (PDO): A change from normal Pacific Ocean sea surface temperatures between the North American coast near Alaska and the north central Pacific Ocean that oscillates over a period of decades.

Pacific High: Surface semipermanent high pressure centered at the latitude of Northern California in the summer and central Baja California in the winter over the Pacific Ocean.

Pangaea: A supercontinent that broke up 250 million years ago formed the seven continents that we now have.

Parameterization: A technique for dealing with subgrid scale processes using the parameters that the weather model can resolve. Parameterization provides the results of these subgrid scale processes without actually simulating them.

Permafrost: A subsurface layer of permanently frozen soil in polar regions.

Permeability: The ability for water to move through open spaces of otherwise solid material.

Persistence Method: A scientific forecasting method that forecasts the same weather in the future as is currently experienced.

pH Scale: A measure of the acidity of water ranging from 0 to 14 where seven is neutral, higher values are alkaline, and lower values are acidic.

Phases of Matter: A categorization of matter based on its state and arrangement of its component particles where all physical properties are uniform.

Pixels: A picture element that makes up the smallest divisible part of an image or picture.

Planetary Boundary Layer: The measurable layer near the Earth's surface where the effects of friction is significant. This layer transitions rapidly to a smoother layer above typically around 1000 m altitude.

Planetary or Rossby Waves: The longwave pattern of ridges and troughs that meander around the world naturally formed in a rotating fluid such as the atmosphere.

Plates: Type of snow crystal that forms at colder temperatures and gives the ground a sparkly appearance. The sparkle comes from light reflecting off the flat side of the plate.

Pleistocene: The period of time in Earth's geological history when the most recent ice ages began.

Polar Cell: Planetary-scale vertical circulation cell of the Earth's atmosphere that extends from the rising branch at 60° latitude to the sinking branch at the poles (90° latitude) in the northern and southern hemispheres.

Polar Easterlies: Prevailing easterly (from east-to-west) winds in the polar latitudes (60° to 90°).

Polar Front: Semipermanent surface boundary between warm subtropical air and cold polar air formed by the convergence of the Ferrel and Polar vertical circulation cells (see Ferrel cell and Polar cell).

Polar Jet: One of two jet streams in both the northern and southern hemispheres, the polar jet stream is normally found between 40° and 60° latitude (see jet streams).

Polar or Inclined Orbit Satellites: Constellation of satellites in low Earth orbit whose orbit crosses the poles or in a circle inclined relative to the poles. The word, inclined, means that it orbits with an angle to the equator where a satellite orbiting around the equator have a 0° inclination and orbits over the poles have a 90° inclination.

Porosity: The amount of open spaces in otherwise solid material.

Positive Feedbacks: A process internal to a system that amplifies an external change.

Potential Energy: The energy of position relative to some energy field.

Precession: The rotation of a rotation axis around a vertical line.

Precision: The spread of the measurements by an instrument when measuring an unvarying parameter.

Pressure Gradient Force: Force caused by a pressure gradient that pushes fluids (including air) from high pressure to low pressure.

Pressure: An applied force perpendicular to an object per unit area caused by atomic or molecular collisions with that object with SI unit N/m^2 or Pascals, Pa; Millibars, mb; and hectopascals, hPa are numerically equal and often used in meteorology as the standard unit.

Prevailing Wind: The usual or average direction that wind blows over some geographical area.

Prime Meridian: The 0° longitude or meridian line that runs through the Royal Observatory in Greenwich, England.

Probabilistic: A system that cannot be exactly determined from causes because of randomness and uncertainty in the initial conditions and processes that lead to the effects. The result can only be determined to some level of probability.

Prognostic Maps (progs): Output future simulated maps from weather model output.

Proxy Data: Data that are not directly measured but are obtained from natural recorders of changes in that data. For example, they can be preserved physical characteristics that can replace absent direct meteorological measurements for observing past climates.

Quasi-Biennial Oscillation (QBO): A 28-29-month oscillation in the direction of the equatorial winds in the stratosphere from easterly to westerly.

Radar Bright Band: A region of higher reflectivity where ice is melting. To the radar a melting snowflake or hailstone looks like a large raindrop and the reflectivity is higher in this region of a storm even though the rainfall rate is less than would be expected if it were fully melted.

Radar: An acronym for Radio Detection and Ranging. Radars are composed of a transmitter and a receiver. The transmitter sends out a radio frequency wave, which reflects off different size objects in the atmosphere. Weather radars are optimized to reflect off raindrops.

Radiation Bands: A range or group of electromagnetic wavelengths often named (e.g. infrared).

Radiation: The transfer of energy via electromagnetic (EM) waves (see Electromagnetic waves).

Radiative-Convective Climate Models: One-dimensional climate models where the variation occurs in the vertical. Energy and mass flux can occur in the vertical, which is often termed convection in meteorology.

Radio frequency Bands: The radiation band with wavelengths between 0.1 m (10 cm) and 1000 m.

Radiometers: An instrument that measures the amount of radiation coming from the direction the instrument is pointing.

Radiosonde: An instrument package that is attached to a weather balloon that contains a radio transmitter to transmit data from the various instruments to a receiver on the ground.

Rain Gauge: A surface-based instrument that measures the accumulation of liquid-based precipitation.

Rain Shadow: An absence of precipitation when plotting the horizontal distribution of precipitation in the area of a mountain much like the absence of light in the area of a tall object in sunlight.

Raindrops: Largely spherical water drops that are large enough to make it to the ground before evaporating.

Rear-Inflow Jet: Melting and evaporation in a trailing stratiform region creates a cold pool of air, which is dense and creates surface high pressure that causes descending air to accelerate forward toward a squall line.

Reduce, Reuse, and Recycle: A phrase used for reducing the amount of trash created and sent to a landfill. The phrase includes three alternatives to creating trash including the reduction of stuff people purchase, reusing items again or for multiple purposes, and recycling the materials to be reused. Composting is sometimes included for recycling organic trash.

Reflectivity: The amount of reflected energy received by a radar.

Regional Scale Climate Model: A technique to dynamically downscale Global Climate Models (GCMs) to local scales by using the GCM as the boundary condition and running a climate model on a regional domain. This technique is similar to how a regional weather model such as the NAM uses the GFS model output to set boundary conditions.

Relative Humidity: The ratio of the measured vapor pressure to the capacity (the amount of water vapor in the air when the air is saturated).

Representative Concentration Pathways (RCPs): A pathway of expected carbon dioxide equivalent concentrations to the year 2100 (and extended to year 2300) to reach expected different energy imbalances based on socio-economic models. The energy imbalances range from 2.6 to 8.5 W/m² in 2100 and those numbers are added to the RCP to define the different scenarios (e.g. RCP 2.6). Climate models use the RCPs as inputs of greenhouse gas increases.

Ridge: A northward bend (southward in the southern hemisphere) in wavy height contours on upper-air maps representing relatively high heights at that latitude.

Rising/Sinking Air: Large scale upward or downward motion of air as opposed to updraft/downdraft, which is a smaller scale upward or downward motion of air (see updraft/downdraft).

Runoff: The movement of water along the surface if the soil is too moist, frozen, or the precipitation rate is too high.

Salinity: Measurement of salt content dissolved in water measured in values of per mille (per thousandth).

Sample Mean: Sum of the data values divided by the number of data values. It is an estimate of the expected or average value of the data values.

Sample Variance: The sum of the squared differences divided by one less than the number of values. It provides an estimate of the magnitude of variations in the data values.

Saturated Adiabatic Lapse Rate: Rate at which saturated air cools in the distance it rises. Saturated air rises with condensation and latent heating causing less cooling than unsaturated air. The saturated (or moist) adiabatic lapse rate has a variable value, but always less than the unsaturated adiabatic lapse rate of 10 °C/km.

Saturation Mixing Ratio: The mixed ratio that would saturate the air at a given temperature.

Saturation Vapor Pressure: The vapor pressure that would saturate the air at a given temperature.

Scattering: Similar to reflection except light can be redirected in any direction when interacting with a scatterer (i.e. small particle of matter) where reflection redirects light in one specific angle.

Scientific Notation: A compact method for expressing large or small numbers (numbers with several significant digits to the left or right of the decimal point) by multiplying a smaller number of digits by a power of ten.

Sea-Level Adjusted Pressure: Station pressure adjusted to the value that would be observed if measured at an elevation of mean sea level.

Sediments in Oceans and Lakes: Sediment at the bottom of oceans and lake have built up over time with each successively deeper layer older than the last. Different sediment layers contain different seeds, pollens, fossils, and other chemicals from which to infer climate.

Semipermanent Highs: High-pressure centers that may not always be in the same region on a day-to-day basis. However, averaging the pressure over a month, these high-pressure centers will show up in their expected locations.

Severe Thunderstorm: A damaging thunderstorm currently defined as producing hail greater than one inch or wind gusts over 50 knots (58 mph).

Shelf Cloud: A cloud that forms when air enters a cumulonimbus cloud along a slant path in a wind-sheared environment.

Short-Range Forecast: Weather forecast that spans the period of 6 hours (0.5 days) to 60 hours (2.5 days) and typically includes precipitation accumulations, wind speed and directions, and exact probabilities of precipitation.

Shortwaves: Atmospheric waves of significantly shorter wavelength than longwaves (see longwaves) that move along with the wind at 700 mb and, therefore, move through the longwave pattern.

Showalter Index: An index for alerting forecasters to severe thunderstorms calculated similar to the lifted index. Unlike the lifted index, the showalter index uses the dry adiabat that runs through the 850 mb temperature instead of the surface temperature (see lifted index).

SI Units: A system of units of measurement based on a standard set of units. In relation to weather and climate the standard units are the second, meter, kilogram, and Kelvin. A series of prefixes including milli-, centi-, deci, deca- hecto-, and kilo- representing thousandth, hundredth, tenth, ten, hundred, and thousand, respectively are also included.

Significant Tornadoes: Tornadoes of EF2 or greater that pose significant risk to even well-built houses.

Single-Cell Circulation Model: Scientific conceptual model of the planetary general circulation that assumes an ocean-covered non-rotating planet that is heated at the equator. Such a planet would have a single vertical circulation cell in the northern and the southern hemispheres and northerly winds in the northern hemisphere and southerly winds in the southern hemisphere.

Skew-T Diagram: A diagram used to plot a weather balloon sounding that has temperature as the x-axis and pressure as the y-axis. Although the pressure grid is horizontal, the temperature grid is not vertical, but skewed diagonally from left-to-right.

Sleet: In the U.S. a type of ice crystal that forms from the freezing of raindrops or the refreezing of partially melted snowflakes, known as ice pellets in Canada.

Sling Psychrometer: An instrument that consists of two liquid-in-glass thermometers mounted side-by-side. One thermometer (dry bulb) measures the air temperature and the other thermometer (wet bulb) measures the wet bulb temperature when an observer slings or spins the thermometers around allowing evaporation from a wet sock on the wet-bulb thermometer. From these two measurements relative humidity can be calculated.

Snow Pellets or Graupel: Small hail formed by the freezing of liquid precipitation onto snowflakes usually formed in cumulonimbus clouds.

Snow Ratio: Average snow accumulation to liquid precipitation ratio used to forecast snow accumulation from liquid precipitation forecasted by weather models.

Snow: Precipitation that forms by deposition and ice crystal growth. Nearly all ice we see on Earth grows six-sided. Depending on temperature and humidity, numerous shapes are possible including needles, dendrites, plates, and columns.

Solar Noon: The moment each day that the sun angle above the horizon is largest.

Soundings: A graph of data from individual weather balloons.

Southern Oscillation: An oscillation in the pressure difference between Australia and South America at the equator. The oscillation is closely related to the Walker Circulation (see Walker Circulation) and El Nino and La Nina.

Spaghetti Plots: Plots of a single weather parameter for every member of an ensemble model run. Because of the spatial variations of the results, the plot looks like cooked spaghetti.

Spectral Models: A type of weather model that uses a spectrum of wavelengths to approximate spatial functions of each model parameter.

Squall Line: A line of thunderstorms forming in front of some atmospheric boundary like a cold front.

Stable Equilibrium: An atmospheric equilibrium where air falls back down to its original height after a small upward push caused by a temperature lapse rate less than the dry (or saturated if the rising air is saturated) adiabatic lapse rate.

Standard Deviation: Square root of the sample variance, which provides an estimate of the deviation of values from a sample mean in units of measure that are the same as the data values.

State of Matter: A categorization of matter based the interaction of its component particles. Solid, liquid, gas, and plasma are distinct states of matter leading to different interactions of the component particles.

Static Stability: Gravitational (or buoyant) resistance to vertical fluid motion typically determined by the difference between the vertical temperature lapse rate and the dry (or saturated if the rising air is saturated) adiabatic lapse rate.

Station Models: A shorthand way of including all the surface weather data recorded at each station on a weather map.

Station Pressure: Pressure observed from a station barometer after all station calibrations are applied.

Stationary Front: A transition zone between two stationary air masses.

Statistically Downscaling: A process used to produce high-resolution data from low-resolution data. The process involves finding statistical relationships between large-scale variables from climate models and observed local scale variables.

Steady State: An assumption used in science that acceleration and development of a feature or object will not occur.

Stefan-Boltzmann Law: Scientific law that relates the energy emitted by an object to its temperature. The emission energy increase with temperature to the fourth power.

Stoke's Law: Scientific law that provides the physical basis for determining how fast spherical objects such as cloud drops fall within a fluid such as the atmosphere.

Storm Surge: The rise in the mean sea level caused by a tropical cyclone's sustained winds.

Stratocumulus: A low altitude layered cumulus clouds. They have a light outline (often referred to as a "silver lining") with little billowy white over the darker base.

Stratosphere: The layer of the Earth's atmosphere above the troposphere that has a negative temperature lapse rate (temperature increases with altitude) usually ending around 50 km above the Earth's surface.

Stratus: Low altitude layered clouds that have little shading differences or contrast across a large part of the sky.

Subducting Tectonic Plates: Area where Earth's tectonic plates of different density are moving toward one another. The more dense plate will sink below or subduct the less dense plate.

Subgrid Scale: Features or processes that are smaller than the model resolution (see model resolution).

Sublimation: Phase change from the solid to the gas state.

Subtropical Jet: One of two jet streams in both the northern and southern hemispheres, the subtropical jet stream is normally found between 20° and 40° latitude (see jet streams).

Sunspots: Temporary dark and relatively cool areas that form on the sun's surface indicating intense magnetic fields that are often associated with more intense solar activity.

Supercell: A type of thunderstorm with a rotating updraft that develops around a rotating mesocyclone and produces a large majority of strong tornadoes.

Supercooled Drops: Liquid drops at temperatures below the freezing point.

Surface Ocean Currents: Continuous flow of surface ocean water over some geographical area.

Synoptic Scale: A spatial range that meteorologists define features that are 100 km or more.

Tectonic Plates: Mass of irregularly shaped solid rock several kilometers thick and spanning to thousands of kilometers in the horizontal that float on the asthenosphere (see asthenosphere). The sum of all the tectonic plates make up the crust (outer layer) of the Earth.

Teleconnections: Environmental effects separated on planetary scales connected to a long-term change.

Temperature: A measure of the kinetic energy of the internal motion of the component particles of matter with SI units of Kelvin, K or degrees Celsius, °C.

Terminal Velocity: Constant velocity achieved when an object falling due to gravity is balanced by air resistance.

Theory of Plate Tectonics: A scientific theory that states that the crust of the Earth is broken up in different tectonic plates. These plates are bounded at the bottom by a plastic layer of the upper mantle known as the asthenosphere. Each plate can move somewhat independently of the other tectonic plates on the asthenosphere.

Theory: A statement or an explanation applicable to a broad range of observations. The breadth of application is developed over many years through experimentation and confirmed by many different scientists (i.e. those that follow the scientific method).

Thermal infrared (IR): The longer IR wavelengths that most things on Earth emit or radiate. Most people associate this with our heat, which is why it is called thermal IR, but everything around average atmospheric temperature ranges emit in the thermal IR.

Thermocline: A layer of rapid cooling with depth that separates the surface water above and the deep ocean below.

Thermohaline Circulation: Deep ocean circulation driven by density differences related to temperature and salinity differences.

Thermometer: An instrument that measures temperature.

Thermosphere: The uppermost layer of the Earth's atmosphere above the mesosphere that has a positive temperature lapse rate (temperature decreases with altitude).

Three-Cell Circulation Model: Scientific conceptual model of the planetary general circulation that assumes an ocean-covered rotating planet that is heated at the equator. Such a planet would have three vertical circulation cells and belts of easterlies in the tropics, westerlies in the midlatitudes, and easterlies in the polar latitudes in the northern and the southern hemispheres.

Tilt of the Earth's Rotation Axis: Angle that the rotation axis of the Earth makes with the orbital plane of the Earth in its transit around the sun.

Topographic of Orographic Lifting: The forced rising of air as it moves toward an obstacle such as a building or mountain.

Tornado Vortex Signature (TVS): A pattern on a Doppler radar velocity mode image caused by rapid rotation within a mesocyclone. The rapid rotation appears as an area of strong winds approaching the radar adjacent to strong winds moving away from the radar within a small area.

Trade Winds: Prevailing northeasterly (northern hemisphere) or southeasterly (southern hemisphere) winds in the tropics and equatorial latitudes (30 °S to 30 °N). They are called trade winds because of the historical impact of these winds on early marine navigation, exploration, and trade.

Trailing Stratiform Region: A region of stratiform clouds that develops behind a squall line from ice falling and melting from tall cumulonimbus clouds.

Training: When thunderstorms continually form over the same area like a train of thunderstorms moving past an area.

Transmission: Transfer of electromagnetic waves through space and matter without absorption or scattering.

Tree Rings: In areas where there is a distinct growing season, trees grow in diameter rapidly compared to the dormant season. When looking at a cross-section of a tree the growing season produces the lighter rings and the dormant season produces the darker rings.

Trend Forecast: A scientific forecasting method based on the assumption that weather systems will not develop or change movement speed and the current weather upstream of a location determines the future weather of that location.

Tropical Cyclones: Centers of low pressure that form in tropical latitudes. They may move into the midlatitudes, but do not form there because of the lower sea surface temperatures and presence of large temperature gradients.

Tropical Depressions: Tropical cyclones initially form a center of low pressure at the surface, and air circulates around the center. Surface wind speeds are less than 34 knots (39 mph). Tropical depressions are assigned a number that counts each depression in a season.

Tropical Storms: Tropical cyclones with wind speeds ranging from 34 knots (39 mph) to 63 knots (73 mph). Tropical storms are assigned alternating male and female names alphabetically restarting each season.

Troposphere: The lowest approximately 10 km (6 miles) of the Earth's atmosphere that has a positive temperature lapse rate (temperature decreases with altitude).

Trough of Warm Air Aloft (TROWAL): Warm sector air in an occluded front that wraps around the center of low pressure.

Trough: A southward sag (northward in the southern hemisphere) in wavy height contours on upper-air maps representing relatively low heights at that latitude.

Typhoons: Tropical cyclone that have surface winds that equal or exceed 64 knots (74 mph) in the western North Pacific Ocean.

Ultraviolet Band: The radiation band with wavelengths between 0.001 μm (1 nm) and 0.1 μm.

Uncertainties: The average root mean squared difference between the measurement of an instrument and the true value of a parameter over several measurements. Uncertainties are usually estimated by the standard deviation of several measurements.

Universal Time Coordinated (UTC): The time zone of the prime meridian, which runs through the town of Greenwich, England.

Unsaturated (or Dry) Adiabatic Lapse Rate: Rate at which unsaturated air cools in the distance it rises and is the same no matter where in the atmosphere the rising air occurs and its value is 10 °C/km (5.5 °F/1000 feet).

Unstable Equilibrium: An atmospheric equilibrium where air keeps rising after a small upward push caused by a temperature lapse rate greater than the dry (or saturated if the rising air is saturated) adiabatic lapse rate.

Updrafts/Downdrafts: Small scale upward or downward motion of air usually referring to air motion in clouds.

Upper-Air Maps: Upper-air weather maps at mandatory levels created from data from every weather balloon launched at the time of the map.

Upwelling: Water from lower down in a lake or ocean that rises to the top. This upwelling water is colder and nutrient rich, which leads to vibrant marine life and cold surface waters.

Urban Heat Island: Effect of urban developed areas on local climate because of the heat generation of industrial areas, impervious materials replacing vegetation, and heat absorption of asphalt and concrete. The urban area appears as an island of some contrasting climate parameter such as average temperature in comparison to the surrounding rural areas.

Vapor Pressure: The amount of pressure in the atmosphere due to water with SI units of millibars, mb.

Vectors: A quantity that requires both a magnitude and its direction

Velocity: A vector quantity where the magnitude is speed with the SI unit of meters per second, m/s.

Vertical Wind Shear: The difference between the wind speeds at two different levels.

Virga: Precipitation that evaporates before it hits the ground

Visible Band: The radiation band with wavelengths between 0.3 μm and 0.7 μm. These wavelengths are visible to human vision; thus these are called the visible radiation band.

Vortex Tubes: Rotating air formed in a strong vertical wind shear environment. The rotation axis is parallel to the ground unlike a tornado, which has a rotation axis perpendicular to the ground.

Walker Circulation: An equatorial atmospheric circulation over the Pacific Ocean between Australia and South America caused by a pressure difference formed by the equatorial surface ocean current that piles warm surface water on the Australian side of the Pacific.

Warm Conveyor Belt: The trajectory air takes within the warm sector of a midlatitude cyclone. It starts out at the surface transporting warm humid air over the warm front, but later when the cyclone forms an occluded front, it can get wrapped around low pressure forming a TROWAL (see TROWAL).

Warm Front: A transition zone where a warmer air mass is advancing into areas that are currently relatively cold.

Warm Sector: The area of surface warm air between the cold and warm fronts in a midlatitude cyclone.

Water Cycle: The flow of water in all its phases through all of Earth's spheres including the atmosphere, biosphere, cryosphere, geosphere, and hydrosphere.

Water Vapor: Water in the gas state or phase.

Watershed: An area that falling precipitation will be confined by land elevation to a single outlet.

Wavelength: The distance from one wave crest to the next.

Weather Hazards Forecast: A weather forecast product produced by the NOAA Weather Prediction Center that covers flooding; heavy ice, rain, or snow; severe storms; excessive heat; high winds; much above/below normal temperatures; significant water waves; wildfires; and drought for the following 3-7 days. NOAA Climate Prediction Center produces a similar product for the following 8-14 days that only covers precipitation, temperature, and wind hazards.

Weather Model: A scientific mathematical tool using initial conditions and the physical laws to calculate future changes in the weather.

Wet Snow: Partially melted snow that is heavy to shovel and prone to aggregation creating large flakes.

Wet-Bulb Thermometer: The temperature a wet-bulb thermometer lowers to when evaporation occurs from a wet sock on the wet-bulb thermometer. This temperature is significant because it is the temperature that air lowers to when precipitation evaporates into it.

Wien's Law: Scientific law that relates temperature to the wavelength at which matter emits the largest amount of energy. The peak emission wavelength is inversely proportional to temperature.

Wind Barb: A station model symbol that provides both the direction with the staff of the barb and the speed with the 'feathers' on the end of the staff. Three different feathers are used: a half line representing 2.5 m/s (5 knots), a full line representing 5 m/s (10 knots) and a pennant representing 25 m/s (50 knots). The decoded wind speed would be the sum of the included feathers.

Wind Vane: An instrument that measures wind direction.

Wind: Air in motion. Convention is to refer to the direction the wind is coming from with the SI unit of m/s with the conventional unit of knot for the speed.

Windward side: Side of the mountain from where the prevailing winds come from.

Work: The transfer of energy by a force as it is accelerating an object.

Zero-dimensional Climate Models: A climate model that has no spatial or temporal dimension. They provide one globally annual mean temperature based on an energy budget.

Zonal: Aligned with the latitude lines.

Index

H

I

isobars, 56

isopleths, 56

isotherms, 67, 150

isotopes of oxygen, 36

J

jet streaks, 157

jet streams, 152

K

Kelvin scale, 5

kinetic energy, 84, 149

Kohler's theory, on cloud formation, 130

Köppen, Wladimer, 44

    climate classification scheme, 44

Kuroshio Current, 175

L

lake-effect snowstorms, 283–288, 296

land use, 336–337

La Nina, 177 178, 200

    U.S. climate effects from, 179

latent heat, 85

latent heating, 319

latitude, 54

    Coriolis force (CF), 109

law of conservation of energy, 84–85, 101

law of conversation of angular momentum, 152, 173

lee sides, of mountains, 47

lifted index, 206

lifting condensation level (LCL), 125, 205, 313

lightning, 300–301

liquid-equivalent precipitation accumulation, 18

liquid-in-glass thermometers, 17

Little Ice Age, 330

longitude, 54

Lorentz, Edward, 230

M

Madden-Julian Oscillation (MJO), 180

mammatus clouds, 132

maps

    projections, 55

    reading of, 54–55

    surface, 55–60

    upper-air, 65, 66–70

maritime air masses, 182

mass, 3, 86

matter, 3

Maunder minimum, 330

melting, 4

mercury barometer, 190

mesocyclone, 307

mesosphere, 8

methane, 332

    emissions by source, 333

midlatitude cyclones, 147, 150–151, 239, 276, 294, 314

    conceptual model of, 167

        development of, 167

        Earth's general circulation, 168–173

        ocean circulation, 173–178

        shortcomings of, 167

    conveyor belt model of, 161, 167

    forecasting of, 152–162

        atmospheric rivers, 161–162

        existence of jet streams, 152–158

        longwaves and shortwaves, 158–161

        upper tropospheric divergence, 152–158

    lifecycle of, 147–149

    polar front theory, 167

    surface-based observations, 148

    vorticities of, 155–156

midlatitude westerlies, 168

Milankovitch cycles, 329–330

mixing ratio, 16

model levels, 218

Model Output Statistics (MOS), 194, 231

model time step, 218

Modular Ocean Model v.4 (MOMv4), 246

moist adiabat, 124

moisture flux, 182

molecular viscosity, 111

Morse, Samuel, 190

mountain snows, 278

Mt. Pinatubo, eruption of, 327

multi-cell thunderstorms, 302–303

    formation of, 303

N

National Center for Environmental Information (NCEI), 35

National Center for Environmental Prediction (NCEP), 216, 229

National Hurricane Center (NHC) hurricane hunter aircraft, 317

National Oceanic and Atmospheric Administration (NOAA)

    Climate Prediction Center (CPC), 245

    National Center for Environmental Prediction (NCEP), 245, 252

    Tropical Prediction Center, 266

National Weather Service (NWS), 41, 301

    National Center for Environmental Prediction (NCEP), 225

natural gas, 332

near IR band, 90

negatively tilted troughs, 157

Newton, Isaac, 11, 105, 125, 168

    law of motion, 11, 105–106

Newton's Laws of Motion, 11, 105–106

    first law, 105

    second law, 106, 112–113, 117

nimbostratus clouds, 23, 64

nitrogen cycle, 247

nitrous oxide, emissions of, 333

Noah Land model, 247–248

Nor'easters, 150–151, 281–283

North Atlantic drift, 175

North Atlantic Oscillation (NAO), 180, 266

North Pole, 109, 150

nowcast, 255–256

nuclear power, 344

O

ocean acidification, 332, 341

ocean circulation

    conceptual models of, 173–178

        surface currents, 174–177

        thermohaline circulation, 177–178

    impact on climate changes, 330–331

ocean-effect snowstorms, 283

ocean surface temperature, 247

offshore flow, 172

omega blocks, 159

1-day extreme precipitation, 41

onshore flow, 172

ordinary single-cell thunderstorms, 299–301

    life cycle of, 301

orographic lifting, 117

outflow boundary, 300

overshooting tops, 202

oxygen isotopes, 36–37

ozone density, 201

ozone-depleting substances, 334

P

Pacific Decadal Oscillation (PDO), 180, 181, 266

Pangaea, 325

    breakup of, 326

partial pressure, 16

Pascal, 11

patterns, concept of, 9

perfluorocarbons (PFCs), 334

permafrost, 332, 338

permeability, 291

persistence forecasting, 191–192

phases of matter, 3

pH scale, 341–342

pixels, 72

planetary boundary layer, 111

planetary-scale oscillations, 266

planetary waves, 158

plate tectonicsm

    events caused by, 327

    theory of, 325–328

Pleistocene, 38

polar cell, 169, 173

polar easterlies, 169

polar front, 147, 152, 167, 170

polar jet, 153

polar orbiting satellites, 72–73

Polar Stereographic maps, 55

polar vortex, 180, 258

porosity, 291

potential energy, 84, 149

precipitation, 182, 300

    determination of rate of, 196

    forecasting of, 142

    formation of, 132–135

        Bergeron process for, 133–135

        collision-coalescence theory for, 132–133

    frozen precipitation

        humidity, role of, 142

        liquid water content of, 142

    snow ratio, 142

    types of

        cold season precipitation, 137–142

warm season precipitation, 135–136

pressure, 11–13

    barometers, 11–13

    unit of measurement, 11

pressure difference, 176

pressure gradient force (PGF), 106–107, 108, 113, 115–116, 125, 157

    derivation of, 107

prevailing winds, 168, 174

prime meridian, 55

prognostication maps (progs), 222

Q

Quasi-Biennial Oscillation (QBO), 180, 258

R

radar (radio detection and ranging), 73

    Doppler radars, 74–75, 195, 197

    dual frequency polarization radar (DPR), 201

    ground clutter, 76

    images of, 73–76

    reflectivity of, 75–76

    as tool for weather forecasting, 195–199

radar bright band, 303

radiation, 88–90

    direct, 97

    indirect, 97

radiation balance, 94–101

    with an atmosphere, 95, 96

    calculation of, 95

    and distribution of temperature on Earth, 96–97

    diurnal cycle, 99–100

        other factors affecting, 100–101

    with no atmosphere, 94–95

    reason for the seasons, 97–99

    solar energy, 94

radiation bands, 89

radiative-convective climate models, 239–242

radiative transfer, 92–94

radioactivity, 88

radio frequency band, 89

radiometers, 6–9

radiosonde (rawinsonde), 7

rain, 135–136

    freezing, 139–142

raindrops, 135

rain gauge, 18

rain shadow, 47

Rapid Radiative Transfer Model (RRTM), 229

rapid refresh (RAP), 299

Rapid Refresh Model (RAP), 229–230, 231

reduce, reuse, and recycle programs, 344

relative density, 15

relative humidity (RH), 16, 129, 143

remote sensing, 24

Representative Concentration Pathways (RCPs), 339, 341, 346

Richardson, Lewis F., 190, 193, 220

Richardson's approximation, 220

Rossby waves, 158, 173

rotation rate, of Earth

    Coriolis force (CF) and, 109

runoff, 182

S

Saffir–Simpson scale, 314

salinity, 177

satellite images

    geostationary orbiting satellites, 71–72, 199–200

    polar orbiting satellites, 72–73

    radar images, 73–76

satellites

    Global Precipitation Measurement (GPM), 200

    polar- and geostationary-orbiting, 71–72, 199–200

    for weather forecasting, 199–202

saturation mixing ratio, 16

saturation vapor pressure, 16

scientific notation, 89

scientific theory, 83

sea ice, 178, 246

sea level

    mean, 53

    rise in, 40–41

sea-level adjusted pressure, 55

seasonal cycles, 31

seasons, reasons for, 97–99

sea surface temperature, 40–41

sediments, in oceans and lakes, 37

semipermanent highs, 171

severe thunderstorms, 301–308

    aerial damage assessments, 301

    definition of, 301

    forecasting of, 308–313

    multi-cell, 302–303

    squall lines, 303–304

    straight-line winds, 301

    supercell, 304–308

    watch/warning, 271

shear vorticity, 155

shelf cloud, 301

short-range ensemble forecast (SREF), 229

Showalter index, 206

SI unit, 3, 5, 84

Skew-T diagram, 70–71, 77, 126, 222, 255, 289

    for environment's stability, 123–125

    for freezing rain, 141

    for sleet, 140

    for snow, 138

    for weather forecasting, 205–207

sleet and ice pellets, 139

sling psychrometer, 17, 18

snow

    columns, 137

    dendrites, 137

    freezing rain and freezing drizzle, 138–142

    needles, 137

    plates, 137–138

    skew-T diagram for, 138

    sleet and ice pellets, 139

    wet snow, 137–138

snowfall, 18, 19

snow ratio, 142

snowstorms and blizzards, 275–283

    Alberta Clipper, 278

    Colorado lows, 278–281

    dendritic growth zone, 284

    Gulf of Alaska lows, 276–278

    Gulf of Mexico and Hatteras lows, 281–283

    lake-effect snowstorms, 283–288

    midlatitude cyclone, 280

    Nor'easters, 281–283

    ocean-effect snowstorms, 283

    threshold conditions for, 279

solar absorption, 239

solar energy, 94

    on Earth's surface, 97

solar flares, 330

solar output, 330

solar photovoltaics, 344

solar power, 344

solar radiation, 239–240

    scattering of, 336

solar radiation absorption, 328

soundings, 65, 70–71

    Skew-T diagram, 70–71

    for thunderstorm forecasting, 70

Southern Oscillation, 177, 180, 183

Southern Oscillation Index, 177

South Pole, 109

spaghetti plots, 228

speed shear, 305

squall lines, 303–304

    derecho, 304

    radar bright band, 303

    rear-inflow jet, 304

    trailing stratiform region, 303

stability and change, concept of, 119–120

states of matter, 3

static instability, 150

station pressure, 55

steady-state assumption, 192–193

Stefan-Boltzmann constant, 91

Stefan-Boltzmann Law, 90–91, 95, 96, 100–102

Stokes' Law, for cloud formation, 130–132

    terminal velocity and, 131

storm prediction mesoanalysis, 284

storm relative helicity (SRH), 311

storm surge, 316

stratocumulus clouds, 22

stratosphere, 8

    effects on surface weather, 258–259

stratus clouds, 18

subgrid scale phenomena, 221

sublimation, 4

subtropical jet, 153

sunspots, 330

    11-year cycle, 330

    history of, 330

    Maunder minimum, 330

supercell, 197

supercell thunderstorms, 304–308

supercooled drops, 134

surface currents, 174–177

Tropic of Cancer, 170

Tropic of Capricorn, 170

troposphere, 8, 66, 206

trough of warm air aloft (TROWAL), 149, 162, 280

turbulence, 194

typhoons, 314

U

ultraviolet (UV), 90

ultraviolet band, 90

Universal Time Coordinated (UTC), 25

upper-air maps, 65, 66–70

upper-air weather data, 65–71

    divergence, 68

    height contours, 67

    isotachs, 68

    isotherms, 67

    mandatory pressure levels, 66

    ridge, 67

    soundings, 65, 70–71

    trough, 67

    upper-air maps, 65, 66–70

upwelling water, 176

urban heat island, 48, 182

U.S. Global Change Research Program, 252

V

vapor density, 15

vapor pressure, 15–17

velocity, 130

vertical wind shear, 207

vertical wind velocity, 222

virga, 135

visible band, 90

volcanic eruptions

    aerosols, 327

    cooling effect caused by, 327

    created by oceanic plates, 327

    effects of, 328

    warming effect caused by, 327

vortex tubes, 304

vorticity

    curvature, 155

    shear, 155

W

Walker circulation, 176–177

    diagram of, 177

warm conveyor belt, 161

warm season precipitation, 135–136

    drizzle, 135

    hail, 136

    rain, 135–136

warm sector, 149

watches and warnings, issuance of, 269–271

water, 15–18

water cycle, 167, 181–182, 247

    effect of land-use changes on, 336

watersheds, 291

water vapor, 16

water vapor transport, 202

wavelength, 89

weather balloons, 7, 66, 67, 70

weather broadcasts, 270

weather codes, on surface weather maps, 60

weather forecasting, 26, 189

    assimilating data for, 216–219

    broadcasting of weather information, 209–210

    by calculating changes in weather parameters, 219–222

    cause-and-effect relationship in, 222

    gathering data for, 215–216

    Global Climate Models for, 194

    instrument-based, 190

Z